The MICHELIN Guide

San Francisco
Bay Area & Wine Country

RESTAURANTS
2011

Manufacture française des pneumatiques Michelin

Société en commandite par actions au capital de 304 000 000 EUR
Place des Carmes-Déchaux — 63000 Clermont-Ferrand (France)
R.C.S. Clermont-Fd B 855 200 507
No part of this publication may be reproduced in any form without the prior
permission of the publisher.

© Michelin, Propriétaires-éditeurs
Dépot légal Octobre 2010
Made in Canada
Published in 2010

Our editorial team has taken the greatest care in writing this guide and checking
the information in it. However, practical information (administrative formalities,
prices, addresses, telephone numbers, Internet addresses, etc) is subject to
frequent change and such information should therefore be used for guidance
only. It is possible that some of the information in this guide may not be accurate
or exhaustive as of the date of publication. Before taking action (in particular in
regard to administrative and customs regulations and procedures), you should
contact the appropriate official administration. We hereby accept no liability in
regard to such information.

The MICHELIN Guide
One Parkway South
Greenville, SC 29615 USA
www.michelinguide.com
michelin.guides@us.michelin.com

Dear Reader

W*e are thrilled to present the fifth edition of our MICHELIN Guide to San Francisco.*

Our dynamic team has spent this year updating our selection to wholly reflect the rich diversity of San Francisco's restaurants and hotels. As part of our meticulous and highly confidential evaluation process, our inspectors have anonymously and methodically eaten through all the city's neighborhoods including the bay area and wine country to compile the finest in each category for your enjoyment. While these inspectors are expertly trained food industry professionals, we remain consumer driven: our goal is to provide comprehensive choices to accommodate your comfort, tastes, and budget. Our inspectors dine, drink, and lodge as 'regular' customers in order to experience and evaluate the same level of service and cuisine you would as a guest.

Furthermore, we have delved deeper into the dining scenes south of San Francisco in order to provide a more thorough selection of notable and unique restaurants in both the Peninsula and South Bay. Don't miss the scrumptious "Small Plates" category, highlighting those establishments with a distinct style of service, setting, and menu; and the further expanded "Under $25" listings which also include a diverse and impressive choice at a very good value.

Additionally, you may now follow our Michelin Inspectors on Twitter @MichelinGuideSF as they chow their way around town. Our anonymous inspectors tweet daily about their unique and entertaining food experiences.

Our company's two founders, Édouard and André Michelin, published the first MICHELIN Guide in 1900, to provide motorists with practical information about where they could service and repair their cars, find quality accommodations, and a good meal. Later in 1926, the star-rating system for outstanding restaurants was introduced, and over the decades we have developed many new improvements to our guides. The local team here in San Francisco enthusiastically carries on these traditions.

We sincerely hope that the MICHELIN Guide will remain your preferred reference to San Francisco restaurants and hotels.

Contents

● Where to **Eat**   10

SFCVB/Phillip H.Coblentz

Contents

SFCVB/Phillip H. Coblentz

Contents

The Michelin Guide

"This volume was created at the turn of the century and will last at least as long".

This foreword to the very first edition of the MICHELIN Guide, written in 1900, has become famous over the years and the Guide has lived up to the prediction. It is read across the world and the key to its popularity is the consistency in its commitment to its readers, which is based on the following promises.

→ Anonymous Inspections

Our inspectors make anonymous visits to hotels and restaurants to gauge the quality offered to the ordinary customer. They pay their own bill and make no indication of their presence. These visits are supplemented by comprehensive monitoring of information—our readers' comments are one valuable source, and are always taken into consideration.

→ Independence

Our choice of establishments is a completely independent one, made for the benefit of our readers alone. Decisions are discussed by the inspectors and the editor, with the most important decided at the global level. Inclusion in the guide is always free of charge.

→ The Selection

The Guide offers a selection of the best hotels and restaurants in each category of comfort and price. Inclusion in the guides is a commendable award in itself, and defines the establishment among the "best of the best."

How the MICHELIN Guide Works

→ Annual Updates

All practical information, the classifications, and awards, are revised and updated every year to ensure the most reliable information possible.

→ Consistency & Classifications

The criteria for the classifications are the same in all countries covered by the Michelin Guides. Our system is used worldwide and is easy to apply when choosing a restaurant or hotel.

→ The Classifications

We classify our establishments using XXXXX-X and 🏨🏨🏨-🏠 to indicate the level of comfort. The 🏵🏵🏵-🏵 specifically designates an award for cuisine, unique from the classification. For hotels and restaurants, a symbol in red suggests a particularly charming spot with unique décor or ambiance.

→ Our Aim

As part of Michelin's ongoing commitment to improving travel and mobility, we do everything possible to make vacations and eating out a pleasure.

The Michelin Guide

How to Use This Guide

Where to **Eat**

Restaurant Classifications by Comfort

More pleasant if in red

X	Quite comfortable
XX	Comfortable
XXX	Very comfortable
XXXX	Top class comfortable
XXXXX	Luxury in the traditional style
▤	Small plates

The Michelin Distinctions for Good Cuisine

Stars for good cuisine

❀❀❀	Exceptional cuisine, worth a special journey
❀❀	Excellent cuisine, worth a detour
❀	A very good restaurant in its category

☺ Bib Gourmand
Inspectors' favorites for good value

Areas or neighborhoods
Each area is color coded...

🔲 el station

Map Coordinates

Average Prices

☺☺	under $25
$$	$25 to $50
$$$	$50 to $75
$$$$	over $75

Restaurant Symbols

🎴	Cash only
♿	Wheelchair accessible
☼	Outdoor dining
☕	Brunch
88	Notable wine list
♨	Notable sake list
🍸	Notable cocktail list
🅿	Valet parking
⏱	Late dining

The Bronx
Chicago ▶ Loop

Yellow Dog Café ☺

A4

American XX

1445 Jasmine Court Dr. (at Lee Blvd.)
Lunch daily
🔲 Addison

Phone: 212-599-0000
Web: www.ilovegolden.com
Prices: $$

Named for the owners' beloved yellow Labrador retriever, this chic cafe exudes warmth from the welcoming waitstaff to the lace cafe curtains, and pet portraits in the dining room. Pride of place is evident in the faces of friendly servers who are happy to accommodate special requests.

You won't be barking up the wrong tree if you order the specialty of the house: prime rib. It is roasted to medium rare (or whatever degree you prefer) and accompanied by the vegetable of the day and mashed Yukon golds tinged with garlic. Fish fanciers can choose among dishes such as sautéed day-boat scallops, grilled wild salmon, and pan-fried catfish.

Hearty portions and beef bones available to take home for your canine buddies bring new meaning to the term "doggie bag."

Jeanine's Uptown

Pizza X

C4

8459 Hart Blvd. (bet. 45th & 46th Aves.)
Tues-Sat dinner only

Phone: 310-454-5294
Web: www.eatjeanines.com
Prices: $$$

Carb lovers flock to the Uptown branch of this local pizzeria chain for thick-crust pies slathered with the house marinara sauce and sprinkled with fresh toppings such as organic spinach and broccoli, artichoke hearts and pancetta.

There's always a line out the door, and patrons rave about the signature pizza, brimming with pepperoni and house-made sausage. Although pizza is the main attraction here, the menu lists a number of traditional pastas as well. Red-and-white-checked tablecloths and Chianti bottles adorn the tables, creating an old-fashioned Italian restaurant ambience. And speaking of Chianti, it's the wine of choice here. The chain takes its name from the owner's daughter, who loves that thick crust, but won't touch meat with a ten-foot pole.

152

A4

Phon
Sub
Wel
Pri

Where to **Stay**

Average Prices	Hotel Symbols	Hotel Classifications by Comfort

Average Prices

Prices do not include applicable taxes

$	under $200
$$	$200 to $300
$$$	$300 to $400
$$$$	over $400

Map Coordinates

Hotel Symbols

149 rooms Number of rooms & suites

&.	Wheelchair accessible
⨍🏋	Exercise room
⊛	Spa
⌇	Swimming pool
⌸	Conference room
⌕	Pet friendly

Hotel Classifications by Comfort

More pleasant if in red

🏠	Quite comfortable
🏠🏠	Comfortable
🏠🏠🏠	Very comfortable
🏠🏠🏠	Top class comfortable
🏠🏠🏠🏠	Luxury in the traditional style

's Palace ❀❀

Italian ✗✗✗✗

ther Pl. (at 30th Street)   Dinner daily

09

asfabulouspalace.com

Home cooked Italian never tasted so good than at this unpretentious little place. The simple décor claims no big-name designers, and while the Murano glass light fixtures are chic and the velveteen-covered chairs are comfortable, this isn't a restaurant where millions of dollars were spent on the interior.

Instead, food is the focus here. The restaurant's name may not be Italian, but it nonetheless serves some of the best pasta in the city, made fresh in-house. Dishes follow the seasons, thus ravioli may be stuffed with fresh ricotta and herbs in summer, and pumpkin in fall. Most everything is liberally dusted with Parmigiano Reggiano, a favorite ingredient of the chef.

For dessert, you'll have to deliberate between the likes of creamy tiramisu, ricotta cheesecake, and homemade gelato. One thing's for sure: you'll never miss your nonna's cooking when you eat at Sonya's.

Manhattan ▶ Chelsea

153

The Fan Inn

🏠🏠🏠

D1

135 Shanghai Street, Oakland

Phone: 650-345-1440 or 888-222-2424
Web: www.superfaninnoakland.com
Prices: $$

45 Rooms
5 Suites

⨍🏋
⊛

Housed in an Art Deco-era building, the venerable Fan Inn ecently underwent a complete facelift. The hotel now fits with the new generation of sleekly understated hotels ering a Zen-inspired aesthetic, despite its 1930s origins.

othing neutral palette runs throughout the property, ctuated with exotic woods, bamboo, and fine fabrics. he lobby, the sultry lounge makes a relaxing place for -mixed cocktail or a glass of wine.

inens and down pillows cater to your comfort, while een TVs, DVD players with iPod docking stations, less Internet access satisfy the need for modern s. For business travelers, nightstands convert to ables and credenzas morph into flip-out desks. inter, fax or scanner? It's just a phone call away. est, the hotel will even provide office supplies.

half of the accommodations here are suites, uxury factor ratchets up with marble baths, ing areas, and fully equipped kitchens. inn doesn't have a restaurant, the nearby early everything you could want in terms of o dumplings to haute cuisine.

San Francisco ▶ Civic Center

315

Where to Eat

San Francisco Convention & Visitors Bureau photo by Phil Coblentz

San Francisco

Castro

Cole Valley • Haight-Ashbury • Noe Valley

It's raining men in the Castro, the world famous "gayborhood" that launched the career of civil rights icon, Harvey Milk, and remains devoted to celebrating the gay and lesbian community (yes, ladies are allowed here too). The hub for all things LGBT—including Gay Pride in June and the Castro Street Fair each October—the Castro is a constant party with a mélange of bars from shabby to chic and dance clubs that honor the ruling class of one-name wonder women—Madonna, Beyoncé, Bette, Babs, and Cher.

The Castro teems with casual cafés to feed its buzzing population of gym bunnies, leather daddies, and drag queens, as well as a flood of vibrant out-of-towners on pilgrimage to mecca. **Café Flore**'s quaint patio is more evocative of its Parisian namesake than the plain-Jane continental fare. But if you go to eat, you're missing the point: This is prime cruising territory with cheap drinks and DJs. There are white napkin restaurants dishing worthwhile cuisine—**Frisée**, **Côté Sud**, and **La Méditerranée**—but the best flavors of the Castro are served on the run.

Thai House and the 24-7 **Baghdad Café** are mainstays for a quick, inexpensive bite, and **Marcello's Pizza** is a satisfying post-cocktail joint. Speaking of booze, San Francisco's first openly gay bar, **Twin Peaks Tavern**, continues to lure. The younger hotties, however, sweat it out at **Badlands** and the **Café**. **Café du Nord** draws hipsters for live music in a former speakeasy built in 1907.

The area is chock-full of darling specialty shops. The **Castro Cheesery** pours fresh-roasted gourmet coffees and offers a small selection of cheese; **Samovar Tea Lounge** brews artisan loose-leaf; and **Swirl**, a sleek space brimming with stemware and accessories, offers tastings of boutique wine varietals. Take home a nosh from Italian foods purveyor **A.G. Ferrari**, or indulge your sweet tooth at **Gelateria Naia** or the kitschy kiosk, **Hot Cookie**.

Nearby Cole Valley is home to **Say Cheese**, full of quality international cheeses and a small stock of sandwiches; and **Val de Cole**, with value table wines galore. On Monday nights, dog-lovers treat the whole family to dinner on the garden patio at **Zazie**.

Counterculturalists, of course, have long sought haven in the hippiefied Haight-Ashbury where, despite recent Gap-ification, head shops and record stores still dominate the landscape. Eschew any notions of fine dining here and join the locals at more laid-back hot spots. **Cha! Cha! Cha!** is a groovy tapas bar flowing with fresh-fruit sangria, and for the morning after, **Pork Store Café** draws a cliquey following for greasy hash browns and hotcakes.

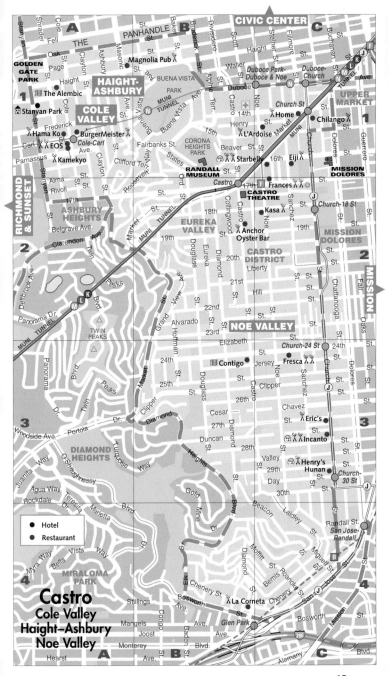

Castro
Cole Valley
Haight–Ashbury
Noe Valley

15

The Alembic

Gastropub

1725 Haight St. (bet. Cole & Shrader Sts.)

Phone: 415-666-0822   Lunch & dinner daily
Web: www.alembicbar.com
Prices: **$$**

Culinary kudos aside, The Alembic is first, foremost, and proudly a watering hole. Bare filament bulbs do little to light the bar fashioned from old Kezar Stadium bleachers, and blackboards are hand scrawled with artisanal whiskeys and ryes. Whether you crave a classic old fashioned or an education on the finer points of small-batch bourbons, these talented bartenders are happy to accommodate.

With passionate cooking and a well-worn vibe, this purveyor of fine moods and local foods fits the term gastropub to a tee. Here, find patrons feasting on braised Wagyu beef tongue sliders prepared *sous vide* or a sweet-tangy whiskey glaze over tender baby back ribs. Unlike most pubs, dinner is worth the lengthy wait; weekend lunches are more low-key.

Anchor Oyster Bar

Seafood

579 Castro St. (bet. 18th & 19th Sts.)

Phone: 415-431-3990   Lunch Mon – Sat
Web: www.anchoroysterbar.com   Dinner nightly
Prices: **$$**

For a warm bowl of chowder on a foggy day, head home to Anchor Oyster Bar, the 1977 mainstay that's always ready with a beer and a bivalve. While the homey bar may not have the soigné hip of its younger neighbors, it does have the solid seafood and cheeky humor (note the adult-themed T-shirts for sale) to keep everyone sated. In fact, the place itself is something of an oyster: clean, a bit briny, some claim it has an aphrodisiac quality, and occasional pearls can be found.

Cozy up at a stainless steel table or the marble-topped bar and check the whiteboard for classics such as steamed shellfish, seafood cocktails, and variations on chowder. Their fresh oysters are always expertly shucked—the only thing that changes here are the daily specials.

BurgerMeister

A1

86 Carl St. (at Cole St.)

Phone: 415-566-1274   Lunch & dinner daily
Web: www.burgermeistersf.com
Prices:

This daddy of burger joints with up-market eats and a low-key vibe stacks up to Bay Area standards with all-natural Niman Ranch beef and eco-friendly packaging. Moreover, these juicy quarter- and half-pounders, cooked to order and tossed on a freshly baked bun, are greatly delicious and make a near mockery of the trendy little slider.

Though not cheap, the "Meister Favorites" (starting at nine dollars) offer quality and creativity, as in the "San Diego" topped with roasted jalapeños and melted pepper jack. Fries come in curly, sweet potato, chili, and roasted garlic varieties; beer-battered onion rings arrive without a trace of grease. Salads and wines by the glass are offered, though milk shakes are more popular here, and are best eaten with a spoon.

Chilango

C1

235 Church St. (bet. 15th & Market Sts.)

Phone: 415-552-5700   Lunch & dinner daily
Web: www.chilangococina.com
Prices:

This unexpected taqueria brings wholesome and sophisticated tastes of Mexico City to the Castro. Black-and-white photos depicting life in Mexico DF evoke the roots of Chef Roberto Aguiar Cruz, who hails from the FiDi restaurant that shares that capital's name. His flavors suit the palate of his people (called *Chilangos*), so expect a complex fare of fresh produce and free-range meats. *Lo siento*, no burritos.

Here most *antojitos* begin with a house-made corn tortilla. Tacos may be stuffed with braised beef brisket or filet mignon, while sliced grilled short ribs and fixings top the *huraches chilango*, an open-faced torta resting on an oval tortilla sandal. *Sopes*, ceviche, and posole complement local wines from Latino vintners.

Contigo

B3

1320 Castro St. (at 24th St.)

Phone: 415-285-0250   Dinner Tue – Sun
Web: www.contigosf.com
Prices: $$

In Noe Valley, Contigo is a meat market for melt-in-your-mouth, hard-to-get heartbreakers. Minds out of the gutter! We're talking about *jamón ibérico*, the prized imported ham, sliced tissue thin. If the pig's not your type, experiment with other *pica pica*, succulent Spanish teasers like octopus salad, local calamars *a la plancha*, and Catalan flatbreads hot from the wood-burning oven. While the flavors hail from Barcelona, Contigo's sensibility is straight-up California: dishes are lovingly concocted from local, sustainable products and served on recycled Heath Ceramics dinnerware atop wood tables salvaged from the old Levi Strauss factory on Valencia Street.

The heated patio and organic garden is a comfy spot for a glass of cava.

Eiji

C1

317 Sanchez St. (bet. 16th & 17th Sts.)

Phone: 415-558-8149   Lunch & Dinner Tue – Sun
Web: N/A
Prices:

Wooden shingle siding layers the tiny tree-flanked façade, marked by a single oblong flag reading "sushi" on one side and "tofu" on the other. You may have shown up for the well-made sushi, but at Eiji Onoda's eponymous eatery, fresh, homemade tofu's the thing. Go for a bowl of silky, made-to-order *oboro*—delicate curds of tofu just separated from the soymilk (before they take their more recognizable square shape). Or try the ethereal, melt-in-your-mouth *ankake* tofu—cold steamed and topped with a tasty *konbu*-soy sauce.

Top off your tofu with accompanying additions such as julienned *shiso*, scallion rings, and freshly grated ginger. *Sunomono*, seafood casseroles, *yosenabe*, and *misonabe* are also on offer—bring your own bowl if you want either *nabe* to go.

EOS

A1

Asian ✗✗

901 Cole St. (at Carl St.)

Phone: 415-566-3063
Web: www.eossf.com
Prices: $$

Dinner nightly

Although it abuts Haight-Ashbury, tiny Cole Valley has its own bohemian charm. Families and young professionals frequent the coffee shops and restaurants along the main drag of Cole Street, where EOS draws diners from all parts of the city.

The restaurant presents two faces, a contemporary dining room and cozy adjoining wine salon, each with separate entrances but serving the same full menu of Asian fare. Order several small portions of tasty Thai salads, curries, or perhaps *poke* rolls (ahi tuna and salmon) and share them family-style. Beverage options include wine flights and inspired sake cocktails.

A dinner here is not complete without a taste of exotic homemade ice cream like Vietnamese coffee, roasted banana, and lychee-coconut sorbet.

Eric's

C3

Chinese ✗

1500 Church St. (at 27th St.)

Phone: 415-282-0919
Web: www.erics.ypguides.net
Prices:

Lunch & dinner daily

A neighborhood favorite and Noe Valley fixture with a line out the door since 1991, Eric's is just the sort of godsend that everyone comes to appreciate. This little house packs its bright yellow, mirrored interior with regulars who feast on Hunan and Mandarin lunches for under $10 (including soup and tea) and dinner for just a few bills more.

Prices belie the portions, so expect ample specialties such as rainbow fish with pine nuts in garlic sauce, or tender Shanghai chicken breast with crispy seaweed and al dente brown rice. While some discerning palates may claim the cuisine is somewhat Americanized, no one denies that it is nonetheless delicious.

Reservations are not accepted (hence the line), but service is as very fast as it is friendly.

Frances ✿

C2

Californian ✕✕

3870 17th St. (bet. 15th & Market Sts.)

Phone: 415-621-3870
Web: www.frances-sf.com
Prices: $$$

Dinner Tue – Sun

Jennifer Yin

After gathering a belt full of notches cooking at celebrated eateries like Aqua, Charles Nob Hill, and Fifth Floor, Chef Melissa Perello finally gets a place to herself with this much buzzed-about new Castro restaurant.

Named for Perello's Texan grandmother, Frances is small and cozy, with a decidedly unflashy, contemporary-rustic décor fitted out with loads of wood, creamy walls, and a tiny bar up front. The service is equally unpretentious, with meals being delivered with minimal fuss in perfect synchronicity. The lively crowd who piles in every night doesn't appear to be looking for long, windy explanations of the food anyways—Perello's talents are better seen, smelled, and tasted.

Kick things off with one of the chef's endlessly creative bouchées (little starters offering a handful of bites), which range from crispy pork trotters to chickpea fries; and then move on to fluffy, impossibly light pillows of ricotta gnocchi tossed with baby asparagus, plump fava beans, green garlic, crunchy croutons, and sautéed morel mushrooms; or perfectly seared Sonoma duck breast in an irresistible reduction, paired with a butter bean ragout with sautéed escarole, homemade sausage, and *croutes*.

Fresca

C3

Peruvian ✗✗

3945 24th St. (bet. Noe & Sanchez Sts.)

Phone: 415-695-0549
Web: www.frescasf.com
Prices: $$

Lunch & dinner daily

Inside this cheery room with a raw bar and open kitchen in back, Fresca offers patrons a unique rendition of Peruvian flavors and creative cocktails to be sampled and sipped amid catchy Latin beats. The front seating area with its bright yellow walls, arched ceilings, skylights, and outdoor views lends a fresh, open feel.

Likewise, the purity of their ingredients is patent in fresh seafood items like crisp and creamy *tequeños* (fried wontons packed with shrimp, crab, and cream cheese, with an aji amarillo aïoli), while the salmon BLT provides a very satisfying sandwich experience, if not authentically Peruvian. A morsel of the ahi mignon or *lomo saltado* further illustrates the concept of culinary invention. Two other locations are equally pleasing.

Hama Ko

A1

Japanese ✗

108 Carl St. (bet. Cole & Stanyan Sts.)

Phone: 415-753-6808
Web: N/A
Prices: $$

Dinner Tue – Sun

Wandering a small Japanese village, you won't find a more authentic and unassuming sushi spot than Hama Ko, a mom-and-pop shop run by a charming Japanese couple. He mans the sushi bar, deftly assembling *nigiri* samplers; she serves the handful of tables in the homespun space with a cheerful smile. This feels like the home of the Japanese grandparents you'll wish you had.

The open kitchen is a touch worn, but the food is super fresh and lovingly prepared. Forget those trendier sushi spots with Americanized fare, and opt for the chef's choice combination platter including melt-in-your-mouth tuna, buttery scallops, and simple maki. While the chef is serious and focused, there will be wide smiles all around when you share how much the meal was enjoyed.

Henry's Hunan 🐶

C3

Chinese 🍴

1708 Church St. (bet. Day & 29th Sts.)

Phone: 415-826-9189

Web: www.henryshunanrestaurant.com

Prices: 💲

Lunch & dinner daily

A bargain lover's dream in a tough economy, this modern Noe Valley outpost ranks as the most stylish and tastiest of Henry's five locations. Brothers Jeff and Eddie run this spot with the charisma and congeniality of a neighborhood stalwart, but the food is what earns the accolades here.

As any capsaicin junkie will tell you, Hunan cuisine equals spicy—and there are plenty of dishes on the menu to fill that bill—as in Henry's special, a stir-fry of chopped chicken, tender shrimp, delicate scallops, and crunchy vegetables tossed in a zesty bean sauce. Still, the kitchen will happily accommodate more timid tastes. No matter spicy or mild, the produce is fresh and flavorful, the cooking is spot-on, and the portions will likely warrant a to go box.

Home

C1

American 🍴

2100 Market St. (at Church St.)

Phone: 415-503-0333

Web: www.home-sf.com

Prices: $$

Lunch & dinner daily

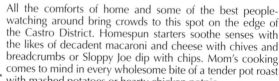

All the comforts of home and some of the best people-watching around bring crowds to this spot on the edge of the Castro District. Homespun starters soothe senses with the likes of decadent macaroni and cheese with chives and breadcrumbs or Sloppy Joe dip with chips. Mom's cooking comes to mind in every wholesome bite of a tender pot roast with mashed potatoes or hearty chicken potpie.

On foggy nights, a roaring fire in the enclosed patio coaxes any chill from the air. Inside, red banquettes, white tile walls, and black lacquer chairs compose the diner-like space, as it caters to its highly supportive, local alternative community. Note that Home is open until midnight, seven nights a week and offers an early bird prix-fixe menu from 5:00-6:00 P.M.

Incanto

Italian XX

C3

1550 Church St. (at Duncan St.)

Phone: 415-641-4500
Web: www.incanto.biz
Prices: $$

Dinner Wed – Mon

Incanto is enchanting. Classic street cars rumble past this quintessential neighborhood spot. Charming and inviting, the refreshed interior is lined with agricultural prints and a trippy Animal Farm-meets-Timothy Leary painting set above the bar. Farm animals aren't just the chosen décor, they are also the chef's forte.

Chef Chris Cosentino is big on the pig, offering a variety of pork-based dishes like pig's trotter with foie gras, pickled green strawberries and jam, ham leg roasted in hay, and whole pig feasts for groups. He is also a master of offal, leaving nothing to waste. The menu spins to the season and is loosely rooted in Italian cooking with a decidedly Californian twist. The wine list is true blue Italian and focuses on a rare selection.

Kamekyo

Japanese X

A1

943 Cole St. (bet. Carl St. & Parnassus Ave.)

Phone: 415-759-5693
Web: N/A
Prices: $$

Lunch & dinner daily

Cole Valley's go-to for sushi lovers since 1996, Kamekyo is an intimate dining room anchored by a polished blonde wood bar and minimalist décor. A lavender ceiling and gold-hued walls warm the space, though the stoic chefs can be chilly. Still, a seat at the counter while the seafood is cleaned could yield a taste that should not be refused.

Deftly cut nigiri, sashimi, and maki make big waves here, but wholesome Japanese favorites including piping hot soba and udon noodles, light and crispy shrimp tempura, teriyaki, perfectly steamed white rice, and budget-friendly lunchtime bento boxes should not be overlooked. For visitors looking to keep with the theme, the Japanese Tea Garden in neighboring Golden Gate Park is just a Prius hop away.

Kasa

C2

Indian ✗

4001 18th St. (at Noe St.)

Phone: 415-621-6940   Lunch & dinner daily
Web: www.kasaindian.com
Prices: ⊜⊗

Indian ex-pats feel right at home at Kasa, which takes pride in authentic, home-style recipes. A minimalist, budget-friendly menu focuses on *thali* plates served on divided steel trays, loaded with chutneys, raita, lentils, and seasoned basmati rice. Try these stuffed into buttery *kati* rolls for a taste of Indian street food. Other staples include locally sourced vegetarian dishes and naturally raised chicken tikka masala, lamb curry, and char-grilled turkey kebabs.

In keeping with the low-key fare, the vibe is self-service casual with a high communal table that is ideal for on-the-go eats. A modern palette and brushed aluminum accents make this a sleek spot for a home cooked meal. In the Marina, check out Kasa's Fillmore Street location.

La Corneta

B4

Mexican ✗

2834 Diamond St. (bet. Bosworth & Chenery Sts.)

Phone: 415-469-8757   Lunch & dinner daily
Web: www.lacorneta.com
Prices: ⊜⊗

A smiley sunshine mural beams atop cheery yellow walls at this awesome taqueria. Upbeat, tidy, and vibrant, La Corneta serves up fresh, fast, and very filling fare from prawn burritos to sautéed salmon fish tacos—cooked to order from fresh fillets. Queue up and mosey down the food line where servers pile your favorite ingredients into a mouthwatering heap of Mexican deliciousness.

Try to tackle the carne asada super burrito—expertly wrapped to contain the gargantuan mix of grilled beef, beans, rice, cheese, guacamole, sour cream, lettuce, tomato, and *pico de gallo*. If the nachos, tacos, burritos, and quesadillas haven't defeated you, end with a warm, sugary *churro*. A word to the wise: any item with the word "super" means it, so grab a knife and fork.

L'Ardoise

French 🍴

C1

151 Noe St. (at Henry St.)

Phone: 415-437-2600
Web: www.ardoisesf.com
Prices: $$

Dinner Tue – Sat

The French accent is thick at L'Ardoise, a petite neighborhood bistro named for the de rigueur chalkboard displaying the daily specials. Dimly lit with antique lamps and awash in burgundy paint, the snug spot draws swish Castro denizens and Noe Valley couples nostalgic for Parisian romance to sit elbow to elbow at zinc-topped tables. Plats du jour might include tiger shrimp ravioli with fresh herbs, or succulent pan-roasted pork tenderloin ready to be washed down with a spicy *Châteauneuf-du-Pape*.

Chef/owner Thierry Clement is to be applauded equally for his knowledgeable, all-French staff and his concise menu of bistro favorites. Savvy locals call ahead for reservations, arrive on the F-Market trolley, begin with charcuterie, and finish with *fromage*.

Magnolia Pub

Gastropub 🍴

A1

1398 Haight St. (at Masonic Ave.)

Phone: 415-864-7468
Web: www.magnoliapub.com
Prices: $$

Lunch & dinner daily

This veteran Haight-Ashbury hangout finally got a shave and haircut, perhaps to the dismay of the neighborhood regulars. While black tufted leather now covers the booths and that old psychedelic mural has been muted with a gold-leaf patina, the windows still sweat with the humidity of brewing beer and the air is heavy with the scent of fresh hops late in the week. Magnolia has long been hailed for its draught micro-brews, which are jotted on a blackboard along with each beer's BUs (bitterness units) in keeping with British pub tradition.

Yet these days, its witty gastropub fare is a formidable draw, with such twists on bar classics as Scotch quail eggs deep fried to golden brown, or sticky-sweet duck wings—a perfect match for anything on tap.

25

Starbelly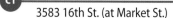

C1

Californian 🍴🍴

3583 16th St. (at Market St.)

Phone: 415-252-7500

Web: www.starbellysf.com

Prices: $$

Lunch & dinner daily

All the stars in foodie heaven collide at Starbelly, a hot spot illuminated by a constellation of watchwords: organic, Californian, pizza, and pork. This last ingredient plays a leading role as house-made bacon, *coppa de testa* (head cheese), and succulent roasted porchetta. Fans of sister restaurant Beretta are familiar with the cerebral pizzas, perhaps topped with autumn squash, sage, and *pepitas*, or Mexican chorizo and sunny eggs.

An instant darling since opening in August 2009, Starbelly boasts a chic, green design with its bowling lane turned communal table and a cozy patio with potted herbs. The Castro clientele is expectedly stylish and, given the menu, impossibly trim. Expect clever wine- and beer-based cocktails as well as a line at the door.

Good food without spending a fortune? Look for the Bib Gourmand 😊.

Civic Center
Hayes Valley • Lower Haight • Tenderloin

The gilded Beaux-Arts dome of City Hall marks the main artery of the Civic Center, where graceful architecture houses the city's finest cultural institutions, including the War Memorial & Performing Arts Center and the Asian Art Museum. On Wednesdays and Sundays, the vast promenade outside City Hall hosts **Heart of the City**, San Francisco's oldest farmer's market. Priced to attract low-income neighborhood families, the market brims with such rare Asian produce as young ginger, Buddha's hand, and bergamot lemons.

Ground zero for California's marriage equality movement and protests of every stripe, City Hall is also prime territory for festivals, including Love Fest; the SF Symphony's biennial Black & White Ball; and the Lao New Year Festival in April. This same mall also witnessed the harvest of Alice Waters' Slow Food Nation Victory Garden in 2008.

With an enormous Asian, and particularly Vietnamese, population in the neighboring Tenderloin, there is an incredible array of authentic dining options, especially on Larkin Street. Mom-and-pop shop **Saigon Sandwiches** leads the way with spicy *bánh mì* made with fresh, crusty baguettes. These tasty subs are only three bucks a pop. Nearby, the *pho ga* at **Turtle Tower** is said to be a favorite of Slanted Door's chef, Charles Phan, while **Bodega Bistro** is

a romantic purple nook with an infusion of French flavors and *pho*.

Best known for a seedy mess of strip clubs, liquor stores, and drug deals, the Tenderloin is a go-to for both a dingy and decadent nightlife. On the site of a former speakeasy, **Bourbon & Branch** is a sexy hideaway with a tome full of classic and creative cocktails. Other sleek lounges with interesting beats and delicious concoctions include the famed **Slide**. This is a rather unique and sophisticated playground despite its unusual

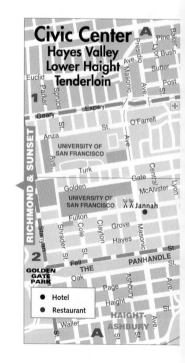

entrance—that's right, a snaking mahogany slide.

West of the Civic Center, Hayes Valley is positively polished, with a coterie of chic design shops and boutiques, as well as an interesting medley of stylish restaurants. The concise menu at **Essencia** includes flavorful Peruvian dishes and unique wines in a pumpkin-hued corner space. **Destino** is a mainstay for *"nuevo Latino"* cuisine, and **Miette Confiserie** is an impossibly charming old-fashioned style candy store jam-packed with hard-to-find European chocolates, salted licorice, taffy, and gelées. Apostles of **Blue Bottle Coffee** get their daily dose at the kiosk on Linden Alley.

To the west, the Lower Haight draws hipsters for foosball and 21 tap beers at **The Page**, sake cocktails at **Noc Noc**, and live shows at the Independent. However, it's the Fillmore Jazz District that lures true music lovers. Settled by African-American GIs at the end of World War II, the neighborhood hummed with jazz greats like Billie Holiday and Miles Davis. Today, with the attempted resurgence of the jazz district, large restaurants present live music and contemporary stars grace the stage. The Fillmore still echoes with the voices of Pink Floyd, Hendrix, and the Dead, and the annual Fillmore Jazz Festival is also a must-see.

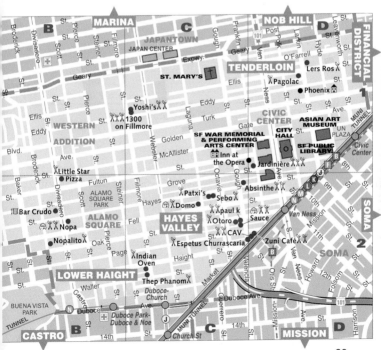

Absinthe

Mediterranean

C2

398 Hayes St. (at Gough St.)

Phone: 415-551-1590   Lunch & dinner Tue – Sun
Web: www.absinthe.com
Prices: $$$

This brasserie is known for its creative cocktails—which, thanks to recent legalization, can now incorporate the restaurant's namesake spirit. (The quaff of choice for artists in mid-19th century France, absinthe was banned in 1912.) Lovers of the arts favor this Absinthe for its corner location near the performing arts center, where it's a hot spot for a pre- or post-performance meal.

French, Californian, and Mediterranean notes play through the theme of the menu. A riff on the classic frisée salad includes bacon, a fried duck egg, caviar, and baby leeks vinaigrette. Pizza topped with young dandelion greens, onion jam, and Cypress Grove goat cheese may solo as a small plate; while entrées like grilled halibut with *pipérade* earn ovations.

Bar Crudo

Seafood

B2

655 Divisadero St. (at Grove St.)

Phone: 415-409-0679   Dinner Mon – Sat
Web: www.barcrudo.com
Prices: $$

Hailed for raw oysters, clams, crawfish, and Dungeness crabs, Bar Crudo was also known for sardines—or at least for its tin-sized room cramped with folks hooked on fresh seafood. To better accommodate a growing school, Bar Crudo has moved to a larger reef, in NoPa, where beautiful mermaid murals make use of long sought-after wall space.

The menu has also spread its fins with such additions as arctic char with wasabi *tobiko*, and Anchor Steamed clams with spicy linguiça. There is no dessert but it's all for the best: artisanal beers pair well with an adventurous octopus salad, or a messy-yet-magical quartet of Louisiana "devil" prawns. Order another round and kick back on the mezzanine, which offers a seagull's view to the zinc bar and open kitchen.

CAV

D2

Californian

1666 Market St. (bet. Franklin & Gough Sts.)

Phone: 415-437-1770

Web: www.cavwinebar.com

Prices: $$

Dinner Mon – Sat

Peek into this beloved wine bar and find connoisseurs nursing an enticing glass of pinot noir, or some other ravishing selection from CAV's compact but well-chosen wine list. A modish niche with a hint of grit, graffiti murals veil the walls and zinc tabletops dot the floors. Filament bulbs, deep red hues, and soft votive candles clinch the allure of this esoteric gem.

Swirled to a table at back, guests peruse an à la carte menu of pig trotters and foie gras. Inspired dishes with top ingredients—homemade potato *agnolotti* with white truffle, Parmigiano Reggiano, and *buerre monté*; beef short ribs with crispy *pommes* Anna, vanilla-glazed Tokyo turnips, and *cuisson* jus; and smoky Brussels sprouts caramelized in lardon and chili—are quite champion.

Domo

C2

Japanese

511 Laguna St. (bet. Fell & Linden Sts.)

Phone: 415-861-8887

Web: www.domosf.com

Prices: $$

Lunch Mon – Fri
Dinner nightly

Just two narrow counters and a prep kitchen dress the space at Domo, a *tobiko*-sized Japanese haunt that serves creative, ingredient-driven cuisine. The constant crowd is as much a sign of fine food as it is of cramped quarters, and the sunny vibe—imagine citrus-hued walls and blonde wood accents—makes up for the lack of elbow room.

Wherever you sit, you'll be treated to a view: one counter faces streetfront windows; the other overlooks the kitchen, where the aroma of torched Kobe beef will make you drool. Make it quick, however, because Domo turns the seats. You'll have no trouble wolfing spicy tuna *crudo* with *sriracha*, cilantro, and avocado; fresh *unagi* sashimi; or the unbeatable $12 lunch special, served with soup and salad.

Espetus Churrascaria

Brazilian 🍴

C-D2

1686 Market St. (at Gough St.)

Phone: 415-552-8792   Lunch & dinner daily
Web: www.espetus.com
Prices: $$

Have a big appetite for meat? Look for carnivore heaven in the Civic Center area at this *rodizio*-style restaurant. "All you can eat" takes on new meaning here, as waiters clad in *gaucho* garb deliver skewers (*espetus* in Brazil) bearing a myriad of grilled meats—Parmesan pork, homemade sausage, chicken thighs, beef sirloin—to your table. You decide when you've had enough: position the wheel at your table to green if you want "more please"; turn it to red when you are "taking a meat break." As accoutrements, a generous buffet overflows with salads, fresh vegetables, and other side dishes.

Lunch provides a more limited selection, while dinner ups the meat ante as well as the prices. Anytime, a glass of malbec complements the grilled and roasted fare.

Indian Oven

Indian 🍴

C2

233 Fillmore St. (bet. Haight & Waller Sts.)

Phone: 415-626-1628   Dinner nightly
Web: N/A
Prices: 🥜

Long a local favorite, Indian Oven dishes up an extensive menu of hearty Northern Indian cuisine. The plate of assorted appetizers makes a good place to start; it teems with large, crisp samosas filled with spiced potatoes and peas; vegetable *pakoras;* and two flavorful *pappadams* served with an array of chutneys and pickles. Entrées encompass classic tandoori chicken; spicy lamb *vindaloo; biryani*; seafood curry; and chicken *tikka masala*, to name just a few.

Tables are cramped in the tiny downstairs dining room (some of the better seats here are next to the open kitchen); for a more intimate ambience, request a table upstairs.

Allow yourself extra time to park, since finding a space can be a nightmare in this Lower Haight neighborhood.

Jannah

Middle Eastern

1775 Fulton St. (bet. Central & Masonic Aves.)

Phone: 415-567-4400   Lunch & dinner daily
Web: www.yayacuisine.com
Prices: $$

With its walls and ceilings painted with bright blue skies and puffy clouds to the Arabic music bleating through the dining room, Jannah is like a trip to the Medina without the jet lag. Bright, upbeat, and full of energy, Jannah's boundaries extend to a pleasing outdoor patio—just right for enjoying the hookah pipes that sit at the ready.

It is California-meets-Middle East on the menu, which features interesting, authentic, and unique dishes. Chef Yaya Salih punctuates his cooking with bold flavors and sweet/savory spices to create his own mark on everything from tabbouleh to *kuzi*—phyllo dough stuffed with lamb, fruit, vegetables, and an enticing blend of spices. Don't dismiss the chef's specials, like smoked spice-crusted trout (*maskoof*).

Jardinière

Californian

300 Grove St. (at Franklin St.)

Phone: 415-861-5555   Dinner nightly
Web: www.jardiniere.com
Prices: $$$

Posh couples and culture vultures have long counted this arts district mainstay as home base for pre- and post-curtain revelry. Downstairs, indulgent regulars unwind on low-slung sofas and nosh on decadent bar bites in j lounge, while Jardinière's upstairs dining room sets the stage for Chef/owner Traci Des Jardins' French-Californian cuisine.

Nestle into a velvet booth beneath the golden dome or grab a two-top near the balustrade that hugs a view of Champagne on ice at the bar below. Wherever you sit, these meals are expertly choreographed. Order oysters or caviar à la carte, or settle in for the chef's seven-course menu with wine pairings. Savor such fare as herbaceous and crispy bacon-wrapped quail or pan-seared duck breast with chestnut spätzle.

Lers Ros

D1

Thai 🍴

730 Larkin St. (bet. Ellis & O'Farrell Sts.)

Phone: 415-931-6917   Lunch & dinner daily
Web: www.lersros.com
Prices: 💰💰

A cheap and tasty meal isn't worth braving this shady stretch of Tenderloin by night. But come daylight, another story unfolds. Lers Ros is a cult favorite lunch spot you can count on. Union Square and Civic Center suits pour over heaping plates of flavorful Thai cuisine; visitors from across town are wise to park in a nearby garage (street parking is nil).

At Lers Ros, you've barely set your menu down before the food arrives. Sample red curry, sweetened with coconut milk and loaded with beef, Thai eggplant, and Kaffir lime leaves; minced chicken stir-fried with basil, garlic, and chili (*pad kra pow kai*); or *pad kee mow*, a spicy pan-fried noodle ensemble topped with juicy pork and bean sprouts. Cool your palate with a sweet and creamy Thai iced tea.

Little Star Pizza

B2

Pizza 🍴

846 Divisadero St. (bet. Fulton & McAllister Sts.)

Phone: 415-441-1118   Dinner Tue – Sun
Web: www.littlestarpizza.com
Prices: 💰💰

This is a hip, chic, and minimalist spot for local 20-somethings to pop in, put some up-to-the-moment music on the jukebox, grab an ice cold P.B.R., and wait for their eponymous Little Star deep dish pies to arrive, topped in creamy spinach, feta, and mushrooms. The Classic deep-dish (sausage, mushrooms, green peppers, and onions) is likewise a favorite, but lovers of thin crust find nirvana in roasted chicken and basil pesto atop a crispy, flaky cornmeal crust.

The dimly lit dining room is always packed, loud, and not a kid-friendly spot, so the Chuck E. Cheese set should stay home with a sitter. Expect waits during prime time, so consider calling for a pie to go. If too packed, give their Valencia Street, or new Albany location in the East Bay a shot.

Nopa

B2

Californian XX

560 Divisadero St. (at Hayes St.)

Phone: 415-864-8643　　　　　　　　　　　　　　　Dinner nightly
Web: www.nopasf.com
Prices: $$

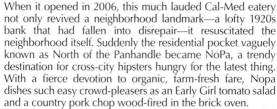

When it opened in 2006, this much lauded Cal-Med eatery not only revived a neighborhood landmark—a lofty 1920s bank that had fallen into disrepair—it resuscitated the neighborhood itself. Suddenly the residential pocket vaguely known as North of the Panhandle became NoPa, a trendy destination for cross-city hipsters hungry for the latest thing. With a fierce devotion to organic, farm-fresh fare, Nopa dishes such easy crowd-pleasers as an Early Girl tomato salad and a country pork chop wood-fired in the brick oven.

Despite the enormity of the space, which boasts a crowded mezzanine and whimsical local art, Nopa is hailed for friendly service and a boisterous vibe; the after-work crowd shares generous portions at the congenial communal table.

Nopalito

B2

Mexican X

306 Broderick St. (at Fell St.)

Phone: 415-437-0303　　　　　　　　　　　　　　　Lunch & dinner daily
Web: www.nopalitosf.com
Prices: 🥖🥖

Is it a zesty edible cactus? Or, little sister to neighboring Nopa? In name, Nopalito is a double entendre, but the ambiguity stops there.

With vibrant Mexican cuisine served in a mellow space, Nopalito's intent is clear: quality food, no strings attached. Organic décor and walls the shade of salsa verde set an unfussy backdrop for family-friendly meals handcrafted with local, sustainable goods. Start with kicky fried chickpeas on the house, followed by thick *totopos*—corn chips tossed with *chile de arbol* salsa and homemade *cotija* cheese.

A seasonal adobo sturgeon taco, washed down with hibiscus-blood orange soda, makes for a rewarding lunch; while a bowl of posole *rojo*, enjoyed on the heated patio, is a belly-warming cap to a night.

35

Otoro

C2

Japanese

205 Oak St. (at Gough St.)

Phone: 415-553-3986
Web: www.otorosushi.com
Prices: $$

Lunch Mon – Sat
Dinner nightly

As any sushi aficionado knows, *otoro* is the Japanese term for the prized yet scarce, melt-in-your-mouth cut of tuna belly that is rich in fat and healthful omega-3 fatty acids. At this tiny Hayes Valley sushi spot, *otoro* is featured among a wide range of raw, composed, and hot dishes.

Slurp through noodle bowls like miso ramen or tempura udon while checking out the dry erase board behind the sushi counter for seasonal offerings, such as seared hamachi belly and monkfish liver pâté. Or, feel free to get creative and suggest your own sushi roll ideas here.

A good selection of sake lines the shelves by the entrance, but if you are new to the field of rice wine, rest assured that the list here is well-illustrated and explained for novices.

Pagolac

D1

Vietnamese

655 Larkin St. (at Ellis St.)

Phone: 415-776-3234
Web: N/A
Prices:

Dinner Tue – Sun

San Francisco's Tenderloin district demands quality restaurants like Pagolac to lure folks to this less savory area. The owners of this tiny and very popular family-run business clearly pour their hearts into both the service and the fresh, vibrant Vietnamese food.

The weathered pink awning may not seem enticing, but once inside you'll be embraced by the friendly staff and captivated by the good food at bargain-basement prices. Do-it-yourself cooking and tableside dining are taken to the next level with the "7 Flavors of Beef," a multicourse feast that you prepare using tabletop firepots and a grill—delicious, unforgettable, and just plain fun. The kitchen is equally happy to oblige those seeking less hands-on eating, with claypots and noodle bowls.

Patxi's

Pizza 🍴

C2

511 Hayes St. (bet. Laguna & Octavia Sts.)

Phone: 415-558-9991
Web: www.patxispizza.com
Prices: $$

Lunch & dinner daily

An exuberant din of neighborhood pizza lovers rocks the rafters at Patxi's, the Hayes Valley outpost of the Palo Alto original. Exposed brick walls, concrete floors, and bright paintings from a nearby gallery give this location a distinctly San Francisco feel, though many of the pies actually nod to Chicago.

While Patxi's does offer cracker-crisp cornmeal pies for thin-crust devotees, deep dish is the main draw here. Expect to wait half an hour or more for that flakey-buttery, two-inch-deep sensation stuffed with gooey cheese; the "Favorite" is heavily heaped with pepperoni, mushrooms, and black olives. Salads and pizzas by the slice play well to the loyal lunch crowd, while half-baked take-home pies are a smart reward at the end of a long day.

paul k

Mediterranean 🍴🍴

C2

199 Gough St. (at Oak St.)

Phone: 415-552-7132
Web: www.paulkrestaurant.com
Prices: $$

Lunch Sat – Sun
Dinner Tue – Sun

It is no wonder that owner Paul Kavouksorian abbreviated his name on the sign above this Hayes Valley restaurant, where Paul K himself directs the well-choreographed service in the intimate dining room, conveniently located near the Opera House in Hayes Valley.

A leisurely weekend brunch may start with "bottomless" bloody Marys and mimosas to accompany the likes of smoked lox Benedict. Dinners may begin with an array of small plates celebrating Mediterranean, North African, and Armenian heritage in *meze* of lamb riblets, kebabs, baba ganoush, cucumbers, olives, feta, and yogurt. *Za'atar* (that intriguing herb and spice mix), sumac, and pomegranates are just a few of the more exotic ingredients that co-star with chicken, lamb, and Syrian-spiced duck.

Sauce

C2

131 Gough St. (bet. Oak & Page Sts.)

Phone: 415-252-1369   Dinner nightly
Web: www.saucesf.com
Prices: $$

In the lively performing arts district, where such dramatic acts as Jardinière and Zuni Café share the stage, Sauce is a quieter number that prefers substance to style. The dining room may be decades overdue for decorating, but the laid back, old wooden bar and hearty American menu—accented by some lighter, California-style choices—lure a consistent group of neighborhood regulars. Offerings may range from refreshing and savory white peach salad to bacon-wrapped meatloaf.

The kitchen is open until midnight daily, so even late-night snackers can pop in for a "PB&J"—sponge cake layered with strawberry preserves, Frangelico peanut butter, and vanilla ice cream. The bar is open till 2:00 A.M., making Sauce a hit for post-theater nightcaps.

Sebo

C2

517 Hayes St. (bet. Laguna & Octavia Sts.)

Phone: 415-864-2122   Dinner Tue – Sun
Web: www.sebosf.com
Prices: $$$

Local sushi lovers craving the quality easily found in New York and L.A. are happy to wait for a coveted spot (no reservations are taken) at the six-seat sushi bar of this Hayes Valley favorite. Trapezoidal tables are the lone design flourish in an otherwise minimalist space, but a glass of crisp, dry sake is all one needs to savor the experience.

Sebo is best known for its hard-to-find fish offerings such as seasonal firefly squid, gizzard shad, and blue fish gracing the nigiri selection. The sashimi omakase is silky, fresh, and pretty looking with its fan of carrots, shredded daikon, and shiso leaves. Cut rolls may appear less refined, but the *maguro* roll with avocado, radish, sesame oil, and sea salt bursts with memorable flavor.

Thep Phanom

Thai 🍴

C2

400 Waller St. (at Fillmore St.)

Phone: 415-431-2526   Dinner nightly
Web: www.thepphanom.com
Prices: $$

Founded in 1986, this little place delivers big flavors. The extensive menu stays true to what the restaurant bills as "authentic Thai cuisine," but also leaves the kitchen leeway to be creative. Thus, the standards like Massaman and Panang curries and pad Thai appear along with "Thaitanic" beef (a spicy stir-fry with a crunch of string beans and green peppers), and "Three's Company" (prawns, scallops, and calamari in coconut sauce). The "dancing" and "weeping" ladies referred to on the Favorites menu are all edible and delicious.

Warmly lit and furnished with simple wood chairs and cloth-covered tables, the small dining room fills up fast. The bar in the back of the room usually bustles with locals coming 'round to pick up carry-out fare.

1300 on Fillmore

American 🍴🍴🍴

C1

1300 Fillmore St. (at Eddy St.)

Phone: 415-771-7100   Lunch Sun
Web: www.1300Fillmore.com   Dinner nightly
Prices: $$$

1300 on Fillmore is pitch-perfect in bridging jazz-era nostalgia with a sultry, urbane vibe. A backlit wall of sepia-toned images and black-and-white photos of jazz greats add smooth notes to the posh leather-clad lounge, while gray and chocolate tones dress the soaring dining room. However, the menu of appetizing American soul food headlines the show and makes this a favorite in the Fillmore Jazz Preservation District.

Come hungry and prepared to devour an array of comfort food. A culinary performance might warm up with cornbread smothered in honey butter and pepper jelly; crescendo at supremely tender maple-braised beef short ribs with buttermilk mashed potatoes; and wind down with a hot apple cobbler. Classic cocktails sing spirited backup.

Yoshi's

Japanese ✗✗

C1

1330 Fillmore St. (at Eddy St.)

Phone: 415-655-5600
Web: www.yoshis.com
Prices: $$$

Dinner nightly

Inside the Fillmore Heritage Center, Yoshi's exhibition kitchen sets the stage for creative sushi in a jazzy interior that's suited to a grand performance hall. The restaurant has a contemporary-industrial aura with polished wood tables, concrete columns, and a sweeping staircase leading to an upstairs club. Moreover, the vast dining room can accommodate a sold out crowd of concert-goers with two lounge areas and a sleek sushi counter.

Service may be slow but the wait is worth it for such expertly prepared dishes as the "High Note," a sushi-sashimi combo including *maguro*, hamachi, and *unagi*; grilled *robata* plates; and rolls like the spicy dragon with shrimp tempura and creamy avocado. A glass from the well-curated sake list perfectly washes it all down.

Zuni Café

Mediterranean ✗✗

D2

1658 Market St. (bet. Franklin & Gough Sts.)

Phone: 415-552-2522
Web: www.zunicafe.com
Prices: $$

Lunch & dinner Tue – Sun

If you haven't idled away an afternoon slurping oysters and sipping champagne in a sunny window seat at venerable Zuni Café, you've never lived in San Francisco. A fixture since 1979 and evocative of a European eatery, Zuni remains at the height of local fashion. A 2009 face-lift made the split-level interior all the more inviting—the revamped mezzanine offers a delicious view.

Serving largely sustainable, ingredient-driven fare, Chef/owner Judy Rodgers seasons her Mediterranean menu with a pinch of California: the rosemary focaccia burger is a favorite; roast chicken is practically famous; and Serrano ham garnished with goat cheese-stuffed black mission figs is divine.

On weekends, denim-clad revelers sip aperitifs at the long, copper bar.

Financial District
Embarcadero • Union Square

Though San Francisco may be famed for its laid-back image, its bustling business district is ranked among the top financial centers in the nation. On weekdays, streetcars, pedestrians, and wildly tattooed bicycle messengers clog the streets of the triangle bounded by Kearny, Jackson, and Market streets. Lines snake out the doors of the better grab-and-go sandwich shops and salad bars at lunch; both day and night, a host of fine-dining restaurants in this quarter cater to clients with expense accounts. Along Market Street, casual cafés and chain restaurants focus on tourists and shoppers.

Despite all that the area has to offer, its greatest culinary treasures may be within the Ferry Building. This 1898 steel-reinforced sandstone structure was among the few survivors

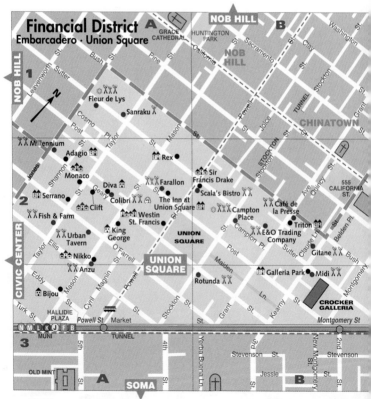

of the 1906 earthquake and fire that destroyed most of the area. It remains a clear neighborhood standout, easily recognized by its 244-foot clock tower rising from Market Street above the waterfront promenade known as The Embarcadero ("boarding place" in Spanish). Renovated in 2004, its soaring interior arcade now makes an architecturally stunning culinary showcase for local and artisanal foods, fine Chinese teas, and everything in between. Known as the **Ferry Building Marketplace**, this is a true foodie pilgrimage and includes Daniel Patterson and Lauren Kiino's **Cane Rosso**—

a quick serve rotisserie and sandwich shop..

The marketplace strives to support the local and artisanal food community by highlighting small regional producers. Among these, two of the most popular are the acclaimed **Cowgirl Creamery** farmstead cheeses and the organic breads of Berkeley's **Acme Bread Company**. Discover exotic, organic mushrooms, medicinals, and themed products at **Far West Fungi**. Patient enthusiasts can even purchase logs on which to grow their own harvest. The legendary **Frog Hollow Farms** also has an

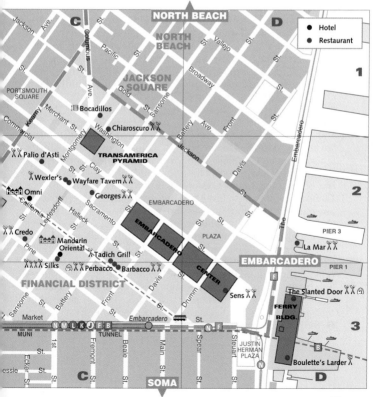

outpost here, offering luscious seasonal fruit as well as organic chutneys and marmalades. **Rechiutti Confections** elevates the art of crafting Parisian-style chocolates and caramels to a level that can only be described as heavenly!

Even the retail offerings are food-themed here, and include a number of cookware shops and home-design boutiques with a northern Californian flair. **4505 Meats** is hugely popular for Chef Ryan Farr's butchery classes, as well as for his smoked artisan hotdogs, sausages, and *chicarrones*.

While this world-class food shopping may whet the appetite, more immediate satisfaction can be found in the building's casual dining spots. **DELICA rf-1** offers beautifully-prepared Japanese fusion foods, from signature sushi rolls to savory croquettes. Grab a seat with the FiDi lunch crowds filling the picnic tables at **Mijita**—run by Traci Des Jardins of Jardinière—to enjoy some Oaxacan chicken tamales or Baja-style fish tacos. Or, take a stool at the bar of the **Hog Island Oyster Company**, whose fresh bivalves are plucked from the Tomales Bay in Marin County—this is a great spot to sit, slurp, and take in the view. Still perhaps the most decadent takeout option may be from **Boccalone Salumeria**, where one can find a full selection of charcuterie that are available for purchase by the platter, pound, or layered in a single-serving "cone" for an unapologetically carnivorous treat.

On Tuesday and Saturday mornings, join the chefs and crowds at the **Ferry Plaza Farmers Market** for organic produce, mouthwatering baked goods, fresh pasta, and more. On market days, stands and tents fill the sidewalk in front of the building and rear plaza that overlooks the bay.

Clusters of FiDi office workers head to the Embarcadero Center (spanning five blocks in the heart of the commercial district with reduced parking rates on weekends) to get their midday shopping fix in the sprawling three-story indoor mall and to grab a quick lunch in one of the complex's 30-some eateries, which range from chain restaurants to little noodle shops. Here you'll also find two longtime local favorites, **See's Candies** and **Peet's Coffee**.

Any serious shopper in San Francisco makes a pilgrimage to Union Square, the area bordering the formal park (named on the eve of the Civil War) on the FiDi's western edge. Here, upscale department stores like Saks and Neiman Marcus preside over the square. While fashionistas flock to the designers, foodies come for the area's profusion of gourmet restaurants. Eateries in this area are also favored by drama lovers, since they are conveniently located near some of the city's most beloved theaters.

Anzu

A2·3

Fusion

222 Mason St. (bet. Ellis & O'Farrell Sts.)

Phone: 415-394-1100   Lunch & dinner daily
Web: www.restaurantanzu.com
Prices: $$$

By the look of its stodgy dress and FiDi digs in the Nikko Hotel, Anzu calls to mind the Mac v. PC commercials wherein a creative type squares off with a corporate suit. Yet in a Clark Kent–style twist, Anzu sheds its uptight guise to reveal powerfully artistic "Euro-Japanese" cuisine guaranteed to impress.

Sample the popular signature sushi, bold with aromatics like shiso or ponzu, but the imaginative and flavorful fusion entrées reveal the menu's true inspiration. Smoky, caramelized, and nearly sweet fresh cod arrives glazed with miso alongside silky pork belly and a crisp daikon cake—the aromas of ginger and barbecue conspire to wake the senses. Also try hamachi with Spanish chorizo and Albariño sauce, or yuzu ginger chicken with *kabocha* risotto.

Barbacco

C3

Italian

220 California St. (bet. Battery & Front Sts.)

Phone: 415-955-1919   Lunch Mon – Fri
Web: www.barbaccosf.com   Dinner Mon – Sat
Prices:

Barbacco's style is matched only by its efficiency. This younger sister of Perbacco (next door) stretches its long, lean interior with the *oomph* of an Italian sports car—think Ferrari red and yellow accents, shiny stainless steel, and contemporary photos with a dizzying sense of motion. Busy FiDi regulars appreciate that the staff is equipped with hand-held POS systems to keep them on the go.

Bustling at lunch, dinner, and for drinks in between, Barbacco serves impeccable trattoria fare as well as takeout bites. Light nibbles include crispy bruschetta topped with smoked *lonza* and marinated Tuscan kale, while pickled peppers, olives, and house-cured salumi make a hearty butcher's salad. As at Perbacco, the rustic house-made pastas are perfection.

Bocadillos

Spanish

C1

710 Montgomery St. (at Washington St.)

Phone: 415-982-2622
Web: www.bocasf.com
Prices: ⊜⊜

Lunch Mon – Fri
Dinner Mon – Sat

   A fiery shade of *piment d'espelette* (a spice made from dried Basque peppers) heats the walls at Bocadillos, Chef/owner Gerald Hirigoyen's tiny tapas bar that pays homage to a *pequeño* Spanish sandwich loaded with big, authentic flavors. At lunch, FiDi suits file in for the $10 duo and choose from hot and cold varieties such as chorizo with walnut spread and parsley; 18-month Serrano ham rubbed with fleshy tomato; and mini lamb burgers with fresh shallot.

High stools around the polished wood bar are a laid back perch to enjoy a glass of Spanish wine, while tapas and salads round out the offering at supper. Come nightfall, votives illuminate a snug uncluttered space where the tables are loaded with baskets of utensils and small plates for sharing.

Boulette's Larder

Californian ✗

D3

1 Ferry Building (at The Embarcadero)

Phone: 415-399-1155
Web: www.bouletteslarder.com
Prices: $$

Lunch Sun – Fri

   Think of this little retail business in the Ferry Building as a foodie's version of an apothecary. Here discover everything from wild Italian fennel and rose petal sugar, to lobster stock or squab sauce—and don't forget to pick up Japanese specialty items like bamboo charcoal and freeze-dried yuzu. Beside the esoteric ingredients (pine needle syrup, anyone?), there are composed salads by the pound, soups by the quart, and mouthwatering pastries.

At breakfast, lunch, and Sunday brunch (the only meals served), eat at either the communal kitchen counter or at tables just outside in the busy hall. Choose the former to watch the chefs prepare a daily changing roster of dishes from local, organic, sustainably-raised products—right before your eyes.

Café de la Presse

B2

French ✗✗

352 Grant Ave. (at Bush St.)

Phone: 415-398-2680
Web: www.cafedelapresse.com
Prices: $$

Lunch & dinner daily

After a fashionable stroll through nearby Union Square, Café de la Presse is a lovely spot to brush up on your French with an après-shopping glass of viognier. The sunny street-front café is dotted with bistro tables and stocked to the rafters with international newspapers and magazines; if you desire to actually speak French, the restaurant's manager is happy to oblige.

Framed reproductions of vintage French posters dress the slightly more formal wood-paneled dining room where Francophiles from near and far nosh on authentic dishes such as Niçoise salad heaped with flaked white tuna, haricot verts, olives, and hard-boiled eggs atop butter lettuce; or traditional steak frites seasoned simply with salt and cracked black pepper. *Bon appétit*!

Chiaroscuro

C1

Italian ✗✗

550 Washington St. (bet. Montgomery & Sansome Sts.)

Phone: 415-362-6012
Web: www.chiaroscurosf.com
Prices: $$

Lunch Mon – Fri
Dinner Mon – Sat

Set across from I.M. Pei's dramatic Transamerica pyramid, Chiaroscuro takes its aesthetic cues from stark architectural forms and the neighborhood's Italian heritage. Austere white walls, dotted minimally with art, rise to a vaulted ceiling; while a concrete banquette with fluffy pillows provides Chiaroscuro with its namesake point of contrast.

Chef Alessandro hails from Roma and takes inspiration from the region: Italian specialties from the open kitchen include homemade carbonara and *spaghetti all'amatriciana* with *guanciale* and San Marzano tomato sauce. Begin with fresh-baked bread and flavored butters or the *insalata de fragole*— a mix of greens, pistachios, and fresh strawberries in balsamic vinaigrette. Viva the friendly service!

Campton Place ✿

Contemporary 🍴🍴🍴

B2

340 Stockton St. (bet. Post & Sutter Sts.)

Phone: 415-955-5555   Lunch & dinner daily
Web: www.camptonplacesf.com
Prices: $$$$

Taj Campton Place

Housed in the Taj Campton Place, an elegant little hotel located just off bustling Union Square, this contemporary restaurant is an expense account kind of place—the mood usually being fairly quiet and sedate, as power players swap cards in a comfortable, upscale setting with low lighting.

Not to say you can't go for a date—the bar, in fact, has a warm buzz to it most nights of the week. And no matter where you sit, you'll want to spend some time with the fantastic wine list, a visionary roundup that offers New and Old World vintages alike.

The food can read simplistically on the menu at times, but make no mistake, the result of Chef Srijith Gopinathan's marriage of Southern Indian spices and Euro-Californian sensibilities is intricate, complex, and delicious. The tasting menus rotate often, but might reveal fresh lumps of tender Dungeness crab paired with caviar, toasted lentil crumbs, diced blood orange, and ruby-red grapefruit, succulent crab claw and mint; an earthy Jerusalem artichoke soup bobbing with a soft-poached farm egg, crispy fried pancetta, and white truffle oil; or an exquisitely fresh piece of arctic char served in a silky mussel vichyssoise.

Colibrí

A2

Mexican 🍴🍴

438 Geary St (bet. Mason & Taylor Sts.)

Phone: 415-440-2737   Lunch & dinner daily
Web: www.colibrimexicanbistro.com
Prices: $$

With wrought-iron chandeliers and lanterns casting a glow on massive mirrors, this warm Spanish Colonial–style dining room feels a world away from the sleek Italian suits and chic French fashions adorning Union Square's boutiques. But when the shopping set craves a margarita, it heads to the mahogany bar at Colibri, a high-end Mexican bistro displaying an impressive array of tequilas and vintage Latino films.

The front of the house buzzes with theatergoers grabbing a bite before a show; at back, larger tables are ideal for leisurely meals. Begin with guacamole mixed tableside then sink your teeth into tender poblano chicken with chocolaty mole. Cooler days call for a fortifying bowl of *posole verde* with braised chicken, plump hominy, and green chili.

Credo

C2

Italian 🍴🍴

360 Pine St. (bet. Montgomery & Sansome Sts.)

Phone: 415-693-0360   Lunch Tue – Fri
Web: www.credosf.com   Dinner Mon – Sat
Prices: $$

At Credo, located in the heart of the Financial District and named for the Latin term "I believe," pinstriped suits can roll up their sleeves. The industrial, loft-style space features clean white walls, scrawled with philosophical quotes, and handmade salvaged wood tables—a refreshing addition to the modern, business savvy neighborhood.

The Italian trattoria menu of thin-crust pizzas, salads, and rustic pastas lends to the warm downtown vibe. And with relatively low prices, hungry execs can indulge in a feast. Look for a flavorful albacore tuna and cannellini bean salad, and pies topped with spicy Tuscan sausage and smoked mozzarella. The dense, flourless chocolate cake is well above average and the bar is ideal for dining solo or post-work drinks.

E&O Trading Company

B2

Asian

314 Sutter St. (bet. Grant & Stockton Sts.)

Phone: 415-693-0303

Web: www.eotrading.com

Prices: $$$

Lunch & dinner daily

Just steps from the dramatic 1970s Chinatown Gate, E&O Trading Company serves a taste of Southeast Asia in an interior that reflects both exotic flavors and Union Square chic. Mammoth glowing lanterns take center stage in the dramatic dining room where Asian artifacts and green bamboo create a steamy vibe that lures both neighborhood professionals for lunch or happy hour as well as tourists at dinner.

The spicy menu offerings are as far reaching as the soaring ceilings. In addition to the notable house infusions, the cocktail crowds sample such appetizers as lemongrass-scented Thai rock shrimp cakes and chicken and pork dumplings with tangy citrus chili sauce. Entrées, like roasted *char siu* black cod, may lack the zest of their creative small plates.

Farallon

A2

Seafood

450 Post St. (bet. Mason & Powell Sts.)

Phone: 415-956-6969

Web: www.farallonrestaurant.com

Prices: $$$

Dinner nightly

Named for the national wildlife refuge that covers a string of islands off the coast, this undersea fantasy is located near Union Square area shops and theaters. Much of the drama lies inside the restaurant, swimming with flamboyant jellyfish chandeliers, glowing kelp-like columns, scallop-shaped booths, and a school of other aquatic elements—all set beneath hand-painted cloistered ceilings that date back to 1924.

Move away from the capricious yet classy design to discover true savoir faire in seafood such as a crispy Chesapeake Bay soft shell crab atop broiled purple tomatoes with a divine roasted duck crouton and herbaceous sauce verte; or grilled Alaskan king salmon with delicate sweet corn ravioli, Romano beans, and crispy apple-smoked bacon.

Fish & Farm

A2

American 〤〤

339 Taylor St. (bet. Ellis & O'Farrell Sts.)

Phone: 415-474-3474   Dinner Mon – Sat
Web: www.fishandfarmsf.com
Prices: $$

This narrow, attractive space flanked by chocolate-brown leather banquettes and marble tables, serves a menu of organic produce and sustainably-raised meat and seafood— all sourced from within a 100-mile radius of the restaurant, when possible. The likes of roasted Pacific halibut with green garlic purée, spring vegetable ragout, wild mushrooms, and Port-shallot reduction; fried Petaluma chicken with Gracie's cornbread; and Liberty ale-battered fish and chips made with local cod sing the praises of American products. Still, the Niman Ranch cheeseburger has the most devout following. One caveat: the valet parking option is only for Hotel Mark Twain guests, so everyone else must allow time for hunting down a coveted spot.

Georges

C2

Seafood 〤〤

415 Sansome St. (bet. Commercial & Sacramento Sts.)

Phone: 415-956-6900   Lunch & dinner Mon – Fri
Web: www.georgessf.com
Prices: $$

Housed in the historic Fugazi building—an Italian bank during the Gold Rush Era—Georges adheres to a philosophic purity in tune with the mod Bay Area. The restaurant takes great pride in its locally sourced ingredients and sustainable fare, while the atmosphere is warmed by recycled design,— envisage tables made of reclaimed Asian rosewood flooring. A window display of fresh fish and shellfish is a not-so-subtle hint of what's to come from the sleek, open kitchen: octopus carpaccio with lemon, capers, and arugula; plump blue nose sea bass with rosemary-roasted fingerling potatoes; and ice cold oysters, ceviche, and clams at the raw bar. A glass wall of wine is mighty alluring, though a sweet *tartufo* chocolate tempts one to a hasty finish.

Fleur de Lys

French 🍴🍴🍴

A1

777 Sutter St. (bet. Jones & Taylor Sts.)

Dinner Tue – Sat

Phone: 415-673-7779
Web: www.fleurdelyssf.com
Prices: $$$$

Fleur de Lys

Honoring a reservation at Fleur de Lys is like a stamp on your passport to a faraway era where serious cooking demanded strictly indulgent décor. Fleur de Lys' lavish dining room is elaborately tented in a patterned textile that drapes heavily down the walls, and a massive floral arrangement rises and blooms toward the pavilion's peak. An ornate Murano glass chandelier looms from the center, keeping watch over the white-clothed tables and the choreography of a well-suited staff.

The vibe is romantic, even if it is a bit old-fashioned. A mixed clientele of affluent locals, theatergoers, and couples toasting special occasions continue to be charmed by Chef Hubert Keller, who has helmed this fine dining mainstay since 1986.

Rich with decadent flavors, Keller's menu is perfect for a big night. His contemporary French dishes may disclose a foie gras torchon topped with thinly sliced duck breast garnished with pineapple gelée, bright peppers, and Marcona almonds; slow-braised Wagyu beef cheeks with a crunchy pretzel crust; and the ever-perfect and piping hot Grand Marnier soufflé. A robust French wine list and tableside Absinthe service only accentuates the drama of Fleur de Lys.

Gitane

Mediterranean

B2

6 Claude Ln. (bet. Bush & Sutter Sts.)

Phone: 415-788-6686
Web: www.gitanerestaurant.com
Prices: $$

Dinner Tue – Sat

Named for its gypsy spirit, Gitane cooks up a sultry atmosphere in a whimsical yet dark and dusky upstairs dining room. Remember to book ahead for a table in this avant-garde, hip, and eclectic space, which fashions a relaxed lounge feel.

Wandering from the Basque country of Spain to the sands of Morocco, Gitane's menu imparts the exotic aromas and techniques from North Africa and the Mediterranean with dishes like white shrimp salad with endives, shaved fennel, and orange vinaigrette; sweet and savory bastilla with duck, chicken, and Moroccan spices; or roasted quail stuffed with chicken mousseline and raisins with a Port demi-glace.

Besides their inventive cocktails, Gitane also boasts a respectable selection of sherry and Madeira.

La Mar

Peruvian

D2

Pier 1 1/2 (at The Embarcadero)

Phone: 415-397-8880
Web: www.lamarsf.com
Prices: $$

Lunch & dinner daily

Pisco cocktails and adventurous ceviches (*cebiches*) are de rigueur at this Pier One-and-a-Half *cevicheria Peruana*, enhanced by Bay views and a waterfront breeze on the patio. While Latin-American culinary star Gaston Acurio owns many international eateries, this is the chef's first foray into North America. A vivid interior mirrors the sparkling flavors of the fresh and balanced mingling of ceviches, like the "chifa" with Mahi Mahi, peanuts, mango, and habanero; or the "chipotle" with scallops, calamari, and shrimp—with habanero adding even more heat to the *leche de tigre*.

Other delicacies include an artistically presented tasting of four *causas* (whipped potato cakes) and tender chicken stew with *aji amarillo*, a fruity yellow pepper indigenous to Peru.

San Francisco ▶ Financial District

53

Midi

B3

Californian ✗✗

185 Sutter St. (at Kearny St.)

Phone: 415-835-6400
Web: www.midisanfrancisco.com
Prices: $$

Lunch daily
Dinner Mon – Sat

Enter through the sleek street-level bar and navigate up the stairs to a dining room where guests people-watch over tartines, fresh salads, and virgin spritzers at this hot spot between the Financial District and Union Square. The business-chic dining room features streamlined wood fixtures, leather and chrome accents, alongside pinstriped banquettes. The design, however, is rendered with balance: pops of hot pink and a flirty, floral mural lend both feminine mystique and *joie de vivre*.

This seasonal menu focuses on fresh, Californian bistro fare. The "Midi quartet" makes a stylish lunch at less than $20, while seasonal dinners may include pan-roasted cod or braised spring lamb. For dessert, the bittersweet chocolate mousse is a decadent must.

Millennium

A2

Vegan ✗✗

580 Geary St. (at Jones St.)

Phone: 415-345-3900
Web: www.millenniumrestaurant.com
Prices: $$

Dinner nightly

Many cultures influence Millennium's vegan cuisine, which bursts with flavor and creativity. A black bean torte with caramelized plantains, pumpkin-honey *papazul*, and English pea samosa may hail from different parts of the world, but all are masterfully made at the hands of Chef Eric Tucker. Even tried and true carnivores trade their steaks for tofu here inside the Hotel California, where the friendly staff is eager to offer advice about the area's best organic markets. Dishes are so tasty that this place is packed most nights, so reserving ahead is advised. Otherwise, hope for a seat at the first-come, first-served bar counter.

Any budget woes will be soothed by the three-course Frugal Foodie menu, offered each Sunday through Wednesday night.

Palio d'Asti

Italian ✗✗

C2

640 Sacramento St. (bet. Kearny & Montgomery Sts.)

Phone: 415-395-9800
Lunch & dinner Mon – Fri
Web: www.paliodasti.com
Prices: $$

♿

Named for Il Palio, a bareback horserace in the Italian town of Asti that harks back to the Middle Ages, this FiDi favorite does not stray from its theme. Equestrian art gallops around concrete columns and across walls, while courtly banners and vibrant coats of arms trumpet contemporary Italian meals of enormous proportions.

The fare hails from various Italian regions and is available in two-, three-, and four-course prix-fixe menus that largely appeal to neighborhood businessmen. Aromatic, authentic, and generous dishes might include hand-rolled penne pasta with herb-rich tomato sauce and Berkshire pork *guanciale*; fennel sausage pizza with smoked mozzarella; or a steaming fisherman's stew with spicy saffron-lobster broth and grilled sourdough.

Perbacco 😵

Italian ✗✗

C3

230 California St. (bet. Battery & Front Sts.)

Phone: 415-955-0663
Lunch Mon – Fri
Web: www.perbaccosf.com
Dinner Mon – Sat
Prices: $$

♿
⅋

Perbacco loosely translates to "good times" in Italian and that's exactly what you'll have when you come here. From the cool marble bar to the sleek furnishings, Perbacco has city chic written all over it. It is urban and up-to-the-minute and its smartly dressed and sophisticated crowd knows it.

The highly professional and knowledgeable staff make this a tightly run ship, while the country Italian cooking is sure to please. The food focuses on the Piemonte region with a little bit of Liguria, and even Provence, thrown in for good measure. It's comfort food for city slickers—truffle herb ricotta gnocchi, rabbit-stuffed *agnolotti*, pappardelle topped with short rib ragù, and slow-roasted veal—all at palatable prices.

Rotunda

Californian ✗✗

B3

150 Stockton St. (at Geary St.)

Phone: 415-362-4777   Lunch daily
Web: www.neimanmarcus.com
Prices: $$$

Upon entering Neiman Marcus from Union Square, cast your eyes skyward to the four-story Belle Époque rotunda. This marvelous architectural opus was crowned the City of Paris department store and built in 1908 on this site. Highlighted in cream and gold with gilded carvings of Poseidon, the soaring oval stained glass dome bears a nautical theme. The eponymous restaurant that sits under the rotunda looks down on Union Square through large windows.

At midday, Rotunda overflows with well-heeled ladies who lunch; the light menu of American fare caters to their tastes, while the upscale prices aim at the credit cards in their designer bags. Count on a complimentary taste of chicken consommé to begin, along with puffy turnovers paired with strawberry butter.

Sanraku

Japanese ✗

A1

704 Sutter St. (at Taylor St.)

Phone: 415-771-0803   Lunch Mon – Sat
Web: www.sanraku.com   Dinner nightly
Prices: ⊛

When it comes to consuming raw fish, it's easy to judge a sushi bar by its cover: sleek can be a misleading synonym for fresh. But San Francisco sushi connoisseurs know that the most outstanding seafood hides out in unassuming corners. Welcome to Sanraku, a no-frills favorite with quick, inexpensive, and quality Japanese bites.

Dressed in bare light walls and blonde wood tables, Sanraku isn't much to look at. But natural light and spunky service keep things upbeat, and ample portions do not disappoint the Western palate. Santa Barbara uni is fresh and creamy, and the sashimi platter is loaded with flavorful fluke, Spanish mackerel, and salmon. With small salads and bowls of miso soup, lunch specials appeal to the local working set.

Scala's Bistro

Italian ✕✕

B2

432 Powell St. (bet. Post & Sutter Sts.)

Phone: 415-395-8555   Lunch & dinner daily
Web: www.scalasbistro.com
Prices: $$

Historic charm radiates from this casually elegant bistro, adjacent to the venerable Sir Francis Drake Hotel a block from Union Square. Classy but not stuffy, Scala's tuxedo-clad servers, original murals, and art deco ceiling conjure the best of the Old World. An open kitchen provides a brick backdrop dangling with antique copper cookware.

Here, Chef Jen Biesty, of *Top Chef* fame, infuses Italian country cuisine with Californian flair in turkey tortellini in a Parmesan *brodo* with vegetables and tarragon *pistou*. The *secondi* course may feature a tender braised Wagyu short rib with creamy celery root purée, gremolata, and parsnip crisps; or *mezzaluna* ravioli stuffed with braised lamb *agrodolce*. Mini-portions of selected desserts allow a last sweet bite.

Sens

Mediterranean ✕✕

D3

4 Embarcadero Center (Sacramento St. at Drumm St.)

Phone: 415-362-0645   Lunch Mon – Fri
Web: www.sens-sf.com   Dinner Mon – Sat
Prices: $$$

Part of a six building complex, 4 Embarcadero Center is the tallest—at 45 stories—of its kind. Visit the promenade level for a meal at Sens, the cavernous restaurant that showcases faux alligator-skin armchairs, flagstone walls, and wood-beamed ceilings draped with fabric. Perhaps best of all, this dining room and its spacious patio enjoy views of the Ferry Building right across the street and the Bay Bridge beyond.

Richly spiced tastes of Turkey, Greece, and North Africa flavor the changing Mediterranean menu. For dessert, honey-cumin *pot de crème* and cocoa-nib panna cotta merely scrape the surface of the sophisticated sweets.

If parking in the garage here, be sure the restaurant validates your ticket or parking may cost as much as the meal.

Silks

C2

Contemporary

222 Sansome St. (bet. California & Pine Sts.)

Phone: 415-986-2020

Web: www.mandarinoriental.com

Prices: **$$$$**

Lunch Mon – Fri
Dinner Wed – Sat

Gold and white linens top the tables at Silks, the resident restaurant at the Financial District's Mandarin Oriental hotel. Here you'll find, what else, but coppery silk drapes and honey silk hanging lamps, as well as luxurious armchairs and booths rich with blue velvet. The effect is a subtly exotic background for Californian cuisine with a distinct Asian inflection.

Prosperous patrons flood the space in anticipation of dishes such as classic green papaya salad, beautifully plated on contemporary whiteware, with the bright colors and vibrant flavors of pink grapefruit and dried red pepper. Confit of Sonoma duck leg has a perfectly rendered, crispy skin that locks in yummy moisture. Sweet tooths should try the coconut sorbet for dessert.

The Slanted Door

D3

Vietnamese

1 Ferry Building (at The Embarcadero)

Phone: 415-861-8032

Web: www.slanteddoor.com

Prices: **$$**

Lunch & dinner daily

Faraway from the struggles of Vietnam, Charles Phan's forever sacred Slanted Door embodies a fortuitous marriage of local bounty kissed with Californian flair and faithful Vietnamese flavors. A virtual emperor of a Bay Area empire, his branches ooze verve and vivacity. Superbly set in the cuisine-centric Ferry Building, the hype still sates at this swank and scenic space.

Cypress tables cradle earthenware parading a litany of Viet delights. Tinged with clean, fresh flavors are tiger shrimp in chili sauce; classic spring rolls; squid sautéed with sweet peppers and jalapeño; lemongrass chicken drenched in roasted chili paste; and cellophane noodles rippling with crab.

The bar lures boisterous beauties with a bevy of beers, cocktails, and teas.

Tadich Grill

Seafood 🍴

240 California St. (bet. Battery & Front Sts.)

Phone: 415-391-1849
Web: www.tadichgrill.com
Prices: $$

Lunch & dinner Mon – Sat

Tadich Grill is as much a spot for history buffs as it is for local foodies: opened in 1849, San Francisco's oldest restaurant retains its antique charm. While there are a few tables, regulars prefer a niche at the long wood bar where they can catch up with fellow barflies and watch the white-coated staff up close.

Try not to fill up on sliced sourdough—the simple dishes are hearty. Mainstays include a creamy Boston clam chowder; large Dungeness crab cakes with steamed baby bok choy; and fresh seafood entrées that may be broiled, pan-fried, sautéed, poached, deep-fried, or baked *en casserole*. Don't forget about the delightful daily specials, which may include seafood cioppino with garlic bread; broiled lobster tail; and corned beef hash.

Urban Tavern

Gastropub 🍴🍴

333 O'Farrell St. (bet. Mason & Taylor Sts.)

Phone: 415-923-4400
Web: www.urbantavernsf.com
Prices: $$

Dinner nightly

Set off the lobby of the large Hilton Hotel, this place is hardly a tavern in the strict sense of the word. However, it is indeed urban; the design is chic and sleek, with warm earthy tones and light wood accents that soften the lines of the room. Tying old and new together is an eye-catching multicolored horse sculpture, cobbled from salvaged automobiles and farm machinery parts.

The inviting bill of fare features classic yet sober pub grub. The Ploughman's board carries a selection of meats and cheese, while a starter of grilled *Caggiano* beer sausage and house-made soft pretzel bun plays well with beer. Homey entrées include fish and chips; braised short ribs; and the Urban Tavern burger with bacon, white cheddar, grilled onions, and potato-onion fries.

Wayfare Tavern

C2

Gastropub ✕✕

558 Sacramento St. (bet. Montgomery & Sansome Sts.)

Phone: 415-772-9060
Web: www.wayfaretavern.com
Prices: $$

Lunch Mon – Fri
Dinner nightly

Maybe it's because big name chef, Tyler Florence of Food Network fame, pays the rent or maybe it's because it's just plain good, but Wayfare Tavern is way cool. This highly anticipated restaurant has caught on quickly with a crowd of movers and shakers and masters of the universe.

Wood floors and furnishings, vintage-style wallpaper, open kitchen with counter seats—it's the embodiment of the new take on Old World pubs.

Californian-American dishes rule the roost. All ingredients are locally sourced and then dressed up with a decidedly talented hand. If you're lucky enough to get a table (reservations are a must), tuck in to yummy dishes like smoked pork chops with roasted fennel and peach pie with goat's milk ice cream and rosemary sugar.

Wexler's

C2

American ✕

568 Sacramento St. (bet. Leidesdorff & Montgomery Sts.)

Phone: 415-983-0102
Web: www.wexlerssf.com
Prices: $$

Lunch Mon – Fri
Dinner Tue – Sat

Blink and you might just miss Wexler's. This diminutive spot has just a sprinkling of tables and a few seats at the bar, but those who plan ahead and make reservations are generously rewarded with inspired southern-influenced cooking.

Inside, it feels like the simple dining room of a slightly quirky art student. Stark white walls are offset by two red chandeliers, while simple metal chairs and stools sit at blonde wood tables.

Dishes exemplify the restaurant's slightly offbeat, but gourmet approach to barbeque-inspired American cuisine. Expect the menu to highlight smoked and roasted flavors in dishes such as barbecue Scotch eggs wrapped in short ribs and served with sweet tea gastrique, pork plate with creamy grits, and smoked collard greens risotto.

Marina
Japantown • Pacific Heights • Presidio

If San Francisco were a university campus, the Marina would be Greek Row: For what it lacks in diversity and substance, it makes up with a nod to those with "new money." The Marina's more sophisticated sister, Pacific Heights, thrives on serious family money and couldn't care less about being edgy.

When the tanned denizens of this beautiful bubble aren't jogging with their golden retrievers at Crissy Field, or sipping aromatic chocolate from the **Warming Hut**, they can be seen pushing designer baby strollers in boutiques or vying for parking in Mercedes SUVs.

Perhaps surprisingly, fine dining is not a hallmark of the Marina. Rather, this socialite's calling card is the quick-bite café **La Boulange** or the **Grove**; the gastropub, à la **Liverpool Lil's** or the **Balboa Café**; and the pickup joint **Perry's**, said to have been among the world's first. In truth, quality cuisine has little to do with a Marina restaurant's success: The locals are delightfully content to follow the buzz to the latest hot spot, whose popularity seems mandated by the number of pretty people sitting at its tables. However, in the Presidio, where Lucasfilm H.Q. rules, creatives and tech geeks opt for convenience at nearby **Presidio Social Club** and **La Terrasse**.

For the Marina's physically fit and diet-conscious residents, food is mere sustenance to the afternoon shopper and a sponge for the champagne and chardonnay flowing at plentiful watering holes. In other words—it's all about the bar scene, baby, and there's a playground for everyone. Oenophiles save the date for the annual ZAP Zinfandel Festival in January. Preppy post-collegiates swap remembrances of European semesters abroad at **Ottimista Enoteca-Café**, **Bacchus Wine Bar**, and **Nectar**. Guys relive their frat house glory days at **Bayside Sports Bar & Grill** or **Harry's Bar**. Well-heeled singles on the hunt for marriageable meat prefer the

fireplace at posh and trendy **MatrixFillmore**.

With a burgeoning Asian culture, Japantown is the exception to the rule. Hotel Tomo got a cool J Pop overhaul and serves all-you-can-eat shabu-shabu at Mums Restaurant and Bar. O Izakaya Lounge riffs on the Japanese novelty for baseball; and the fabulous Sundance Kabuki Cinema serves a range of treats in their two full bars. Also in abundance here are hugely sought after Japanese cultural events, local shopping, and scores of schools.

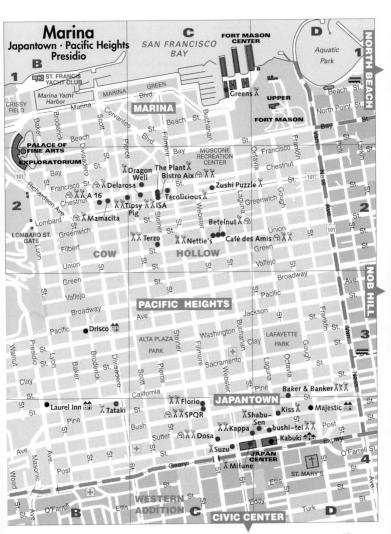

A 16

B2   Italian XX

2355 Chestnut St. (bet. Divisadero & Scott Sts.)

Phone: 415-771-2216   Lunch Wed – Fri
Web: www.a16sf.com   Dinner nightly
Prices: $$

With a wood-burning oven, house-cured meats, and swags of chili hanging out to dry, A16 feels more Campania than Marina despite its local hipster crowd. Pour in a list of seductive Southern Italian wines, curated by owner Shelley Lindgren, and A16 could be a cozy roadside retreat on the Italian highway that inspired its name.

Chef Liza Shaw steers the laid-back but precise kitchen, turning out soulful Southern Italian fare with northern Cali influence. Pizzas are blistered to a delectable crisp and heaped with faithfuls like earthy mushrooms and smoked mozzarella; pastas and meatballs are divine; and entrées like roasted stuffed quail are delicious crowd pleasers. Dessert may bring a fig and raspberry *crostata* with ricotta gelato and crunchy pistachios.

Baker & Banker

D3   Californian XXX

1701 Octavia St. (at Bush St.)

Phone: 415-351-2500   Dinner Tue – Sun
Web: www.bakerandbanker.com
Prices: $$

Baker & Banker is at once a new old favorite, the kind of husband-wife-owned eatery that feels like it's been there for years. Opened in 2009, the space oozes warmth in hues of espresso and honey while framed mirrors reflect chalkboards scrawled with beer and wine specials.

Both husband (Jeff Banker) and wife (Lori Baker) are in the kitchen, though they do regularly pop out to assure your satisfaction. Judging by their harmonious cuisine, this is a happy marriage indeed.

These approachable yet refined meals may begin with sweet potato rolls and creamy butter enhanced with *fleur de sel*, followed by nettle fettuccine or soy and mirin-braised black cod. Excellent desserts, like the kumquat sticky toffee pudding, are the couple's pride and joy.

Betelnut

C2

A s i a n ✕

2030 Union St. (bet. Buchanan & Webster Sts.)

Phone: 415-929-8855   Lunch & dinner daily
Web: www.betelnutrestaurant.com
Prices: $$

This bustling open kitchen cranks out great Far Eastern street-food delicacies, with focus on small plates designed for sharing and pairing with perhaps a Tsing Tao or Elephant beer. Sample grilled pancakes with hand-pulled Mongolian hoisin pork; *bien pow* chicken with dried Sichuan chilis and almonds; Sri Lankan clay pot curried fish; and myriad other options for those with an asbestos palate.

Its mysterious vibe, sultry lighting, and lazy bamboo fans over streetfront Dragonfly Lounge earn this Marina favorite major points for ambience, though service is often lukewarm. Nevertheless, a red lacquered bar is a sleek spot for creative cocktails and the upstairs dining room is constantly packed with festive revelers—reservations are recommended.

Bistro Aix

C2

M e d i t e r r a n e a n

3340 Steiner St. (bet. Chestnut & Lombard Sts)

Phone: 415-202-0100   Dinner nightly
Web: www.bistroaix.com
Prices: $$

Marina locals who missed their favorite neighborhood eatery are relieved at the return of Bistro Aix, which closed briefly for a welcome renovation. Opened again in April 2010, Aix is back and better than ever, welcoming loyalists with the scent of an oak-burning grill. A reclaimed redwood banquette lines the back dining room where tables are topped with cotton dishcloth napkins; the back atrium is sunny, framing a decade-old olive tree, giving Aix the *au naturel* aroma of Provence.

Southern French fare has a Californian accent. Expect such dishes as tender squid on white bean crostini with flavorful *persillade*; fresh salmon *a la plancha* perfectly prepared; and a very high-quality dark chocolate cloud cake with whipped crème fraîche and toasted almonds.

bushi-tei

D4

1638 Post St. (bet. Buchanan & Laguna Sts.)

Phone: 415-440-4959
Web: www.bushi-tei.com
Prices: **$$$**

Lunch & dinner daily

On a strip of Japantown marked by authentic storefronts and few traces of English, bushi-tei speaks its own language. The performance begins with a glass of "micro-structured electrolysis water with a pH of 8.5-9.5, an indication of extreme detail in Chef Seiji Wakabayashi's French fusion kitchen. Dramatic acts include foie gras with *kabocha* squash *pot de crème*, or tender lamb loin balanced atop haricots verts and black rice galette. Chilled sake and interesting wines make witty accomplices.

A 16-seat glass communal table hogs the stage, but the candlelit set is actually intimate. Rustic wood wall panels date to 1863 Japan, and a mini mezzanine is ideal for private omakase tastings.

For a modest meal, try bushi-tei bistro across the street.

Café des Amis

C2

2000 Union St. (at Buchanan St.)

Phone: 415-563-7700
Web: www.cafedesamissf.com
Prices: **$$**

Dinner Mon – Sat

The Chanel suit wearing clan clamors for a table at the lovely Café des Amis. Serving classic French dishes in an authentic setting, this faddy restaurant has already captured the hearts of the city's who's who. Even if you didn't have your assistant book a reservation in the highly coveted mezzanine, you can still be part of the scene with a seat in the first-come, first-served bar area.

The traditional French dishes are enough to bring Proust to tears. From bouillabaisse and *pot de feu* to steak frites, duck *rillettes*, and salad Niçoise, it is just what any Francophile yens for. Mussels in white wine broth with tomato *brunoise* are simple, but deliciously plump, while tender, juicy chicken Ballotine is roasted just enough to crisp the skin.

Delarosa

Italian

C2

2175 Chestnut St. (bet. Pierce & Steiner Sts.)

Phone: 415-673-7100
Web: www.delarosasf.com
Prices: $$

Lunch & dinner daily

Pizza and beer prove their very happy (and economy-proof) marriage at this posh neighborhood darling from the owners of Beretta and Starbelly. The challenging parking is a boon to the deep-pocketed local hipsters, who walk here in droves to keep the small place packed.

Inside the modern space in grey and tangerine hues, trendsters hoping to see and be seen line the blonde wood communal tables. A selection of 15 draught beers complements the Roman-style crispy pizzas decked with house-cured meats. The ever-popular margarita is worth the upgrade to their silky *burratta* cheese for a few bucks more.

The kitchen also turns out an array of antipasti, including beet carpaccio and crab *arancini*; pastas; and Italian gelato spiked with grappa.

Dosa

Indian

C4

1700 Fillmore St. (at Post St.)

Phone: 415-441-3672
Web: www.dosasf.com
Prices: $$

Lunch & dinner daily

Emily and Anjan Mitra's Dosa in Pacific Heights outshines its Valencia Street sibling with a larger space, more opulent contemporary design, inviting bar, and vibe that verges on the euphoric. Tones of burnt orange, tangerine, chocolate, and mustard dress the urban setting, while the dancing gold deity Shiva oversees it all.

This larger offering of Southern Indian cuisine includes a reasonably priced four-course tasting menu at dinner. Crisp curls of fennel-studded *pappadam* make a fine introduction to an array of *dosas* filled with everything from the classic masala (creamy spiced potatoes, onions, and cashew nuts), to mouth-searing habañero-mango chutney. For a unique variation, try the tomato, onion, and chili *uttapam*, and let the flavors seep in.

Dragon Well

C2

Chinese ✗

2142 Chestnut St. (bet. Pierce & Steiner Sts.)

Phone: 415-474-6888   Lunch & dinner daily
Web: www.dragonwell.com
Prices:

Sandwiched between the posh boutiques and trendy eateries of Chestnut Street, Dragon Well is a modest favorite for fresh Chinese served continuously from 11:30 A.M. until 10:00 P.M. The cozy space sports well-worn wood floors, close tables, and skylights that shed light onto butter-yellow walls. Scenes of Chinese life overlook the fully Western clientele who pack the house at lunch to feast on somewhat Americanized fare. Made with the freshest ingredients, dishes include flavorful tea-smoked duck with plump steamed buns and hoisin sauce; stir-fried chicken and black beans with red bell pepper and chili sauce; and a crisp "bird's nest" of scallops, calamari, and prawns with sugar snap peas, carrots, and ginger. Dragon Well is also terrific for takeout.

Florio

C4

Italian ✗✗

1915 Fillmore St. (bet. Bush & Pine Sts.)

Phone: 415-775-4300   Dinner nightly
Web: www.floriosf.com
Prices: $$

On a tree-lined avenue bursting with trendy retailers, this European-style bistro tips its hat to an earlier time, when neighborhood haunts served soul warming classics with a smile of genuine hospitality. Expect to see the well-stocked bar at the front of the house filled with familiar residents ordering "the usual." At back, parchment paper lines wooden tables and conversation bubbles over the low cling clang rising from the semi-open kitchen.
The menu offers first-class travel between Italy and France, featuring such traditional fare as butternut squash ravioli with fresh thyme and earthy chanterelles, or juicy rosemary steak in tarragon béarnaise with crispy frites. New- and old-world varietals as well as wine by the carafe offer good values.

Greens

Vegetarian 🍴

C1

Building A, Fort Mason Center

Phone: 415-771-6222
Web: www.greensrestaurant.com
Prices: $$

Lunch Tue – Sun
Dinner nightly

Zen is the theme that unites all aspects of this local institution, established in 1979 by disciples of the San Francisco Zen Center. This means inventive organic vegetarian cuisine, with much of the pristine produce coming from the Zen Center's Green Gulch Farm. Recipes from Mexico (black bean chili), North Africa (tagine with couscous, ginger, and saffron), and Asia (stir-fry with grilled tofu) influence the imagination of Executive Chef Annie Somerville. On the unique wine list, labels from boutique, bio-dynamic, and organic vintners vie for attention.

The Zen ambience extends to the dining room, which commands a stellar view of the marina and Golden Gate Bridge. Patrons are strongly encouraged to maintain the mood by turning off their cell phones.

ISA

French 🍴🍴

C2

3324 Steiner St. (bet. Chestnut & Lombard Sts.)

Phone: 415-567-9588
Web: www.isarestaurant.com
Prices: $$

Dinner Mon – Sat

ISA's new owners, Elias and Sameera Memon, were wise to keep this quaint Marina eatery just as it was before, with a petite candlelit interior that houses just a few tables, an L-shaped bar, and a romantic back patio covered in climbing ivy. People-watching from the front windows is a popular evening pastime but, really, the best thing about ISA is its weekday prix-fixe.

The Cal-French cuisine comes with extensive choices to make up a $30 three-course meal: sink your teeth into grilled squid with a brush of honey and dusting of cinnamon and cloves; pan-roasted free range chicken with zesty herbs stuffed beneath its crispy skin; and amaretto *semifreddo* garnished with crunchy cookies. Arrive before 7:00 P.M. to take advantage of $5 wines by the glass.

Kappa

C-D4

J a p a n e s e ❌❌

1700 Post St. (at Buchanan St.)

Phone: 415-673-6004

Web: www.kapparestaurant.com

Prices: $$$$

Dinner Mon – Sat

Kappa necessitates a call ahead: not only will you need precise directions to find this obscure Japantown hole-in-the-wall, but the chef only cooks for expected guests. The omakase—an $85 tasting suggested for novices of traditional *koryori* cooking—must be ordered a day in advance. A true mom-and-pop spot, Kappa specializes in intricate small plates with homespun Japanese style.

Served by the lady of the house, who dons a traditional kimono, expect such dishes as bonito atop roasted eggplant in dashi; high grade sashimi; and fried corn fritters. The à la carte menu, penned in Japanese calligraphy, is tough to discern even in English. Thankfully, the husband/wife duo is happy to guide your experience, with the hope that you will become a regular.

Kiss

D4

J a p a n e s e

1700 Laguna St. (at Sutter St.)

Phone: 415-474-2866

Web: N/A

Prices: $$$

Dinner Tue – Sat

On the fringe of Japantown, this matchbox-sized sushi-ya run by the same husband-and-wife team for over a decade continues to thrive under the radar. Chef Naka San prepares all food himself, which is eased by the fact that there are only three small tables—grab one of the five counter seats to behold the chef's kitchen, alongside the local cognoscenti of Japanese food.

Aptly referencing the acronym to "keep it short and simple," Kiss is at its best when highlighting the pure flavors of its pristine fish. Forego the regular sushi menu in favor of one of the two omakase offerings. Both feature a delicious culinary adventure, lingering over jewels such as a silky warm egg custard in a broth floating with shellfish, and perhaps the city's freshest nigiri.

Mamacita

Mexican ✕

B2

2317 Chestnut St. (bet. Divisadero & Scott Sts.)

Phone: 415-346-8494   Dinner nightly
Web: www.mamacitasf.com
Prices: $$

The name is Mexican and, despite major Californian influence, so is the cuisine's inspiration. Still, Mamacita is a bona fide gringo hangout for affluent Marina youngsters, hipsters, players, and cougars who pose among them. Upbeat, loud, and festive with starry lanterns and photos of Mexican life, these close quarters are a non-issue for the under-40 crowd fueled by top-shelf margaritas.

That said, Mamacita's creative combinations and bold flavors are legitimately delicious. Seared ahi tuna "tacos" arrive in clever jicama wraps with persimmon-apple *pico de gallo*. Mixed into the towering heap of house-made chips, even the ubiquitous *chilaquiles* are fresh with pulled roasted chicken, sautéed spinach, and poblano chili *rajas* tossed in chipotle cream.

Mifune

Japanese ✕

C4

1737 Post St. (bet. Buchanan & Webster Sts.)

Phone: 415-922-0337   Lunch & dinner daily
Web: www.mifune.com
Prices: ⊕⊕

A trip to the Kintetsu Restaurant Mall in Japantown is a serious cultural journey. After rummaging around Hello Kitty and Nijaya Market, hunker down at Mifune for a steaming bowl of homemade noodles. The sleek red and black dining space is lined with crib-like booths that bustle with a mostly Asian clientele and hip adolescents donning MP3 earbuds. Yet draw your attention back to those noodle bowls, where freshly prepared udon, ramen, and soba served hot or cold, swim in your choice of savory broths and toppings.

Try the jumbo shrimp udon—perfectly cooked noodles served alongside tempura-fried vegetables and shrimp, with gingered soy sauce for dipping. A small selection of sushi and cut rolls are also on offer, in addition to daily lunch specials.

Nettie's

C2

Seafood ✗✗

2032 Union St. (bet. Buchanan & Webster Sts.)

Phone: 415-409-0300
Web: www.nettiescrabshack.com
Prices: $$

Lunch & dinner daily

With farm tables and weathered cottage chairs, Nettie's is the only "shack" you'll find in this neighborhood. Tables are adorned with mallets and rolls of paper towels for blotting fingers still buttery with the conquest of grilled, local Dungeness crab. While this particular crustacean is king, a messy lobster roll, served with homemade chips, is delish; on Sundays, clambakes or crab feeds bring a smorgasbord of seasonal shellfish with satisfying sides; and barbecue brisket is an option for land lovers. Don't miss such homespun desserts as caramel apples and s'mores.

The surfer-chic vibe belies the place's pedigree: the shack's namesake, Annette Yang, has worked such fine dining rooms as Spruce; Chef Brian Leitner did five at Chez Panisse.

The Plant

C2

Vegetarian ✗

3352 Steiner St. (bet. Chestnut & Lombard Sts.)

Phone: 415-931-2777
Web: www.theplantcafe.com
Prices:

Lunch & dinner daily

The name has changed from Lettus Café Organic, but the concept remains the same at this eco-friendly eatery that aims to keep both their (mostly feminine) patrons and the planet healthy. Vegetarian and vegan options abound, beginning with a breakfast stack of blueberry pancakes. Lunch and dinner bring sandwiches, veggie burgers, shiitake mushroom spring rolls, and an array of smoothies. The menu also remembers those craving meatier choices, with the likes of mango-lime chicken panini.

The Plant is popular with business people, families, and single diners, who can opt to sit in the simple dining room, at the counter, or sidewalk tables. If rushed, grab a pre-packed meal from the to go cooler. Also try waterfront dining at their Pier 3 location.

Shabu-Sen

Japanese 🍴

D4

1726 Buchanan St. (bet. Post & Sutter Sts.)

Phone: 415-440-0466   Lunch & dinner daily
Web: N/A
Prices: 🍪

Founded in 1906, San Francisco's Japantown is among the oldest in America; on this district's main street is Shabu-Sen. With modest décor and prices to match, the restaurant keeps decision-making to a minimum by focusing on two styles of dishes: shabu-shabu and *sukiyaki*. These preparations derive from the Japanese practice of families gathering in front of a fire to share a meal together.

To join in this experience, order from the half-dozen combinations of beef, pork, chicken, tiger prawns, sushi-grade scallops, and premium beef. Then, cook your ingredients with seasonal vegetables or noodles in a pot of rich, aromatic broth boiled right at the table. Homemade sesame and ponzu dipping sauces are served by helpful and amiable Japanese waitresses.

Sociale 😋

Italian 🍴🍴

A4

3665 Sacramento St. (bet. Locust & Spruce Sts.)

Phone: 415-921-3200   Lunch Tue – Sat
Web: www.caffesociale.com   Dinner Mon – Sat
Prices: $$

Burrowed behind a wisteria corridor fringed with flowers and shops, Sociale is *the* destination for family feasts and frolicking with friends. A dandy dining room pleases patrons with peach banquettes and walls warmed with black-and-white photos. Augmenting the space is an attractive arch, but their gorgeous garden rules the roost.

Frenzy-free, the patio is a perfect perch for relishing Italian classics crafted with crazy Cali flair. Laughter rises up in the air as tickled diners dive into such sophisticated surprises as yellow wax beans tossed with strawberries, pancetta, and goat cheese; *malfaddini* flirting with clams, *grechetto*, chili, and spinach; and a chocolate oblivion cake crowned with olive oil, sea salt, and amaretti cookies.

SPQR

Italian 🍴🍴

1911 Fillmore St. (bet. Bush & Pine Sts.)

Phone: 415-771-7779	Lunch Sat – Tue
Web: www.spqrsf.com	Dinner nightly
Prices: $$	

Just as Rome had many Caesars, so has the guard changed at SPQR, a rustic Italian eatery that takes its name from *Senatus Populesque Romanus* (Latin for "the senate and people of Rome"). Chef Matt Accarrino is flexing major culinary muscle, inviting adventurous eaters to dine on crispy pig's ear with pickled green tomatoes, jalapeño, and radish; while pan-fried halibut cheeks, tomatoes, and fried capers may literally just melt in the mouth.

Another welcome change: SPQR now takes reservations, though walk-ins might find a seat at the Carrara marble bar with a view to the open kitchen. Weekend brunches are inventive with clever cocktails to match. No matter the meal, remember the *vino*—owner/wine director Shelley Lindgren (of A16) is a maestro.

Suzu

Japanese 🍴

1581 Webster St. (at Post St.)

Phone: 415-346-5083	Lunch & dinner daily
Web: N/A	
Prices:	

A trip to the Japan Center is a lesson in San Francisco's stellar cultural diversity. When you've finished devouring the many Japanese cookbooks and manga at the bookstore, find physical nourishment at Suzu, where regulars slurp their sustenance in the form of fresh soba, udon, and ramen noodles. Thirteen varieties of ramen are cooked al dente, including spicy *mabo* in pork broth and Tokyo ramen with green onion, bamboo shoots, roast pork, and a boiled egg.

Noodled out? Meats are served over rice *donburi* style, and there are a few sushi and sashimi dishes too. Service is brusque, demand is high, and tables are small and sparse. In case of a full house, jot your name on the legal pad at the door. A bowl of buckwheat soba with curry chicken is worth the wait.

Spruce ✿

Mediterranean 🍴🍴🍴

A4

3640 Sacramento St. (bet. Locust & Spruce Sts.)

Phone: 415-931-5100
Web: www.sprucesf.com
Prices: $$$

Lunch Mon – Fri
Dinner nightly

Frankie Frankeny

Never mind parking on Sacramento Street in charmed Laurel Heights: the affluent neighborhood draws citywide aficionados of food, wine, and fashion (high-end boutique Susan is across the street). Instead, pull up to the valet and spend your spare moments perusing Spruce's gourmet takeout shop—a great spot for a pastry or coffee to go. But you're really here for the full Spruce experience, a culinary must that has kept tables packed since its opening.

Entering the grand interior, it's easy to see why San Francisco's highfalutin types treat this dining room as their own. Here, socialites kiss-kiss amid chocolate mohair walls, which soar to a vaulted ceiling, and faux ostrich chairs that evoke visions of plush handbags. A busy bar and black-and-white street photography, however, keep Spruce's feet on the ground.

The Mediterranean cuisine strikes a happy balance with local, seasonal product and house-made charcuterie. Solid à la carte fare may include spring pea ravioli in lemony, herbaceous *nage* or crispy duck confit with radicchio and poached pears. The burger is a local favorite. And don't worry—with such a creative wine and cocktail program, the vibe could never be utterly stuffy.

Tacolicious

Mexican

C2

2031 Chestnut St. (bet. Fillmore and Steiner Sts.)

Phone: 415-346-1966   Lunch & dinner daily
Web: www.tacolicioussf.com
Prices:

Marina dwellers craving Mexican street food head to Tacolicious and gratify a juicy temptation. Evocative prints, votive candles, and wrestling figurines add local flavour to the "bar" vibe. Once just a taco stand, it unfolds a throng of inventive tacos in the former Laiola space.

Free your forks and with your fingers plunge into fleshy tacos with the freshest ingredients. The shot-and-a-beer chicken tacos; the taco of the week with fried chicken or grilled filet mignon aside caramelized onions, arugula, and poblano salsa; and tuna tostadas with chipotle mayonnaise and avocado are kissed with spice and all things nice.

A lick from the homemade sauce spectrum (chipotle, tomatillo, habañero) and a sip from the slew of tequilas will keep grown-ups jaunty.

Tataki

Japanese

B4

2815 California St. (bet. Broderick & Divisadero Sts.)

Phone: 415-931-1182   Lunch Mon – Fri
Web: www.tatakisushibar.com   Dinner nightly
Prices: $$

In an area famed for plentiful organic eats, Tataki puts the rest to eco-shame as one of North America's first sustainable sushi bars. Not only are the impeccable rolls and fresh, delicate sashimi thoughtfully prepared, the ingredients are strictly considered in terms of fishing practices—whether diver- or line-caught, netted or trapped, farmed or wild, domestic or imported. Start with a flavorful kampachi or seaweed salad, tossed with paper-thin cucumber and sesame vinaigrette. Top it off with a bowl of soba noodles or an arctic char and avocado roll that holds together to the perfect finish.

Tataki also pays it forward with take-home sustainability guides from the Monterey Bay Aquarium. This is a bite-size gem with big heart and a teeny footprint.

Terzo

Mediterranean ✗✗

3011 Steiner St. (bet. Filbert & Union Sts.)

Phone: 415-441-3200   Dinner nightly
Web: www.terzosf.com
Prices: $$

Like its North Beach sister Rose Pistola, this charming Cow Hollow restaurant explores Mediterranean cuisine, wandering far afield to Spain, Portugal, Morocco, and the South of France. Warmth permeates the trendy dining space, with communal tables and a custom-made zinc bar. In the open kitchen, everything is based on flavorful, local organic products; this is serious cooking that exhibits a very skilled hand.

Chef Mark Gordon's daily changing menu focuses on small plates like Hungarian pork and kale sausages, or the signature free range chicken *spiedini*, as well as vegetarian choices like roasted winter vegetables in brown butter and sage. The limited selection of larger plates may include roasted wild mahi mahi with spinach and Meyer lemon relish.

Tipsy Pig

Gastropub ✗✗

2231 Chestnut St. (bet. Pierce & Scott Sts.)

Phone: 415-292-2300   Lunch Sat – Sun
Web: www.thetipsypigsf.com   Dinner nightly
Prices: $$

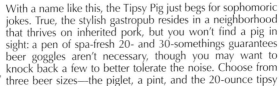

With a name like this, the Tipsy Pig just begs for sophomoric jokes. True, the stylish gastropub resides in a neighborhood that thrives on inherited pork, but you won't find a pig in sight: a pen of spa-fresh 20- and 30-somethings guarantees beer goggles aren't necessary, though you may want to knock back a few to better tolerate the noise. Choose from three beer sizes—the piglet, a pint, and the 20-ounce tipsy pig—then soak up your lager with a pretzel dipped in smoky cheddar or beer-battered onion fritters. More sophisticated dishes like Alaskan halibut with Meyer lemon beurre blanc are nearly superb.

With flat screen TVs and a vintage saloon vibe, this is very much an adult bar, although there is a special menu for *les petits cochons*.

Zushi Puzzle

Japanese

1910 Lombard St. (at Buchanan St.)

Phone: 415-931-9319   Dinner Mon – Sat
Web: www.zushipuzzle.com
Prices:

Zushi Puzzle's diminutive façade is easy to miss as you're making your way down Lombard Street, but the cognoscenti know to head for this regularly packed Japanese place. Even solo diners are routinely turned away if they don't have a reservation.

What's the lure? Terrific fresh fish, and lots of it. Between the printed menu and the dry-erase board, the restaurant offers more than five dozen maki (think Romeo and Juliet: salmon and avocado topped with thinly sliced scallop, *tobiko*, and spicy sauce). Chef Roger Chong lords over the sushi bar—the best seats in the house—where freshly grated wasabi graces each plate.

Parking in this area can be a hassle, and often there's a line to get in, but a bit of advance planning brings its own reward here.

Look for our symbol ♨, spotlighting restaurants with a notable sake list.

Mission
Bernal Heights • Potrero Hill

The sun always shines in the Mission, a bohemian paradise dotted with palm trees and home to artists, activists, and a vibrant Latino community. Graffiti murals line the walls of funky galleries, thrift shops, and bookstores; and sidewalk stands burst with Mexican plantains, nopales, and the juiciest limes this side of the border.

The markets here are among the best in town: **La Palma Mexicatessan** brims with homemade *papusa*, chips, and fresh Mexican cheeses. **Lucca Ravioli** stocks imported Italian goods, while **Bi-Rite** is a petite grocer popular for fresh flowers and prepared foods. Across the street find **Bi-Rite Creamery**, a cult favorite for ice cream.

Countless bargain *mercados* and dollar stores might suggest otherwise, but the Mission is home to many a hipster hangout. **Dynamo Donuts** on 24th Street is the place for delectable flavors like apricot-cardamom, chocolate-star anise, banana de leche, and maple-glazed bacon apple. **Walzwerk** charms with East German kitsch, and **Bissap Baobab** is *the* go-to for Senegalese eats. Mission pizza reigns supreme—thin crust lovers wait in line at **Pizzeria Delfina**—they serve a wicked pie with crispy edges blistered just so.

To best experience the flavors of the Mission, forgo the table and chairs and pull up a curb on Linda Street, where a vigilante street food scene has incited a revolution on Thursday nights. The **Magic Curry Kart** plates $5 steaming rice dishes, while the **Crème Brûlée Cart** torches fresh custards, some spiked with Bailey's Irish Cream, *à la minute*. The alley buzzes with locals noshing homemade pastries, empanadas, and Vietnamese spring rolls until the grub runs out.

For an affordable dinner in a more civilized fashion, **Mission Street Food** serves an ever-changing menu, prepared by bona fide guest chefs, at **Lung Shan** on Thursdays and Saturdays. Credited with inspiring the area's street food movement, the group donates all profits to hunger- and food-related charities like La Cocina, the Mission's own "incubator kitchen" that supports aspiring, low-income restaurateurs.

The city's hottest 'hood also offers a cool selection of sweets. A banana split is downright retrolicious when served at the Formica counter of 90-year-old **St. Francis Fountain & Candy**. The sundaes are made with **Mitchell's Ice Cream**, famous in SF since 1953. Modish flavors—think foie gras and salted licorice—are in regular rotation at the newer **Humphrey Slocombe**.

Dance off your indulgences on Salsa Sunday at **El Rio**, the dive bar with a bustling back patio, or join the hip kids for DJs and live bands at **Elbo Room** and **12 Galaxies**. For rooftop imbibing, **Medjool** is unparalleled. The lesbian set shoots pool at the **Lexington Club**.

On the late night, growling stomachs brave harsh lighting at numerous taquerias, many of which are open till 4:00 A.M. Go see for yourself: Try the veggie burrito at **Taqueria Cancun**; tacos at **La Alteña**; and mind-blowing meats—*lengua* or *cabeza*, anyone?—at **El Farolito**. During the day, **La Taqueria**'s carne asada burrito is arguably the best. And **El Tonayense** taco truck, to quote one blogger, is of course "da bomb!"

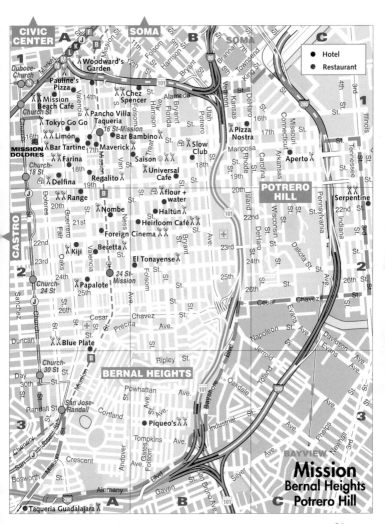

Mission
Bernal Heights
Potrero Hill

Aperto

C1

Italian 🍴

1434 18th St. (at Connecticut St.)

Phone: 415-252-1625
Web: www.apertosf.com
Prices: $$

Lunch & dinner daily

There is no resisting the open arms and warm kitchen at Aperto, the Potrero Hill spot whose apt name is Italian for "open." A casual neighborhood vibe and daily chalkboard specials set the tone for convivial Italian meals that might include chicken liver pâté on grilled bread drizzled with olive oil, or *radiatore* (spiral pasta) tossed with osso buco ragù of braised pork. Seasonal pastas and *secondi* change regularly with Californian flourishes appearing throughout.

Like its East Bay sister restaurant Bellanico, Aperto is also open to children: a five dollar kids' special features any shape pasta, either plain or with three choices of simple sauce. The wine list is equally accommodating with more than 15 good value varietals available by the glass.

Bar Bambino

A1

Italian 🍴

2931 16th St. (bet. Mission St. & Van Ness Ave.)

Phone: 415-701-8466
Web: www.barbambino.com
Prices: $$

Lunch Tue – Sat
Dinner nightly

Packed with clinking glasses though often void of elbowroom, Bar Bambino is a local darling with design that shines in a particularly rough part of town that happens to house some of its hottest and hippest tables. A welcoming marble bar and communal table dominate the narrow space, while a glass enclosed *salumeria* showcases artisanal cheeses and house cured meats.

With more than 35 labels by the glass, Bar Bambino's wine program is an unmistakable highlight. The Italian cuisine is somewhat inconsistent, but small plates and antipasti are pleasant to share. Handmade pasta shines as twisted tubes of *trofie* with sweet Italian sausage—paradise in a bowl. Braised beef brisket with porcini, cocoa, and horseradish gremolata sates heartier appetites.

Bar Tartine

Californian

 A1

561 Valencia St. (bet. 16th & 17th Sts.)

Phone: 415-487-1600
Web: www.bartartine.com
Prices: $$

Lunch Sat – Sun
Dinner Tue – Sun

One could survive on the bread alone at Bar Tartine—the sophisticated sister to nearby Tartine Bakery. It is crusty and utterly delicious, but it's just the beginning at this wildly popular spot where seasonal dishes headline.

The interior conjures a European lodge, with a black-and-white dining room, wood floors, soft candlelight, and elk antler chandelier offering chic rusticity. Behind the scenes, the kitchen practices farm-to-table principles by using local, sustainable, and organic products in finessed dishes that perfectly reflect Californian sensibilities, as in dates stuffed with Pt. Reyes blue cheese and drizzled with honey; or beef filet with succulent bone marrow and onion soubise. House-made sodas and cocktails are well worth trying.

Beretta

Italian

A2

1199 Valencia St. (at 23rd St.)

Phone: 415-695-1199
Web: www.berettasf.com
Prices: $$

Lunch Sat – Sun
Dinner nightly

Beretta delivers a bang-up performance with its thin-crust pizzas and shared Italian dishes. This well-loved spot is perpetually jamming with Mission hipsters who pack the place for its relaxed vibe and fantastic food at reasonable prices. From meatballs like *Mamma* used to make to tender lamb chops and daily entrée specials, there's plenty on the menu, but pizzas always emerge as the champion.

The quarters are tight (elbow-to-elbow at the bar and communal tables), but it's all part of the friendly spirit. Besides, the menu is designed for sharing. Just make sure you call dibs on the last slice of wild mushroom and spicy *coppa* topped pizza.

Call ahead for a coveted spot on the waiting list, since reservations are for large groups only.

Blue Plate

American 🍴🍴

A2

3218 Mission St. (bet. 29th & Valencia Sts.)

Phone: 415-282-6777   Dinner Mon – Sat
Web: www.blueplatesf.com
Prices: $$

Despite San Francisco's outdoorsy image, there is nary a restaurant patio in sight on the dawn of a rare warm day. That's why Missionites have been heading to Blue Plate for more than a decade, where potted plants and blossoming fruit trees overhang café tables in the garden and the kitchen serves mostly organic Cal-Med cuisine inspired by the season.

Inside, the narrow space is cool, casual, and ambient with local art lining the walls and skinny-jeaned regulars chowing tasty comfort fare. Chef/owner Cory Obenour's Mediterranean flavor combinations shine in dishes such as grilled Monterey Bay squid with lemon juice and sorrel chiffonade; and slip-from-the-bone pork osso buco cooked in red wine with wilted chard, porcini, and seasoned walnuts.

Chez Spencer

French 🍴🍴

B1

82 14th St. (bet. Folsom & Harrison Sts.)

Phone: 415-864-2191   Dinner nightly
Web: www.chezspencer.net
Prices: $$$

Set amid warehouses and automotive repair shops of the Mission, this neighborhood darling is easy to miss. Look for the large wooden gate, walk through the garden terrace and covered patio until you reach this lofty dining room. Under the skylights and soaring arched wooden beams, two kitchens and a wood-burning oven are as integral to the space as the patrons.

Owned by Chef Laurent Katgely, and named for his son, Spencer, the prix-fixe and à la carte menus offer classic French fare with Californian freshness, as in lobster and truffles cappuccino royal, wood-roasted sturgeon, or smoked duck breast à la Lyonnaise with poached eggs and bacon lardons.

For French food fast, look for Spencer on the Go "mobile bistro" at the corner of Folsom and 7th streets.

Delfina

Italian

A1

3621 18th St. (bet. Dolores & Guerrero Sts.)

Phone: 415-552-4055   Dinner nightly
Web: www.delfinasf.com
Prices: $$

Some things, like the popularity of Delfina, never change. This Italian joint is as busy as ever. Delfina relies heavily on Californian ingredients and sensibilities, but the menu is strictly Italian from start to finish. The casual space and warm staff make you feel like an old pal; they even fuss over you with attentive service. Eating solo? The long counter overlooking the dining room is the perfect spot.

You don't need a lot of dough to enjoy the delicious dishes. Chicken liver crostini with *giardiniera*, risotto Milanese with oxtail sugo, and mint tagliatelli topped with fresh porcini mushrooms are just some of the goods you'll sup and sample.

The next door pizzeria bustles with the same energy as its more sophisticated sister Delfina.

El Tonayense

B2

Mexican

3150 24th St. (at Shotwell St.)

Phone: 415-550-9192   Lunch & dinner daily
Web: www.eltonayense.com
Prices:

Devout local foodies often chow lunch in the curbside shadow of one of El Tonayense's popular taco trucks. But those who prefer to dine at simple wood tables and worn rattan chairs visit the original El Tonayense, perhaps the city's best taqueria.

Prepare your palate for the bold wallop of deep flavors and spice that elevates these corn tortillas, piled high with tender, intensely seasoned meats. Try the smoky carne asada with roasted red chile salsa, or juicy *al pastor* with fresh cilantro and onions. Four varieties of their outstanding homemade salsas are available at the bar, though most have already found nirvana in the amount splashed atop their order. While the tacos really shine here, burrito junkies relish a variety of enormous wraps.

Farina

Italian ✗✗

A1

3560 18th St. (bet. Guerrero & Valencia Sts.)

Phone: 415-565-0360
Web: www.farinafoods.com
Prices: $$

Lunch Fri – Sun
Dinner Tue – Sun

Large front windows offer an alluring first glimpse of Farina's chicly spare, contemporary veneer and boisterous vibe. But only a reservation can reveal the ethos of this ever-buzzing Mission hot spot where a wait is to be expected even if you called ahead.

Farina's raison d'être may be the infamously addictive focaccia, fresh from the bread oven, topped with the likes of prosciutto, *stracchino* cheese, and dandelion leaves. House-made pasta is likewise a draw, perhaps including tender *pansotti* noodles stuffed with ricotta and drizzled with creamy walnut pesto. First-timers would be wise to snag a seat at the marble counter for a primo view of the open kitchen, where the making of fresh Genovese and Ligurian cuisine is akin to performance art.

flour + water

Italian ✗

B2

2401 Harrison St. (at 20th St.)

Phone: 415-826-7000
Web: www.flourandwater.com
Prices: $$

Dinner nightly

It's easy to sniff out a pizza joint in the Mission, where piquant pepperoni grease saturates the paper plates and the air itself. However, flour + water gives the pie a different spin. In an industrial corner space, high ceilings and concrete floors are expected; meanwhile, an antler light fixture and original artwork that echo the life aquatic are a chic awakening—a must for the Mission's latest culinary darling.

In the kitchen, savory Neapolitans surpass the easy-as-pie implications of flour + water's name: Each is creatively topped and then fire licked for two minutes in an oven hotter than Hades. The menu's real stars, though, are seasonal pastas like sweet pea tortellini with mint, and ambitious starters— think warm potato and lamb's tongue salad.

Foreign Cinema

International **XX**

A2

2534 Mission St. (bet. 21st & 22nd Sts.)

Phone: 415-648-7600
Web: www.foreigncinema.com
Prices: $$

Lunch Sat – Sun
Dinner nightly

Date night is a wrap at Foreign Cinema, the Mission's art house eatery that projects international films and cult classics onto a white brick wall on the heated courtyard patio. (A movie schedule is available online.) After dinner, get your contemporary art fix in the adjoining gallery and finish with a nightcap at László, the restaurant's Soviet-themed annex bar. Understated modish furnishings keep the films in focus, but Foreign Cinema's international translation of Mediterranean fare is worthy of the center stage. At dinner, couples share tuna tartare tossed in ginger-lime vinaigrette or moist swordfish with wilted greens and tangy, herb-rich *gremolata*. At brunch, locals give fried eggs deglazed with balsamic or the Champagne omelet two thumbs up.

Haltún

Mexican **X**

B2

2948 21st St. (at Treat Ave.)

Phone: 415-643-6411
Web: www.haltunsf.com
Prices: 🍲🍲

Lunch & dinner daily

This newcomer to the Mission might be Mexican, but don't expect the typical quesadilla and burrito affair. Instead, Haltún specializes in Mayan dishes not often seen on other menus. Need to get out of a snit? The cheery dining room with bright orange walls and tiled floors as well as the warm, friendly service will definitely banish bad moods.

The authentic, home-style food is flavorful, fresh, and filling, so even though chips and salsa arrive right away, don't stuff yourself just yet. Save your appetite for dishes like *pol-can*, fried corn dumplings stuffed with lima beans and crushed pumpkin seeds, or *diabla* shrimp in chile chipotle sauce. *Pollo pibil*, chicken marinated and glazed with annatto seed sauce, is fingerlicking good.

Heirloom Café

B2

2500 Folsom St. (at 21st St.)

Phone: 415-821-2500	Lunch Fri – Sat
Web: www.heirloom-sf.com	Dinner Mon – Sat
Prices: $$$	

San Francisco foodies may have a new mecca in Heirloom Café, a recent favorite melding the Mission's indie spirit with a vintage interior aesthetic—think wallpaper, worn wood floors, and natural light. The open kitchen lends to a feeling of warmth and bustle, and the limited menu feels a bit like dinner at home—that is, if you happen to be a highly skilled chef.

Seasonal dishes are perfectly prepared and might include housecured gravlax with grilled artisan bread; pillowy gnocchi atop sweet corn and fennel sausage; and roasted halibut with mushrooms, English peas, and creamy cauliflower purée. At dessert, black pepper syrup jazzes up moist olive oil cake with compote of *fraise du bois*. Order a Châteauneuf-du-Pape from the expertly curated wine list.

Kiji

Japanese

A2

1009 Guerrero St. (bet. 22nd & 23rd Sts.)

Phone: 415-282-0400	Dinner Tue – Sun
Web: www.kijirestaurant.com	
Prices:	

From the sushi chefs to the servers, a pride of place infuses this Japanese spot, which stands between the Mission District and Noe Valley. Pride shines through in the food as well. Raw offerings such as toro, nigiri, or kanpachi carpaccio (Japanese amberjack arranged on a banana leaf and topped with thin slices of jalapeño, a drizzle of olive oil, and a crunch of sea salt) will satisfy sushi lovers; but the extensive menu goes way beyond sushi. Plump, seared Hokkaido scallops, for instance, are flavored with a pleasant ponzu reduction, while black cod is marinated in sweet miso and broiled.

The varnished wood bar is the place to sit and if you want to go completely Japanese, complement your meal with a sampling from the well-stocked sake collection.

Limón

A1

Peruvian

524 Valencia St. (bet. 16th & 17th Sts.)

Phone: 415-252-0918
Web: www.limon-sf.com
Prices: $$

Lunch Tue – Sun
Dinner nightly

When fire closed Limón's doors in 2009, regulars satiated their cravings for flavorful Peruvian fare at newly opened sister restaurant, Limón Rotisserie. The offshoot remains popular for juicy rotisserie chicken, particularly at lunch, but loyalists are thrilled to be back in Limon's bi-level space painted a zesty lime green.

The draw of Limón has long been its attention to detail, from skillfully prepared plates down to a notably dishy staff. But the real spice is in the bold cuisine, which ranges from traditional ceviches to flaky empanadas stuffed with braised sirloin and chopped hard-boiled eggs. Entrée delights include a plump fillet of fish and shrimp cooked in garlicky *aji amarillo*; don't miss the crispy fried yucca drizzled with *chimichurri*.

Maverick

A1

American

3316 17th St. (at Mission St.)

Phone: 415-863-3061
Web: www.sfmaverick.com
Prices: $$

Lunch Sat – Sun
Dinner nightly

Posters of the 1950s TV series *Maverick* grace the brown-and-orange walls of this Mission eatery named for the 1800s Texas cattle rancher, Samuel Maverick. The diminutive space has a single high table overlooking a semi-open kitchen at front and close-knit wood tables that scatter the rest of the dining room.

The culinary vibe is hipster American and the patrons, who might fit that same description, are mostly from the neighborhood. Familiar comfort fare might include a crispy corn tostada topped with shrimp, black beans, and slaw; and a grilled Berkshire pork chop, glazed in honey and bourbon, served with cornbread stuffing and candied pecans. At dessert, what better way to cap a night than with warm and chewy cookies dipped in a cool glass of milk?

89

Mission Beach Café

A1

198 Guerrero St. (at 14th St.)

Phone: 415-861-0198
Web: www.missionbeachcafesf.com
Prices: $$$

Lunch daily
Dinner Mon – Sat

Heard the buzz about the amazing homemade pies? We bet you did. But lucky for locals (and us) there's even more to this delightful neighborhood fave than fantastic pastries. Dive right in to the delectable goodness with crispy lemon-saffron risotto cakes, topped with tea-smoked albacore, fried quail eggs and caviar, drizzled with chili crème fraîche and basil oil.

Catch an all-BBQ menu every Tuesday night with tasty offerings like pulled pork sandwiches and grilled chicken. Tuck in a napkin or two for the fall-off-the-bone pork ribs, fig wood smoked, served with baked beans, crunchy coleslaw, and grilled baby corn. Can't decide on sweet? Get spoiled with a trio of desserts—lavender-honey cheesecake; strawberry rhubarb pie; and pear-plum pie.

Nombe

A2

2491 Mission St. (bet. 20th & 21st Sts.)

Phone: 415-681-7150
Web: www.nombesf.com
Prices: $$

Lunch Sat – Sun
Dinner Wed – Mon

Mission regulars set off for Japan at Nombe, a boisterous *izakaya* where the noise level soars as flights of *junmai* sake flow. It's one of those spots where you might land by chance and then stay forever—and with a sake sommelier dutifully pairing sips to authentic fare, hanging around seems the polite thing to do.

Casual groups share high quality, seasonal plates like charred fava beans scented with lavender sea salt or miso-flavored fresh black cod. Seared Wagyu beef *tataki* with ginger and garlic is a juicy option, but the *tsukune* yakitori is an unmistakable showstopper: the tender chicken meatballs with mirin-soy glaze come with a silky five-minute egg for dipping, lined up alongside grilled chicken thighs herbaceous with shiso and sour plum sauce.

Pancho Villa Taqueria

Mexican

 A1

3071 16th St. (bet. Mission & Valencia Sts.)

Phone: 415-864-8840   Lunch & dinner daily
Web: www.panchovillasf.com
Prices:

Choice is chief at Pancho Villa, so scope the menu and come ready to make brisk decisions. This masterful Mexican taqueria presents a parade of burritos, tacos, quesadillas, nachos et al. With wrapper and protein in hand, head for the beverage display. An immaculate and colorful salsa bar with myriad condiments will spin you right round like a record. There is no table service here, so grab the first seat in sight. As the mariachis gently lilt, dive into a fit-for-a-family super burrito, jammed with rice, beans, *chile verde* chicken, *pico de gallo*, cheese, guacamole, and sour cream; classic chips and salsa made divine with a melange of zippy ingredients; and a side order of a *flauta* filled with chicken, fried, and then bathed in a tomato-chile sauce.

Papalote

Mexican

 A2

3409 24th St. (bet. Poplar & Valencia Sts.)

Phone: 415-970-8815   Lunch & dinner daily
Web: www.papalote-sf.com
Prices:

With a cheerful dining room awash in primary hues and playful kites (*papalotes*) flying overhead, this is the kind of taqueria your mom has always wished for—one that garnishes its menu with fresh ingredients and truly healthy choices. The art filled Mexican grill may find critics among Mission locals who prefer gritty authenticity, but sometimes breaking tradition just tastes good.
Here, taqueria mainstays have a northern Californian soul: vegetarian burritos share table space with spicy-sweet mole chicken, fresh fish, and carne asada tacos, all topped with crisp romaine lettuce, guacamole, ripe Roma tomato, and even refreshing jicama. Vegans are also welcome; Papalote offers soy chorizo and grilled tofu as lightweight alternatives to meat.

Pauline's Pizza

Pizza   🍴

A1

260 Valencia St. (bet. Duboce Ave. & 14th St.)

Phone: 415-552-2050   Dinner Tue – Sat
Web: www.paulinespizza.com
Prices: $$

Along busy Valencia Street, recognize Pauline's by the crowds sitting on the interior benches, hungry for a delectable pizza and a free table (this budget-friendly hot spot takes no reservations).

Thin and crisp yet doughy inside, these handmade crusts may be strewn with "eccentric" toppings ranging from andouille and linguiça sausage to Kalamata olives and French goat cheese. Fans of Pauline's crust can even buy a three pack of frozen shells to go. The restaurant's Berkeley garden and Star Canyon Ranch provide a year-round supply of greens and vegetables that comprise the fresh salads.

Local enthusiasts know to check online after 3:00P.M. to hear the nightly specialty pizzas and salads, before walking over—thus avoiding the challenging parking.

Piqueo's

Peruvian   🍴🍴

B3

830 Cortland Ave. (830 Cortland Ave.)

Phone: 415-282-8812   Dinner nightly
Web: www.piqueos.com
Prices: $$

Big flavor comes in tiny packages at Píqueo's, a small eatery in a Bernal Heights bungalow with cozy candlelight and walls the shade of ripe avocado. Neighborhood types sit at the counter for a view to the open kitchen where Chef/owner Carlos Altamirano deploys unusual Peruvian produce in dishes that seem to burst in the mouth.

Adventurous diners new to these enticing flavors will enjoy the learning experience. For the full effect, sample an array of small plates including crunchy wontons filled with creamy minced shrimp; fried white bean cake with sliced plantain and silky egg; and a roast beef sandwich with garlicky *aji* and sweet potato fries. Wash it down with a *chicha morada*, a drink made from the pulp of Peruvian purple maize.

Pizza Nostra

Pizza

B1

300 De Haro St. (at 16th St.)

Phone: 415-558-9493   Lunch & dinner daily
Web: www.pizzanostrasf.com
Prices:

Who says the French can't do pizza, eh? In a brightly hued corrugated building on Potrero Hill, the mini French empire ruled by Jocelyn Bulow invaded Italy, actually he snagged award-winning *pizzaiolo* Giovanni Adinolfi from the Italian Riviera. Counter seating provides an up-close view of the action in the open kitchen, where 12 inch Neapolitan pies are crisped to perfection and turned out with bottles of chili-infused olive oil, an array of antipasti, and a few entrées. The thin crust Calabrese pizza with *salame pepperoncino* and sliced *cipolla* onions is a worthwhile knife-and-fork endeavor.

Dark wood banquettes and an all-European staff add polish to the laid-back space but, on a sunny day, locals prefer to kick back alfresco on the lively patio.

Range

Contemporary

A2

842 Valencia St. (bet. 19th & 20th Sts.)

Phone: 415-282-8283   Dinner nightly
Web: www.rangesf.com
Prices: **$$**

Mission locals feel at home at Range, a neighborhood bistro with a friendly, low key vibe and glimpses of the busy kitchen. Divided into various cozy dining areas with low beamed ceilings and bare filament lights, the hipster hot spot is at once intimate and always packed. Brown leather banquets and rustic florals keep the setting simply elegant—a comfortable backdrop for showcasing contemporary American meals.

The seasonal menu may begin with creamed leeks topped with a toasty brioche, poached farm egg, and fragrant truffle butter. This dish may be stellar, but the juicy maple-glazed pork roast, served with wilted collards and yam gratin, is also worth a taste. Finish with a pink lady apple tart made unique with flowery cardamom ice cream.

Regalito

Mexican

A1

3481 18th St. (at Valencia St.)

Phone: 415-503-0650
Web: www.regalitosf.com
Prices: $$

Lunch Sat – Sun
Dinner Tue – Sun

Spanish for "little gift," Regalito Rosticeria has a polish unique to the Mission, where Mexican food is synonymous with humble taquerias and markets. Here, Regalito is *the* neighborhood spot for market driven fare in a stylish atmosphere, clean and bright with chartreuse accent walls and vibrant art.

A long wood counter peeks into the open kitchen, where seasonal fare is carefully crafted from mostly organic produce and free range meats. A roasted half chicken is sublimely tender and smothered in nutty mole *negro*, while habañero salsa and fresh avocado garnish smoky, grilled *carnitas*. Flavors are more refined than bold, but these premium ingredients are prepared with skill, as if to enhance the pure flavors and complement the contemporary space.

Serpentine

Californian

C2

2495 3rd St. (at 22nd St.)

Phone: 415-252-2000
Web: www.serpentinesf.com
Prices: $$

Lunch daily
Dinner Tue – Sat

Serpentine is every bit a product of its environment. The Dogpatch eatery fuses finely with the neighborhood's cool architecture and sense of recycled design with a wide cement bar, steel accents, and wooden furnishings in a sun-filled space. The dining room snakes comfortably throughout the lofty venue, with ample tables for large parties, and fewer bar tables perfect for sharing small plates.

Service is intimate and warm, and the cuisine is equally pleasant. A seasonal grilled artichoke arrives halved, charred, and laden with Dungeness crab salad; while a delectable risotto rests beneath an abundance of snap peas, Chantenay carrots, and fiddlehead ferns. For dessert, the spongy buttermilk cake with huckleberry purée and Meyer lemon curd is a hit.

Saison ✿

Californian ☓☓

B1

2124 Folsom St. (bet. 17th & 18th Sts.)

Phone: 415-828-7990
Web: www.saisonsf.com
Prices: $$$$

Dinner Tue – Sat

Naseema Khan

Hiding behind an easy-to-miss wood gate in the Mission, Saison is perfect northern California or even Provençal chic, with a flagstone courtyard dotted with potted trees and warmed by a blazing stone hearth. Strings of lights twinkle over the outdoor space, adding to the whimsy and charm of the arena. Pillows and pashminas are on hand to ward off the evening chill.

Inside, Mission industrial meets country cottage with cracked concrete floors, white vaulted ceilings, and just a handful of redwood-topped tables are dressed with paper menus and single sunflowers blooming in slim vases. Given the toasty nature of this foodie haunt, reservations are required well in advance—particularly if you seek a seat at the four-person chef's table in the open kitchen.

Chef/owner Joshua Skenes lives up to his pedigree, dishing his perfectly prepared Californian cuisine as an eight-course prix-fixe with thoughtful wine pairings. Expect such daily and seasonal whims as vegetable *brunoise* suspended in Douglas fir and smoke gelée; tender abalone with coastal herbs and artichoke *citronne*; seared, silky bone marrow; and tangy rhubarb sorbet with milk granite.

95

Slow Club

Californian

 2501 Mariposa St. (at Hampshire St.)

Phone: 415-241-9390
Web: www.slowclub.com
Prices: $$

Lunch daily
Dinner Mon – Sat

 With a somewhat obscure address and an urban-warehouse air, Slow Club is a bona fide hipster hangout. Chicly underdressed with polished concrete floors, exposed metal eye beams, and unremarkable wood furnishings, the Potrero Hill joint would border on ubiquity, but for its aura of having coined the look first. The reasonable prices are unexpected for the well-executed fare sent from the tiny open kitchen.

At lunch, eco-chic locals and business types nosh baby spinach salads with caramelized bacon and grated tangy apple, or sandwiches that run from a basic-but-tasty burger to roasted turkey, avocado, and garlic aïoli on a warm torpedo roll. Dinner is a more ambitious foray, with dishes such as grilled pork loin with savory nettle bread pudding.

Taqueria Guadalajara

Mexican

 4798 Mission St. (at Onondaga Ave.)

Phone: 415-469-5480
Web: N/A
Prices: ⊜

Lunch & dinner daily

Sitting at a carved wood table inside this Outer Mission favorite, imagine yourself at the center of a Guadalajaran town square: Mexican architectural façades loom in floor-to-ceiling murals on three walls, while the aromas of flavorful grilled meats waft from the open kitchen.

Queue up at the counter and order the inexpensive, fresh, and generously portioned menu. Tacos may be filled with adobo-marinated pork or grilled carne asada along with minced white onion and cilantro. Intrepid eaters should dare to try the chicken super burrito, overloaded with the works. With a focus more on grilled meats than on accoutrement, the self-serve salsa bar is a popular stopover. Complement meals with perhaps the city's best *horchata*, redolent with cinnamon and rice.

Tokyo Go Go

Japanese ✗

A1

3174 16th St. (bet. Guerrero & Valencia Sts.)

Phone:	415-864-2288	Dinner nightly
Web:	www.tokyogogo.com	
Prices:	$$	

Welcome to Tokyo Go Go, where blazing lights, thumpin' techno beats, and palate-pleasing bites draw in a hip and stylish set from around the Mission. Toss aside any expectations of traditional Japanese and get motoring for innovative flavorsome fusion instead. Sure, you can have your beloved nigiri, but opt for one of the splendid specialty rolls too, like the *kamikaze* (spicy tuna and crunchy asparagus rolled and topped with albacore tuna, scallions, and tangy ponzu), or the fish taco roll (battered, fried fish, avocado, cilantro, onion, tomato, jalepeño, and chipotle aïoli).

Brought your battalion of buddies? Fill the table with "shared plates" like smoky miso-marinated black cod; tempura sweet onion rings; Tokyo garlic shrimp; or the Kobe beef *tataki*.

Universal Cafe

Californian ✗

B1

2814 19th St. (bet. Bryant & Florida Sts.)

Phone:	415-821-4608	Lunch Wed – Sun
Web:	www.universalcafe.net	Dinner Tue – Sun
Prices:	$$	

Universal Café is one of those contagiously cute places where everyone seems to chill out and be cheerful. The sunny dining room has a bustling open kitchen, a few counter seats ideal for solo diners, and a rustic-urban feel that suits its industrial-cum-residential neighborhood. One could call the spot a bit European, but with a market driven daily menu and on-the-ball staff, this café is très San Francisco.

First rate organic ingredients shine in simple preparations. At lunch, seasonal fare hinges on crisp grilled flatbreads and entrée salads, laden with the likes of hearty avocado and winter citrus. Dinner brings the hugely popular steak frites, but brunch is Universal's true claim to fame. Bring your morning paper and enjoy the wait outdoors.

Woodward's Garden

 American

 A1

1700 Mission St. (at Duboce St.)

Phone: 415-621-7122   Dinner Tue – Sat
Web: www.woodwardsgarden.com
Prices: $$$

Woodward's Garden may sit on the site of San Francisco's first amusement park in a location that, frankly, has little curb appeal—views to the 101!—but this hidden gem somehow manages to retain a vintage charm that lures a coterie of locals questing a quiet meal on the town. The mainstay feels just a bit like your grandma's house, with peeling paint, comfortable worn furnishings, and an antique chandelier.

The old-fashioned ambience sets a sweet stage for home-style fare that changes with the season. Savor farmers' market-fresh ingredients in dishes such as herbed polenta served in an iron crock with tender mushrooms, fresh thyme, and oozing Tallegio; and red wine-braised Sonoma duck leg aromatic with stewed Bing cherries and earthy turnips.

Nob Hill
Chinatown • Russian Hill

In company with the Golden Gate Bridge and Alamo Square's "Painted Ladies," Nob Hill is San Francisco at its most iconic. Historic cable cars chug up the dramatic grades that lead to the top, with familiar chimes tinkling in the wind and brass rails checking tourists who dare to lean out and take in the sights. The Powell-Mason line offers a peek at Alcatraz; and the California Street car stops right at the gilded doors of Grace Cathedral.

Once a stomping ground for Gold Rush industry titans, this urbane quarter—sometimes dubbed "Snob Hill"—echoes of mighty egos and ancestral riches. It is home to white-glove buildings, ladies who lunch, and opulent dining rooms. Named for the 1800s railroad magnates, the **Big Four** is a stately hideaway known for antique memorabilia and nostalgic chicken potpie. Extravagant **Top of the Mark** is beloved for bounteous brunches and panoramic vistas. **Le Club**, a lush supper room and cocktail lounge inspired by the private clubs of yore, is a VIP haunt in an exclusive residential high-rise. For a total departure, kick back with a Mai Tai (purportedly invented at Oakland's Trader Vic's in 1944) at the **Tonga Room & Hurricane Bar**, a tiki spot with a live thunderstorm inside the Fairmont Hotel.

RUSSIAN HILL

Downhill toward Polk Street, the vibe mellows as heirloom splendor gives way to Russian Hill, chockablock with boutiques, dive bars, and casual eateries that cater to regular groups of mostly twenty-something singles. Good, affordable fare abounds at **Café Rex**, and **Street. Nick's Crispy Tacos**, the tacky taqueria turned nighttime disco, is a perennial fave. For dessert, try the sinful chocolate earthquake from **Swensen's Ice Cream** flagship parlor, which is still *so* 1948.

A handful of haute foodie shops whet the palate of resident young professionals. **Cheese Plus** stocks more than 300 international cultures, artisan charcuterie, and chocolate; across the street, the **Jug Shop** is a mecca for micro-brew beer and southern hemisphere wines. Dining at the eternally delish and inexpensive **House of Nanking** is a rare experience. Don't bother ordering from the menu; the owner often takes menus out of diner's hands and orders for them.

CHINATOWN

For a change of pace, head to Chinatown, whose authentic markets, dim sum palaces, and souvenir emporiums spill down the eastern slope of Nob Hill in a wash of color and Cantonese characters. Here you'll find some of the city's finest and crave-worthy barbecue pork buns at the area's oldest dim sum house, **Hang Ah Tea Room**, and a bevy of quirky must-sees. Fuel up on oven-fresh 95-cent custard tarts at **Golden Gate Bakery**, but save room for samples at **Golden Gate Fortune Cookie Company**, where you can watch the prophetic little sweets in the making. The Mid-Autumn Moon Festival brings mooncakes, a traditional pastry stuffed with egg yolk and lotus seed paste. Unwind at **Imperial Tea Court**, a sanctum that offers *gàiwan* and *gongfu* tea presentations and a retail offering of classic accoutrements. Gastronomes, take home a taste of Chinatown at the Wok Shop for Asian cookware, linens, and tools.

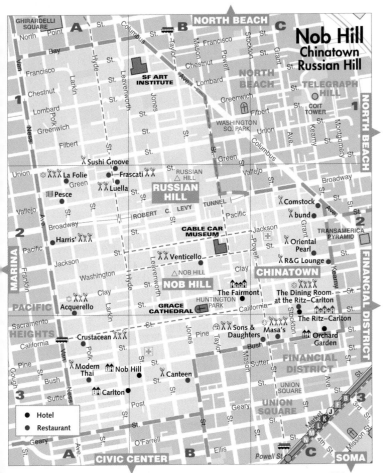

Acquerello ⚛

Italian 𝖃𝖃𝖃

1722 Sacramento St. (bet. Polk St. & Van Ness Ave.)

Phone: 415-567-5432   Dinner Tue – Sat
Web: www.acquerello.com
Prices: $$$

Marty Kelly

There's still a hushed reverence observed in this former chapel, but now it's for Suzette Gresham-Tognetti's clever Italian cooking. Make your way past the eclectic mix of storefronts that make up this patchwork area of Nob Hill, and you'll find Acquerello nearly hidden behind a small, windowless façade and a discreet awning. Don't mind the humble entrance; inside, it's an entirely different story.

The beautiful wooden beams that once supported the steeple are hand-painted now, sloping down into pretty, sunset-colored walls; the soft thrum of classical music drifts down from the speakers, and into a room quietly buzzing with murmuring couples and graceful managers checking in on tables. It is never too crowded here—reservations seemingly spread out generously as not to rush the guests.

Dinner, depending on your appetite, arrives in 3, 4, 5, or 6 courses, and might include tender lobster *panzarotti*, steeping in a spicy lobster sauce drizzled with piquant chili oil; succulent pork loin rolled in sage and lemon, and paired with charred *puntarelle* and an otherwordly pumpkin purée; or creamy, ethereally light vanilla panna cotta with preserved figs and toasted Marcona almonds.

bund

Chinese 🍴

C2

640 Jackson St. (bet. Kearny St. & Wentworth Pl.)

Phone: 415-982-0618
Web: N/A
Prices: 💱

Lunch & dinner daily

On chilly San Francisco days, Chinatown savants (and a few tourists who wandered in the right direction) slurp belly-warming juicy buns, aka soup dumplings, at bund. Though these particular morsels want an extra kick of ginger, the tender pork and quality dough remind us why they command a cult following. The dining room here is cleaner than its neighbors', the friendly owners are ever-present, and the Shanghainese cuisine is a nice departure from the neighborhood's ubiquitous Cantonese menus. Such dim sum options as a flaky turnip puff make for divine snacking, and vegetarians will rejoice in a spinach stir-fry with fresh bamboo shoots.

Reasonable prices, generous portions, friendly service, and tasty food make bund a no-brainer.

The ❀ award is the crème de la crème. This is awarded to restaurants which are really special for their cuisine.

103

Canteen

San Francisco ▶ Nob Hill

B3

Californian 🍴

817 Sutter St. (bet. Jones & Leavenworth Sts.)

Phone: 415-928-8870
Web: www.sfcanteen.com
Prices: $$

Lunch Fri – Sun
Dinner Tue – Sat

Sit yourself down at the lime green counter and watch Chef Dennis Leary work his magic before you in an open kitchen. Sublime, seasonal dishes are concocted right before your eyes, in a mesmerizing display of choreographed chaos. The diner-like space is tiny—four booths and a few seats at the forever packed counter—so waits can be lengthy—but, it's worth it.

Steaming Parker house rolls start things off right, while tasty bites like halibut gravlax (thinly sliced and salt-cured, beneath diced green tomatoes, avocado, and celery) hit the spot. Twirl your tongs around carbonara—capellini noodles, diced ham, chopped herbs, egg yolk, Parmesan, and chili pepper; and as a special treat, stop in on a Tuesday night for the chef's three course prix-fixe.

Comstock

C2

Gastropub 🍴

155 Columbus Ave. (at Pacific Ave.)

Phone: 415-617-0071
Web: www.comstocksaloon.com
Prices: $$

Lunch & dinner Mon – Sat

Named for the legendary Comstock Lode—the mining jackpot that launched the 19th century Gold Rush—Comstock is a historically correct homage to Americana and the classic cocktails—think Sazerac and Manhattan—that are legendary in their own right. The saloon has served as a watering hole since 1907, and its refreshed pressed tin ceilings and carved wood bar feel like they've been there as long.

Comstock is a bar first and foremost but, in the San Francisco foodie tradition, also serves quite good pub grub. Soak up the suds with salty fried fava beans tossed in chili oil; plump corn and jalapeño fritters; and, at dinner, the much loved chicken-fried rabbit. If the booze and bites don't take you back, take a gander at the antiques and old-time portraits.

Crustacean

A3

Asian XXX

1475 Polk St. (at California St.)

Phone:	415-776-2722	Lunch Sun
Web:	www.anfamily.com	Dinner nightly
Prices:	$$$	

On the third floor of a nondescript Nob Hill building, Crustacean is the kind of place that could be easily overlooked. However, once you discover this stylish and comfortable Vietnamese gem sparkling with secret family recipes, consider yourself a regular.

Matriarch Helene An started out as a princess in Vietnam, but she and her family were forced to leave Saigon in the wake of the Communist invasion in 1975. Their restaurant dynasty, which began in San Francisco with Thanh Long, has branched into three locations of Crustacean. Since its 1991 opening, critics and regulars have been clamoring for the "secret specialties," such as garlic noodles and the whole crab roasted with garlic and spices, both prepared in the locked kitchen within the kitchen.

Frascati

A2

Mediterranean XX

1901 Hyde St. (at Green St.)

Phone:	415-928-1406	Dinner nightly
Web:	www.frascatisf.com	
Prices:	$$	

Named for a bucolic hilltop town overlooking Rome, Frascati is a charming and friendly neighborhood treasure. Sidewalk tables enjoy the chimes of passing cable cars, while lovers prefer romantic mezzanine seating on cooler nights. The interior bursts with boisterous Russian Hill regulars who nosh on seasonal Mediterranean fare paired with wines from California and Italy.

Begin with plump and beautifully grilled sardines accented with Meyer lemon aïoli and micro-greens, or sample wild mushroom bruschetta with goat cheese fondue and bacon. Entrées focus on proteins, such as pan-seared *branzino* with herbed polenta and candy cap mushrooms.

Frascati is a popular spot and parking is near impossible. Fortunately, the cable car stops right out front.

The Dining Room
at the Ritz-Carlton

Contemporary XXXX

C2

600 Stockton St. (at California St.)

Phone: 415-773-6198   Dinner Wed – Sun
Web: www.ritzcarltondiningroom.com
Prices: $$$$

The Ritz-Carlton, San Francisco

It's hard not to feel like the Queen of England settling into one of the stately cushioned chairs that flank The Dining Room at the Ritz-Carlton's impeccably appointed tables. Like the ultra-exclusive digs it calls home, everything about this beacon of fine dining is larger than life, with a dining room fitted out and draped in luxurious gold and burgundy fabrics, glowing chandeliers, and china so infallible it would make a Frenchman blush.

The royal treatment hardly stops at the décor—the incredibly professional, polished service staff has an eagle's eye for detail and is uniformly gracious. So let SoMa have its hip, because you'll be expected to don a jacket here, thank you very much.

Critically-acclaimed Chef Ron Siegel's creative, contemporary menu rotates seasonally, but might kick off with a luscious amuse-bouche of slow-poached quail egg topped with osetra caviar and brioche croutons; a small plate of tender black truffle ravioli, paired with melt-in-your mouth Kobe beef and laced with port reduction and a light Parmesan foam; or perfectly sautéed Blue Bream, topped with seared foie gras, fresh pomegranate seeds, and roasted Musque de Provence (a type of pumpkin).

Harris'

Steakhouse

 A2

2100 Van Ness Ave. (at Pacific Ave.)

Phone: 415-673-1888   Dinner nightly
Web: www.harrisrestaurant.com
Prices: $$$$

Look at the crowds inside this pricey Nob Hill steakhouse and dare to forget there is a recession. Nothing has changed for decades here, including the classic interior with its mahogany wood bar, half-moon-shaped booths, and bustling service. Perhaps that's why Harris' is still so sought-after: when times get tough, folks seek refuge in the tried-and-true.

Steaks are serious business here, as the aged midwestern corn-fed beef hanging in the display window attest. The meat is as good as ever, the sides of mashed potatoes huge, and the Caesar salads are served with whole anchovies on top.

The Pacific Lounge, where martinis and live jazz are de rigueur, may be the best spot to dine, even if the tables aren't as comfortable as in the main room.

Luella

Mediterranean

 A2

1896 Hyde St. (at Green St.)

Phone: 415-674-4343   Dinner nightly
Web: www.luellasf.com
Prices: $$

The parking can cause heartburn, but the food and service at Luella make it worth the frustration. Better yet, hop aboard the Powell & Hyde Street cable car for a little old-fashioned, and stress-free, commute.

Ben and Rachel de Vries run the show at this charming, if often boisterous, place. From Coca-Cola-braised pork shoulder and ahi tuna tacos with mango salsa to beef Wellington, this menu covers it all. The food is seriously delicious, but casual pizzas, pastas, and a children's menu prove that this place doesn't take itself too seriously. Dessert is worth saving room for with selections like miniature banana cream pies with Valrhona chocolate sauce and orange and sweet ricotta fritters. The three-course prix-fixe is a real deal.

La Folie

 French XXX

A2

2316 Polk St. (bet. Green & Union Sts.)

Phone: 415-776-5577   Dinner Mon – Sat
Web: www.lafolie.com
Prices: $$$$

La Folie

Tucked into the stylish patchwork of hotels and eateries that makes up modern-day Russian Hill, Chef Roland Passot's family-run mainstay has earned its keep by turning out expertly prepared classic French haute cuisine with a good dose of Californian sensibility manifested in the vegetarian tasting menu.

Some of La Folie's prosperous guests may opt to linger in the adjoining, stylish lounge for an aperitif and haute bar bites before settling into velvet banquettes in a beautiful, wood-paneled dining room dotted with honey-hued curtains and fresh cut flowers. Service is equally sophisticated; the sommelier and waiters adeptly walk the line between professionalism and personality.

The tasting menus whirl with the season, but may feature tempura-fried duck egg with a fluffy sweetbread blini in black truffle sauce, served with shaved asparagus salad; succulent fillets of black bass, pan-seared and paired with smooth fava bean purée, a baked razor clam, Brussels sprout leaves, and bone marrow ragout; or plump medallions of quail wrapped in crispy potato threads and stuffed with rare squab breast and mushrooms, then plated with a fried quail egg, sautéed baby carrots, and haricot verts.

Masa's ✿

Contemporary ✕✕✕✕

C3

648 Bush St. (bet. Powell & Stockton Sts.)

Phone: 415-989-7154   Dinner Tue – Sat
Web: www.masasrestaurant.com
Prices: $$$$

Masa's

Tucked behind a miniscule, blink-and-you'll-miss-it glass awning just north of Union Square, the best way to find Masa's is by knowing it's connected to the Hotel Vintage Court. There's a reward inside for all your hard efforts: an impossibly sexy lair fit for a hipster king, with stunning chocolate walls, striking Toile de Jouy chairs, and bright red lampshades.

With style dripping from the walls in this manner, you have to ask: does the food get lost? Quite the opposite, with the talented, meticulous Gregory Short manning a kitchen that proffers a wide range of specialty ingredients into its contemporary, French-influenced menu.

There is no à la carte option, but diners can choose from a five- or nine-course menu with vegetarian selections available in both versions. The nightly lineup changes seasonally but might reveal creamy pillows of potato gnocchi studded with baby artichoke hearts, caramelized sunchokes, tiny bits of fermented black garlic, and shaved Parmigiano Reggiano; or three small Australian lamb chops, roasted to juicy, rosy pink perfection and paired with fluffy mint couscous, toasted green chickpeas with cumin, and yogurt mousse fragrant with garlic and dill.

Modern Thai

1247 Polk St. (at Bush St.)

Phone: 415-922-8424
Web: www.modernthaisf.com
Prices:

Lunch & dinner daily

In the cheery colonial-style dining space, shades of raspberry sherbet and lime vivify stark white walls, while colorful Gerber daisies adorn glass-topped tables. An enclosed porch affords sunny street side views and a great spot to tuck into some cheap and tasty Thai. Pumpkin lovers rejoice—this gourd is prepared in all kinds of delicious ways, whether shredded and deep-fried with sesame and coconut, or cubed in a luscious, creamy curry. Specialties like crispy calamari with cashews or roasted duck with lychee curry are equally worthy, as are the fishcakes—golden, crispy pancakes of minced fish, silver rice noodles, and shiitake mushrooms.
Exotic desserts like blueberry *roti* or the MT sundae with purple yam and coconut ice cream are a perfect finale.

Oriental Pearl

760 Clay St. (bet. Grant & Kearny Sts.)

Phone: 415-433-1817
Web: www.orientalpearlsf.com
Prices:

Lunch & dinner daily

At Portsmouth Square, Chinese elders gather to play cards or dominos, smoking cigarettes amid hovering crowds. Across the way, a gem of an eatery lures in those locals, where gracious servers clad in red bow ties serve up authentic, delicious Hong Kong-style Chinese at budget-friendly prices. With no dim sum cart in sight, everything is ordered straight off the menu and served fresh from the kitchen. Dim sum menus are for two or more so eating turns into a team sport tackling delights like lightly fried chive, spinach, and shrimp dumplings. The house special meatball—a blend of chicken, shrimp, mushrooms, and Virginia ham wrapped "dumpling style" in a poached egg white, all tied together with a thin green onion, is something of a little treasure.

Pesce

Seafood

A2

2227 Polk St. (bet. Green & Vallejo Sts.)

Phone: 415-928-8025
Web: www.pescesf.com
Prices: $$

Dinner nightly

From Venice, Italy, comes the tradition of *cicchetti*, small appetizers served in wine bars all over that city. Here atop Russian Hill, San Franciscans can savor these little bites too, honestly interpreted by Pesce's chef and owner, Ruggero Gadaldi (also of Antica Trattoria, down the block).

Here, *cicchetti* arrive either cold or hot—just remember to check the blackboard for daily specials. Refreshing *gamberoni* (white shrimp sautéed with spices) plated with a frisée salad, pecorino, ricotta salata, and mint may be among the cold offerings, while *tonno* puttanesca (herb-crusted tuna in a spicy tomato sauce) is a warm plate highlight. Though meats do appear on the menu, Pesce stays true to its moniker with seafood dishes predominating.

R & G Lounge

Chinese

C2

631 Kearny St. (bet. Clay & Sacramento Sts.)

Phone: 415-982-7877
Web: www.rnglounge.com
Prices:

Lunch & dinner daily

Deceptively large R & G Lounge is a true standout, especially in comparison to its sketchier Chinatown neighbors. The wood-paneled subterranean dining room is uncommonly clean and lined with tanks full of the freshest seafood around. During the lengthy season, whole salt-and-pepper Dungeness crab is the signature dish, while kung pao prawns please the lunch crowd year-round. Landlubbers enjoy familiar classics such as hot and sour soup or lemon chicken.

The menu is extensive and service is especially prompt, but newbies should stand their ground and take time to peruse the offerings. Solo diners should beware that they may be seated among strangers at the round communal tables. At dinner, parking is validated in the Portsmouth Square garage.

Sons & Daughters

C3

Contemporary 🍴🍴

708 Bush St. (bet. Mason & Powell Sts.)

Phone: 415-391-8311
Web: www.sonsanddaughterssf.com
Prices: $$

Dinner Wed – Sun

The layout is cozy, but the food serious; the flavors are sophisticated and the prices, reasonable. This SF brainchild has it all. Already showing signs of brilliance, stylish Sons & Daughters wears handsome leather chairs, twinkling chandeliers, and a deep purple ceiling. Begging to be the spotlight is a central kitchen that barely fits three cooks.

Shelves lined with canisters of herbs and spices hint at star flavors in a four-course affair that may include a foie gras torchon with absinthe, blackberry gelée, and candied almond shavings. The kitchen also bestows thoughtful à la carte compositions including a scallop resting on a bed of maitakes, drizzled with veal-jasmine broth; or roasted lamb and chanterelles blessed with root beer jus.

Sushi Groove

A2

Japanese 🍴

1916 Hyde St. (bet. Green & Union Sts.)

Phone: 415-440-1905
Web: www.sushigroove.com
Prices: $$

Dinner nightly

This fishbowl of a Hyde Street space is forever packed with friends who crave raw seafood in creative preparations. The soft glow of the sunset behind neighboring homes casts a warm spell, and the intimate space may be boisterous with groups catching up after work. Parking is a trick, so call ahead to see about valet.

Sushi Groove also has popular locations in SoMa, Walnut Creek, and Mexico City, so the place must be doing something right. A fresh *ahi poke* salad is layered with thinly sliced cucumber, mango, and papaya; translucent *hirame* nigiri drapes over cool rice; and the maki are tantalizing—try the tuna *caliente* with garlic, jalapeño, and *tobiko*. Those looking for cooked fare can find comfort in a glass of sake and try to enjoy the party.

Venticello

Italian 𝒳𝒳

B2

1257 Taylor St. (at Washington St.)

Phone:	415-922-2545	Dinner nightly
Web:	www.venticello.com	
Prices:	$$$	

Concierges in the Nob Hill luxury hotels eagerly recommend this charming restaurant, whose name is Italian for "little breeze." Indeed, this place is a breath of fresh air, from the rustic, cozy dining room in terra-cotta hues that conjures a Tuscan farmhouse, to the menu of well-made Italian favorites.

This cuisine adheres to the restaurant's decidedly Italian philosophy: *chi mangia bene, vive bene* (he who eats well, lives well). True to this philosophy, everyone is well-fed after polishing off *pizzette* fresh from the cobalt blue-tiled wood-fired oven, plates of homemade pasta dishes like spaghetti carbonara or cheese ravioli, as well as outstanding specials.

Parking spaces are precious in this neighborhood, so use the valet or take the cable car.

Hotels and restaurants
change every year,
so change your Michelin
Guide every year!

North Beach
Fisherman's Wharf • Telegraph Hill

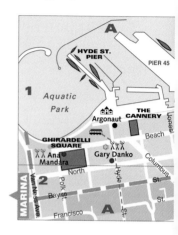

Nestled between bustling Fisherman's Wharf and the steep slopes of Russian and Telegraph hills, North Beach owes its lively nature to the Italian immigrants who settled here in the late 1800s. Many of these were fishermen from the Ligurian coast; the seafood stew they made on their boats evolved into the quintessential San Francisco treat, cioppino—a must-order in this district. Though Italians are no longer in the majority here, dozens of pasta places, pizzerias, coffee shops, and bars in North Beach attest to their idea of the good life. At the annual North Beach Festival in mid-June, a celebrity pizza toss, Assisi Animal Blessings, and Arte di Gesso (chalk art) also nod to the neighborhood's Italian heritage. **Fog City Diner** remains a popular stop for tourists after a ferry to Alcatraz or a walk along The Embarcadero.

Today the majority of North Beach's restaurants and bars lie along Columbus Avenue. Be sure to check out the quarter's Italian delis, like **Molinari's**, whose homemade salami has been a local institution since 1896. Pair some imported meats and cheeses with a bottle of wine for a perfect picnic in nearby Washington Square Park.

Hanging out in North Beach can be a full-time job, which is what attracted a ragtag array of beret-wearing poets to the area in the 1950s. These so-called beatniks—Allen Ginsberg and Jack Kerouac among them—were eventually driven out by busloads of tourists. Bohemian spirits linger on at such landmarks as the City Lights bookstore, and next door at **Vesuvio**, the original beatnik bar.

You won't find many locals there, but Fisherman's Wharf, the mile-long stretch of waterfront at the foot of Columbus Street, ranks as one of the city's most popular tourist attractions. It may teem with souvenir shops, street performers, rides, and other attractions, but you should go—if only to feast on a sourdough bread bowl filled with clam chowder, and fresh crabs cooked in huge steamers right on the street.

When here, sample a piece of edible history at **Boudin Bakery**. This old-world bakery may have bloomed into a large modern operation—complete with a museum and bakery tour—but

North Beach
Fisherman's Wharf
Telegraph Hill

SAN FRANCISCO BAY

FISHERMAN'S WHARF

PIER 41
PIER 39
PIER 43½

AQUARIUM OF THE BAY

- ● Hotel
- ● Restaurant

SAN FRANCISCO BAY

Jefferson
St.
Taylor
Mason
Powell
Stockton
Kearny
St.
Point
Bay
Francisco
St.
Embarcadero
LEVI'S PLAZA
Sansome
PIER 29
The Embarcadero
Albona
Chestnut
NORTH BEACH
TELEGRAPH HILL
COIT TOWER
Battery
PIER 5
Greenwich
Lombard
St.
Montgomery
Grant
Kearny
St.
Filbert
WASHINGTON SQ. PARK
Café Jacqueline
Piperade
Front
St.
Davis
Trattoria Contadina
Rose Pistola
Maykadeh
The Embarcadero
Union
Iluna Basque
Green
St.
Jones
Taylor
Mason
Bohème
Columbus
Ave.
St.
RUSSIAN HILL
Vallejo
Powell
Stockton
the house
Coi
Broadway
Lafitte
RUSSIAN HILL
Tommaso's
Kokkari Estiatorio
ROBERT C. LEVY TUNNEL
Broadway
Quince
Bix
Drumm
Leavenworth
Pacific
St.
Grant
Pacific
Gold St.
Jackson
JACKSON SQUARE
Washington
EMBARCADERO PLAZA
Jackson
NOB HILL
CHINATOWN
TRANSAMERICA PYRAMID
EMBARCADERO CENTER
Washington
NOB HILL
Clay
Ave.
FINANCIAL DISTRICT
Sacramento

they still make their sourdough bread fresh each day, using the same mother first cultivated here from local wild yeast in 1849.

Nearby on North Point Street, Ghirardelli Square preserves another taste of old SF. This venerable chocolate company, founded by Domingo Ghirardelli in 1852, now flaunts its delectable wares at the **Ghirardelli Ice Cream and Chocolate Manufactory**. Here you can ogle the original chocolate manufacturing equipment while you enjoy a hot-fudge sundae. Don't leave without taking away some sweet memories in the form of their chocolate squares.

Albona

B2

Italian ✗✗

545 Francisco St. (bet. Mason & Taylor Sts.)

Phone: 415-441-1040
Web: www.albonarestaurant.com
Prices: $$

Dinner Tue – Sat

This old-school charmer, located on a residential block of North Beach, is the place to go for Istrian cuisine. A fusion of Italian and Eastern European influences, the dishes here find their roots in the Croatian town of Albona, which sits high on a cliff overlooking the Adriatic Sea.

Start with Italian, as in a bowl of seafood linguini brimming with fresh mussels, clams, shrimp, and whitefish. The tradition is to follow pasta with a meat dish, perhaps a hearty mustard-crusted rack of lamb.

Closely spaced, linen-topped tables, low lighting, and friendly service fashion an intimate atmosphere favored by local couples. If driving, take advantage of the restaurant's valet service; otherwise, parking is hard to come by in this area.

Ana Mandara

A1

Vietnamese ✗✗

891 Beach St. (at Polk St.)

Phone: 415-771-6800
Web: www.anamandara.com
Prices: $$

Lunch Mon – Fri
Dinner nightly

Situated in the well-tread and touristy Ghirardelli Square area, Ana Mandara is indeed a "beautiful refuge," as its name suggests. Colonial Vietnam comes alive in the Southeast Asian temple décor, replete with silk lanterns, rattan furnishings, trickling fountains, and leafy palms. The upstairs mezzanine lounge, where live music entertains Thursday through Saturday nights, provides a lovely perspective of the scene below.

Courteous servers clad in traditional silk gowns deliver such delicacies as sweet Dungeness crab soup with hand cut noodles; seared salmon with fresh mango and tamarind sauce; and spicy ginger chicken served atop a bed of snow peas. A quick lunch option for $16 offers the choice of an appetizer and entrée from a limited selection.

Bix

American

 C·D3

56 Gold St. (bet. Montgomery & Sansome Sts.)

Phone: 415-433-6300
Web: www.bixrestaurant.com
Prices: $$$

Lunch Fri
Dinner nightly

Pass through the nondescript brick façade, follow the cryptic entry, and find yourself in the bygone supper club era, paying homage to jazz great Bix Beiderbecke. The dining room exudes fanciful charm with lofty columns, rich mahogany panelling, and a baby grand. Lull at the bar where tenders satiate with much shaking and stirring; then sweep up the staircase and into a scenic booth.

Elegant servers enhance the throwback tone, reciting—perhaps to the backdrop of live jazz shows—a menu of revived classics like hearty onion and oxtail soup; crisp, golden cakes of chicken hash drizzled with a mascarpone sauce; and syrupy banana bites on ice cream. Deviled eggs with truffles and chives, and Maine lobster spaghetti add to the delicious nostalgia.

Café Jacqueline

French

C2

1454 Grant Ave. (bet. Green & Union Sts.)

Phone: 415-981-5565
Web: N/A
Prices: $$$

Dinner Wed – Sun

Those looking for a quick meal needn't read any further. This café specializes in slow food—soufflés to be exact. Seductively puffed and airy—and sized for two—these savory creations are flavored with ingredients such as Gruyère cheese and white corn; brie and broccoli; and salmon and asparagus. While you're waiting for your soufflé to emerge from the oven, sample a salad or a bowl of the terrific French onion soup. Dessert brings more soufflés, these rich and sweet, heady with intense chocolate or Grand Marnier.

You have to walk through the kitchen on your way to the loo. There you'll see diminutive Chef Jacqueline Margulis passionately whipping up her signature dish—as she has for more than 25 years—kept company by an enormous bowl of fresh eggs.

Coi ✿ ✿

Contemporary 🍴🍴🍴

C3

373 Broadway (bet. Montgomery & Sansome Sts.)

Phone:	415-393-9000
Web:	www.coirestaurant.com
Prices:	$$$$

Dinner Tue – Sat

Dwight Eschliman

If this North Beach temple of fine dining isn't already on your food-faves list, it should be. Tucked into a seedy neighborhood, Coi (pronounced "kwah") only needs you to make the first step into their minimally marked façade. The rest of your wonderfully serene dining experience is up to them—the polished staff quietly buzzing about the sleek dining room, with its soothing earth tones and minimalist lines; the small oohs and ahs as Chef Daniel Patterson's divine and delicious creations hit the table dish after dish.

And oh, how many dishes there are: don't let the restaurant's seasonal double-digit tasting menu (the only thing you can order) throw you off. Discerning gourmands of all ages book their tables weeks in advance for a brush with this level of fine foodie perfection.

Known for twisting pristine ingredients into creative combinations, a spin through the recesses of Patterson's endlessly inventive mind might unearth sinful specialties like a silky, fennel-studded buttermilk panna cotta topped with cherry blossom gelée and fennel fronds; or faintly crisped abalone strips rolling around with raw asparagus ribbons, a veal jus reduction, fresh mint, and Seville orange zest.

Gary Danko ✿

Contemporary ✗✗✗

A1

800 North Point St. (at Hyde St.)

Phone:	415-749-2060	Dinner nightly
Web:	www.garydanko.com	
Prices:	**$$$$**	

Kingmond Young Photography

Like a white dove in a flock of pigeons, this beautiful, haute brasserie is a world apart from the Fisherman's Wharf, the fanny packing tourist hood it calls home. So come on in, shake off the crowds and let the soft jazz music, sexy curved booths, and fresh cut roses envelope you into Gary Danko's soothing universe for a bit. The best is yet to come.

Named for the multi-talented chef who owns it, this always buzzing restaurant packs them in every night of the week for good reason. Danko made a name for himself working his formidable skills into technically complex dishes like perfectly al dente risotto, chock-a-block with fresh rock shrimp, tender chunks of lobster, pristine vegetables, and creamy Parmesan; or succulent, pan-fried duck breast with lemon pepper, paired with carrot and ginger purée, roasted baby turnips, braised rhubarb, carrots, and tender duck leg confit.

The flexible menu offers a scrumptious roster of à la carte offerings as well as the ability to creatively compose one's own three, four, or five-course tasting menu. Grape connoisseurs will want to take a second to check out the wine list, which plays patriot with an unusually large American selection.

119

the house

Asian ✗

C3

1230 Grant Ave. (bet. Columbus Ave. & Vallejo St.)

Phone: 415-986-8612
Web: www.thehse.com
Prices: $$

Lunch Mon – Sat
Dinner nightly

At the heart of Italian North Beach stands a tiny Asian eatery known for colorful fusion flavors and known simply as the house. Blonde wood furnishings and minimal décor create a pleasant vibe without detracting from the cuisine, while efficient servers recount the daily specials. Listen closely before making hasty decisions.

The meal begins with tangy marinated cucumbers and such appetizers as steamed shrimp-and-chive Chinese dumplings on a vibrant bed of carrot, beets, and radish. Slurp a bowl of udon with grilled chicken and toasted nori or sample more unique fare: wasabi noodles topped with teriyaki-glazed grilled salmon are a house specialty and worth the wait for a table. The house also offers a nice choice of tea, beer, and wines by the glass.

Iluna Basque

Basque

B2

701 Union St. (at Powell St.)

Phone: 415-402-0011
Web: www.ilunabasque.com
Prices: $$

Dinner nightly

Overlooking Washington Square and surrounded by the area's lively nightlife, Iluna Basque is the pleasant, candlelit brainchild of Chef Mattin Noblia—the *Top Chef* charmer whose trademark red neckerchiefs are sold here for charities. On the menu, his Basque roots shine through with small plates to be enjoyed with wine.

Like the modest Spanish wine list, the tapas here are appetizing and affordable—dine reasonably on the likes of warm shrimp and potato croquettes with aïoli or roasted mussels. Those seeking larger plates should try the "petites entrées" which include wood oven-baked, spicy Basque chicken with chorizo, and *pipérade* with sautéed Serrano ham and a poached egg.

On weekdays, take advantage of the two-for-one drinks at happy hour.

Kokkari Estiatorio 😋

Greek ✗✗

D3

200 Jackson St. (at Front St.)

Phone: 415-981-0983
Web: www.kokkari.com
Prices: $$

Lunch Mon – Fri
Dinner Mon – Sat

Easily one of San Francisco's most sensuous dining destinations, Kokkari lures guests back again and again with a roar in the cavernous wood-burning fireplace, plush mismatched armchairs, and an exhibition kitchen in the taverna-style back room. Ambient lighting and moderate space between tables make Kokkari a prime spot for dates and special occasions, so reservations are highly recommended.

Standout Greek and Mediterranean specialties include grilled lamb riblets with lemon and oregano; flaky *spanakotiropita* stuffed with spinach, feta, leek, and dill; and tender pan-roasted halibut steak with sweet corn, peppers, zesty olives, and herbs. Finish the evening with a stone ground Greek coffee heated in a traditional copper urn over piping hot sand.

Lafitte

French ✗✗

D3

Pier 5, The Embarcadero (at Broadway)

Phone: 415-839-2134
Web: www.lafittesf.com
Prices: $$

Lunch & dinner daily

It is quite fitting that Lafitte is named for an 18th century French pirate, since Chef/owner Russell Jackson is something of a renegade. This culinary revolutionary even ran an underground supper club for years before bringing his irreverence to North Beach. With concrete floors, granite tables, exposed ductwork, and a display kitchen, open the dictionary to industrial chic and you may find a picture of Lafitte. There's a palpable energy about this place, even without the piped in French music and jazz.

Farm fresh California meets funkified French here, so don't come expecting anything but surprises. The menu shifts daily and dishes like Padron peppers with *boquerones* vinaigrette and NY strip sandwich with caramelized onions have been known to appear.

121

Maykadeh

Persian ✗✗

470 Green St. (bet. Grant Ave. & Kearny St.)

Phone: 415-362-8286
Web: www.maykadehrestaurant.com
Prices: **$$**

Lunch & dinner daily

At Maykedeh—a name referring to Persian taverns of yore where poets and mystics converged to dine and drink—gracious service and generous portions abound. A burgundy and gold awning crowns the entrance; while inside, Middle Eastern songs and scents linger amid banquettes and linen-draped tables that accommodate crowds savoring the foods of their homeland.

Meals start with a plate of raw onion, fresh basil, and feta cheese—trust in these new, refreshing combinations, salads, and dips laced with alluring Middle Eastern flavors. Sample the rich *kashke bademjan*, an eggplant and garlic spread with warm pita, then a tender skewer of *koobideh*—fresh ground lamb and beef with warm Persian spices. Valet the car to avoid the Telegraph Hill parking conundrum.

Piperade

Basque ✗✗

1015 Battery St. (bet. Green & Union Sts.)

Phone: 415-391-2555
Web: www.piperade.com
Prices: **$$**

Lunch Mon – Fri
Dinner Mon – Sat

Soft Spanish melodies sooth the air at Piperade, where the brick façade, weathered oak floors, and communal shepherds' table evoke a Basque boarding house of yore. This cozy spot is home to Chef Gerald Hirigoyen, who hails from the French Basque country but cooks with both San Franciscan and Northern Spanish sensibilities.

Since "Hiri" oversees every detail, expect a top notch experience. The namesake *pipérade*, or pepper stew, arrives with Serrano ham and poached egg, while scrambled eggs accent an aromatic garlic soup with shrimp and lardoons. *Merguez* sausage and tender braised fennel accompany expertly prepared and sublimely juicy lamb chops. Peruse and sample from their 200 carefully selected wines while enjoying patio seating on a warm evening.

122

Quince ✿

Italian 🍴🍴🍴🍴

C3

470 Pacific Ave. (bet. Montgomery & Sansome Sts.)

Phone: 415-775-8500
Web: www.quincerestaurant.com
Prices: $$$

Dinner nightly

Sara Remington

The location has changed, but the endless stream of town cars crammed with the Who's Who still line up nightly outside Michael and Lindsay Tusk's beloved Quince. Can you blame them? The refined regulars have three excellent reasons to stay loyal to the husband-and-wife duo: a warm, polished, and professional staff; a compact but carefully assembled wine list boasting a healthy by-the-glass and half bottle selection; and elegant, mouthwatering Italian fare.

Make that four: the new digs, in a beautiful brick building overlooking Pacific Avenue, ain't so bad either—the interior pitch-perfect sophisticated, with a contemporary design and big, glossy windows made for two-way people watching (you can even watch the cooks from the sidewalk).

Though he grew up in New Jersey, Michael Tusk's travels to Southern France and Italy after finishing culinary school are likely the inspiration behind Quince's ever rotating menu, which may feature tender, perfectly al dente half moons of *cjalson* pasta packed with house smoked ricotta and laced with plump sultana raisins; or a succulent, albeit curiously small, dish of rabbit rendered four ways, each more deliciously complex than the next.

123

Rose Pistola

Italian XX

C2

532 Columbus Ave. (bet. Green & Union Sts.)

Phone: 415-399-0499
Web: www.rosepistolasf.com
Prices: $$$

Lunch & dinner daily

An unmistakable North Beach favorite, Rose Pistola pays tribute to the Ligurian Coast immigrants who once settled the neighborhood. Here, expect to feast on Northern Italian cuisine that focuses on seafood from independent and local fisherman, imported and house cured *salumi*, as well as meats from the rotisserie grill. The menu changes often but might include cracker-crisp pizza topped with salty prosciutto and fresh mozzarella; and nicely seasoned grilled octopus with Tuscan white beans, fennel, and arugula.

A large open kitchen and wood-burning oven warm the comfortable dining room with blue-and-white tile floors and an elegant bar mixing plenty of drinks. Service is typically friendly and sidewalk tables are preferred among locals with pets.

Tommaso's

Italian X

C3

1042 Kearny St. (bet. Broadway St. & Pacific Ave.)

Phone: 415-398-9696
Web: www.tommasosnorthbeach.com
Prices: $$

Dinner Tue – Sun

California pizza kitchens love to celebrate the bounty of the season, turning out pies with toppings that would boggle a red-blooded Italian (snow peas and sauerkraut?). Not so at Tommaso's, the family-friendly North Beach mainstay where the wood-fired pizzas hail straight from the old country. The chewy thin crust pies are heaped with sausage, meatballs, salami, and Prosciutto di Parma. Fancy pants can sample garlic and clams or chicken and artichoke.

Set against a bright mural depicting the Bay of Naples, dinners at Tommaso's might also include a meaty antipasto plate loaded with rosemary ham and *bresaola*, or classic tiramisu. A fixture in the neighborhood since 1935, this fortress is a refreshing escape from seedy North Beach nightlife.

Trattoria Contadina

Italian X

1800 Mason St. (at Union St.)

Phone: 415-982-5728   Dinner nightly
Web: www.trattoriacontadina.com
Prices: $$

For a neighborhood trattoria where the décor is rustic, the vibe is lively, and the staff is universally welcoming, look no further than the corner of Mason and Union streets. Inside, linoleum floors and signed photographs of celebrities create a homey feel, while outside you can hear the clanging of cable cars on the Powell-Mason line—which stops right outside the restaurant.

The food is equally honest and appealing, pleasing patrons as it has since opening in 1984. Classic preparations of veal and chicken on the menu may not veer from tradition, but they guarantee generous portions and consistent quality. Count on a few daily specials to round out the selection, as well as pasta entrées that are also available in half orders as appetizers.

Look for our category 🍲, small plates.

Richmond & Sunset

Here in the otherworldly outer reaches of San Francisco, the foggy sea washes up to the historic Cliff House and Sutro Baths; in spring, cherry blossoms blush at the breeze in Golden Gate Park; and whimsical topiaries wink at pastel row houses in need of fresh paint. Residents seem inspired by a sense of zen not quite found elsewhere in town, whether you happen upon a Japanese sushi chef or a Sunset surfer dude.

A melting pot of settlers forms the culinary complexion of this quiet urban pocket. The steam wafting from bowls of piping hot *pho* is nearly as thick as the marine layer, while many of the neighborhoods' western accents hail from across the pond.

The Richmond, however, has earned the nickname "New Chinatown" for a reason. A bazaar for the adventurous cook, Clement Street bursts with cramped sidewalk markets where clusters of bananas sway from the awnings and the spices and produce are as vibrant as the nearby Japanese Tea Garden in bloom. While the Bay Area mantra "eat local" doesn't really apply here, sundry international goods abound—think kimchi, tamarind, eel, live fish, and pork buns for less than a buck. Curious foodies find global delicacies: This is the place to source that 100-year-old egg. A gathering place for sea lovers,

Outerlands is perfect when in need of warmth, food, shelter, and "community."

There is a mom-and-pop joint for every corner and culture. The décor is nothing to write home about and, at times, feel downright seedy. But you're here for the cuisine, which is usually authentic: Korean barbecue at **Brothers Restaurant**; Burmese at **B Star Bar**; *siu mai* at **Shanghai Dumpling King** and **Good Luck Dim Sum**; as well

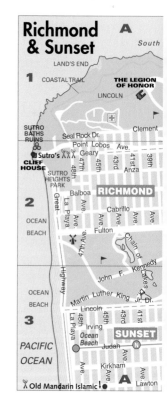

as an intoxicating offering of tequila and mescal at **Tommy's Mexican Restaurant**. For dessert, it's Asian kitsch: **Polly Ann Ice Cream** has served such flavors as durian, jasmine tea, and taro for years, while young club kids nibble Hong Kong–style sweets late night at **Kowloon Dessert Café**.

SUNSET

A touch more gentrified than neighboring Richmond, Sunset—once a heap of sand dunes—retains a small-town vibe that's groovy around the edges. In the early morning, locals line up for fresh bread and pastries at **Arizmendi Bakery**, then wash down their scones at the **Beanery** around the corner. **Katana-Ya** and **Hotei** offer soul-warming bowls of handmade noodles for lunch. While tourists taking in the sights at the DeYoung Museum or the Academy of Sciences might grab a bite at the **Academy Café**, loyalists to **L'Avenida Taqueria** take their burritos to the park. Don't miss dinner at the **Moss Room**, the new hot spot from Chefs Loretta Keller and Charles Phan.

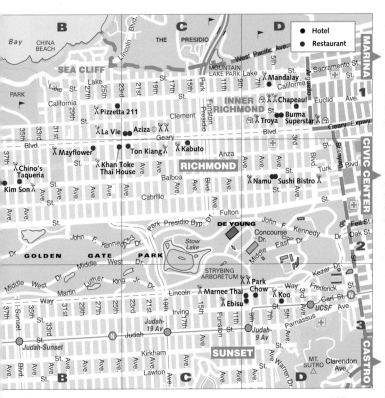

Aziza ✿

Moroccan 🍴🍴

C1

5800 Geary Blvd. (at 22nd Ave.)

Phone: 415-752-2222
Web: www.aziza-sf.com
Prices: $$

Dinner Wed – Mon

Deborah Jones Studio

There's a low-lit sensuality at play within the walls of Aziza: red glass chandeliers and iron mosaic lamps cast a mysterious glow over intricately laced wooden tables; Moorish archways lead to photos of Arabian stallions overlooking intimate banquette nooks; bright ceramic tiles gild a bar that features exotic specialty cocktails. What will it be tonight? A "strawberry" (*moscato d'asti*) or an "apple" (rosemary, maple sugar, and tequila)?

With food this good, why not try both? You might be here for a while. Marrakech-born Chef/owner Mourad Lahlou has a deft hand with his hometown fare, turning classic Berber tagines and vegetable stews on their heads by employing fresh, seasonal Californian ingredients.

Dinner might include a plate of freshly seared scallops, grilled sea eel, plump Manila clams, and octopus strewn across a neat column of crunchy *puntarelle*, diced saffron and leek marmalade, and earthy Hon-shimeji mushrooms; a fluffy mound of couscous laced with sweet prawns, tender grilled chicken, and lean lamb sausage; or a gorgeous tower of rose flavored panna cotta, topped with hibiscus granite, a thin citrus tuile fashioned into a bow, and a flutter of tiny black mint leaves.

Burma Superstar

Burmese ✗

D1

309 Clement St. (bet. 4th & 5th Aves.)

Phone: 415-387-2147
Web: www.burmasuperstar.com
Prices: 😊😊

Lunch & dinner daily

With a far-flung address and a mob at the door, the name Burma Superstar aptly reflects its status as one of the city's hottest hipster destinations.

Many of its traditional Burmese dishes—with flavorful influences from Thailand, India, and China—are prepared tableside in portions ample for sharing, making this fun for small, adventurous groups.

Never heard of *mohinga* or *poodi*? Fear not: the über-friendly staff is ready to expand your culinary education with the likes of rainbow salad's 22 ingredients, including green papaya and four kinds of noodle, tossed together in perfect harmony. Also try perfectly wok-roasted calamari with lemon-chili sauce or stir-fried chili lamb on a banana leaf. Note that sibling, B Star Bar, is just down the street.

Chapeau!

French ✗✗

D1

126 Clement St. (bet. 2nd & 3rd Aves.)

Phone: 415-387-0408
Web: www.chapeausf.com
Prices: $$

Dinner Tue – Sat

Upon arriving at Chapeau!, stylish women are welcomed with a kiss-kiss from Monsieur and Madame Gardelle, the husband-wife team that runs a strictly French ship. A long banquette and close-knit tables span the boisterous dining room that, with an ambient amber glow, is equally romantic and spirited for date nights.

Chef/owner Phillipe Gardelle is as often shaking hands in the dining room as he is in the kitchen, where he prepares such classic Gallic cuisine as porcini-crusted sweetbreads, fresh seafood bouillabaisse, and hearty *cassoulet de Toulouse*. At the end of a meal, the chef may even turn up tableside for a round of applause. On weekdays, early birds put their hands together for the under $30 prix-fixe from 5:00 P.M. to 6:00 P.M.

129

Chino's Taqueria

B2

Mexican ✗

3416 Balboa St. (bet. 35th & 36th Aves.)

Phone: 415-668-9956
Web: www.chinostaqueria.com
Prices: ⊜⊜

Lunch & dinner daily

Big flavors at small prices draw the masses to Chino's. Burritos take center stage, bulging with ingredients such as spicy chicken, carne asada, and chile verde. Additional toppings include beans, rice, guacamole, sour cream, or all of the above. Cheese lovers should request it right away, so the staff can warm it on the tortilla before the stuffing begins. Last, but not least, opt for either the mild green tomatillo sauce or the tongue-tingling red sauce, and dig into the tidy, foil-wrapped result, which bursts with flavor in each juicy bite. Just save room for that brown bag of crispy chips.

There is some seating in the sunny yellow room, but we recommend grabbing a burrito or a jumbo quesadilla to go, and heading west to enjoy it on the beach.

Ebisu

D3

Japanese ✗

1283 9th Ave. (at Irving St.)

Phone: 415-566-1770
Web: www.ebisusushi.com
Prices: ⊜⊜

Lunch & dinner Tue – Sun

For nearly 30 years, Steve Fujii and his wife Koko, have run this favorite sushi-ya, one block from Golden Gate Park. The refreshed décor is sophisticated and contemporary, with a polished wood sushi bar and sleek accents.

Lovers of wacky rolls (and reasonable prices) know this is the place to experiment. With names like Potato Bug (cucumber and freshwater eel inside-out roll), and Tootsie Roll (deep-fried halibut wrapped in soybean paper), these creations push the limits of tradition. Starters are likewise deliciously innovative, as in smoked scallop carpaccio with sizzling blood orange vinaigrette or steamed monkfish liver—foie gras of the sea.

Premium imported sakes have high prices to match, but less expensive sake samplers are also available.

Kabuto

J a p a n e s e ✕

C2

5121 Geary Blvd. (bet. 15th & 16th Aves.)

Phone:	415-752-5652	Lunch Tue – Sat
Web:	www.kabutosushi.com	Dinner Tue – Sun
Prices:	$$	

Named for a helmet worn by the noble samurai, Kabuto is dead serious about sushi. Seafood arrives from Japan daily to land beneath the deft blade of these *itamae*, whose skills command respect. Check the whiteboard for the day's freshest catch and watch quietly at the blonde wood counter as the chef transforms simple fish into an artful sushi experience.

Each bite is a complete flavor adventure, so please, heed the occasional "no soy sauce" decree—sushi is best enjoyed without a scowl from the chef. With such clever concoctions, this advice is worth obeying. Sample *hirame* "Jerry" with Japanese clover, ponzu jelly, and wasabi cream; tempura-coated albacore wrapped in a crêpe with crispy nori; or sliced fresh hamachi with cilantro and jalapeño slivers.

Khan Toke Thai House

T h a i ✕

B2

5937 Geary Blvd. (bet. 23rd & 24th Aves.)

Phone:	415-668-6654	Dinner nightly
Web:	N/A	
Prices:		

This slice of old Siam treats diners to authentic Thai food, music, and culture. Before entering, guests are asked to remove their shoes; sit cross-legged on floor cushions; or have their legs dangling in wells below the hand-carved wooden tables.

Extensive, diverse, and unique, the menu travels through Thailand in the likes of *tom yam* soup with chicken, lemongrass, and cilantro; and *pong pang*, a combination of seafood sautéed with lemongrass, hot chilis, and the chef's secret spicy sauce. Neatly dressed servers can help guide you on your journey.

The ambience, set about with Thai artifacts and a lovely Asian garden out back, makes a perfect romantic rendezvous. Reasonable prices will leave you with enough money to tip the shoeman when you leave.

Kim Son

B2

Vietnamese ✗

3614 Balboa St. (bet. 37th & 38th Aves.)

Phone: 415-221-3811   Lunch & dinner daily
Web: N/A
Prices: 🍴

After a day at Ocean Beach, a piping hot bowl of *pho* from Kim Son is a surefire way to melt the San Franciscan summer chill. Handwritten on dry erase boards, the daily Vietnamese specials, such as the fresh raw beef with a squeeze of lemon (a Southeast Asian version of carpaccio) augment the enormous menu, and are well worth a try. Barbecued pork chops with an omelet over broken rice are delightful—especially when dipped in sweet-and-sour sauce.

Hanging paper lanterns and a few potted plants are the only embellishments to speak of, but the hospitality and efficiency of this family-run eatery make up for the lack of aesthetic. Seven dollar lunch specials are an unbeatable deal—with portions so hearty you may even have leftovers for dinner.

Koo

D3

Japanese ✗

408 Irving St. (bet. 5th & 6th Aves.)

Phone: 415-731-7077   Dinner Tue – Sun
Web: www.sushikoo.com
Prices: 🍴

Located in quiet, and often foggy, Inner Sunset, Koo's tiny sushi counter and tastefully minimalist dining space fills on a regular basis with a coterie of connoisseurs.

Rolls, sized to be easily managed with chopsticks, such as the Tokyo Crunch (hamachi, *unagi*, cucumber, and *tobiko* covered by spicy *tenkatsu*), and the Best Roll (tempura asparagus and avocado wrapped in salmon and thinly sliced lemon) illustrate the tasteful tweaking at which Chef Kiyoshi Hayakawa excels. Tried and true plates of beef *tataki* and miso-marinated black cod are meant for sharing, while selections from the grill—marinated artichokes; jalapeño stuffed with hamachi and served with a side of lime aïoli— add a non-traditional twist not normally found in local sushi haunts.

La Vie

C1

Vietnamese ✗

5830 Geary Blvd. (bet. 22nd & 23rd Aves.)

Phone: 415-668-8080
Web: N/A
Prices: 🍪

Lunch & dinner Tue – Sun

A tank full of playful koi greets visitors to this unassuming Vietnamese spot in the Outer Richmond. In the back of the sparsely decorated room, tanks swim with Dungeness crabs, whose immediate future is rather dim, but all the brighter for diners who order them roasted whole with garlic noodles. This dish may be a bit on the pricey side, but split among friends it becomes a delicious—if messy—party. The menu of moderately priced fare includes the likes of crunchy salt and pepper calamari; tender five-spice chicken with tangy tamarind sauce; steaming bowls of *pho*; cold noodle salads; and loads of vegetarian dishes.

Parking in this area can be a nightmare, so do as many locals do, and take advantage of La Vie's thriving take-out service.

Mandalay

D1

Burmese ✗

4348 California St. (bet. 5th & 6th Aves.)

Phone: 415-386-3895
Web: www.mandalaysf.com
Prices: 🍪

Lunch & dinner daily

Opened in 1984 in Inner Richmond, Mandalay lays claim to being the oldest Burmese restaurant in the city. Today it is experiencing resurgence in popularity, so be prepared to wait for a table.

Familiar fans of authentic Burmese cuisine will find plenty to please their palates here, reveling in these zesty, spicy, and tangy dishes that often include catfish or coconut. For something completely different, discover the Burmese salad—a virtual cacophony of flavor, with pickled mango, cucumber, and toasted garlic in one version; crunchy tea leaves, roasted peanuts, plum tomatoes, jalapeño peppers, and crispy fried lentils in another.

Holiday decorations displayed year-round add kitsch to a large dining room lined with tropical plants, trees, and fresh flowers.

133

Marnee Thai

D3

1243 9th Ave. (bet. Irving St. & Lincoln Way)

Phone: 415-731-9999
Web: www.marneethai.com
Prices: $$

Lunch & dinner daily

The city's food field may be packed, but Marnee Thai stands tall with its authentic array of affordable, fresh, and creative Thai tidbits. Within an earshot of Golden Gate Park, stroll past the anonymous façade and into a snug dining room coupled with gracious service and creative food. Dodge the rumbling open kitchen by grabbing a seat in back where curvy orange tabletops with dainty orchids evoke a bit of Siam.

The exotic menu includes mildly spiced angel wings with a chili-garlic sauce; golden triangles laden with pumpkin, potato, and curry in crispy wrappers; and palate-pleasing *pad kee mao*, pan-fried noodles tossed with thinly sliced beef, chili, garlic, tomato, and basil. Vegetarians frolic in the inventive and tasty selection of dishes.

Mayflower

B2

6255 Geary Blvd. (at 27th Ave.)

Phone: 415-387-8338
Web: www.mayflower-seafood.com
Prices: $$

Lunch & dinner daily

A mostly Asian clientele attests to the authenticity of Mayflower, a Cantonese dim sum house that sits opposite the golden dome of the Holy Virgin Russian Orthodox Church. Westerners beware: authenticity in Chinese cuisine brings recipes that may challenge the uninitiated palate—think goose webs; fish maw; and plump marinated duck tongues meant to be devoured, soft bones, cartilage et al.

Yet timid eaters should fear not, for there are plenty of delectable familiar options, as in crispy spring rolls; barbecue pork buns; and shrimp-and-pork *siu mai*. Shark fin dumpling soup and soft-shell crab with spicy salt are only moderately adventurous. Given the many aquariums, know that the seafood is fresh and these hearty portions won't break the bank.

Namu

D2

A s i a n

439 Balboa St. (at 6th Ave.)

Phone: 415-386-8332
Web: www.namusf.com
Prices: $$

Lunch Sat – Sun
Dinner nightly

This tale began with a food cart named Happy Belly in Golden Gate Park. From there, brothers Dennis, David, and Daniel Lee opened Namu, where slate, bamboo, and wood combine to create a modern Zen oasis. The name means "tree" in Korean, a fitting moniker for a spot where the bar is fashioned from a fallen cypress tree.

The versatile menu focuses on Japanese and Korean dishes and uses all natural meats and local organic produce. Dinner is divided into categories that range from "raw" offerings of scallop carpaccio and "crispy" tempura, to "comfort" foods in bowls of Namu ramen, as well as innovations like KFC (Korean fried chicken). Nab the Korean tacos (with short ribs and kimchi mayo wrapped in nori) at the Ferry Plaza's Thursday and Saturday markets.

Old Mandarin Islamic

A3

C h i n e s e

3132 Vicente St. (bet. 42nd & 43rd Aves.)

Phone: 415-564-3481
Web: N/A
Prices: ☏☏

Lunch Fri – Mon & Wed
Dinner nightly

On cool days, these interior windows perspire from the steam coming off the Beijing-style hot pots; this popular spot is guaranteed to help shake off any chill.

In keeping with what is Halal, or permissible to eat under Islamic law, these bubbling pots may be filled with slices of beef and lamb or fish, but no pork. Feel free to add vegetables like spinach, cabbage, and rice noodles, all simmering in a pot of broth placed over an open flame, making this the perfect meal for a group. Intrepid eaters should try the *na si mi*, "extremely hot pepper," a dish so brazenly fiery that it is hailed as the spiciest in the city. Beyond hot pots, the menu covers a world of offerings; those in the know go for the lamb dishes, or beef and green onion pancakes.

Park Chow

American 🍴🍴

D3

1240 9th Ave. (bet. Irving St. & Lincoln Way)

Phone: 415-665-9912 Lunch & dinner daily
Web: www.chowfoodbar.com
Prices: $$

Next door to Golden Gate Park, this branch of the Chow chain (which has three other locations in the area) is the quintessential neighborhood restaurant. On sunny days, locals fill the sidewalk tables, while others head up to the deck with its retractable roof.

From wontons to pork chops to chicken strips and burgers for "Good Little Kids," the eclectic menu offers something for every member of the family. Three homey, healthy meals a day, with service all day long, means you can drop in for organic farm-fresh eggs for weekday breakfasts, daily changing sandwiches at lunch, or wood oven-baked lasagna and grilled entrées for dinner. End meals comfortably by digging into a flaky, homemade apple pie while gazing into the crackling fire.

Pizzetta 211

Pizza 🍴

B1

211 23rd Ave. (at California St.)

Phone: 415-379-9880 Lunch Wed – Sun
Web: www.pizzetta211.com Dinner nightly
Prices: 🍂

Thin-crust devotees continue to pack this quaint, stripped-down pizzeria hideaway, with limited indoor seats at a premium on a cool day—though a few sidewalk tables help accommodate overflow.

No one is pampered here: place an order at the counter, pick up your own utensils, napkins, and grab a seat during the five short minutes before the pizza arrives. Artisanal pies change daily and veer from the cerebral (squash blossom, cherry tomato, chive, goat cheese, and citrusy *agrumato*) to the humble Margarita. The daily menu prides itself on supporting local, organic producers, so check the appetizer, salad, and calzone specials, as well as the fresh-baked dessert display.

Get the pizza chef to crack a smile and you'll become the talk of the Outer Richmond.

Sushi Bistro

D2

Japanese 🍴

445 Balboa St. (at 6th Ave.)

Phone: 415-933-7100
Web: www.sushibistrosf.com
Prices: $$

Dinner nightly

An excellent value for the money, Sushi Bistro is still a hit after several years. The restaurant sits on a quiet block in the Inner Richmond, where a young and boisterous clientele fills the sunny room's closely clustered tables.

Unique rolls are the main draw here. Expertly done, these signature offerings take on a pleasing Latino and Caribbean twist. Names reflect the chef's sense of humor, as in the Magic Mushroom (chopped salmon and yellowtail mixed with macadamia pesto and topped with mushrooms, then flash-fried); and the Monster-in-Laws (chopped spicy albacore, cucumber, and green onion topped with yellowtail, jalapeño, and ponzu sauce). Pleasure-seeking purists will be equally satisfied by the relatively large portions of sashimi and nigiri.

Sutro's

A2

Californian 🍴🍴🍴

1090 Point Lobos Ave. (at Ocean Beach)

Phone: 415-386-3330
Web: www.cliffhouse.com
Prices: $$$

Lunch & dinner daily

San Francisco literally begins at Sutro's, perched on the city's westernmost tip with a legacy to rival its bird's eye view of the spectacular Pacific Coast. Housed in the third incarnation of the 1909 Cliff House, Sutro's is named for the nineteenth century Sutro Baths, whose neighboring ruins can still be explored. Today, antiques and memorabilia such as old-fashioned swimwear fill the downstairs dining room in salute to the area's storied past.

Sutro's seafood-rich Californian cuisine lives happily in the present and has finally grown worthy of its sensational setting. Such dishes as herb-roasted chicken "under a brick" and Loch Duart salmon over plump hummus ravioli are enough to distract from the surfers and crashing waves at Ocean Beach nearby.

137

Ton Kiang

C2

Chinese 🍴

5821 Geary Blvd. (bet. 22nd & 23rd Aves.)

Phone: 415-752-4440   Lunch & dinner daily
Web: www.tonkiang.net
Prices: 💲💲

Upstairs or down, the focus here is on dim sum and Hakka cuisine. The Hakka people migrated across their country from Northern China, many of them settling in the Guangdong Province near the Ton Kiang, or East River.

Once seated at a round table, equipped with a lazy Susan for sharing dishes, you'll be bombarded by a flurry of female servers proffering steamed, fried, blanched, and roasted miniature delights with little explanation (though there is a diagram on each table to help you identify your choices). The density of the crowd, which gets chaotic on weekends, dictates the level of service.

No prices are posted for dim sum, but never fear; the total bill here may well add up to less than what you'd pay for just an entrée elsewhere.

Troya 🅑

Mediterranean 🍴

D1

349 Clement St. (at 5th Ave.)

Phone: 415-379-6000   Lunch Fri – Sun
Web: www.troyasf.com   Dinner nightly
Prices: $$

The face that launched a thousand ships also inspired one of San Francisco's great Mediterranean eateries. Troya is named in honor of the fabled city Troy and the icons that perished in her wake. This incarnation is a touch less dramatic, with simple Greek and Turkish cuisine served in a sunny corner space with classical-style art.

A six-seat bar offers a welcoming break from the battles of the day. Relax with beautifully golden and flavorful falafel set atop hummus, tzatziki, and spicy tomato sauce; tender lamb shish kebabs; or, on a foggy day, a steaming crock of moussaka topped with a béchamel brûlée. In lieu of the expected baklava, try the flaky nightingale's nest: a walnut-stuffed filo pastry with vanilla ice cream, pistachios, and honey.

SoMa

Peek behind the unassuming doors of the often-gritty façades prevalent in SoMa, the neighborhood South of Market, and discover a trove of creative talent. While you won't find the oodles of sidewalk cafés and storefronts ubiquitous to more obviously charming enclaves, SoMa divulges gobs of riches—from artistic diamonds in the rough to megawatt culinary gems—to the tenacious urban treasure seeker.

RESIDENTIAL MIX

A diverse stomping ground that defies definition at every corner, SoMa is often labeled "industrial" for its hodgepodge of converted warehouse lofts. Or, with a mixed troupe of artists, photographers, architects, dancers, and designers now occupying much of SoMa's post-industrial real estate, you might also call it "artsy."

In reality, dynamic SoMa wears many faces: Youths in concert tees navigate their skateboards around the pitfalls of constant construction, fueled by "Gibraltars" from cult classic **Blue Bottle Café**. Sports fans of a different sort converge for Giants baseball and **Crazy Crab'z** sandwiches at AT&T Park. In the Sixth Street Corridor, an immigrant population enjoys tastes of home at such authentic dives as **Tu Lan**, the Vietnamese hole-in-wall favored by the late Julia Child. Just blocks away, a towering crop of luxury condominiums draws a trendy Yuppie set keen to scoop up modern European furnishings at the SF Design Center and dine at equally slick restaurants—think of **Roe**, which doubles as an after-hours nightclub.

ARTS

Since SoMa is perhaps most notable for its arts scene—this is home to the San Francisco Museum of Modern Art, countless galleries, Yerba Buena Center for the Arts, and the Daniel Libeskind–designed Contemporary Jewish Museum—neighborhood foodies crave stylish culinary experiences to match their well-rounded worlds. Art and design play a key role in the district's most unique dining and nightlife venues; and naturally, the neighborhood is fast welcoming new and avant garde restaurant concepts. Not far from the Jewish Museum, is **Mint Plaza**—step into this charming gathering spot for a bite, perhaps a respite, or to simply read a book. Post-dinner, art evangelists hit **111 Minna**, a gallery turned late-night DJ bar, or the wine bar at **Varnish Fine Art**. Down the street, **Ducca** plays on a Venetian theme with a lush lounge and whimsical paintings of the ducal couple.

Speaking of Ducca, the restaurant inside the Westin Market Street, hip hotel restaurants and bars are prolific in SoMa, in part because of proximity to the Moscone Convention Center. While there is are myriad upscale watering holes to choose from, a batch of casual joints has sprung up of late. **Good Pizza**, inside the Good Hotel, offers crispy artisan pie by the slice, while **Custom Burger/Lounge**, at Best Western Americana, piles gourmet toppings such as Point Reyes Blue Cheese and black olive tapenade onto patties of Kobe beef, salmon, and lamb. **Perry's**, the "meet market" made famous in Armistead Maupin's *Tales of the City*, is enjoying a second home in the Hotel Griffon on Steuart Street. At the InterContinental San Francisco, **Bar 888** pours more than 100 *grappe* to taste.

SoMa is home to a veritable buffet of well-known restaurants with famous toques at the helm. But the fact that these boldface names can also be found in the food court at the mall is testament to the area's democratic approach to food: There is high-quality cuisine to be here had at workaday prices. Here, wondrous things can be found between two slices of bread. Tom Colicchio's **'wichcraft** is a popular lunch spot among area professionals, and former Rubicon star Dennis Leary can actually be spotted slinging sandwiches at **The Sentinel**. Chef Charles Phan has expanded his empire of Asian eateries in the neighborhood to include **Out the Door**, in Westfield San Francisco Centre, that dishes up tantalizing Vietnamese fare in a flash.

For budget gourmands, SoMa brims with cheap eats. Westfield Centre houses an impressive food court with plenty of international options. Nearby, museumgoers can refuel with a fragrant cup of tea at **Samovar** or try a micro-brew beer at **Thirsty Bear Brewing Company**. Take a peaceful stroll around South Park, and make sure you stop by **Mexico au Parc**, where the *sopes* run out by noon. Ballpark denizens get their burger fix at brewpub **21st Amendment**.

NIGHTLIFE

This is all to say little of SoMa's buzzing nightlife, whose scene traverses the red carpet from sports bar to DJ bar, hotel lounge to ultra-lounge, and risqué dinner theater that runs the gamut from drag (at **AsiaSF**) to Dutch: The Amsterdam import **Supperclub** serves a racy mixed plate of performance art and global cuisine—in bed. Oenophiles should definitely pop by **Terroir**, the witty little wine bar on Folsom that stocks more than 700 organic old-world varietals. For more boisterous imbibing, **Bossa Nova** bursts with the flavors of Rio. Soak up your *cachaça*, SoMa style, with a Nutella banana pancake from the 11th Street trailer, **Crêpes a Go-Go**.

SoMa

- ● Hotel
- ● Restaurant

NOB HILL

CHINATOWN

NOB HILL

UNION SQUARE

UNION SQUARE

Four Seasons

Palomar

Fifth Floor

Tropisueño

The Mosser

Lark Creek Steak

Chez Papa Resto

OLD MINT

MOSCONE CENTER WEST

54 Mint

Luce

InterContinental

MARINA

TENDERLOIN

CIVIC CENTER

ASIAN ART MUSEUM

CITY HALL

UN PLAZA

SF PUBLIC LIBRARY

SF WAR MEMORIAL & PERFORMING ARTS CENTER

Civic Center

Heaven's Dog

Van Ness

Basil Canteen

Manora's Thai Cuisine

MISSION

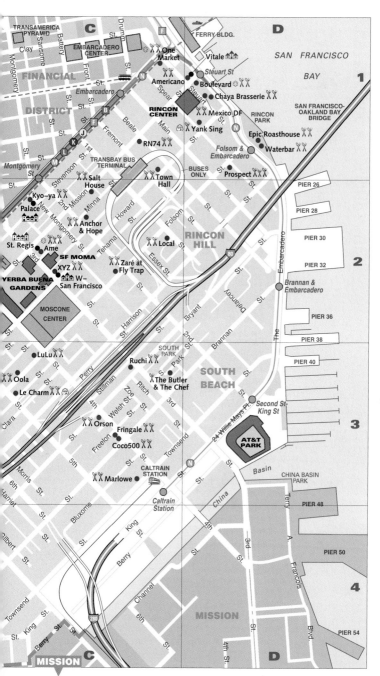

Ame

Contemporary 𝕏𝕏𝕏

C2

689 Mission St. (at 3rd St.)

Phone: 415-284-4040   Dinner nightly
Web: www.amerestaurant.com
Prices: $$$

Joe Fletcher

Tucked inside the posh St. Regis hotel, on Mission Street just south of Market, Ame cuts as sleek a figure as you'd expect from this neck of SF—with a tony brick and glass façade; a custom-designed sashimi bar; and floor-to-ceiling windows draped in gauzy curtains.

What kicks this lovely restaurant high above the trendy water mark is the killer Japanese-influenced fusion food. Husband-and-wife restaurateurs Hiro Sone and Lissa Doumani are absolute masters at their craft, and they bring a certain holistic beauty to the dining experience. This is serene, superb eating from head to toe with no page left unturned.

The dinner menu dances to the season, but might reveal dishes like halibut cheeks, pan-fried to golden perfection with crispy panko, then paired with poached asparagus and buttery sautéed morel mushrooms; grilled Maine lobster glossed with yuzu-brown butter and topped with silky mounds of fresh uni and wilted Chinese kale; or irresistibly creamy pistachio ice cream doused with vibrant green tea and accompanied by crispy butter cookies. Wash it all down with an inventive sake cocktail off the extensive sake list, and you might just spring for a room at the St. Regis.

Americano

D1

Italian ✗✗

8 Mission St. (at The Embarcadero)

Phone: 415-278-3777
Web: www.americanorestaurant.com
Prices: $$$

Lunch Mon – Fri
Dinner Mon – Sat

Follow the trajectory from frat pack to FiDi corner office and you'll eventually land in the circular lounge at Americano, the Hotel Vitale hub for happy hour seeking young execs. A lengthy bar and gorgeous outdoor patio boasting views of the Bay Bridge and Embarcadero make this the neighborhood's most conducive restaurant for cocktailing.

Though the setting emphasizes libations and a trendy, contemporary vibe, do not overlook the very solid Italian fare served in the earth-toned dining room. Crafted with superior seasonal ingredients, the menu might include tasty crowd pleasers like grilled bruschetta piled with creamy white bean purée and silky duck confit; a delightfully crisp-crusted pizza; or perfectly grilled rib eye with an earthy porcini rub.

Anchor & Hope

C2

Seafood ✗✗

83 Minna St. (bet. 1st & 2nd Sts.)

Phone: 415-501-9100
Web: www.anchorandhopesf.com
Prices: $$$

Lunch Mon – Fri
Dinner nightly

Harbored in a restored warehouse, Anchor & Hope's exposed brick walls, lofty ceilings, rope-wrapped support beams, and "fish eating fish" mural fashion a stylish nautical ensemble. Busy, boisterous, and wildly popular among loyal locals and rowdy groups, this is not your date-night dwell.

Steered by the team behind Salt House and Town Hall, an open kitchen nets a medley of outrageously fresh seafood treats like blackboard special oysters and shellfish; deep-fried calamari with basil and a Thai-chili dipping sauce; spice-crusted scallops atop couscous, fennel, and curry; and a decadent chocolate blackout cake with shards of salted almond-pistachio brittle.

A sip from their great selection of beers will perfectly quench this aquatic affair.

Basil Canteen

Thai

B4

1489 Folsom St. (at 11th St.)

Phone: 415-552-3963
Web: www.basilthai.com
Prices: 💰

Lunch Mon – Fri
Dinner nightly

Exposed brick and steel I-beams dominate the interior of this former 1912 Jackson Brewery building, where the industrial vibe is all SoMa and the flavors are otherworldly. More exotic than piquant, the spices used here lend inspired creativity to Bangkok-style street food. Grab a seat at the long, communal table (quiet types will prefer the mezzanine), and sip a crisp lemongrass cocktail while you peruse the casual yet complex menu. *Satay* selections far outshine the more conventional chicken-on-a-stick; Chinese sausage and star anise plum sauce add zest to a blue crab roll; and pork lovers will not want to miss the *khao moo daeng*, crispy house-cured pork belly and roast pork with star anise gravy.

Fiery condiments are available for heat seekers.

Chaya Brasserie

Fusion

D1

132 The Embarcadero (bet. Howard & Mission Sts.)

Phone: 415-777-8688
Web: www.thechaya.com
Prices: $$

Lunch Mon – Fri
Dinner nightly

A dramatic swath of the Bay Bridge fills the Embarcadero-facing windows at Chaya Brasserie, the San Francisco sister to three L.A. locations. Here, contemporary crystal chandeliers, leather banquettes, and exposed steel beams hint at this maritime cuisine's Euro-Japanese style. Proximity to the FiDi and convenient valet parking makes it a popular haunt for business lunches, while dinner brings a mix of locals (who come for the sushi) and tourists (who come for the view).

A bright exhibition kitchen plates specialty sushi rolls like the vegetarian caterpillar with refreshing daikon and pickled burdock; and flavorful entrées like Hawaiian butterfish with sautéed mushrooms and tomato. Desserts can miss their mark, but happy hour is typically happening.

Boulevard ✿

D1

Californian ✗✗

1 Mission St. (at Steuart St.)

Phone:	415-543-6084	Lunch Mon – Fri
Web:	www.boulevardrestaurant.com	Dinner nightly
Prices:	$$$	

Boulevard

It's best to think of restaurant years in terms of cat years—a decade or so of frisky cheer, and you can thank your lucky stars. Much longer, and it's usually downhill from there. Not so with Nancy Oakes' beloved Boulevard, which is still the apple of SF's eye more than a decade and a half since it swung open its doors.

So how does this perennial It Joint keep it going? It could be the restaurant's sweet corner location, occupying the ground floor of the Audiffred Building and offering killer views of the Bay Bridge. Or it could be the easy, loft-like charms of Pat Kuleto's interior design, or the crackerjack waitstaff, which always manages to stay a step ahead of the game.

But the smart money is on Oakes' delicious and highly local Californian menu, which changes to the season but might include a repertoire of deliciousness as in a creamy pile of Vialone Nano rice studded with roasted beets, gorgonzola *dolce*, red-skinned walnuts, and white Oregon truffle; fresh, locally caught rock cod, perfectly pan-roasted to golden brown and paired with local shelling beans and salty chorizo; or a creamy profiterole paired with a decadently caramelized apple terrine.

Chez Papa Resto

Mediterranean

B2

Mediterranean 🍴🍴

414 Jessie St. (bet. Market & Mission Sts.)

Phone: 415-546-4134
Web: www.chezpapasf.com
Prices: $$

Lunch & dinner Mon – Sat

Part of the expansive Jessie Street face-lift, this Chez Papa outpost has fast become a savvy stalwart in the evolving Mint Plaza area. More chic than its Potrero Hill step sister, this SoMa darling possesses a warm, lively ambience, unpretentious vibe, and a clear touch of class.

The staff here is predominantly French; thus the simple, expertly prepared dishes offer authentic accents. Crispy frog legs with Reisling sauce, toasted cumin, fried capers, and lemon zest; or roast monkfish bouillabaisse with shrimp, clams, mussels, fingerling potatoes, sea beans, and rouille may be among the Provençal favorites.

Whether it was the delicious food or ample array of pastis displayed behind the bar, you'll leave feeling better than when you arrived.

Coco500

C3

Californian 🍴🍴

500 Brannan St. (at 4th St.)

Phone: 415-543-2222
Web: www.coco500.com
Prices: $$

Lunch Mon – Fri
Dinner Mon – Sat

This casually hip SoMa spot continues to draw hefty crowds for lunch and dinner, as the loud buzz from happy patrons in the minimalist setting will attest. Chocolate, blue, and caramel tones color a room decorated with work by local artists, while the handsome teak and Italian glass-tile bar beckons with cocktails made from freshly squeezed organic juices.

Chef/owner Loretta Keller has cobbled a Californian menu with dinner offerings broken into several categories. For example, items to be shared at the table might include the baked salt cod *brandade*; truffled squash blossom flatbread; or selections of "California Dirt" starring tasty vegetable sides. Lunch items favor sandwiches, soups, and wood-oven pizzas.

Epic Roasthouse

Steakhouse ✗✗

D1

369 The Embarcadero (at Folsom St.)

Phone: 415-369-9955
Web: www.epicroasthousesf.com
Prices: $$$

Lunch Thu – Sun
Dinner nightly

With a name like Epic, it's a safe bet that this Pat Kuleto roasthouse is a thrilling endeavor. Situated on the iconic Embarcadero with matchless views of the Bay Bridge, Epic is a massive and pricey tourist attraction. Exposed pipes and ductwork are inspired by a saltwater pump house that battled the fires of the 1906 quake; however, leather banquettes, plush carpets, and a fireplace lend an air of classic comfort.

This is just the ambience you'd want for imbibing a full-bodied merlot with your filet of beef, seasoned with salt and pepper and garnished with glazed baby carrots. Don't forget the sides! Garlic oil and red chili flakes add smoke to grilled *broccolini*, and the scent of truffle adds that *je ne sais quoi* to buttery whipped potatoes.

Fifth Floor

Contemporary ✗✗✗

B2

12 4th St. (at Market St.)

Phone: 415-348-1555
Web: www.fifthfloorrestaurant.com
Prices: $$$

Dinner Mon – Sat

Dressed in ivory leather, rich lacquered wood, and a kiss of lipstick red, Fifth Floor's star has begun to fade even though her polished appearance remains. Gone is a marquis chef and, with him, the jet-set clientele. Today, the leading lady may feel a bit forsaken, with only a few dark suits courting her creamy banquettes.

With bizarre flavor combinations and presentations that expose the kitchen's skill, the cuisine seems to have passed its prime. Still, reminders of Fifth Floor's glory days can be glimpsed in well-choreographed service and in the reserve of rare wines waving a handkerchief from their gleaming tower. Pay your respects with an excellent wine and a warm almond tart. This grande dame is still sweet on the finish.

149

54 Mint

Italian ✗✗

B2

16 Mint Plaza (at Jessie St.)

Phone: 415-543-5100

Web: www.54mint.com

Prices: $$

Lunch & dinner Mon – Sat

Amid the towering walls of the historic Old Mint, 54 Mint evokes a distant *ristorante* overlooking an ancient piazza. Its shelves, stocked with artisanal olive oil, spices, and hanging hams guarding a jumbo wheel of Parmigiano Reggiano, complete the allusion. Still, this is a passionately run, contemporary space with brick and whitewashed walls, streamlined furnishings, and leather-clad stools at the granite-topped bar.

On the menu, antipasti invite you to savor the simplicity in aged cheeses and house-cured meats. Fresh, house-made pastas abound, from linguini and ravioli to gnocchi with rich meat ragù. Abundant seafood offerings, like crisp *arancini* purple with squid ink and other pleasant game dishes complete the frequently changing menu.

Fringale

French ✗✗

C3

570 4th St. (bet. Brannan & Bryant Sts.)

Phone: 415-543-0573

Web: www.fringalesf.com

Prices: $$

Lunch Tue – Fri
Dinner nightly

With its friendly service, consistency, and just plain good food, the currently reinvigorated SoMa restaurant scene can take a lesson from Fringale. Though the Basque cuisine features French accents, there is no fussiness here; as ever, dishes are unpretentious and approachable as they throw the stereotypes out the window.

The menu may feature offerings such as sautéed prawns in pastis and sun-dried tomatoes; or poached black cod with *pipérade*, artichokes, olives, and *piment d'Espelette*. Food here embraces the bold flavors and rustic quality of traditional Basquaise cooking.

It is fitting that this small dining room offers a certain undeniable romance, and that it is typically jammed at night, with a line of diners stretching out the door.

Heaven's Dog

B3

Chinese ✗✗

1148 Mission St. (bet. 7th & 8th Sts.)

Phone: 415-863-6008
Web: www.heavensdog.com
Prices: 💰💰

Dinner nightly

If there is one rule in naming an Asian restaurant, it should be to avoid the word "dog" at all costs. Chef Charles Phan is winking at custom and is certain to get away with it: as chef/owner of the renowned and beloved Slanted Door, this sly dog is already a household name. On the ground floor of the SoMa Grand condo tower, Heaven's Dog serves finger foods with Chinese flair in an offbeat downtown setting. Friends crowd around cypress tables on orange leather banquettes and share such snacks as pork belly buns or grilled lamb skewers dusted with sesame, cumin, and chilies.

Snacks pair well with designer cocktails or a grassy sauvignon blanc. Noodle soups for the soul are ladled at the bar overlooking the exhibition kitchen.

Kyo-ya

C2

Japanese ✗✗

2 New Montgomery St. (bet. Jessie & Market Sts.)

Phone: 415-546-5090
Web: www.sfpalacerestaurants.com
Prices: $$$

Lunch & dinner Mon – Fri

At home in downtown's Palace Hotel, Kyo-ya's chic, simple dining room and straightforward Japanese fare are more down-to-earth than the lavish surrounds. The mood is tranquil with a few vibrant works of art and a long sushi bar overlooking sparse tables dotted with fresh flowers. Efficient service pleases the mostly corporate clientele who arrive here to conduct midday business.

An ample selection of sake complements the chef's nigiri omakase, which features very fresh, unadorned fish. Savor delicious toro, crab, and salmon simply garnished with only a bit of spicy wasabi. Large sushi pieces are something of a mouthful and, with few fireworks, Kyo-ya's prices can seem high. The quality of the fish, however, out-swims most competitors.

151

Lark Creek Steak

B2

Steakhouse

845 Market St. (bet. 4th & 5th Sts.)

Phone: 415-593-4100
Web: www.larkcreeksteak.com
Prices: $$$

Lunch & dinner daily

Set off the rotunda on the fourth floor of the Westfield Centre, Lark Creek Steak appeals to savvy shoppers who save money on the sales so they can splurge on a meal here. Farm-fresh American fare and a good wine list add up to this perfect respite from rifling through the racks at Nordstrom.

Local farms and ranches provide many of the ingredients for Chef John Ledbetter's seasonal à la carte menu. Easily the best steaks found in a Bay Area mall, Lark Creek's grass-fed boneless ribeye and certified Angus filet mignon—among other choices—come with house-made sauces like red wine butter, creamy fresh horseradish, or the signature steak sauce. Vanilla cheesecake with Crackerjack crust will furnish the sugar rush for a few more hours of shopping.

Le Charm

C3

French

315 5th St. (bet. Folsom & Shipley Sts.)

Phone: 415-546-6128
Web: www.lecharm.com
Prices: $$

Lunch Tue – Fri
Dinner Tue – Sun

True to its name, this high-ceilinged spot is a perennial charmer. A tiny copper-topped bar sits off the foyer, while paper-covered tables cluster in the small dining room. On the courtyard, umbrellas shade the sun-dappled space between walls laced with trellised vines.

As if to offer respite to both French expats on a budget and novices to the cuisine, this kitchen adheres to the classics that everyone will appreciate. Offerings may include endive and walnut salad with Roquefort cheesecake and pear; baked escargot with parsley butter; or cassoulet with duck confit, pork belly, and Toulouse sausage. Provençal influence adds vegetables and *plats du jour* to the menu.

Adding to the pleasure, Le Charm's prices reflect the good value of simpler days.

Local

Italian

C2

330 1st St. (bet. Folsom & Harrison Sts.)

Phone: 415-777-4200
Web: www.sf-local.com
Prices: $$

Lunch Tue – Fri & Sun
Dinner Tue – Sun

Local elevates the humble pizza joint. This contemporary loft-like space finds European inspiration in its urban minimalist décor comprised of polished concrete floors, aluminum chairs, Carrara marble tiles, and Mondrian-inspired doors. Only in San Francisco could a spot named "local" look so utterly cool.

Local has a small wine shop and gourmet food store at the front, but it is the California-influenced Italian fare that draws in the crowds. The menu focuses on perfectly browned, crispy, wood burning oven-fired, thin-crust pizza dough. Even the rustic pasta dishes come served with a round of flash baked pizza dough—ideal for soaking up those last flavorful bits of spicy wine and tomato sauce left in a deep bowl of their *linguine allo scrigno*.

LuLu

Mediterranean

C3

816 Folsom St. (bet 4th & 5th Sts.)

Phone: 415-495-5775
Web: www.restaurantlulu.com
Prices: $$

Lunch & dinner daily

Visitors traveling to SF in packs or locals hosting the whole family for a weekend on the town should head to this SoMa mainstay with enough space (and an ample bar) to accommodate an entire army. Arched ceilings cap a voluminous interior that is as amenable to business lunches as large scale celebrations, and the Provençal fare is served family style to guarantee a convivial good time.

A roaring rotisserie and wood-burning pizza oven draw the eye into the exhibition kitchen, where seasonal ingredients are king. Thin-crust pizzas may be topped with slices of spring asparagus, while fresh field greens with tangy vinaigrette accompany a bison burger on a green onion bun. Don't miss out on such hearty side dishes as earthy, roasted *kabocha* squash.

153

Luce ❀

B3

888 Howard St. (at 5th St.)

Lunch & dinner daily

Phone: 415-616-6566
Web: www.lucewinerestaurant.com
Prices: $$$

Rien van Rijthoven

By day this modern SoMa restaurant, tucked into the ground floor of the InterContinental San Francisco hotel, plays up its casual side; by night, those who wander into its elegant lair will find a first-class dining experience by way of Chef Dominique Crenn's heavenly cooking.

Make your way through bustling Bar 888—a grappa-centric lounge, ideal for a pre-dinner cocktail or happy hour sip—and you'll find a stunning dining room fitted out with hand-blown Italian glass orb lamps and shining marble and granite floors. Service is polite, polished, and perfectly attentive—a nice upgrade from previous years, when the service fell just short of the food. These days, it's a match made in heaven.

A seasonal chef's tasting menu is available nightly (a recent 11-course dinner clocked in at around $85), and a seasonal à la carte menu boasting a number of options is available as well. Dinner might include a fan of perfectly roasted abalone dusted with sea salt and paired with caramelized pork belly, spring onion, and yuzu broth; or a tender roulade of roasted squab, surrounded by butter-sautéed chanterelles, roasted pear, vanilla-port reduction, and fluffy dollops of brioche veloute.

Manora's Thai Cuisine

Thai 🍴

1600 Folsom St. (at 12th St.)

Phone: 415-861-6224
Web: www.manorathai.com
Prices:

Lunch Mon – Fri
Dinner nightly

Large appetite, small budget? Grab your loose change and get your growling belly to Manora's, where bountiful portions of tasty Thai keep locals coming in herds. Quick service and super cheap specials (soup, fried rice, and two main courses for under 9 bucks) make this a go-to spot for lunch, though dinner lingers in this league. Start off with a bowl of creamy *gai tom ka*, a tangy, traditional Thai soup of coconut milk, lemon, and cilantro quivering with tender chunks of stewed chicken. Next, order up a plate of scrumptious garlic pork—marinated and char-grilled to tender perfection—or the *gai kraprao*, a stir-fry of ground chicken, chili, garlic, and fresh basil.

Quench your thirst with a tall glass of creamy Thai iced-tea—a cool remedy for a warm day.

Marlowe

Californian 🍴🍴

330 Townsend St., Ste. 230 (bet. 4th & 5th Sts.)

Phone: 415-974-5599
Web: www.marlowesf.com
Prices: $$

Lunch Mon – Fri
Dinner Mon – Sat

Locals who lamented the loss of Aussie wine bar South are now making merry at Marlowe, the rustic-chic bistro that opened in its place. Re-imagined with white penny-tile floors, faux-ostrich banquettes, and a wall of front windows inscribed with whimsical food and wine quotes, the tiny Townsend Street spot is already packed with regulars, so do plan in advance.

If there is a wait, hit a barstool and nurse a crisp glass of Riesling—it will pair well later with a "snack" of sea-salty Brussels sprout chips, or seared black cod smeared with sautéed spinach and spring vegetables. Marlowe's market-driven menu has much to crave, including a decadent burger. Finish with an upside-down apple crisp beneath bourbon ice cream and a crumbled oatmeal cookie.

Mexico DF

D1

Mexican

139 Steuart St. (bet. Mission & Howards Sts.)

Phone: 415-808-1048
Web: www.mex-df.com
Prices: $$

Lunch Mon – Fri
Dinner nightly

Revolving digital artworks, rich textiles, and low lighting are just the first clues that Mexico DF is a world away from San Francisco's beloved taquerias. The vibe here is contemporary and the cuisine a bit westernized, but primo ingredients guarantee that DF is anything but run-of-the-mill.

Friendly service echoes the warmth of brick walls, velvet, and leather accents in the streetfront lounge, where the FiDi set shares small plates over rounds of mojitos and margaritas at happy hour. For those who stay to dine, meals are festive and flavorsome. Soft corn tacos may be heaped with moist, ancho chile-braised leg of lamb, while the *huarache de Costilla*, a griddled masa cake laden with smoky short ribs and *cotija* cheese, is quite simply delicious.

Oola

C3

Californian

860 Folsom St. (bet. 4th & 5th Sts.)

Phone: 415-995-2061
Web: www.oola-sf.com
Prices: $$

Dinner nightly

Night owls lounging in high-backed suede booths, ambient light, and pounding club music set the scene at this chic and sophisticated SoMa hot spot. The restaurant actually takes its moniker from Chef/owner Ola (pronounced ooh-la) Fendert, who turns out bold Californian cuisine with superlative ingredients from start to finish.

With an urban vibe and well-executed fare—think moist salmon with fennel confit or baby back ribs that slip right off the bone—Oola lures a crowd to its chic open dining room and loft upstairs. Call ahead for a reservation or chance a seat at the backlit bar. But be warned: with dinner served until midnight on weekdays and Saturdays till 1:00 A.M, Oola is a popular choice for a post-party snack. Doors close at 2:00 A.M.

One Market ❀

Californian 🍴🍴

C1

1 Market St. (at Steuart St.)

Phone:	415-777-5577	Lunch Mon – Fri
Web:	www.onemarket.com	Dinner Mon – Sat
Prices:	$$$	

John A. Benson

Visitors making their way to San Francisco's restyled waterfront area are in for a real treat when they set their dinner sights on this spacious brasserie. With enormous windows facing the Bay Bridge and Ferry Building, and a cushy corner spot along bustling Market Street, One Market is obviously sitting on some prime real estate.

But this popular restaurant didn't build its fan base resting on its location laurels. Once inside, you'll find a masterful staff and easy brasserie's good looks—think mile-high ceilings, gorgeous stone-tile floors, and wrought-iron chandeliers. Not to mention partner/Chef Mark Dommen's bustling, semi-exposed kitchen, which pushes out exceptional regional Californian fare loaded with all kinds of creative surprises.

A plate of grilled octopus, deliciously caramelized in all the right places, is topped with a cloud of soy foam and paired with puréed edamame and pin pricks of semi-sweet soy glaze; while a house-made cavatelli arrives perfectly chewy and puddled in a delicate lamb and tomato sauce topped with a creamy quenelle of homemade ricotta; and a chocolate tart is topped with three batons of ripe banana sporting an irresistible caramelized crust.

157

Orson

C3

508 4th St. (at Bryant St.)

Phone: 415-777-1508
Web: www.orsonsf.com
Prices: $$

Lunch Tue – Sun
Dinner Tue – Sat

Industrial-chic Orson continues to evolve, though the thirty-somethings crowding the oval bar still revel in the pumping club music. This up-tempo vibe mirrors the contemporary cuisine by Chef/owner Elizabeth Faulkner.

The ever-popular duck fat fries served with brown-butter béarnaise, wood-fired mussels in spicy coconut broth, and creatively decked pizzas with caramelized fennel, roasted garlic ricotta, and pecorino, make perfect mates for "$5 Classic Cocktail Hour." Fans know not to skip the whimsical dessert selection such as the buttered popcorn ice cream sundae; strawberry red rum cake with berry lime sorbet; or the "midnight at the oasis" assortment with chocolate fudgesicle, devil's food cake, milk pudding, and nibby chocolate streusel.

Prospect

D1

300 Spear St. (at Folsom St.)

Phone: 415-247-7770
Web: www.prospectsf.com
Prices: $$

Dinner nightly

Amid the contemporary glass-and-steel façade of the posh Infinity towers, massive wood doors hint at a warmer interior dressed in unexpected earth tones and natural fibers. No expense was spared in the architecture of Prospect, which feels a touch corporate in all its shiny newness. Still, Heath ceramic tableware, reclaimed wood floors, and wrought-iron chandeliers add enough coziness to make Prospect a worthwhile culinary retreat.

Cuisine here also fits the laid-back but well-appointed vibe: the American fare is sophisticated but balanced with familiar, rustic ingredients. Dinner may include buffalo carpaccio with fried oysters and aïoli studded with *tasso* ham; organic chicken and sausage with broccoli-cheddar grits; and chocolate root beer cake.

RN74

C1 — Californian ✗✗

301 Mission St. (at Beale St.)

Phone: 415-543-7474
Web: www.rn74.com
Prices: $$$

Lunch Mon – Fri
Dinner nightly

Named for Burgundy's main *route nationale*, Michael Mina's RN74 is an intoxicating Millennium Tower spot for a singular wine experience. A handful of rare labels beckon from an old-school train station schedule board, while vaulted ceilings, iron rafters, and antique lanterns further evoke a European station. When a wine sells out, letters flip to reveal another bottle. Market wines are displayed on additional boards, where white lights signal the vintages that guests are drinking. A space this sleek draws a buzzing clientele.

The concise, carefully considered menu may include roasted shrimp with green apple and citrus butter; or grilled *loup de mer* with mussels, artichokes, and chorizo; with interesting lounge bites like maitake mushroom tempura.

Ruchi

C3 — Indian ✗✗

474 3rd St. (bet. Bryant & Stillman Sts.)

Phone: 415-392-8353
Web: www.ruchisf.com
Prices: ㉚

Lunch & dinner Mon – Sat

The name literally means "taste," so it's not surprising that Ruchi delivers a powerful lip-smacking punch to the taste buds. The focus is on Southern Indian flavors at this SoMa newcomer. *Dosas*, those thin, lacy, crispy little pieces of heaven, are a "don't miss." Try the Mysore masala *dosa* with crushed potato filling and spicy chutney on the side—yum! Stews and curries account for most of the menu, but this isn't anything like your *nani* used to make. Instead, the stews are pungent and flooded with rich flavors and tender, juicy meats.

Nab a table in the back and watch the action in the open kitchen. With all of those bubbling pots of curries and other concoctions, it may look a bit more like a coven, but there's nothing evil about these tasty treats.

159

Salt House

C2

American 🍴🍴

545 Mission St. (bet. 1st & 2nd Sts.)

Phone: 415-543-8900
Web: www.salthousesf.com
Prices: $$

Lunch Mon – Fri
Dinner nightly

It's a little bit country, a little bit rock and roll here, where amusing yet chic country touches abound (find milk bottles used for water and jars in place of dessert plates) and everyone seems to be having fun. From the communal counter and lively bar to the bustling open kitchen, Salt House has a palpable energy. The service is efficient and professional, yet manages to make everyone in the crowd feel cosseted. However, this house is packed, so reservations are a good idea.

The menu has an appealing mix of citified comfort food. Your country cousin surely never cooked like this, with dishes that may include a refreshing salad of smoked trout with beets and tart grapefruit, or a modern interpretation of roasted pork pozole in chile broth.

The Butler & The Chef

C3

French 🍴

155A South Park St. (bet. 2nd & 3rd Sts.)

Phone: 415-896-2075
Web: www.butlerandthechef.com
Prices:

Lunch Tue – Sun

Take a late morning stroll through South Park, the urban green surrounded by studios and neighborhood eateries, and you'll stumble upon vintage enamel tables crowding the sidewalk in front of The Butler & The Chef, a devil-may-care café with a sunny façade and blue awning. There's probably a pooch enjoying the shade beneath an outdoor bistro chair, adding to the convincingly Parisian air of this quaint spot, billed as "the cheapest roundtrip to France."

Try freshly baked pastries for a *petit dejeuner*. Lunch brings savory stuffed crêpes, *croques*, and golden quiches with daily ingredients, like shrimp and spinach. Channel your inner francophile and savor it with a glass of champagne. Or join the locals and take your hot dog gratiné to the park.

Town Hall

American ✕✕

C1

342 Howard St. (at Fremont St.)

Phone: 415-908-3900
Web: www.townhallsf.com
Prices: $$

Lunch Mon – Fri
Dinner nightly

If the town hall is an American tradition that's always been and always will be, then Town Hall may be true to its name. By now a San Francisco culinary institution, the SoMa mainstay has something for everyone. A spacious patio is your first sign of the convivial hospitality to come, and an exposed brick interior with metal chandeliers keep the vibe going.

The flavor of the kitchen is American, of course, with unassuming yet crave-worthy fare. Crispy artichokes and Meyer lemon dress up Dungeness crab salad; fresh cilantro and shaved radish garnish flavorful pulled pork enchiladas with goat cheese and *tomatillo* salsa; and warm beignets, with espresso ice cream and chicory streusel, beg you to order dessert—even when you couldn't possibly.

Tropisueño

Mexican ✕

B2

75 Yerba Buena Ln. (bet. Market & Mission Sts.)

Phone: 415-243-0299
Web: www.tropisueno.com
Prices:

Lunch & dinner daily

Shaded by the dramatic, blue steel wing of the Contemporary Jewish Museum, Yerba Buena Lane is becoming a foodie destination for local art junkies and tourists alike. Tropisueño has something for everyone. At lunch, a taqueria-style counter serves tacos and *tortas* to professionals on the run; for those with time for a knife and fork, the super burrito *mojado* is a saucy siesta-inducer.

The restaurant dresses up a bit for dinner, delivering Latin American dishes like ceviche and tender chicken with *mole poblano*. A small salsa bar brims with jalapeños, sliced radishes, and tangy tomatillo salsa to pile on the mercifully thin chips.

But that's nothing compared to the expansive mahogany bar that oozes fine tequila and top-shelf margs.

Waterbar

D1

Seafood ✗✗

399 The Embarcadero (at Harrison St.)

Phone: 415-284-9922
Web: www.waterbarsf.com
Prices: $$$

Lunch & dinner daily

It's all in the name at Waterbar. This scenic restaurant enjoys a prime location on the Embarcadero with stunning views of San Francisco Bay. It's the kind of place that impresses out-of-towners and clients, especially on warmer days when outdoor seating is available. Inside, floor-to-ceiling fish tanks are the focal point and lend a sophisticated under-the-sea feel to the dining room.

Of course, seafood anchors the comprehensive bill of fare, which even includes a separate daily shellfish menu featuring selections from across the country as well as fantastic desserts. Prix-fixe lunch and oyster specials are reasonable ways to sample the goods, and the bar menu has small plates all day. Not hungry? Just drink in the view at the swanky bar.

XYZ

C2

Californian ✗✗

181 3rd St. (at Howard St.)

Phone: 415-817-7836
Web: www.xyz-sf.com
Prices: $$$

Lunch daily
Dinner Mon – Sat

This restaurant in the W San Francisco serves both a trendy setting and excellent, creative cuisine—while remaining a SoMa hot spot. The sleek décor changes with the seasons, featuring artful floral compositions, contemporary canvases, high-backed circular booths, and two-story windows framing Third Street.

The menu follows suit with the talented kitchen's clear devotion to superlative seasonal cooking that highlights both modern Mediterranean and Californian flair. Bright, bold flavors are coaxed from top-of-the-line local products in crab *arancini* with sweet peppers and citrus aïoli; or chicken ragù *strozzapreti* (pasta) with English peas and pecorino.

"W" could also stand for wine, with more than 600 international labels on their outstanding list.

San Francisco ▶ SoMa

Yank Sing

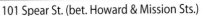
Chinese ✗

D1

101 Spear St. (bet. Howard & Mission Sts.)

Phone: 415-957-9300
Web: www.yanksing.com
Prices: $$

Lunch daily

Two tiny words will rouse any San Franciscan on Saturday morning: dim sum. The city's soup dumplings are legendary, and no one does them quite like Yank Sing, where Shanghai dumplings are stuffed with moist ground pork and a burst of juicy broth. Lengthy weekend waits are testament to each morsel's yummy goodness.

In the airy urban space, carts manned by servers wired with earpieces and mikes are loaded with steamed and fried delights then wheel up to tables in rapid fire. Barbecue pork buns are smoky and tender; caramelized pot stickers are a standout; and sesame balls filled with sweet mung paste are a sticky, lovely finish. Over-ordering is a hazard here; mind that prices add up quickly.

Take heart in validated parking in the subterranean garage.

Zaré at Fly Trap

Middle Eastern ✗✗

C2

606 Folsom St. (bet. 2nd & 3rd Sts.)

Phone: 415-243-0580
Web: www.zareflytrap.com
Prices: $$

Dinner Mon – Sat

Sliding into the Fly Trap, the 1906 eatery with tin ceilings and antique accents, downtowners can't help but feel at home at the end of a long day. That's just how Chef/owner Hoss Zaré felt when he bought the place in 2008: this was the first kitchen to hire Zaré when he arrived from Iran in 1986.

Today, though the historic vibe remains, the chef is infusing the Fly Trap with savory flavors from his home—think cinnamon-braised lamb tongue or sumac couscous with Dungeness crab. "Meatball Mondays" are a vegan's nightmare, with well-spiced two-pound beef and veal balls, stuffed with a meaty surprise. Try pairing it with a heady Lebanese red.

For dessert, crispy milk *torrijas* are plated with rosewater-scented hot chocolate and homemade marshmallows.

163

East Bay

East Bay

Berkeley is legendary for its liberal politics and university campus that launched the 1960s Free Speech Movement. Among foodies, this is a Garden of Eden that sprouted American gastronomy's leading purist, Alice Waters, and continues to be a place of worship. Waters' Chez Panisse Foundation has nurtured the Edible Schoolyard, an organic garden and kitchen classroom for students; she also founded Slow Food Nation, the country's largest festival of slow and sustainable foods. Since Waters is credited with developing Californian cuisine, her influence can be tasted in myriad restaurants. But, one needn't look much further than Berkeley's "gourmet ghetto." The North Shattuck corridor is aromatic with fresh-roasted joe from **Village Grounds** and fab take out from **Grégoire** and **Epicurious Garden**.

This strip houses co-ops like the **Cheese Board Collective**; the **Cheese Board Pizza Collective**; and the **Juice Bar Collective**. On Thursday afternoons, the **North Shattuck Organic Farmers Market** is crammed with local produce.

La Note's brioche *pain perdu* is lovely; **Tomate Café** proffers a Cuban breakfast on a pup-friendly patio; and **Caffe Mediterraneum** is the SF birthplace of the caffe latte. Berkeley is also home to **Acme Bread Company** and Chef Paul Bertolli's handcrafted **Fra'mani Salumi**.

Oakland doesn't quite carry the culinary panache of neighboring Berkeley, but the workaday city has seen a revival of its own with new businesses and condos. **Jack London Square** has stunning views of the bay, and crows the area's chief tourist destination for dining, nightlife, and a **Sunday Farmers and Artisan Market**. **Fentons Creamery** has served ice cream for 115 delicious years.

Taco junkies congregate on International Blvd. for a taco feast; **Tacos Sinaloa** and **Mariscos Sinaloa** are known for chorizo and fish tacos, respectively. Downtown, crowds nosh on Po'boys at **Café 15**; in Temescal, **Bakesale Betty** serves crispy chicken sandwiches atop ironing board tables. After work, the **Trappist** pours over 160 Belgian and specialty beers. On Sundays, oyster mongers line up at **Rudy Figueroa's** at the **Montclair Farmer's Market** for bivalves shucked to order. In August, the Art & Soul Festival brings a buffet of world flavors, as does the Chinatown Streetfest with curries and barbecue meats.

In Rockridge, the quaint shopping district between Oakland and Berkeley, boutiques and eateries abound. **Tara's Organic Ice Cream** serves unique flavors, like chile pistachio or basil, in compostible cups. **Market Hall** is a gourmet shopper's paradise with sustainable catch at **Hapuku Fish Shop**, specialty groceries at the **Pasta Shop**, a bakery, produce market, and coffee bar.

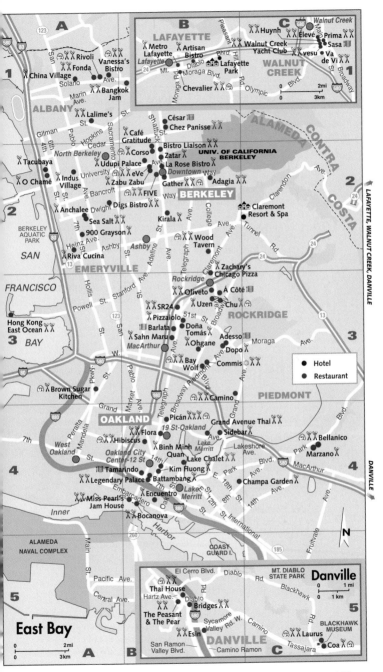

À Côté

Mediterranean

B3

5478 College Ave. (bet. Lawton & Taft Aves.), Oakland

Phone: 510-655-6469   Dinner nightly
Web: www.acoterestaurant.com
Prices: **$$**

With a convivial communal table, semi-open kitchen, and blazing wood-fired oven, few can find fault with this Rockridge favorite. The small tables are close but comfortable, and the patio—sunny in the summer, heated in winter—guarantees a party year-round. Few reservations are accepted so there is often a wait, but the borough's cheeky shops are a pleasant way to pass the time. Singles might score seats at the bar.

Seasonal Mediterranean small plates are both simple and satisfying. Dip into a steaming *bollito* of sliced braised beef brisket soaking in rich broth or sample chunks of grilled lamb with pomegranate glaze. Finish with fluffy ricotta fritters, crisp gold and served with a trio of sweet sauces. Forty wines by the glass make pairing a snap.

Adagia

Californian

B2

2700 Bancroft Way (bet. College & Piedmont Aves.), Berkeley

Phone: 510-647-2300   Lunch Tue – Fri
Web: www.adagiarestaurant.com   Dinner Tue – Sat
Prices: **$$**

Leaded glass windows, wrought iron chandeliers, a massive fireplace, and custom-made communal table inside Tudor-style Westminster House create a fittingly Hogwarts atmosphere for the academic crowd from neighboring U.C. Berkeley—just beware that eavesdropping here may make you smarter. This restored 1926 landmark designed by architect Walter Ratcliff is still owned by the Presbyterian Church; its Great Hall, where ministers once entertained dignitaries, now holds Adagia.

Californian and Mediterranean compositions here earn high marks, as in tuna and watermelon *crudo*; habañero coulis and black salt; or garlic and coffee braised beef cheeks. Between lunch and dinner, the restaurant offers a snack menu and stately place to study.

Adesso

Italian

4395 Piedmont Ave. (at Pleasant Valley Rd.), Oakland

Phone: 510-601-0305
Dinner Mon – Sat
Web: www.dopoadesso.com
Prices: $$

Carnivores rejoice: this is a meaty restaurant. Sister to nearby Dopo, Adesso boasts more than 30 varieties of house-made *salumi*, a selection of artisanal pâtés—served in thick slices—and jars of creamy rillettes just begging to be spread over toasty croutons. Antipasti, panini, and *piadina* (flatbread wraps) are all made with talent, quickly served, and priced to please.

Its wraparound bar, flat screen TV, foosball table, high windows overlooking Piedmont Avenue, and chill, watering hole vibe lure a consistent afterwork crowd. Try an original cocktail with freshly muddled fruit, or opt for a dusky red that pairs well with meat. Then again, you'll have time to try both while waiting for a coveted table at this first-come, first-served eatery.

Anchalee

Thai

1094 Dwight Way (at San Pablo Ave.), Berkeley

Phone: 510-848-4015
Lunch & dinner daily
Web: www.anchaleethai.com
Prices:

Catering to its colorful college set, Berkeley is rife with cheap ethnic eateries, but Anchalee's fresh, flavorful fare deems it a worthy stand out. Wooden tables perch on hard wood floors, while olive green walls, exposed brick, and pendant lights create a calm vibe. This is quality Thai where creative dishes like basil squid and garlic salmon fried rice make for exciting picks alongside trusty standbys like pad Thai and satay. And almost every item—except for seafood—is under ten dollars. Tuck into the *yum nuer*, a tender beef salad with mint and cilantro; or the spicy red curry green bean chicken (opt for the nutty brown rice).

Herbivores rave about the steamed radish cakes and green papaya salad. Wash it all down with a creamy Thai iced tea.

169

Artisan Bistro

Californian ✗

B1

1005 Brown Ave. (at Mt. Diablo Blvd.), Lafayette

Phone: 925-962-0882   Lunch & dinner Tue – Sun
Web: www.artisanlafayette.com
Prices: $$$

Located east of Berkeley, the upscale town of Lafayette is named for the French Marquis who aided America during the Revolutionary War. Were he still around, Lafayette would certainly find nostalgia for his homeland in Artisan's straightforward bistro fare. Seasonal ingredients headline in the likes of a flaky piece of halibut served over wilted spinach and sautéed morels, with English peas adding a sweet note. A luscious Meyer lemon tart crowned with fresh blackberries and candied lemon zest provides the pièce de résistance.

The bistro's craftsman-style cottage includes a spacious brick patio strewn with umbrella-shaded tables. Inside, the space is divided into several small rooms, where the majority of loyal patrons seem to know each other.

Bangkok Jam

Thai ✗✗

B1

1892 Solano Ave. (bet. Fresno Ave. & The Alameda), Berkeley

Phone: 510-525-3625   Lunch & dinner daily
Web: N/A
Prices: 💰💰

Taking up residence in Boran Thai's former digs, this ritzy replacement kicks it up a notch with fresh, creative twists on classic Thai. Vibrant paintings and vivid photos brighten the walls, while milky glass chandeliers illuminate a chic, modern space. If those luscious scents of coconut, basil, and lemongrass don't have your mouth watering, sate your buds with a "wrap and bite"—roasted coconut, peanuts, lime, ginger, and diced shrimp cradled in lettuce leaves, served with a savory ginger sauce. Or tuck into crispy shrimp and cream cheese wontons ("dress up prawns") aside pineapple sweet and sour sauce.

Fresh produce and organic ingredients weave their way into a menu of salads, curries, noodle, and rice dishes; and affordable prices to boot.

Barlata

Spanish

B3

4901 Telegraph Ave. (at 49th St.), Oakland

Phone:	510-450-0678
Web:	www.barlata.com
Prices:	

Dinner nightly

Canned food gets a bad rap. So in the tradition of so-wrong-it's-right culinary phenomena, Barlata celebrates the *lata*—which is, you guessed it, a can. Still, there's nothing lowbrow about Chef/owner Daniel Olivella's Spanish tapas, many of which are presented in recycled tins and priced around $8 a pop. The Catalan native, who also owns B44 in San Francisco, conjures the Iberian Peninsula with nearly 40 savory small plates like seafood piquillo peppers or fennel sausage stuffed with baby squid. Inventive dishes include lamb meatballs with squid, chocolate, and tomato sauce. Thematic artwork also tributes the tin, and hanging imported hams lend authenticity to the eclectic vibe.

Canned tuna, *pimenton*, anchovies, and the like are available to go.

Battambang

Cambodian

B4

850 Broadway (bet. 8th & 9th Sts.), Oakland

Phone:	510-839-8815
Web:	N/A
Prices:	

Lunch & dinner Mon – Sat

Named for Cambodia's second largest city, Battambang is beloved by foodies with a taste for authentic cooking—which, oddly, is tough to find among the area's many Asian eateries. Fresh orchids and perky yellow walls enliven the modest room, where charming servers are proud and knowledgeable of the cuisine. Thai and Vietnamese influences are evident across the extensive menu; though these well-seasoned dishes are less spicy, that jar of garlic-chili sauce on each table allows self-spice gratification.

Expect the likes of charbroiled meats, pan-fried lemongrass catfish, and the vegetarian favorite *trorb aing* (smoky roasted eggplant in spicy lime sauce), as well as specialties that some may find intimidating, but others are sure to find delicious.

Bay Wolf

B3

Californian ✗✗

3853 Piedmont Ave. (at Rio Vista Ave.), Oakland

Phone: 510-655-6004
Web: www.baywolf.com
Prices: $$

Lunch Tue – Fri
Dinner Tue – Sun

In a wood-shingled house on Piedmont Avenue, Bay Wolf has been an Oakland icon since the 1970s. Even then, this quaint little haunt was at the forefront of the Slow Food movement and today still serves the kind of seasonal Californian fare that warms the soul: a rustic duck pâté is spread on toasty Acme bread with capers and cornichons, and celery root purée lends a little sweetness to grilled steelhead trout and crispy onions.

Chef/owner Michael Wild continues to run this show, greeting neighborhood regulars who crowd the heated patio and dining room, which is split in two by a small, central bar. Simple desserts are a pleasant cap to the meal. With layers of lemon curd and champagne gelée, the lime panna cotta is a mandatory indulgence.

Bellanico

C4

Italian ✗✗

4238 Park Blvd. (at Wellington St.), Oakland

Phone: 510-336-1180
Web: www.bellanico.net
Prices: $$

Lunch & dinner daily

A small wonder in Glenview, Bellanico is a kid- and foodie-friendly eatery tucked into a former flower shop with a new open kitchen and a warm palette. The Italian cuisine is both rustic and elegant: seasonal starters may include a savory goat cheese and pink peppercorn panna cotta with tomatoes and peaches, or juicy pork saltimbocca with fresh sage, prosciutto, and fig *agrodolce*. Entrée prices are a hearty welcome for budget-conscious gourmands.

For petite gourmands, bambino-sized pasta dishes are available with a choice of toppings. Parents can thank the owners' own tots, whose combined names form the amalgamation Bellanico. There is also a four-course dinner tasting menu for $26 that will appease the indecisive.

Binh Minh Quan

Vietnamese ✗

B4

338 12th St. (bet. Harrison & Webster Sts.), Oakland

Phone: 510-893-8136
Web: N/A
Prices:

Lunch & dinner daily

First-timers are wise to bring their reading glasses and a hearty appetite to appreciate this very authentic view of Vietnam. The sprawling menu features more than 130 items, including 30 dishes with super sticky, nutty "broken" rice; soups that surpass expectations; and specialties seasoned with mounds of fresh, exotic herbs. Culinary adventurers are bound to relish delicacies like curried frog and grilled wild boar, while couples and larger groups can delight in sharing the seven-course beef tasting prepared in fire pots at the table. Even timid diners should explore the curious drinks selection of fruit shakes made with durian, jackfruit, and soursop.

Bamboo wainscoting and mini-tiki hut roofs fashion a comfortable, unembellished setting.

Bistro Liaison

French ✗✗

B2

1849 Shattuck Ave. (at Hearst Ave.), Berkeley

Phone: 510-849-2155
Web: www.liaisonbistro.com
Prices: $$

Lunch & dinner daily

The concept of a bistro developed in Paris as a small restaurant serving simple, inexpensive meals in a modest setting. Bistro Liaison follows this time honored model with its L-shaped banquette that runs along the back wall below a narrow mirror, hand painted with French phrases.

Here, Chef Todd Kneiss (a former protégé of Roland Passot) approaches simplicity with a deft hand to create "French food for the soul" that celebrates its most traditional dishes. His *ris de veau*, coq au vin, *bouillabaisse*, or steak frites are sure to elevate the mood of any expat. Dessert and cocktail selections are rubber stamped on the white butcher paper that covers each table.

For regulars and Berkeley residents, a wine club and periodic cooking classes are also offered.

Bocanova

B4

55 Webster St. (at Jack London Square), Oakland

Phone: 510-444-1233
Web: www.bocanova.com
Prices: **$$**

Lunch & dinner daily

This tremendous piece of real estate housed in a 1920s icehouse, with towering ceilings, an open kitchen, ample bar, and oversized windows peering onto Jack London Square, is also a promising newcomer to its waterfront locale. The space is suited to success with ample seats at the bar, on the patio, or at group friendly communal tables.

The pan-American cuisine focuses heavily on ocean dwellers and old-world tastes mixed with New World creativity. Flavors are bright in such dishes as halibut ceviche with cilantro and *ají Amarillo*, and bowls of Yucatan seafood stew are perfectly prepared, yet other offerings are still finding their sea legs. Save room for dessert: the roasted banana cake with cashew brittle and red pepper sauce is a triumphant end.

Bridges

B5

44 Church St. (at Hartz Ave.), Danville

Phone: 925-820-7200
Web: www.bridgesdanville.com
Prices: **$$**

Lunch Mon – Fri
Dinner nightly

Robin Williams' fans may remember Bridges' cameo appearance in the 1993 hit *Mrs. Doubtfire*, but this Danville starlet stakes its true claim to fame in a consistent appeal to an East Bay audience. The cinematic setting is geared to special occasions with tangled vines and a trickling waterfall weaving romance on the patio. Inside, a mural of grand bridges spans one of the few walls not occupied by soaring windows.

Neighborly hospitality lends a small town vibe. The cuisine, however, explores the globe from Europe to Asia and back home again. Start with a hearty salad or a shrimp and avocado quesadilla; then, journey on with sautéed mahi mahi dressed in tangy pineapple salsa. The creamsicle parfait is a dressed up end to a most enjoyable ride.

Brown Sugar Kitchen

American

A3

2534 Mandela Pkwy. (at 26th St.), Oakland

Phone:	510-839-7685	Lunch Tue – Sun
Web:	www.brownsugarkitchen.com	
Prices:		

From afar it looks as if a giant wedge of sweet potato pie landed smack in the center of industrial West Oakland. This slice of "new style down home" goodness is French trained Tanya Holland's opus—where organic and soul foods meet in a heavenly convergence of sheer belly bliss. Even if you have to wait for a table, think you can resist the brown sugar pineapple-glazed baby back ribs, or smoked chicken and shrimp gumbo? We doubt it. Try the talented chef's take on a beloved Harlem classic: crispy buttermilk fried chicken, perfectly done, nestled aside a delicate, crunchy cornbread waffle kissed with brown sugar butter and apple cider syrup. The smart wine list features mainly African-American vintners and the bounty of rustic desserts changes frequently.

Café Gratitude

Vegan

B2

1730 Shattuck Ave. (at Virginia St.), Berkeley

Phone:	415-824-4652	Lunch & dinner daily
Web:	www.cafegratitude.com	
Prices:		

On the restaurant-rich strip of Shattuck Avenue known as the "gourmet ghetto," Café Gratitude keeps Berkeley's bohemian spirit alive and well—quite literally, since this healthful cuisine is completely vegan and mostly raw.

Rest assured that before the organic elixirs and the likes of zucchini lasagna layered with cashew "ricotta" have the opportunity to comfort you, the waitstaff will. Servers offer menu affirmations such as "you are divine." Quirky and cute the first time, by the end of a multicourse meal—when you are also "fabulous," "insightful," and "lovely"—you will either be at a higher level of self-affirmation, or totally over the kitsch.

A vegan Mexican sibling, Gracias Madre, has a budding following in SF's Mission District.

Camino

Californian ⚔

3917 Grand Ave. (at Sunny Slope Ave.), Oakland

Phone: 510-547-5035
Web: www.caminorestaurant.com
Prices: $$

Lunch Sat – Sun
Wed – Mon dinner only

Courtesy of Chez Panisse graduate Chef Russell Moore, Camino fills its Basque-style dining room with pressed tin ceilings, enormous wrought iron chandeliers, and communal tables fashioned from locally salvaged redwood trees. Exposed brick and dark wood beams add to the homespun feel.

Along a brick wall, the expansive open kitchen provides evening long entertainment with cooks shelling fresh beans before adding them to bubbling pots over the fire, or turning a roasting leg of lamb over the flames, adding smoke-tinged flavors to the air. The menu changes nightly, featuring typically less than 10 dishes, such as a grilled local squid with cucumbers, chili, and basil; or local albacore aside green beans, potatoes, saffron, garlic, and pounded oregano.

César

Spanish 🍽

1515 Shattuck Ave. (bet. Cedar & Vine Sts.), Berkeley

Phone: 510-883-0222
Web: www.barcesar.com
Prices: $$

Lunch & dinner daily

Chez Panisse remains a Berkeley big ticket, but don't underestimate this lively neighboring tapas bar with all the Californian influence, indie soul, and simple cooking with Alice Waters alums running the show. Amusingly, the eatery is named for filmmaker Marcel Pagnol's character César, a café owner who sets about reuniting the estranged family of Honoré Panisse.

Spanish-style tapas may begin with *patatas rellenas*, or potatoes stuffed with spicy chorizo and bathed in *queso urgelia*, continuing with fresh fish or beef *a la plancha*, or *bocadillos*. The seasonal paella may be slow to develop but is rich in reward. Be sure to cap off meals with a selection from their black book of sherries, Madeiras, and Ports.

A larger Latino sib is in nearby Oakland.

Champa Garden

Asian

B4

2102 8th Ave. (at 21st St.), Oakland

Phone: 510-238-8819
Web: www.champagarden.com
Prices:

Lunch & dinner daily

Couched in a residential area of Oakland's edgy San Antonio neighborhood, Champa Garden lures locals inside with its aromatic Southeast Asian cuisine, inexpensive prices, and courteous service. The setting may not impress, but authentic tastes of Vietnam, Laos, and Thailand infuse the appealing dishes.

An abundant offering of noodle soups, pan-fried noodles, seafood entrées, fried rice, and curries pack the value-driven menu. Starters standout in the fried rice ball salad (*nam kaow*), where a symphony of flavor and texture reveals itself in this blend of crispy fried rice, crumbles of preserved pork, green onions, chilis, and lime juice. To eat it, wrap the rice mixture in the Romaine leaves provided, along with some fresh mint and cilantro.

Chevalier

French

B1

960 Moraga Rd. (at Moraga Blvd.), Lafayette

Phone: 925-385-0793
Web: www.chevalierrestaurant.com
Prices: $$

Lunch Tue – Fri
Dinner Tue – Sat

This little Lafayette neighborhood spot captures the warmth and charm of Southern France in its delightful seasonal dishes. Ignore the strip mall location and request a seat on the enchanting semi-circular patio, which winds around a fragrant garden stocked with herbs, flowers, and hedges for privacy. With white clothed tables and soft French background music, the patio encourages romantic dinners on a warm evening.

The chef's passion fires the authentic fare, with appetizers of silky and tender escargots de Bourgogne in a pool of buttery garlic and parsley. Entrées may include roasted Colorado lamb with a spicy chorizo ragout and tarragon-lamb jus, followed by traditional desserts such as tarte Tatin, rich with the flavors of caramel and butter.

177

Chez Panisse

Californian

B1

1517 Shattuck Ave. (bet. Cedar & Vine Sts.), Berkeley

Phone: 510-548-5525 — Dinner Mon – Sat
Web: www.chezpanisse.com
Prices: $$$$

Chez Panisse is a perfect fit within Berkeley's gourmet ghetto. Housed in a vine-covered Craftsman-style bungalow, it may seem surprising that this place is responsible for one of America's biggest food revolutions. Then again, this is Berkeley, a place known for its table-turning agendas.

Wood beams, antiqued mirrors, copper light fixtures, and large floral arrangements create a rustically appealing dining room.

Everyone from hippies to hotties has been frequenting this bold-faced restaurant since 1971. The three- and four-course prix-fixe menus change nightly and are based solely on fresh, organic, and seasonal products. This is serious American cooking and includes treats like King salmon carpaccio or a wood-grilled duck breast with pickled cherries.

China Village

Chinese

A1

1335 Solano Ave. (at Pomona Ave.), Albany

Phone: 510-525-2285 — Lunch & dinner daily
Web: www.chinavillagesolano.com
Prices:

High tolerance for tongue-numbing, lip-scorching spice? China Village will happily oblige. Local Chinese diners flock to this Albany spot for fiery, authentic Mandarin and Sichuan style cuisine, where classics like Kung Pao share the menu with more exotic offerings like thousand chili chicken and boiled kidney. For another spicy spectacle, try the West Sichuan style fish fillet: bedecked with a startling number of dried red chilies, the server filters them out, leaving a moderately piquant soup of delicate whitefish, cellophane noodles, and tasty broth.

The modest space, divided into a few pleasant, banquet style dining rooms with artfully decorated tables and tanks of live Dungeness crabs, is ideal for large groups and families.

Chu

B3

5362 College Ave. (bet. Bryant & Manila Aves.), Oakland

Phone: 510-601-8818   Lunch & dinner daily
Web: www.restaurantchu.com
Prices: $$

A universe away from Oakland's grittier Chinatown, Chu serves urbane Chinese fare in Rockridge style. Dramatically dressed in black and white with high ceilings and sleek leather chairs, the restaurant draws its aesthetic influence from contemporary Chinese art.

Owners Dana and Philip Chu, also the proprietors behind Berkeley's Kirin, take an equally modern approach to cuisine. The open kitchen conceives such exotic fare as green onion pancakes laden with thin slices of flavorful smoked salmon, cilantro, and hoisin sauce; *ching hua* chili prawns laced with tongue-tingling Sichuan pepper; and expertly refined versions of classics such as pot stickers and spring rolls. In lieu of dessert, try a lychee oolong tea beautifully presented in an iron pot.

Coa

C5

3421 Blackhawk Plaza Circle (at Camino Tassajara), Danville

Phone: 925-984-2363   Lunch & dinner daily
Web: www.coarestaurant.com
Prices: $$

Wrought-iron chandeliers dangling from vaulted brick ceilings and elegant swans gliding along the aquatic landscape are hints that Coa, at ritzy Blackhawk Plaza, isn't your average taqueria. Here, affluent couples pause from shopping to sip top shelf margaritas; their children may be found feeding tortilla chips to the ducks on the waterfront patio.

Inside, Latin beats reverberate against sunburned floors as the kitchen turns out contemporary Mexican cuisine bursting with flavor. Serrano and chipotle peppers heat ahi tuna *tostaditos*, while creamy cheese sauce complements a plump rock shrimp relleno. For dessert, sugar-dusted churros are fun for the whole family: The fried straws arrive with rum-scented *horchata* and salted caramel anglaise.

Commis ✿

3859 Piedmont Ave. (at Rio Vista Ave.), Oakland

Phone: 510-653-3902   Dinner Wed – Sun
Web: www.commisrestaurant.com
Prices: $$$

Aaron Stienstra

Before opening this fantastic solo project in Oakland, Chef James Syhabout worked his way through some of the world's most legendary kitchens, including El Bulli, The Fat Duck, Manresa, and Plumpjack Café. All that studying paid off, for Commis—which loosely means "trainee chef" in French— is the kind of upscale neighborhood spot you dream about: laid back, sexy, and serious about its food.

Housed in the former Jojo space, the narrow interior boasts a centerpiece kitchen that makes every table in the sleek, sparsely decorated room feel like a chef's table—and Syhabout has been known to occasionally trot the food over himself. Hardcore foodies will want to sit at the wood counter, which offers great views of the small crew of cooks, each of them sporting the blue pin-striped *commis* apron.

A highly seasonal, three course prix-fixe dinner offers several options for each course and might include juicy corned pork jowl on a pristine little salad sporting black trumpet mushrooms, braised chicory, and broccoli rabe blossoms; wild guinea fowl with a confit of cèpes laced under the crispy skin; or a warm pumpkin custard sporting black liquorice cream, root beer reduction, and *pepitas*.

Corso

B2

Italian ✗

1788 Shattuck Ave. (bet. Delaware & Francisco Sts.), Berkeley

Phone: 510-704-8003

Web: www.trattoriacorso.com

Prices: **$$**

Dinner nightly

In the birthplace of Californian cuisine, Berkeley's Corso is a journey to Tuscany. The rustic little eatery bears the stamps of travel: framed trattorie menus and wine lists offer a glimpse at co-owner Wendy Brucker's extensive "research," collected during her wanderings in the Renaissance city, Florence. In the homey dining room, a granite-topped bar offers a view to the open kitchen where Florentine specialties are testament to Brucker's quest for authenticity. Savory pizzas are thin and true to traditions, while the *pollo al burro*—crispy skin-on chicken sautéed liberally in butter—is revelatory. The wines, of course, are all Italian and available by the carafe.

At brunch, toasted *panettone* with butter and jam is a sweet start to the weekend.

Digs Bistro

A2

American ✗✗

1453 Dwight Way (bet. Sacramento St. & San Pablo Ave.), Berkeley

Phone: 510-548-2322

Web: www.digsbistro.com

Prices: **$$**

Dinner Thu – Mon

Word of mouth draws Berkeleyites to this unpretentious bistro, which started out as an "underground" restaurant in the manager's home. Now housed in a converted residence, Digs is a quaint spot for an evening out. Its four-seat zinc bar and small dining area are accented by arched openings and avocado-green tables; a beehive oven fire adds warmth in the winter months.

One can measure a kitchen staff by how well they roast a chicken, and here the cooking is spot on. Digs' version turns out succulent, with a crispy skin and a rich chicken jus studded with baby shiitake mushroom caps.

Parents love the first Monday of every month, when the bistro staff will supervise their kids so the adults enjoy a peaceful dinner—though the scene can get chaotic.

Doña Tomás

Mexican

B3

5004 Telegraph Ave. (bet. 49th & 51st Sts.), Oakland

Phone: 510-450-0522   Dinner Tue – Sat
Web: www.donatomas.com
Prices: **$$**

Follow the freshly fashioned Yupsters through revitalized Temescal, which is fast becoming Oakland's own up and coming arts community, to this Mexican highlight of the local culinary scene. Upbeat Latin music pulses through the dining room, and the later it gets, the higher the volume climbs. Evenings may begin with a margarita at the small corner bar and end with coffee on the inviting back courtyard.

Regional Mexican and Californian cuisines offer seasonal flair, fusing into favorites like *antojitos* of *sopes* with poblano cream, chanterelle, and crimini mushrooms; or *entradas* of plump chile rellenos stuffed with raisins, pinenuts, and queso.

While the price tag is higher than the neighborhood taqueria, quality is what stands out here.

Dopo

Italian

B3

4293 Piedmont Ave. (at Echo St.), Oakland

Phone: 510-652-3676   Lunch & dinner Mon – Sat
Web: www.dopoadesso.com
Prices: **$$**

Locals may come here for the artisanal Neapolitan pies, but Dopo is much more than a pizza place. Thank Oliveto veteran Jon Smulewitz. His concise daily menu holds to the basic tenet of Californian cuisine: simple, fresh, and local. Diners who stand in line to eat here—despite an expansion a few years ago that doubled the seating capacity—agree that a panini filled with a breast of fried Hoffman Farm hen, and house-made pasta or pâté are worth the wait. Then again, the namesake Dopo pizza (tangy tomato sauce, oregano, mozzarella, Pecorino Romano, chile flakes, and optional anchovies) always wins raves.

Claim a seat at one of the closely spaced pine tables, or at the aqua-tiled dining counter that wraps around the bar from the open kitchen.

Élevé

Vietnamese ✕✕

C1

1677 N. Main St. (1677 N. Main St.), Walnut Creek

Phone: 925-979-1677
Web: www.eleverestaurant.com
Prices: $$

Lunch Tue – Fri
Dinner Tue – Sat

Across from City Hall in Walnut Creek, Élevé has broad portrait windows that invite the hungry wanderer. Inside, where natural light and a stunning quartzite bar lend a welcoming, modern vibe, cocktail hounds appreciate such creative pours as the "Sleepy Head," a concoction of brandy, ginger, and mint; while burled wood tabletops are a warm surface for family-style Vietnamese meals.

The fusion cuisine is laden with crisp flavors in entrées such as spicy steak salad with watercress, daikon radish, and jalapeños; and chicken *zao lan* with yellow coconut curry, mushrooms, and sweet onion. Vegetarians will find plenty of dishes to satisfy them, including garlic tofu and spicy root curry. Noodle lovers must also try sister restaurant Pho84 in Oakland.

Encuentro

Vegetarian ✕

B4

202 2nd St. (at Jackson St.), Oakland

Phone: 510-832-9463
Web: www.encuentrooakland.com
Prices: 🪙🪙

Lunch Mon – Fri
Dinner Wed – Sat

While many Bay Area restaurants go hog wild for meaty menus showcasing charcuterie and porchetta, Chef/owner Eric Tucker continues to practice the art of high vegetarian cuisine. Also of San Francisco's veggie haven, Millenium, Tucker is sprouting his newest venture in Jack London Square where Encuentro is a welcome addition to the burgeoning neighborhood.

Natural light fills the tiny corner spot where rugs warm the concrete floors and a handful of tables and wine counter seating yield a cozy getaway from the din of the square. Vegans may feast on pâtés made from nuts and truffled mushrooms, while others take their tomato bread pudding with a regal crown of Humboldt Fog cheese. The wine bar is a mellow spot for deviled eggs and roasted nuts.

Esin

✗✗

B5

750 Camino Ramon (at Sycamore Valley Rd. W.), Danville

Phone: 925-314-0974   Lunch & dinner daily
Web: www.esinrestaurant.com
Prices: $$

From its plot in Danville's Rose Garden marketplace, Esin feels fresh with soft yellow walls and dark wood trim, as if it just sprouted yesterday. In fact, Esin is actually a transplant that flourished for 10 years in San Ramon.

Here, it continues to please crowds with well-executed, homey fare that takes a cue from the Turkish roots of Chef/owner Esin deCarion, whose name means "inspiration." Working together with her husband and co-owner, this kitchen team turns out such Cal-Med dishes as apple-cured gravlax with grilled bread and caperberry butter; and fillet of Petrale sole cooked meunière-style with lemon-caper beurre blanc. Desserts are tasty and homemade, like the rich and subtly sweet banana cream pie with a dark chocolate cookie crust.

eVe 😊

✗✗

B2

1960 University Ave. (bet. Martin Luther King Way and Milvia St.), Berkeley

Phone: 510-868-0735   Dinner Tue – Sat
Web: www.eve-berkeley.com
Prices: $$

Not quite what you'd expect from a college town eatery, eVe whispers of a romance inspired by its owner—Christopher and Veronica Laramie, who fell in love at Le Cordon Bleu in Paris, work in tandem at the stoves. Their ambitious Californian cuisine mingles with French fundamentals and molecular gastronomy, and the overall theme is fresh and flavorful.

Dressed in black-and-white textiles with dark stone tables, eVe's modern aura complements contemporary fare. A the whim of the mister and missus who might personally deliver your sous vide farm egg, the menu changes every few days. An intimate dining room puts the focus on the menu, where $11 items might include lamb with Israeli couscous and pea gazpacho, and vanilla goat's milk panna cotta.

FIVE

B2

2086 Allston Way (at Shattuck Ave.), Berkeley

Phone: 510-845-7300   Lunch & dinner daily
Web: www.five-berkeley.com
Prices: $$

Housed in the sparkling Hotel Shattuck Plaza, a glossy checkered floor leads the way to FIVE's panache dining room—a stylish feast for the eyes with towering columns and discreet red jewel tones that illuminate the bright space. The sophisticated setting is relaxed and comfortable, but taste is assured, given the influence and brief stint by talented Chef Scott Howard.

Though he is off to another venture, much of his expertise remains with dishes like braised pork belly with cider vinegar glaze and apple-walnut salad; short rib pot roast with horseradish-Yukon gold purée and red wine jus; or creamy macaroni and cheese starring orzo and braised morel mushrooms topped with tangy tomato jam. Be sure to save room for freshly made, homespun desserts.

Flora

B4

1900 Telegraph Ave. (at 19th St.), Oakland

Phone: 510-286-0100   Lunch & dinner Tue – Sat
Web: www.floraoakland.com
Prices: $$

Finding its name in its location, Flora's attractive black and cream dining room and long curving bar are housed in the nostalgic 1931 Oakland Floral Depot Building—an art deco gem faced in cobalt blue terra-cotta with silver trim that drips down the façade like water. Run by Dona Svitsky and Chef Thomas Schnetz—of Doña Tomás (Oakland) and Tacubaya (Berkeley)—Flora proves that this team can reach well beyond Latin American fare.

Organic ingredients from local growers pepper the seasonal menu with the likes of brie *agnolotti* and chanterelle mushrooms; olive oil-poached ahi tuna with tomato-pepper fondue; or suckling pig two ways with corn, plums, and green onion. Remember the caramel pudding for dessert, topped with a divine sprinkle of *fleur de sel*.

Fonda

A1

1501 Solano Ave. (at Curtis St.), Albany

Phone: 510-559-9006	Lunch Sat – Sun
Web: www.fondasolana.com	Dinner nightly
Prices: $$	

Part of the restaurant empire of Haig and Cindy Krikorian, this festive Albany hot spot showcases creative Latin American cuisine and drinks to match. A long inviting bar offers views of the open kitchen, while the upstairs mezzanine sports a comfortable, lounge-y feel with its upholstered chairs. Mavens of the late-night scene drop in for happy hour, which starts here after 9:00 P.M. every night.

The original menu spotlights favorites such as Veracruz-style seafood cocktail with Caribbean white shrimp, mahi mahi, and avocado; or grilled skirt steak with Manchego onion rings and mojo Colorado. Drop in Friday through Sunday for an afternoon "siesta" menu featuring rum cocktails and a selection of tapas, or go earlier for their weekend brunch.

Gather 😊

B2

2200 Oxford St. (at Allston Way.), Berkeley

Phone: 510-809-0400	Lunch & dinner daily
Web: www.gatherrestaurant.com	
Prices: $$	

An alumnus of the San Francisco vegetarian institution Millenium, Gather's Chef/owner Sean Baker plays well to the UC Berkeley campus just across the street. But here, Gather is welcoming to all: Fish and meat play supporting roles to such headliners as the ever-changing vegetarian "charcuterie," which composes an artist's palette of creative bites like braised wild mushroom bruschetta and vibrant beet tartare.

Blackboards near the exhibition kitchen showcase ingredients from local farms, and studious patrons will appreciate a source book that Gather keeps on hand for in-depth review. Those less interested in the origin of their young chicken "under a brick" can revel in a rowdy collegiate vibe and soak up organic cocktails and biodynamic wines.

Grand Avenue Thai

 B4

Thai XX

384 Grand Ave. (bet. Perkins St. & Staten Ave.), Oakland

Phone: 510-444-1507
Web: www.grandavenuethai.com
Prices:

Lunch Mon – Sat
Dinner nightly

This chic yet unassuming neighborhood favorite just steps from Lake Merritt fills daily with the Oakland workaday crowd looking for a lunchtime pick-me-up. Brightly hued walls don vivid oil paintings created by a friend of the chef, and each table is topped with fresh, cheerful flowers.

This is a comfortable atmosphere for sampling contemporary Thai cuisine, but spice lovers may be disappointed—the kitchen turns down the heat to suit the American palate. Dishes are nonetheless packed with flavor: a lemongrass tilapia is pan-fried with Thai basil and sweet red chili sauce, while green chicken curry is redolent with coconut milk and kaffir lime. Straightforward service and attention to detail makes this an ideal spot for a quick but satisfying bite.

Hibiscus

 B4

Caribbean XX

1745 San Pablo Ave. (at 18th St.), Oakland

Phone: 510-444-2626
Web: www.hibiscusoakland.com
Prices: $$

Lunch Wed – Fri
Dinner Wed – Mon

Something special is brewing in Sarah Kirnon's kitchen. The Barbados-raised chef wields her island-inspired talent like a fiery wand, transforming locally sourced products into plates of Caribbean and Creole-style deliciousness. Island grooves flow through the dining room, where smoky brown walls display floral paintings while white linens and rattan seating create a warm elegance. Begin with rock shrimp and egg salad featuring chopped romaine, pimiento-stuffed olives, and hearts of palm in a sugarcane vinaigrette. Next, nosh on Miss Ollie's Fried Chicken—tender pieces snuggled between zesty potato salad on one side and sautéed kale and sweet corn on the other.

Refresh with homemade ginger limeade, and save room for panna cotta with drunken cherries.

Hong Kong East Ocean

A3

Chinese

3199 Powell St., Emeryville

Phone: 510-655-3388
Web: www.hkeo.us
Prices:

Lunch & dinner daily

Cantonese dishes, fresh seafood, and dim sum are the main reasons crowds flock to this massive pagoda-roofed restaurant that flanks the Bay. Here, diners enjoy fantastic views of the nearby marina, Bay Bridge, and San Francisco skyline through the large windows that define the space.

This place is meant for family-style dining, so bring a few relatives or friends and try the special set menu available for four, six, or eight. Or choose from the regular bill of fare, which includes fish from the massive tanks along one wall. At lunchtime, opt for dim sum; check off a sampling of items from the written list, and moments later they parade from the kitchen one by one.

Plenty of banquet rooms accommodate groups from business meetings to birthday parties.

Huynh

C1

Vietnamese

1512 Locust St. (at Bonanza St.), Walnut Creek

Phone: 925-952-9898
Web: www.huynhrestaurant.com
Prices:

Lunch Mon – Fri
Dinner nightly

The culinary baby of husband-wife owners Kim Huynh and Hung Tran, Huynh is an alluring respite from tony Walnut Creek, with hanging parchment lanterns, silk screens, and a palette of lemongrass and mustard. Cheerful Buddhas keep watch over the six-seater bar where green tea martinis and lychee cosmos add to the tropical vibe, and trickling fountains bestow a serene backdrop for Vietnamese gastro adventures.

Dishes are reasonably priced and packed with flavor. A spicy steak salad is loaded with mint, jalapeños, cilantro, and peanuts; while the tender *ga sai gon*, or chicken thighs are dressed in a smoky homemade sauce evocative of barbecue and mole. Vegetarians will find plenty to feast on, including classic imperial rolls and satisfying soups.

Indus Village

Indian

A2

1920 San Pablo Ave. (bet. Hearst & University Aves.), Berkeley

Phone: 510-549-5999
Web: www.indusvillage.net
Prices:

Lunch & dinner daily

With carefully crafted curries, tasty lamb dishes, tandoor specialties, and Indian and Pakistani recipes at bargain-basement prices, Indus Village is the answer to any foodie seeking a casual and inexpensive South Asian meal.

Regulars check out the day's specials on the whiteboard at the entrance, walk up to the counter, place their order, and seat themselves in the bright, ornate chairs; food is delivered to them when it is ready. There is table service too, but it's brisk and no-nonsense, keeping the focus on the food rather than formality. Vibrant and evocative wall murals depict the desert life of India and Pakistan.

Next door, the restaurant's grocery is well-stocked with all the items you need to recreate your favorite dishes at home.

Kim Huong

Vietnamese

B4

304 10th St. (at Harrison St.), Oakland

Phone: 510-836-3139
Web: N/A
Prices:

Lunch & dinner Wed – Mon

Set at the intersection of 10th and Harrison streets, Kim Huong corners the market on good, light Vietnamese fare in this area. There may not be much that is noteworthy about the large, airy, sunny-hued room, but the food is another matter.

Great care shines through in a beef noodle broth, or *pho*, studded with pieces of gelatinous tripe, sheets of beef flavored with just a bit of sweet fat, and beef balls redolent with aromatic herbs. Quickly sautéed slices of white meat chicken are brightened with pungent ginger, while tart green papaya, sweet mango, and dried shrimp are tossed with fried shallots, cilantro, soy sauce, and lemongrass to fashion a perfect salad. The staff is friendly and attentive, under the watchful eye of the charming owner.

Kirala

Japanese

B2

2100 Ward St. (at Shattuck Ave.), Berkeley

Phone: 510-549-3486
Web: www.kiralaberkeley.com
Prices:

Lunch Mon – Fri
Dinner nightly

Playing world beats and named for Mother Nature, Kirala is a natural selection for Berkeley types craving sushi and *robata* delicacies. Daily market specials are displayed on a whiteboard above the bar, which is staffed by experts who take great care in their perfectly steamed sticky rice—topped with hamachi or blood red *maguro*—steaming bowls of soba and udon, and robust grilled items such as skewered baby lobster tails, bacon-wrapped asparagus, and chicken-stuffed mushrooms.

True to Japanese form, the dining room is restrained yet sophisticated, and the service is pleasant. Their eclectic music selection (reggae, jazz, and Latin) peps up the sophisticated vibe.

Kirala is also a stone's throw from Berkeley Bowl, the neighborhood's market mecca.

Lake Chalet

Seafood

B4

1520 Lakeside Dr. (bet. 14th & 17th Sts.), Oakland

Phone: 510-208-5253
Web: www.thelakechalet.com
Prices: **$$**

Lunch & dinner daily

In a remodeled boathouse on Lake Merritt, Lake Chalet impresses with refined American classics that promise to inspire its beach-destination competitors with large portions of carefully prepared, familiar fare in a setting that is infinitely "travel-friendly" but never touristy.

The tremendous space hosts tables upstairs and down, as well as on the picturesque pier in the company of gulls and geese. On a sunny day, the serene view from the 80-foot marble bar is attractive to out-of-towners looking for an escape from urban Oakland. The menu depends on where you sit (more formal in the dining room, casual outdoors), but expect such favorites as fresh oysters; petrale sole *piccata* with fried capers and spicy cress; and a luscious coconut cream pie.

Lalime's

International ✗✗

A1

1329 Gilman St. (bet. Neilson & Peralta Aves.), Berkeley

Phone: 510-527-9838   Dinner nightly
Web: www.lalimes.com
Prices: **$$**

♿ Owners Haig and Cindy Krikorian still know how to throw a party. Like sister restaurants Sea Salt and T-Rex Barbecue, Lalime's is a local favorite, drawing an affable crowd of regulars who congregate upstairs for lively meals near the bar, fireplace, and semi open kitchen. Couples and quiet types prefer the downstairs dining room where citrus-hued walls add a friendly vibe and storefront windows offer a view of the neighborhood.

The staff is attentive and knowledgeable of the cuisine, which marries diverse cultural influences with California's seasonal-organic philosophy. Dishes may include squab with apple, chestnut, and bacon bread pudding; Idaho pork "prime rib" with honey mustard glaze; and Maine lobster cake with satsuma oranges and curry aïoli.

La Rose Bistro

French ✗

B2

2037 Shattuck Ave. (at Addison St.), Berkeley

Phone: 510-644-1913   Lunch Mon – Fri
Web: www.larosebistro.com   Dinner nightly
Prices: **$$**

♿ Painted with pastel hues and pastoral murals, La Rose is equally good for a casual lunch, family get-together, or romantic evening out. Hai and Quynh Nguyen's laid back bistro is located in Berkeley's theater district (on the one way, north bound bit of Shattuck), attracting drama lovers as well. A meal here begins with fresh-baked French bread and an herbaceous cilantro-pesto for dipping. Then come consistently well-prepared French classics, such as *entrecôte frites* and duck confit with Madeira sauce. Californian touches stand out in succulent roasted medallions of pork with honeyed apples and rosemary jus.

Lunch may offer sandwiches such as the *pain bagnat* stuffed with tuna, olives, anchovies, and egg, as well as a full complement of main courses.

Laurus 😊

Mediterranean Mediterranean ✗✗

C5

3483 Blackhawk Circle Dr. (at Tassajara Ranch Dr.), Danville

Phone: 925-984-2250   Lunch & dinner daily
Web: www.laurussf.com
Prices: $$

Dressed in hues of olive and bay leaf, draped in tawny curtains that open to koi ponds and fountains, Laurus is the Mediterranean sister of the Verve Group's Coa and Stomp, all at Blackhawk Plaza. A wall of windows illuminates the spacious dining room where the Green Fairy, contained in an absinthe dispenser, flutters on a curved stone bar.

The clipboard menu is served all day, perhaps featuring braised wild boar Bolognese atop al dente tagliatelle to pair with wines selected from Italy, Spain, and France. Truffled honey mustard glazes a crispy half chicken served with a sophisticated mac 'n' cheese made with *cavatelli*. Like much of the menu, desserts are kid-friendly, as in flaky apple tart topped with granola, aged cheddar, and caramel gelato.

Legendary Palace

Chinese ✗✗

B4

708 Franklin St. (at 7th St.), Oakland

Phone: 510-663-9188   Lunch & dinner daily
Web: N/A
Prices: ☜☜

In the heart of Oakland's Chinatown, this restaurant boasts two floors of dining space and seats more than 600. The building, which dates back to 1917, was remodeled as a literal palace of Chinese cuisine. Inside, the restaurant is surprisingly elegant; gold curtains frame floor-to-ceiling windows, and sparkling chandeliers dangle overhead.

At lunchtime, dim sum carts circulate amid the closely spaced tables on both levels, offering a treasure trove of tasty little gems that do not disappoint, including dumplings, noodles, meats, and pastries. For dinner, the à la carte selection spotlights Cantonese specialties, and seafood (Pacific lobster, geoduck clams, Chinese ling cod) fresh from the aquarium tanks that line the back corners of the main room.

Marzano

Pizza

C4

4214 Park Blvd. (at Glenfield Ave.), Oakland

Phone: 510-531-4500	Lunch Sat – Sun
Web: www.marzanorestaurant.com	Dinner nightly
Prices: $$	

Make a reservation at Marzano, the cozy neighborhood pizza joint that bursts with as much local flavor as the tomatoes for which it is named. Reclaimed wood chandeliers and antique glass wine casks hang from the exposed beam ceiling above the rustic dining room, where personal space is at a premium. While there are a few entrées like pan-roasted Alaskan cod and chicken *all' arrabiata* (all under $15), the blistered pies are the true draw. Blazed to a crisp in minutes in the 800-degree wood-fired brick oven, pizzas range from a classic margherita to such seasonal creations as spring onion with pecorino, pancetta, and rosemary.

Nibbles like Meyer lemon and green garlic *arancini* are simply lovely, as is Strauss soft-serve ice cream for a *dolce* finish.

Metro Lafayette

Californian

B1

3524 Mt. Diablo Blvd. (bet. 1st St. & Oak Hill Rd.), Lafayette

Phone: 925-284-4422	Lunch & dinner daily
Web: www.metrolafayette.com	
Prices: $$	

With an upscale clientele, relaxed atmosphere, and straightforward cuisine, this neighborhood hot spot serves both small town atmosphere and big city food. The mood is boisterous at the front bar, where locals gather for evening cocktails. More subdued are the sleek indoor dining room and the umbrella-shaded outdoor terrace. Vine-covered walls and potted trees ensconce this spot teeming with families and friends.

Seasonal and local are the watchwords for this Californian-style cuisine. French and Asian influences energize dishes such as duck confit spring rolls with spicy lime dipping sauce, and Penn Cove *moules frites* with white wine, garlic, and herbs. At dinner, a three-course fixed menu offers value and numerous options for each course.

Miss Pearl's Jam House

B4

1 Broadway (at The Embarcadero), Oakland

Phone: 510-444-7171   Lunch & dinner daily
Web: www.misspearlsjamhouse.com
Prices: $$

If Jack London Square is an unsuspecting locale for exotic island cuisine, Miss Pearl's Jam House suspends disbelief. Past the palm-lined waterfront terrace, enter this maze of dining rooms bedecked with tropical tchotchke, heirlooms, and animal prints. Sample a sassy special cocktail, like Miss Pearl's rum punch, to accompany live music on weekends.

Conceived by Chef Joey Altman, who helmed the original location in San Francisco, this New World cuisine is both fun and familiar. Flavors of Cuba, the Caribbean, and the Bahamas tickle the palate at Miss Pearl's, which might also be the pearly gates for fried food aficionados—look for Creole shrimp poppers and crisp sweet plantains with creamy lime sauce. Jerk chicken lovers are also in heaven.

900 Grayson

A2

900 Grayson St. (at 7th St.), Berkeley

Phone: 510-704-9900   Lunch Mon – Sat
Web: www.900grayson.com
Prices: ☜

A noteworthy stop on the East Bay hamburger circuit, 900 Grayson makes their version from all-natural beef, topped with double-smoked bacon, white cheddar, shoestring onions, and homemade barbecue sauce. Herbed fries come on the side. Elsewhere on the menu, the Demon Lover—a take on the Southern favorite fried chicken and waffles—coats a boneless chicken paillard in a peppery breading and plates it alongside a buttermilk waffle, with your choice of country-style gravy or Vermont maple syrup. Accompanying bottles of hot sauce give it the final kick. Vegetarians are just as happy to substitute seitan for the chicken.

This quaint family-friendly café, with its raspberry-colored façade and tree-shaded back patio, serves breakfast, lunch, and brunch.

O Chamé

Asian

 A2

1830 4th St. (bet. Hearst Ave. & Virginia St.), Berkeley

Phone: 510-841-8783   Lunch & dinner daily
Web: N/A
Prices: $$

This upscale noodle house is the go-to place for savvy locals. Those in the know order bento boxes off the menu; this lunchtime treat, available on a first-come, first-served basis, consists of fluffy white rice, pickled vegetables, and an entrée such as grilled salmon. If dining in, earthenware dishes come arranged with satisfying starters like sweet white corn and green onion pancakes, or seared tuna with braised leeks. Noodle bowls are the highlight among main courses. Hearty and healthy, these attractive bowls swim with the likes of buckwheat soba noodles and plump roasted oysters; or thick udon, pork tenderloin, spinach, and *takuan* (a pickle made from daikon radishes).

The pleasant outdoor patio is great for people-watching on a nice day.

Ohgane

Korean

B3

3915 Broadway (bet. 38th & 40th Sts.), Oakland

Phone: 510-594-8300   Lunch & dinner daily
Web: www.ohgane.com
Prices:

Lovers of Korean food in Oakland pop over to Ohgane during their midday break for a tasty bargain: the bounteous lunch buffet priced at around $10. Extensive and constantly refilled, the buffet features items from fried mackerel and *bi bim bap* to buckwheat noodles. Their barbecued meats, cooked over mesquite wood, are a specialty of the house and a favorite with the local Korean crowd. Accompaniments include soups, salads, noodles, rice, and assorted kimchi such as crunchy cubed daikon, fiery with vinegar, red chili paste, and garlic. Sliced fruit finishes off the meal.

In addition to the buffet, a large selection of à la carte dishes rounds out the menu at both lunch and dinner. Diners cook many of the meats themselves on the tabletop grills.

Oliveto

East Bay

 Italian

B3

5655 College Ave. (at Shafter Ave.), Oakland

Phone: 510-547-5356
Web: www.oliveto.com
Prices: $$

Lunch Mon – Fri
Dinner nightly

Occupying prime Rockridge real estate at the corner of the European-style gourmet hub known as Market Hall, Oliveto begins with a café offering an all-day menu and lovely perch to sip wine while awaiting a date. However, its true rustic Italian glory lies above you at day's end, up the winding staircase, in a dining room anchored by a wood-burning oven and Californian sensibilities.

While everyone here made reservations, the guests enjoying the coveted window seats overlooking Rockridge made them first. Nevertheless, there is plenty to enjoy in the elegantly secluded space serving Slow Food dishes of pastas and wild game in Northern Italian style. The menu may include the likes of spaghetti with goose cracklings or grilled wild boar sausages.

Picán ☺

Southern

B4

2295 Broadway (at 23rd St.), Oakland

Phone: 510-834-1000
Web: www.picanrestaurant.com
Prices: $$

Dinner nightly

Showcasing a menu of down-home favorites with a distinctively Californian touch and the largest bourbon portfolio in the Bay Area, it's no surprise this classy uptown newcomer is an instant success. Owner Michael LeBlanc, a New Orleans native and former executive at Polaroid, offers his vision of Southern-focused dining in a grand and lofty space done in warm shades of chocolate and copper.

A mouthwatering tour of the South sizzles in a delightful range of specialties from Atlanta transplant Chef Dean Dupuis, beginning with complimentary honeyed-buttered cornbread. The menu's temptations may go on to include grilled Berkshire pork chop with smoked pork belly, hoppin' john, chow chow, or Southern fried chicken with tableside truffled honey service.

Pizzaiolo

Pizza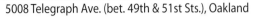

B3

5008 Telegraph Ave. (bet. 49th & 51st Sts.), Oakland

Phone: 510-652-4888
Web: www.pizzaiolooakland.com
Prices: $$

Dinner Mon – Sat

Couples and small groups populate Pizzaiolo's main room, while solo diners line the polished wood bar at this perennial East Bay favorite. All come for the blistered, thin crust pizzas piled with toppings that epitomize California. Combinations suit the seasons, as in a warm weather version touting summer squash with pounded parsley, garlic oil, and Grana Padano. As you would expect from an alumna of Chez Panisse, founder Charlie Hallowell updates his menu daily.

A peek into the open exhibition kitchen reveals the wood-burning oven that turns out those mesmerizing pies. Outside, two spacious patios are just right for playing a game of bocce by day, or basking in the moonlight come nightfall. Some say the staff has moxie; others call it attitude.

Prima

C1

1522 N. Main St. (bet. Bonanza St. & Lincoln Ave.), Walnut Creek

Italian

Phone: 925-935-7780
Web: www.primaristorante.com
Prices: $$$

Lunch Mon – Sat
Dinner nightly

At the heart of Walnut Creek's downtown shopping district sits this stalwart and its adjoining wine shop. Diners may choose from the front space anchored by a large wood-burning oven, a room next to the wine cellar, and a back bar area. Setting the sultry mood are skylights, fireplaces, and flickering candlelight. Outside, a large enclosed patio overlooks the sidewalk.

Prima remains a local favorite for Italian fare—with good reason. The market fresh menu focuses on the likes of asparagus, baby beets, and quail eggs combined winningly with Meyer lemon vinaigrette. This may be followed by tender sheets of spinach pasta filled with fresh herb-infused ground lamb. Exceptional and extensive, the wine list revels in Italian reds.

Riva Cucina

A2

Italian

800 Heinz Ave. (at 7th St.), Berkeley

Phone: 510-841-7482
Web: www.rivacucina.com
Prices: $$

Lunch Mon – Fri
Dinner Tue – Sat

Translated as the point where land and water meet, Riva marries Italian hospitality with Berkeley industrial chic. The interior echoes a former spice factory with exposed brick and ductwork, but owners Massi and Jennifer Boldrini have warmed the space with citrusy paint and velvet curtains. The Northern Italian fare is crafted with mostly local, organic ingredients—even the restaurant's patio is redolent with fresh herbs and vegetables. (The planters also serve as lessons in healthy eating for the nearby preschool.) If this sounds very California, it is; these influences can be seen in such dishes as free range chicken in Dijon, lemon, and herbs.

For a more authentic taste of Italy, opt for handmade pastas like tagliatelle with *ragù alla Bolognese*.

Rivoli

A1

Californian

1539 Solano Ave. (bet. Neilson St. & Peralta Ave.), Berkeley

Phone: 510-526-2542
Web: www.rivolirestaurant.com
Prices: $$

Dinner nightly

Recycled cork wainscoting and parchment lanterns lend an earthy, Japanese vibe to Rivoli, which backs up to a lush "secret" garden framed by dramatic windows. The potted plants, climbing ivy, and fronds are a pretty, natural contrast to the interior's white linen-topped tables, which provide a clean backdrop for northern Californian fare with a shake of Italian seasoning.

Start with a "napoleon" of butter-poached shrimp and crab flavored with Pernod lobster sauce and a crisp puff pastry garnish, then dive in deeper with a fillet of salmon grilled and perched atop potato and celery root purée. Save room for the light and tangy mascarpone cheesecake with shortbread cookie crust, sautéed apples and pears, and a drizzle of sweet rhubarb sauce.

Sahn Maru

Korean

 B3

4315 Telegraph Ave. (bet. 43rd & 44th Sts.), Oakland

Phone: 510-653-3366
Web: N/A
Prices: $$

Lunch & dinner Wed – Mon

The Korean translation of Sahn Maru, "top of the mountain," is more indicative of its status than location; of the neighboring Korean restaurants, it is pricier yet far more unique than the rest. Still, this quaint, homey, and casual spot impresses with quality ingredients and skillful recipes that cannot be found anywhere else—proof is in the black goat stew served in a stoneware pot with lovely, pungent dipping sauce. Further proof is the the fact that the majority of guests converse with the servers in Korean. *Banchan* such as kimchi and marinated mushrooms lead to heartier entrées like braised pork with dates and sweet potato.

As if to reinforce the authenticity, Korean TV plays in the background, and Korean tchotchkes adorn the walls.

Sasa

Japanese

 C1

1432 N. Main St. (bet. Cypress St. & Lincoln Ave.), Walnut Creek

Phone: 925-210-0188
Web: www.sasawc.com
Prices: $$

Lunch & dinner daily

In the 1910 brick building that once housed Walnut Creek's meat market, this Japanese *izakaya* is a trip to both another time and place. A trickling water feature greets you at the entry, which opens to a cozy lounge with lit stone tables. A mix of stone and wood warms the interior dining room, while sunlight drenches the patio in warmer months.

The tradition of Japanese hospitality is palpable, with several small plates and sake samplers to bolster conversation. Snack on fresh sushi from Tokyo's Tsukiji fish market or on such cooked items as seafood *kara-age*, a mixed fry of tender calamari, ice fish, asparagus, and jalapeños. At lunch, nosh on classic combos like chicken teriyaki with crunchy shrimp and vegetable tempura, sashimi, and miso soup.

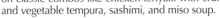

Sea Salt

Seafood

A2

2512 San Pablo Ave. (at Dwight Way), Berkeley

Phone: 510-883-1720
Web: www.seasaltrestaurant.com
Prices: $$

Lunch & dinner daily

A relaxed seaside vibe reigns at this Berkeley favorite where, thanks to a recent expansion and remodel, the look is cool with high ceilings, exposed brick walls, and aquatic hues throughout. At happy hour, slurp dollar oysters at the raw bar or alfresco on the large patio; stick around for late night bites till midnight.

From the semi-open kitchen comes an ocean-centric fare perhaps including calamari classically combined with plump butter beans in basil-almond pesto; grilled local sardines; and pan-seared Tsar Nicoulai sturgeon with pork and smoked black pepper aïoli. Regulars loyal to owners Haig and Cindy Krikorian (also of Lalime) relish seasonal desserts like subtly spiced pumpkin cheesecake with a gingerbread crust and licorice anglaise.

Sidebar

Gastropub

B4

542 Grand Ave. (bet. Euclid Ave. & MacArthur Blvd.), Oakland

Phone: 510-452-9500
Web: www.sidebar-oakland.com
Prices: $$

Lunch Mon – Fri
Dinner Mon – Sat

Amber pendant lamps, pumpkin walls, and a copper-topped bar cast a warm glow on Sidebar, the casually sophisticated Lake Merritt spot with Mediterranean verve. Friendly patrons crowd the communal table or grab at a seat at the counter for a view into the open kitchen, where upscale pub grub draws influence from Italy, France, and Spain. Run by husband-wife team Mark Drazek and Barbara Mulas, Sidebar is resplendent with homespun hospitality.

At lunch, opt for dressed up sandwiches or a crisp polenta cake with Manchego and Parmesan; dinner brings more wholesome fare like baked pastas and grilled Hawaiian swordfish. Late afternoon brings "in between" bites, like well-bred burgers topped with fried egg or Maytag blue, served with oven-baked fries.

SR24

American

East Bay

 B3

5179 Telegraph Ave. (at 51st. St.), Oakland

Phone: 510-655-9300   Lunch & dinner Mon — Sat
Web: www.sr24food.com
Prices: **$$**

Set adrift in an ocean of cars just off state route 24, SR24 is far more welcoming than its cramped Temescal address might suggest. Plush throw pillows dot a long wood banquette lit with dusky red chandeliers, and classic American films flicker above the tiny bar and hint at the chef's sustainable take on American cuisine.

At happy hour, Oakland hipsters swig PBR and nosh appetizers to a soundtrack of '80s punk. Meal times bring a daily pizza and a single plump *raviolo*—stuffed, perhaps, with goat cheese and leeks—that is simply irresistible. Of course, deep-fried pumpkin "jojos," served in a fryer basket lined with newsprint, are also tough to pass up. Culminate with a trio of petite pies—think all-American key lime, banana cream, and lemon meringue.

Tacubaya

Mexican

A2

1788 4th St. (bet. Hearst Ave. & Virginia St.), Berkeley

Phone: 510-525-5160   Lunch daily
Web: www.tacubaya.net   Dinner Wed — Mon
Prices: 🍪

Not your run-of-the-mill taqueria, Tacubaya occupies a corner along Berkeley's popular 4th Street shopping area. Line up at the counter and peruse the menu items written on the large chalkboard before placing an order. Tasty varieties of tacos, *tortas*, tamales, and tostadas headline at lunch. Better yet, come early—the place opens at 10:00 A.M. for *desayuno*—and start the day with chorizo and eggs, *chilaquiles*, and churros (Mexican doughnuts).

A sibling to Doña Tomás in Oakland, this colorful spot is painted in bright red, pink, orange, and blue shades. Take a seat at the long wood bar, and watch the cooks press fresh tortillas as they prepare your meal. Cookie jars and cake plates near the register display homey sweets to tempt you for dessert.

Tamarindo

Mexican

B4

468 8th St. (at Broadway), Oakland

Phone: 510-444-1944
Web: www.tamarindoantojeria.com
Prices:

Lunch & dinner Mon – Sat

One need not speak Spanish to know this cheerful *antojeria* is a "place of little cravings." Sunlight spills from the sidewalk patio into the cozy dining room where potted palms and a communal table lend a homey vibe. In this family run *cocina*, the house matriarch, Gloria Dominguez, sees to every last detail—from the affable mood and the authentic Mexican small plates, to the recently added tequila bar next door.

These *antojitos*, or "little whims," make it a fun spot to over order and share with friends. Start the fiesta with their popular guacamole and house-made *totopos*, then turn up the heat with *chilaquiles* in chipotle salsa; crisp quesadillas stuffed with squash blossoms, jack cheese, and roasted poblano; or the chef's fresh ceviche of the day.

Thai House

Thai

B5

254 Rose Ave. (bet. Diablo Rd. & Linda Mesa Ave.), Danville

Phone: 925-820-0635
Web: www.thaihousedanville.net
Prices:

Lunch Mon – Fri
Dinner nightly

Want to feel like you're dining in the home of your Thai friends? Visit Thai House, a quaint restaurant just off the beaten path in Danville. This retreat is sheltered within a tranquil cottage filled with blooming flowers, antique chandeliers, and hand-carved wood details. The smiling staff make guests feel warm and comfy in this appropriately named place.

How spicy can you take it? Hopefully a bit more than usual because they have a one- to four-star system, and the heat kicks in at level 2. The menu is huge and can be a bit overwhelming, but just ask for help and you'll be steered in the right direction. Some of the highlights include tender shrimp in a flavorful hot and sour soup, and juicy chicken simmered in coconut milk and *massaman* curry.

The Peasant & The Pear

International 🍴🍴

B5

267 Hartz Ave. (at Linda Mesa Ave.), Danville

Phone: 925-820-6611
Web: www.thepeasantandthepear.com
Prices: $$

Lunch Sun
Dinner Tue – Sun

Danville's The Peasant & The Pear nods to the original Parisian bistro, where simple slow cooked foods were served in a modest setting. Within these buttery walls adorned with a few framed photos and dark wood wainscoting, locals get their fill of double cut pork chops and Chianti-braised lamb shank with provolone polenta.

Like a traditional bistro, The Peasant & The Pear feels as familiar as the well-worn dining room of a favorite relative. The petite zinc bar is an easy perch to sip and gab with Chef/owner Rodney Worth as your charming host. When not in the kitchen, he can be found shooting the breeze with regulars who appreciate his American culinary accent in such dishes as prawns *a la plancha* and quesadilla with Brie and spiced-pear chutney.

Udupi Palace

Indian 🍴

B2

1901 University Ave. (at Martin Luther King Jr. Way), Berkeley

Phone: 510-843-6600
Web: www.udupipalaceca.com
Prices: 💰

Lunch & dinner daily

For those unfamiliar with the dosa, the sheer size of these thin, crispy, rice and lentil flour pancakes here is a wonder to behold. Flavorful fillings may include the likes of turmeric-spiced potatoes and creamy spinach. This vegetarian and vegan menu goes on to list Southern Indian specialties that dig much deeper than the standard potato- and pea-stuffed samosas. Breads are reinvented again when presented as puffed pillows of poori or *batura*, and paratha stuffed with a choice of ingredients.

Udupi Palace shies away from calorie-dense ghee, and the students from U.C. Berkeley who frequent this place appreciate the lighter fare that results—as well as the takeout option. Their location in the Mission gives popular competition a run for its money.

Uzen

B3

Japanese ✗

5415 College Ave. (bet. Hudson St. & Kales Ave.), Oakland

Phone: 510-654-7753
Web: N/A
Prices: $$

Lunch Mon – Fri
Dinner Mon – Sat

The ethos of Uzen lies in simplicity. Hardly bigger than a bento box, its decor relies on sunshine from the skylights by day and, at night, pendant lights glistening over fresh fish at the sushi bar. The slanted bar seats fewer than a dozen, still there are more guests than there are menu items. Expect just a few choices of uncomplicated seafood with a happy lack of gimmicky maki.

A couple of cooked teriyaki dishes at times disappoint, though steaming noodle bowls are a treat on cool Oakland nights. But truly, Uzen does sushi best. With deep pink *maguro* and hamachi right from the sea with a dab of wasabi, there is little left to be desired.

Just be sure to keep your eyes peeled in Rockridge: this triangular storefront is equally simple to miss.

Va de Vi

C1

Fusion ✗✗

1511 Mt. Diablo Blvd. (near Main St.), Walnut Creek

Phone: 925-979-0100
Web: www.vadevi.com
Prices: $$

Lunch & dinner daily

When denizens of Walnut Creek crave a light nosh paired with global wines, they head to the lusciously fresh Va de Vi—a hugely hip spot around town. With more than 16 different varietals available by the glass, the taste (3 ounces), or in flights of three, this über popular yet relaxed bistro's focus on wine is true to its Catalan moniker.

Dishes like the wonderfully flavored anise-scented duck confit, or a crispy *chile relleno* filled with melted *queso fresco*, sweet corn, and fresh cilantro, demonstrate the menu's international tone and scope.

An oak-barrel ceiling covers the long room, accented by wood cabinetry and tile floors. Outdoor seating lines the sidewalk, but the back patio is near majestic, with tables surrounding a venerable oak tree.

Vanessa's Bistro

Vietnamese ✕✕

A1

1715 Solano Ave. (at Tulare Ave.), Berkeley

Phone: 510-525-8300   Dinner Wed – Mon
Web: www.vanessasbistro.com
Prices: $$

Chef Vanessa Dang keeps a hands-on approach in her Berkeley kitchen, crafting an innovative and unique menu of French-accented Vietnamese tapas cuisine that is at once all her own. What appears on the plate stays true to its mouthwatering menu description, as in crisp, succulent honey marinated quail; flavorful and refreshing duck confit lettuce wraps; and perfectly fried salt and pepper prawns. For beverages, check out the bamboo-lined bar's cocktail selection (lychee martini, anyone?), and be sure end any meal with a Vietnamese coffee.

This is a hospitable place for sharing with friends. In fact, bring a large group with the hope of conquering more of the menu. In 2010 Walnut Creek denizens were the lucky recipients of Vanessa's Bistro 2.

vesu

International ✕✕

C1

1388 Locust St. (at Cypress St.), Walnut Creek

Phone: 510-280-8378   Dinner nightly
Web: www.vesurestaurant.com
Prices: $$

In posh Walnut Creek, vesu is a modern, worldly beauty. Her curved wood façade opens to a smart interior, where shades of gray, black, and white belie the restaurant's warmth. Slide into a plush leather banquette beneath filament bulbs and check into a global journey that dishes flavors of Latin America and the Orient.

Peruse the various small plates over an exotic cocktail: The jalapeño-infused "Hot Lips" is a spicy, boozy diversion. Share worthy snacks include heritage pork "cracklins" with black vinegar dipping sauce, while traditionally portioned entrées, such as a forest mushroom "hot pot," will sate the hearty eater. For dessert, don't miss the apricot *crostada* "pudding cake" with a quenelle of brown butter gelato and almond praline crumble.

Walnut Creek Yacht Club

C1

Seafood ✗✗

1555 Bonanza St. (at Locust St.), Walnut Creek

Phone: 925-944-3474
Web: www.walnutcreekyachtclub.com
Prices: $$$

Lunch & dinner Mon – Sat

Despite its lack of both water and yachts, the (landlocked) Walnut Creek Yacht Club does manage to serve some of the best seafood in the East Bay area. The chef's brother-in-law owns Osprey Seafood Company, guaranteeing that everything at this casual seafood favorite is superbly fresh.

Start with raw oysters or a pound of steamers while perusing the menu of expertly prepared, boldly seasoned, and simply great seafood. Creative combinations may include the silky, rich yellowfin tuna, seared and fanned over a refreshing jicama salad and chili-lime cream. Less ambitious palates can opt for the "Dockside" fish selection, where items are prepared to your liking with a choice of sauces and sides. Save room for the all-American peanut-butter chocolate tart.

Wood Tavern

B2

Californian ✗✗

6317 College Ave. (bet. Alcatraz Ave. & 63rd St.), Oakland

Phone: 510-654-6607
Web: www.woodtavern.net
Prices: $$

Lunch Mon – Sat
Dinner nightly

On a block aromatic with fresh produce and just-baked bread, Wood Tavern is like buttah—seriously, those of high cholesterol and crash diets need not apply. Artisan charcuterie and cheese boards are divine for soaking up a glass and you'll find many an Oakland foodie indulging in hearty happy hours. And why not? With lofty ceilings, sage walls, and streetfront windows, Wood Tavern is a quintessential up-market neighborhood joint.

Nab a seat at the chef's counter for a view of the open kitchen, where Mediterranean comfort is the fare du jour. Nosh on crisp pork belly "Lyonnaise" with poached egg and frisée or the favorite pan-roasted half chicken with fingerling potatoes and garlic confit. Save room for the Tavern's beloved root beer float.

Zabu Zabu

Japanese

 B2

1919 Addison St. (bet. Martin Luther King Jr. Way & Milvia St.), Berkeley

Phone:	510-848-9228	Lunch Mon – Fri
Web:	www.zabu-zabu.com	Dinner nightly
Prices:		

"All u can shabu-shabu" at Zabu Zabu may sound like a silly Seussian culinary come-on, but try telling that to the budget-conscious UC Berkeley smarty-pants who pack the place. Even if the hot pot meals and group dining concept are a bit novel for the intellectual locale, Zabu Zabu's wide array of thinly sliced meats, vegetables, and choice of seafood are undeniably alluring.

Each table is embedded with a burner where festive DIY diners dip their selections into steaming broth. The method is best suited to sharing among friends, but there are plenty of options for the single diner including briny seaweed salad with a refreshing crunch; creative sushi rolls; noodles; and small plates of golden brown pork *gyoza* with a sweet-spicy dipping sauce.

Zachary's Chicago Pizza

Pizza

 B3

5801 College Ave. (at Oak Grove Ave.), Oakland

Phone:	510-655-6385	Lunch & dinner daily
Web:	www.zacharys.com	
Prices:		

Every pie is delivered with pride at this employee-owned pizzeria, which recently celebrated its 25th anniversary. Lovers of Chicago-style deep-dish pizza don't mind waiting 30 to 40 minutes for the cheesy, gooey, calorie-laden Nirvana that is Zachary's signature stuffed pie. Many of the combinations of toppings that are slathered over tangy tomato sauce are also available on a thin cornmeal crust—though not the favorite spinach and mushroom.

Great for families, this no-frills place is always bustling (there are other locations in Berkeley and San Ramon). Consider calling ahead to place your order to cut down the wait for a table once you arrive. Another way to avoid the wait is to order a "half-baked" pizza to take away and cook in your oven at home.

Zatar

B2

Mediterranean 🍴

1981 Shattuck Ave. (bet. Berkeley Way & University Ave.), Berkeley

Phone: 510-841-1981
Web: www.zatarrestaurant.com
Prices: $$

Lunch Fri
Dinner Wed – Sat

Though it is set in Berkeley, Zatar transports diners to the Mediterranean with the colorful murals and collection of hand-painted ceramic platters that adorn the walls. Husband-and-wife team Waiel and Kelly Majid do Berkeley proud in their certified green business by harvesting vegetables from their organic garden, composting raw kitchen scraps, and feeding any vegetarian food remains to their laying hens.

Zatar's name refers to the traditional Middle Eastern spice mixture—made from sesame seeds, oregano, thyme, and sumac—used here in a variety of dishes. The dinner menu recites a litany of vegetable spreads and dolmas to start; grilled leg of lamb, pistachio and spring herb chicken, and sea bass with sesame-*harissa* sauce make satisfying entrées.

Your opinions are important to us. Please write to us at:
michelin.guides@ us.michelin.com

San Francisco Convention & Visitors Bureau photo by Phil Coblentz.

Marin

Marin

Journey north of the Golden Gate Bridge and entrée the sprawling Marin County. Draped along the breathtaking Highway 1, coastal climates hallow this region with abounding agricultural advantages. Snake your way through the ground, and find that food oases are spread out. But when fortunate to 'catch' them, expect fresh and luscious seafood, oysters, and cold beer...slurp! Farm-to-table cuisine is the par in North Bay and they boast an avalanche of local food purveyors.

Begin with the prodigious cheese chronicles. Visit the quaint and rustic **Cowgirl Creamery** where "cowgirls" make delicious, distinctive, and artisan cheeses. By producing only farmstead cheese, they help refine and define artisan cheesemaking...respect! Turn the leaf to cheese wizard **Laura Chenel**. Her baby, chevre, is a scrumptious goat cheese full of nuance and zing. For a more lush and heady blue cheese, dive into the divine 'Original Blue' at **Point Reyes Farmstead Cheese Co**. The cheese conte continues at **Adante Dairy**, where they churn out every type of cheese imaginable; and the fertile process at **Bellwether Farms** uses first-class milk to produce a quintessential cheese. These driving and enterprising cheesemakers live by *terroir*. Restaurants here follow the European standard and offer cheese before, or in lieu of a dessert course. The ideal is simply magical...end of story!

From tales of cheese to Ranch romances, **Niman Ranch** is at the crest. They tell the story of environmentally-sustainable farming, and provide the most wholesome and finest tasting meats to a sweeping nexus of establishments from farmers and grocery stores, to a plethora of stellar restaurants. Although petite in comparison, **Marin Sun Farms** is towering. A magnified butcher shop, their heart, hub, and soul lies in the production of local and natural-fed livestock for the hamlet.

Ravenous after hours of scenic driving and the ocean waft? Rest at **The Pelican Inn**. Their hearty stew of English country cooking and wide brew of the English 'bar' will leave you craving more of the bucolic. Carry on your hiatus and stroll into the olive tree orchard **McEvoy Ranch** a dairy farm reincarnated into olive oil utopia. The piece de resistance here is their rich and peppery extra virgin olive oil in the Tuscan style. Like most thirsty travelers, let desire lead you to **Three Twins Ice Cream**. A lick of their organically-produced creamy goodness will bring heaven to earth.

Waters off the coast here provide divers with exceptional hunting ground, and restaurants across the country seek the same including lush oysters, clams, and mussels. The difficulty in obtaining a hunting permit, as well as the inability to retrieve the large savory mollusks, makes red abalone a treasured species, especially in surrounding Asian restaurants. Yet, despite such hurdles, seafood is the norm at most restaurants in Marin County. One such gem is **Sam's Anchor Café** known for their superb seafood and glorious views. If seafood isn't your thing, entice your palate with authentic and sumptuous Puerto Rican flavors at **Sol Food**.

Marin County is known for its deluge of local organic ingredients carried in the numerous farmers' markets. The marriage of food and wine is best expressed at Sausalito's own "Tour de Cuisine" and The Marin County Tomato Festival. Magnificent Marin, with its panoramic views, is one of the most sought after locales and celebrities abound. Thus, some diners may have a touristy mien; however, it is undeniable that restaurants and chefs are blessed with easy access to the choicest food and local food agents.

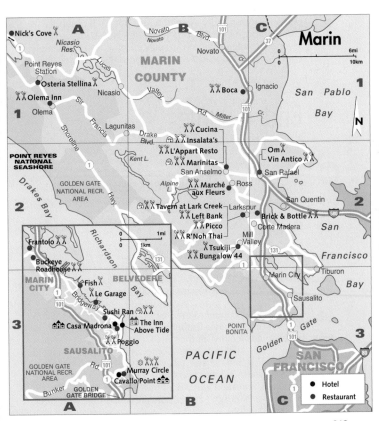

Boca

Steakhouse ✗✗

340 Ignacio Blvd. (bet. Alameda Del Prado & Enfrente Rd.), Novato

Phone: 415-883-0901
Web: www.bocasteak.com
Prices: $$

Lunch Mon – Fri
Dinner nightly

Decked with timber, rawhide, and leather—oh my!—Boca is just the kind of pared-down yet upscale steakhouse that casual Marinites might keep on their speed dial. And while reservations might be a good idea on Tuesday nights when bottle prices are slashed in half, Boca's interior brick walls and bovine art beg you to just come on down.

Helmed by George Morrone, a Jersey boy with Argentine roots, Boca dishes steaks and seafood with sultry Latin appeal. A grass-fed skirt steak is grilled over hardwood and hangs out with a crisp, salty-skinned baked potato. Its Latin flavor comes through in a trio of *chimichurries*. Non-beef eaters can savor the roasted shrimp with spicy cilantro butter, or sample empanadas and *bocadillos* with fabulous duck fat fries.

Brick & Bottle

American ✗✗

55 Tamal Vista Blvd. (bet. Council Crest Dr. & Chicksaw Ct.), Corte Madera

Phone: 415-924-3366
Web: www.brickandbottle.com
Prices: $$

Lunch & dinner daily

Chef Scott Howard has made his mark on a number of restaurants in the Bay Area, but he's finally landed at Brick & Bottle. This Marin native delivers his signature jazzed-up comfort food to this restaurant inside the Marketplace strip mall.

The gleaming copper-topped bar, open kitchen, and warm dining room decked in leather booths, dark wood, and leather paneling are a draw on their own, but looks aren't the only thing at this affable respite. Come armed with an appetite for crowning and creative takes on America's favorite foods, like the white cheddar and braised short rib grilled cheese sandwich. Smoked Gouda orzo mac and cheese is definitely not from a blue box, and pizzas are amped up with duck confit and onions.

Buckeye Roadhouse

American

A2

15 Shoreline Hwy. (west of Hwy. 101), Mill Valley

Phone: 415-331-2600   Lunch & dinner daily
Web: www.buckeyeroadhouse.com
Prices: $$

Forget spa food; there are few things more decadent than a succulent, grilled double-cut Berkshire pork chop after an invigorating stomp through the Marin Headlands. Hike over to Buckeye Roadhouse to savor one of the Bay Area's most delicious traditions, perhaps served with a side of creamy chive-mashed potatoes and tangy apricot chutney. Lighter dishes may include house-smoked chicken and local blue cheese jazzing up a salad with green apples, celery, and currants.

True, the Buckeye is located on a Highway 101 on-ramp, but the historic lodge charms with rich wood paneling, deep leather booths, and a roaring fire in the hearth. The sophisticated American fare, delivered by vested servers, pairs well with classic cocktails and enjoys a loyal following.

Bungalow 44

American

B2

44 E. Blithedale Ave. (at Sunnyside Ave.), Mill Valley

Phone: 415-381-2500   Dinner nightly
Web: www.bungalow44.com
Prices: $$

Little Mill Valley is resplendent with trendy boutiques, cute shops, and great restaurants like this local favorite. In the evening, the vibrant bar scene is jammed with young couples who leave the kids with the nanny and congregate here for a night out. Their lively conversations can overwhelm the space, so those seeking a quieter evening should shoot for a table in the tented dining area or in the main room past the open kitchen.

The menu plays with American dishes, so mouths water for cayenne-spiced onion rings and artichoke fritters with tarragon aïoli; while the signature kickin' fried chicken draws fans of its own. Salad aficionados feast on the smoked-duck Cobb; heartier appetites may favor a Kobe beef burger cooked on the wood-fired grill.

Cucina

B2

510 San Anselmo Ave. (at Tunstead Ave.), San Anselmo

Phone: 415-454-2942   Dinner Wed – Sun
Web: www.cucinarestaurantandwinebar.com
Prices: $$

For a case of the warm fuzzies along this quaint main strip of San Anselmo, try this charming and welcoming trattoria, courtesy of the folks behind Jackson-Fillmore in San Francisco.

Sunny walls, terra-cotta floors, and a blazing wood-burning oven warm the family-friendly dining room, where the staff greets regulars by name and everyone with a smile. Garlicky tomato bruschetta is a tasty start, compliments of the house. The ever-changing menu may feature rustic dishes such as chicken ravioli; or gnocchi with asparagus, fontina cheese, and white truffle oil. These homey preparations are simple, genuine, and uncomplicated. Kids love the pizza margherita, and few can turn down the tiramisu.

The wine bar at back is a perfect post-dinner spot.

Fish

A3

350 Harbor Dr. (off Bridgeway), Sausalito

Phone: 415-331-3474   Lunch & dinner daily
Web: www.331fish.com
Prices: $$

To sate a hankering for sustainable seafood and family-friendly feasts served in a bright and airy space overlooking a picturesque Sausalito harbor, go to Fish. Order at the counter and then pick your perch—broad window walls flood the interior with sunlight and aquatic views, while outdoor picnic tables beckon with toe-dipping proximity to the water.

This casual, cash only joint serves generous portions composed of organic ingredients to satisfy the whole family. Tangy homemade lemonade is a refreshing companion to grilled tilapia tacos with a mound of fresh cilantro or Anchor Steam-battered cod with rustic wedge "chips."

On your way out, check out the small fish market counter where various raw goods are just waiting to be cooked at home.

Frantoio

Italian ✗✗

A2

152 Shoreline Hwy. (Stinson Beach exit off Hwy. 101), Mill Valley

Phone: 415-289-5777
Web: www.frantoio.com
Prices: $$

Dinner nightly

What this restaurant lacks in location, it makes up for with its delicious Northern Italian cuisine. Frantoio, the Italian word for "olive press," makes its very own olive oil on-site in November and December. Two granite wheels, weighing in together at 3,200 pounds, are used to crush organic olives; you can watch the process behind a large window in back of the dining room.

On bustling nights, the high ceilings reverberate with the sounds of animated conversations over spreads like spinach gnocchi, pan-seared day boat scallops, or perhaps a wood oven-roasted leg of lamb. Olive oil, of course, finds its way into many of the dishes. For a finale, the moist chocolate tower cake wins raves, as does the tiramisu spiked with grappa.

Insalata's

Mediterranean ✗✗

B2

120 Sir Francis Drake Blvd. (at Barber Ave.), San Anselmo

Phone: 415-457-7700
Web: www.insalatas.com
Prices: $$

Lunch & dinner daily

In both name and spirit, this establishment pays homage to Chef Heidi Krahling's father, Italo Insalata. The ivy-covered exterior welcomes guests to an airy dining room filled with larger than life paintings of fruit—reminders that this restaurant exalts a familial love of cooking with fresh, local products.

Tastes of the Mediterranean sparkle in the chilled avocado and cucumber soup, or roasted honey-glazed pomegranate duck breast. Herbivores relish in the Middle Eastern-inspired vegetarian platter; this seasonal mélange, served with Turkish yogurt and couscous, regularly emerges from the open kitchen. A deli area in back offers a large selection of cooked and cold foods to go.

Insalata's Latin cousin, Marrinitas, is located just down the road.

217

L'Appart Resto

French ✗✗

636 San Anselmo Ave. (636 San Anselmo Ave.), San Anselmo

Phone: 415-256-9884
Web: www.lappartresto.com
Prices: $$

Lunch daily
Dinner Mon – Sat

Looking for *un peu de la France* in Marin County? Look no further than the charming L'Appart Resto. This little French café is quickly becoming a hugely loved and popular spot in the artsy town of San Anselmo.

It's light and airy inside, where the Gallic influence can be seen everywhere from the front patio enhanced with flower boxes to the brick accent walls, simple furnishings, and banquettes. Of course, the spacious patio is *the* place to be when the sun shines.

Like the amiable setting, the food is casual French to a tee. Simple, but well-prepared selections like smoked salmon *tartine*, drizzled with crème fraîche and served with a salad; or seared ahi tuna atop a chewy ciabatta roll prove that you don't need to be fancy to be flavorful.

Left Bank

French ✗✗

507 Magnolia Ave. (at Ward St.), Larkspur

Phone: 415-927-3331
Web: www.leftbank.com
Prices: $$

Lunch & dinner daily

In the 1913 Blue Rock Inn along the quaint main street of this storybook village, find this classic, spacious bistro—part of Roland Passot's (of La Folie fame) consolidated chain—featuring pressed-tin ceilings, a lengthy bar, and large colorful posters. This may be a far cry from the Rive Gauche in Paris, but French comfort food here stays as true to tradition as anywhere along St.-Germain-des-Près.

With northern Californian accents, the classic menu retains an intense focus on seasonal ingredients. Thus an artisanal tarte flambée is topped with glorious heirloom tomatoes and basil *pistou*; and *crevettes Provençales* uses Fisherman's Daughter Wild Sonora Coast shrimp, garlic, tomatoes, and olives, finished with Pernod and crisp, lacey frisée.

Le Garage

Mediterranean

A3

85 Liberty Ship Way #109, Sausalito

Phone: 415-332-5625
Web: www.legaragebistrosausalito.com
Prices: $$

Lunch daily
Dinner Mon – Sat

Don't let the fire engine red doors and servers clad in mechanic getups fool you. As the name suggests, Le Garage is an old carport with Provençal polish. Perched at the tip of Liberty Ship Way—picturesque with palms, bobbing dinghies, and a briny sea breeze—this is a feel-good bistro serving simple Mediterranean eats both inside and on a cozy heated patio. The owners hail from SF's Chez Papa, and recently opened L'Appart Resto in San Anselmo.

Start with mussels *du Mistral* or Loch Duart salmon atop sautéed green onions and Niçoise olives. Finish with Nutella panna cotta dusted with bittersweet chocolate, delight in the French staff, and conjure visions of an evening at water's edge in Nice.

Limited seating and irresistible charm make reservations a must.

Marché aux Fleurs

Mediterranean

B2

23 Ross Common (off Lagunitas Rd.), Ross

Phone: 415-925-9200
Web: www.marcheauxfleursrestaurant.com
Prices: $$$

Dinner Tue – Sat

You have not died and gone to the South of France, so don't let your taste buds fool you. It may seem like it, but you are still firmly planted in Marin County in the town of Ross. Named for the celebrated farmer's market in Provence, this French restaurant charms the pants off locals with its farm-fresh cuisine and attractive setting.

Aptly named, since the kitchen works exclusively with products sourced from local farmers, this place turns out consistently delicious, Mediterranean-inspired dishes. There's a little bit of cheer on every plate, whether it contains the bacon-wrapped and Grana cheese-stuffed Medjool dates; gnocchi with sweet white corn and foraged mushrooms; or local king salmon with Bloomsdale spinach and green garbanzo beans.

Marinitas

Latin American 🍴

B2

218 Sir Francis Drake Blvd. (bet. Bank St. & Tunstead Ave.), San Anselmo

Phone: 415-454-8900

Lunch & dinner daily

Web: www.marinitas.net

Prices: $$

Rustic antlers, a warm stone fireplace, and exposed wood beams crisscrossing lofty ceilings give Marinitas, named for *la gente* of Marin, a cozy cantina feel. Focusing on seasonal ingredients, Chef/owner Heidi Krahling cooks authentic Mexican and Latin American dishes just like *tia* used to make. Juicy carne asada tacos burst with flavor and vegetable enchiladas are bold and savory in green *pepian* mole. A dash of ancho chili spices up moist chocolate cake.

Upbeat Latin tunes encourage festive imbibing at the long, friendly bar, where the wine list features mostly South American varietals. Fresh squeezed juices and the house sweet-and-sour mix add zest to margaritas concocted with specialty tequilas. Homemade corn chips and salsas are on the house.

Nick's Cove

Seafood 🍴

A1

23240 Hwy. 1 (near Miller Park), Marshall

Phone: 415-663-1033

Lunch & dinner daily

Web: www.nickscove.com

Prices: $$$

You can arrive by car or by boat (there's a dock next door), but just get here. Nick's Cove overlooks Tomales Bay and is adjacent to Point Reyes National Seashore. It just doesn't get more picturesque than this and it's all within an hour from the city.

Great views, friendly service, and fresh fish are all on tap at this enjoyable spot. Every table has a view, but seats on the wraparound porch are the most coveted. As expected, it's seafood, seafood, seafood. Barbecue oysters, thick and yummy clam chowder, crispy local cod and chips, and Arnold Palmers with house-made lemonade and herbal tea to wash it all down make this place feel like vacation on a dinner plate.

Feel like extending the visit? Nick's Cove rents out its charming cottages too.

Murray Circle ✿

Californian XXX

A3

601 Murray Circle (at Fort Baker), Sausalito

Lunch & dinner daily

Phone: 415-339-4750
Web: www.murraycircle.com
Prices: $$$$

Kodiak Greenwood

Nestled into the Cavallo Point Lodge in Fort Baker, near the Marin County base of the Golden Gate Bridge, guests winding the meandering road that leads to Murray Circle might be tempted to think getting there is half the fun. With sweeping views of the Bay, cityscape, and the Golden Gate Bridge, the road trip to this restaurant is worth the gas money alone.

Thankfully, things just get better once you arrive. Housed in a historical three story Colonial building, Murray Circle shows off its early 19th century heritage with its meticulously stamped metal ceilings, leaded glass windows, and wagon wheel-inspired light fixtures.

And then there's the divine food. Chef Joseph Humphrey worked in Napa Valley before heading south, bringing his talent, creativity, and obsession with local, seasonal ingredients with him. A textbook example of the farm-to-table movement, Murray Circle's menu spins seasonally but may include dishes like pillowy potato gnocchi with freshly sautéed prawns, served over a warm salad of caramelized chestnut segments, Brussels sprouts, and creamy salsify purée; or tender slices of slow-roasted pork loin, with baby red abalone and black-eyed peas.

221

Olema Inn

A1

Californian ✗✗

10000 Sir Francis Drake Blvd. (at Hwy. 1), Olema

Phone: 415-663-9559   Lunch & dinner daily
Web: www.theolemainn.com
Prices: $$$

Situated just off the lushly wooded Sir Francis Drake Boulevard, the Olema Inn is a sweet, country-cut outpost ideal for lighthearted dining on a sunny day. Much like a ranch, the inn has a charming porch, and its dining room blurs onto a spacious shaded patio overlooking a grove of fruit trees and gardens. If you must sit inside, wood furnishings and white walls keep with the serene, bucolic vibe.

The relaxed, friendly atmosphere is conducive to easygoing Californian meals. Dishes may reveal a Niman Ranch burger with caramelized onions, smoky bacon, and pungent Point Reyes blue cheese; and flaky halibut perched on tender wax beans, baby potatoes, and roasted cherry tomatoes. Pair your burger with a glass of Pey-Marin pinot noir for a perfect couple.

Om

C2

Indian ✗

1518 4th St. (at E St.), San Rafael

Phone: 415-458-1779   Lunch & dinner Mon – Sat
Web: N/A
Prices:

Patrons at this family-run spot focus their attention on the food, knowing that all their senses will delight in Om's fragrant rice-based South Indian cuisine. They might begin with the bright red chicken *anjappa*—yummy cubes of boneless meat marinated in yogurt and spices, then deep-fried—and move on to *dosas*. Made from rice and lentil flour, dramatic dosas come sliced and easy to eat. A pancake-like *uttapam* is smaller and more delicate, studded with a variety of components. Sambar and coconut chutney accompany just about everything.

The all-you-can-eat lunch buffet is wildly popular, and bargain-priced for Marin County. If you have time to spare, order off the menu; the service will be slower, but the dishes will be worth waiting for.

Osteria Stellina

A1

11285 Hwy. 1 (at 3rd St.), Point Reyes Station

Phone: 415-663-9988   Lunch & dinner Wed – Mon
Web: www.osteriastellina.com
Prices: $$$

After slurping oysters at Tomales Bay, cruise down to Point Reyes Station and grab a seat at Osteria Stellina. As befits the tiny charmer of a rural town, Stellina has a rustic aspect and relaxed feel. The newcomer is luxuriating in a bit of buzz among area foodies, who come to relish the Italian eatery's local, organic, and seasonal offerings.

Order Hog Island oysters from the raw bar (if you haven't had enough already) or delight in eating your greens: braised collards, chard, and dandelion come with rosemary-infused cannellini beans and a drizzle of olive oil. Pasta lovers will appreciate perfectly al dente fusilli, while meat lovers can dig into a slow-cooked pork osso buco from Niman Ranch. Even if the pork doesn't wow, the mashers are a hit.

Picco

B2

320 Magnolia Ave. (at King St.), Larkspur

Phone: 415-924-0300   Dinner nightly
Web: www.restaurantpicco.com
Prices: $$

For the optimum Picco experience, dine with a group to relish the range of Chef/owner Bruce Hill's contemporary small plates menu. Amid the exposed rafters, brick, and redwood accents, dishes are graciously placed in the middle of the table to ease and encourage sharing. The menu changes frequently, and skillful preparations may include butter-roasted fennel with grain mustard vinaigrette; seasonal risotto made from scratch every half hour; or farro-dusted Chatham haddock with olive oil mashed potatoes and melted leeks. Marin Mondays' offerings highlight local products from area farms.

Those who prefer not to share can visit Pizzeria Picco next door for wood-fired, thin-crust pies; or Zero Zero in SoMa for pizza, pasta, and organic soft-serve ice cream.

Poggio

Marin

A3

Italian ✗✗

777 Bridgeway (at Bay St.), Sausalito

Phone: 415-332-7771
Web: www.poggiotrattoria.com
Prices: $$

Lunch & dinner daily

Just as its name translates, Poggio is indeed a "special hillside place." The Casa Madrona Hotel houses this Northern Italian restaurant, with its mahogany archways, plush booths, terra-cotta tiles, and buzzing bar. Dining here is pure joy in warmer months, when French doors swing open to offer views of the serene Sausalito yacht harbor across the street.

Having cooked in the Italian regions of Tuscany and Lombardy, Chef Peter McNee brings authenticity to a menu that incorporates the freshest Californian products. Offerings such as light lamb and ricotta meatballs; a salad of persimmon, cracked almonds, autumn lettuces, and goat cheese crostini; or spinach ricotta pillows with beef ragù are all enhanced by herbs and greens from their terraced garden.

R'Noh Thai

B2

Thai ✗✗

1000 Magnolia Ave. (bet. Frances & Murray Aves.), Larkspur

Phone: 415-925-0599
Web: N/A
Prices:

Lunch Mon – Sat
Dinner nightly

"Rising sun" is a fitting translation for this serene spot, where a calming vibe, cheery service, and robust flavors uplift and satisfy. The bi-level space rocks rich red walls with framed photos of water lilies on one level, and billowing white fabric under a sunny skylight on the other.

Get your caffeine fix with a creamy Thai iced coffee; when you're ready to chow, choose from any number of delightful curries, salads, soups, noodles, or rice dishes, many of which are prepared with local and organic products. Buttery *samosas* stuffed with chicken, peas, potatoes, and spices are full of flaky golden goodness (note the beautifully carved radish blossom on the side). A small back deck overlooking a marshland and bird sanctuary adds to the tranquility.

Sushi Ran

Japanese ✗✗

A3

107 Caledonia St. (bet. Pine & Turney Sts.), Sausalito

Phone: 415-332-3620
Web: www.sushiran.com
Prices: $$

Lunch Mon – Fri
Dinner nightly

These twin wood bungalows nestled on a picturesque main drag might appear to be pure Sausalito; but inside, the two houses (one open daily, the other reserved for dinner and private parties) echo loudly of Japan. A blonde wood sushi bar dominates the space accented with decorative ceramic plates, kanji brushed on dangling banners, and artistic florals that evoke the minimalist beauty that Japan has honed so well.

Of course, superior sushi and lunchtime bento boxes keep foodies coming back. Innovative maki and tempura reflect influences from California and the Pacific Rim. Don't miss the outstanding seven-piece omakase, which might highlight an excellent flying fish with ponzu and ginger or a torched barracuda with daikon radish and scallions.

Tavern at Lark Creek

American ✗✗

B2

234 Magnolia Ave. (at Madrone Ave.), Larkspur

Phone: 415-924-7766
Web: www.tavernatlarkcreek.com
Prices: $$

Lunch Sun
Dinner nightly

After twenty years in the restaurant business, the exterior of Tavern at Lark Creek is the same as it always was—a charming yellow Victorian shaded by majestic redwoods. Inside, however, it is much more casual with a pared-down interior and an eclectic menu highlighting comfort foods galore. The motto here could be "light on the wallet, full in the belly" with offerings like panko-crusted mac 'n' cheese croquettes served with cheddar fondue; and Spanish chorizo in the sweet company of a Mexican chocolate crostini.

While change is clear throughout, it remains a local favorite, with a bustling bar serving creative cocktails and value wines on tap. The patio outside is a great spot to enjoy this farm-to-table fare.

Tsukiji

B2

Japanese

24 Sunnyside Ave. (at Parkwood St.), Mill Valley

Phone: 415-383-1382
Web: www.tsukijisushimv.com
Prices: **$$$**

Lunch Tue – Fri
Dinner Tue – Sun

Enclosed by a serene porch in the heart of Mill Valley, Tsukiji is a peaceful sushi spot with outdoor dining in warmer months. Trickling waterfalls recall the Japanese ethos, but a large menu of boldly flavored sushi is more suited to the local American palate. Settle into one of two small dining rooms or pull up a chair at the bar—don't miss the à la carte specials for the day's freshest fish.

Formerly of Sausalito's acclaimed Sushi Ran, the chef turns out such specialty maki as spicy tempura tuna with lemon and red chili aïoli and a typical Dynamite roll of hamachi, albacore, salmon, and scallions. True sushi lovers will enjoy assorted nigiri: Silky toro, *hirame*, and hamachi are served with just rice, wasabi, and pickled ginger.

Vin Antico

C2

Italian

881 4th St. (bet. Cijos St. & Lootens Pl.), San Rafael

Phone: 415-454-4492
Web: www.vinantico.com
Prices: **$$**

Lunch Tue – Fri
Dinner Tue – Sun

With rich fabrics, noir leather, and plentiful candles ablaze, Vin Antico exudes big city sophistication in a small town setting. Perhaps inspired by Tuscany's venerable reputation for art, museum-quality works by local painters adorn the brick walls. Meanwhile, Northern Italian culinary masterpieces are crafted in the exhibition kitchen—solo diners should grab a seat at the chef's counter for maximum viewing pleasure. The atmosphere is laid-back and the meals are satisfying, with such gourmet ingredients as smoked duck breast and hazelnut-rolled goat cheese topping seasonal *pizzetine*.

Homemade pastas might include organic parsley fettuccine or leek- and lobster-stuffed ravioli. The small wine bar is a jovial spot for a glass of Italian *vino*.

Jay Graham

Peninsula

Peninsula

The Peninsula may not be internationally heralded for celebrity chefs and groundbreaking Californian cuisine but, with a diverse population rich in Asian cultures, the area is laden with neighborhood eateries and bountiful markets that appeal to locals craving authentic cuisines.

Those seeking a taste of the East can scoop up inexpensive seafood and links of *longaniza* alongside the Filipino population at Daly City's **Manila Oriental Market** or practice the art of chopstick wielding at one of the many Japanese sushi bars, ramen houses, and *izakaya*. Chinese food fans tickle their fancies with traditional sweets such as assorted moon cakes and yolk pastries at San Mateo's cash-only **Sheng Kee Bakery** or the **Kee Wah Bakery** in Milpitas, while sugar junkies of the Western variety chow authentic Danish pastries at Burlingame's **Copenhagen Bakery**, also known for its special occasion cakes.

In addition to harboring some of the Bay Area's most impressive Cantonese and dim sum houses, Millbrae is a lovely spot to raise one last toast to summer. The Millbrae Art & Wine Festival is a cornucopia of wicked fairground eats—think gooey cheesesteak, Cajun-style corndogs, and fennel-scented sausages. Wash it all down with a glass of wine or a cold microbrew, and kick up your heels to the tune of a local cover band.

If, however, it is cooking classes that you seek, head to **Draeger's Market** in San Mateo and sign up for "Indian Cooking Boot Camp" or a lesson in baking "Rustic Italian Breads." While there, also sample artisan and specialty goods and pick up some wine and cheese to go.

Speaking of take-home deliciousness, Half Moon Bay is a must-stop for insanely fresh, seasonal ingredients. Load up on gorgeous fruits and vegetables at the many roadside stands on Route 92 and don't miss the town's **Coastside Farmers Market** where you'll find local bounty including Harley Farms goat cheese, from nearby Pescadero, and organic eggs from **Green Oaks Creek Farm** up in the Santa Cruz Mountains.

If seafood is more your speed, **Barbara's Fish Trap**, just north in Princeton by the Sea, serves fish 'n' chips overlooking the harbor. And after all that healthy fish and produce, pork ribs are in order at last: Join locals and tourists at **Gorilla Barbeque**, which serves meaty combos and down-home sides out of a bright orange railroad car on Cabrillo Highway in Pacifica.

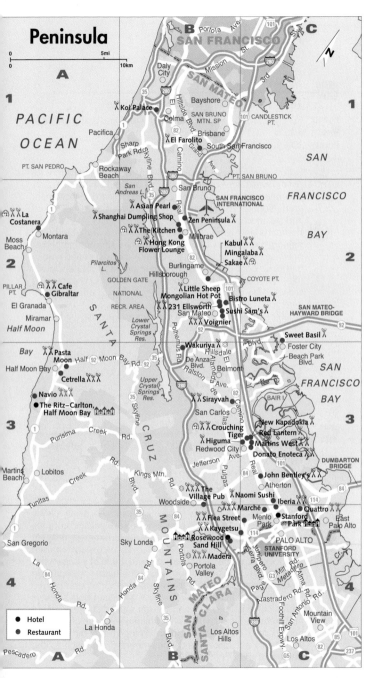

Peninsula

0 — 5mi
0 — 10km

A **B** **C**

PACIFIC OCEAN

SAN FRANCISCO

Daly City

Koi Palace

Pacifica

Colma

SAN BRUNO MTN. SP

Bayshore

CANDLESTICK PT.

El Farolito

Brisbane

South San Francisco

PT. SAN PEDRO

Rockaway Beach

Sharp Park Rd

Skyline Blvd

San Andreas L.

San Bruno

SAN FRANCISCO INTERNATIONAL

PT. SAN BRUNO

SAN FRANCISCO BAY

La Costanera

Moss Beach

Montara

Asian Pearl

Shanghai Dumpling Shop

Zen Peninsula

The Kitchen

Millbrae

Hong Kong Flower Lounge

Kabul

Mingalaba

Sakae

PILLAR PT.

Cafe Gibraltar

El Granada

Miramar

Half Moon

Pilarcitos L.

Hillsborough

GOLDEN GATE NATIONAL RECR. AREA

Burlingame

Little Sheep Mongolian Hot Pot

231 Ellsworth

San Mateo

COYOTE PT.

Bistro Luneta

Sushi Sam's

SAN MATEO-HAYWARD BRIDGE

Voignier

Bay

Pasta Moon

Half Moon Bay

Lower Crystal Springs Res.

Wakuriya

Half Moon Bay Rd.

Hillsdale

De Anza Blvd.

Belmont

Alameda de

Ralston

Foster City

Beach Park Blvd.

Sweet Basil

SAN FRANCISCO BAY

Cetrella

Navio

The Ritz-Carlton, Half Moon Bay

Upper Crystal Springs Res.

Skyline Blvd.

Sirayvah

San Carlos

BAIR I.

Purisima Creek

Kings Mtn. Rd.

Crouching Tiger

Higuma

Redwood City

New Kapadokia

Red Lantern

Martins West

Donato Enoteca

DUMBARTON BRIDGE

Martins Beach

Lobitos

Creek

Jefferson Ave.

John Bentley's

Atherton

The Village Pub

Naomi Sushi

Iberia

Quattro

Tunitas Creek

Woodside

Marché

Menlo Park

Stanford Park

East Palo Alto

San Gregorio

Flea Street

Kaygetsu

Rosewood Sand Hill

Madera

PALO ALTO

STANFORD UNIVERSITY

Sky Londa

Portola Valley

La Honda Rd.

Portola Rd.

Skyline Blvd.

Mountain View

La Honda

Los Altos Hills

280

Los Altos

Pescadero Rd.

SAN MATEO

SANTA CLARA

● Hotel
● Restaurant

231

Asian Pearl

B2

Chinese ✘

1671 El Camino Real (at Park Pl.), Millbrae

Phone:	650-616-8288
Web:	N/A
Prices:	

Lunch & dinner daily

Follow the Chinese locals and true dim sum devotees to Asian Pearl, take a number, and line up to sit among strangers in a banquet-style hall where the service can be downright gruff. Nonetheless, what awaits is a moveable feast of baked and steamed delights.

Pushcarts and whirling server trays bring a veritable buffet right to your table. Choose from steamed shrimp dumplings; pork spareribs with nutty sesame oil; sweet-and-smoky barbecue pork buns; and sticky rice noodle rolls deliciously filled with minced beef, ginger, and scallions. If something seems to be missing, just ask a server for a particular menu item and you shall receive it within minutes.

Asian Pearl also offers an à la carte menu for those who prefer to stick out from the crowd.

Bistro Luneta

B2

Filipino ✘

615 E. 3rd Ave. (bet. Eldorado & Delaware Sts.), San Mateo

Phone:	650-344-0041
Web:	www.bistroluneta.com
Prices:	

Lunch & dinner Tue – Sun

Although San Francisco boasts a wealth of Asian dining choices, Bistro Luneta will have adventurous palates dropping their *dan dan* noodles for the likes of *tapsilog*—a heaping plateful of thinly sliced marinated beef, fried garlic-infused sticky rice, crumbly salt-cured egg, and a side of vinegar jelly. Chef Emmanuel Santos, whose path to the kitchen was initiated by cooking alongside his great-grandmother, prepares unique specialties that include Manila-style barbecued pork skewers with pickled papaya; soy and vinegar sauced chicken adobo; and crème brûlée flavored with Philippine-grown coffee.

Served in a clean and modern dining room, the cooking here takes an upscale and contemporary approach to the traditional dishes of the Philippines.

Cafe Gibraltar

Mediterranean ✗✗

A2

425 Avenue Alhambra (at Palma St.), El Granada

Phone: 650-560-9039   Dinner Tue – Sun
Web: www.cafegibraltar.com
Prices: $$

Delicious and affordable are an enviable duo in today's restaurants, and this oceanside café is beloved by diners along the San Mateo County coast. Borrowing from the Middle East, the charming décor offers sunny colors and Moorish elements, as well as a wall of tented booths and low tables where guests sit cross-legged on cushions, North African-style.

Since 1998, Chef Jose Luis Ugalde has led this open kitchen, turning out a variety of fresh, flavorful, and aromatic dishes that hail from almost every country along the Mediterranean Sea. From Catalonia comes wood-roasted venison loin with a spiced sour cherry-red wine glaze; while Portuguese dishes may feature caplana with duck confit, potatoes, mushrooms, and onions in a *sofregit*-white wine sauce.

Cetrella

Mediterranean ✗✗✗

A3

845 Main St. (at Spruce St.), Half Moon Bay

Phone: 650-726-4090   Lunch Sun
Web: www.cetrella.com   Dinner Tue – Sun
Prices: $$$

If not for the striped banquettes and contemporary accents, Cetrella could be of another place and time—encapsulated in a gold-flecked Mediterranean villa with exposed wood beams peering down on private dining rooms, a glass-encased cheese pantry, wood-burning fireplace, and wine cellar with more than 400 international vintages.

Possibly the most stylish restaurant in Half Moon Bay, Cetrella also serves some of the town's most sophisticated fare. Its market-driven menu might feature red wine-braised lamb ravioli with bitter dandelion greens, or a perfectly seasoned fillet of salmon with bacon-wrapped potato gratin. Desserts fall short of Cetrella's savory accomplishments; opt instead for a nightcap on the terrace.

Crouching Tiger

Peninsula

C3   Chinese ✗✗

2644 Broadway St. (bet. El Camino Real & Perry St.), Redwood City

Phone: 650-298-8881   Lunch & dinner daily
Web: www.crouchingtigerrestaurant.com
Prices: 🍲

Crouching Tiger is Redwood City's hidden dragon, capable of breathing intense fires, as evidenced by the red chili pepper icons burning the menu. Sichuan lovers can scorch their palates and sweat their brows with a dish of *Xingjian* lamb, stir-fried with dried red chilis and sliced jalapeños.

It's hotter than Hades, but wickedly delicious. Sizzling dishes are also just as they sound, so shyer tongues are wise to opt for appealing Mandarin and Hunan classics like pot stickers, fried wontons, and sweet-and-sour pork.

Watery eyes and fiery tongues find solace in the cooling effects of trickling fountains and flat screens looping aquatic images and slideshows of mouthwatering delicacies. As hot as this food may be, note that the service can be cold.

Donato Enoteca

C3   Italian ✗✗

1041 Middlefield Rd. (bet. Jefferson Ave. & Main St.), Redwood City

Phone: 650-701-1000   Lunch & dinner daily
Web: www.donatoenoteca.com
Prices: $$

Executive Chef Donato Scotti brings the cuisine of his native Northern Italy to Redwood City. Located next to City Hall, the *enoteca* has proven itself to be a popular addition to the town's dining scene. When the weather is warm, locals love to eat on the alluring and spacious outdoor patio, shaded by umbrellas and decorated with potted plants. Indoor options include the chic but rustic main dining room and the lounge-like wine bar.

A bowl of house-made *agnolotti* stuffed with ground sausage and veal is as appealing as a wood-fired pizza or a sautéed Mediterranean sea bream. The menu changes weekly, according to the market and the chef's whim.

Compact and well-chosen, the wine list offers a solid range of Italian varietals.

El Farolito

 B1

Mexican ✗

394 Grand Ave. (at Maple Ave.), South San Francisco

Phone: 650-737-0138   Lunch & dinner daily
Web: www.elfarolitoinc.com
Prices: 💰💰

San Franciscans are welcome to wait in line at the Mission's location of El Farolito, where super burritos are a tasty cult classic. But, just minutes south of town, this San Francisco locale serves the same satisfying fare to a local working class that is happy to walk right up to the counter and order their hearts' content.

Cleaner than most of El Farolito's outposts, the dining room (if you can call it that) is all about cheap, yummy eats. If the massive grilled chicken burrito packed with black beans, rice, and cheese isn't enough to satiate you, take a gander at shrimp ceviche tostadas; slightly spicy green chile pork tacos; or crispy *taquitos* with smoky carne asada. Cinnamon *horchata* is a sweet addition to a meal—never mind the Styrofoam cup.

Flea Street

 C4

Californian ✗✗

3607 Alameda de las Pulgas (at Avy Ave.), Menlo Park

Phone: 650-854-1226   Dinner Tue – Sun
Web: www.cooleatz.com
Prices: $$$

 This classy café is Menlo Park's darling, though its name may not spark the appetite. The white, cottage-like restaurant sits on a slope, so there are also several tiers of dining space inside, offering an intimate ambience equally conducive to celebrating a special occasion or staging a first date. Outside, a pretty patio provides alfresco dining for its droves of loyal regulars on warm days.

Savory courses are highlights here. Locally grown, seasonal, and primarily organic products lend their simple clean flavors to the Californian cuisine, perhaps featuring Dungeness crab sweet potato cake with roasted cauliflower and crispy capers; or pasture-raised chicken with delicata squash, *guanciale*, raisins, and chickpeas in a zinfandel beurre blanc.

Higuma

C3

540 El Camino Real (bet. Hopkins & Whipple Aves.), Redwood City

Phone: 650-369-3240   Lunch Mon – Fri
Web: N/A   Dinner Mon – Sat
Prices:

A meal in this popular neighborhood sushi spot housed in a cute little bungalow on El Camino Real is a straightforward affair, and one that caters to midday crowds of Japanese businessmen and the local high-tech and medical industry. Friendly service, reasonable prices, and good ingredients ensure that the place stays packed for weekday lunch.

The chef's sushi assortment emerges as an ungarnished array of neat packages of fresh fish placed atop rice. A large bowl of fragrant and spicy miso ramen makes a fine meal on its own.

Seats at the tiny sushi bar are at a premium here, but small tables that huddle close together are also available in the dining room. Echoing the restaurant's name, images of Japanese brown bears (*higuma*) decorate the space.

Hong Kong Flower Lounge

B2

51 Millbrae Ave. (at El Camino Real), Millbrae

Phone: 650-692-6666   Lunch & dinner daily
Web: N/A
Prices:

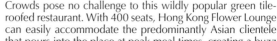

Crowds pose no challenge to this wildly popular green tile-roofed restaurant. With 400 seats, Hong Kong Flower Lounge can easily accommodate the predominantly Asian clientele that pours into the place at peak meal times, creating a buzz that suggests the city for which the lounge is named.

Dim sum is the main attraction for lunch. Servers bearing trays and rolling carts stream out of the kitchen with a parade of jewel-like treats: potstickers; fluffy dumplings filled with the likes of barbecued pork or steamed shrimp; or Chinese broccoli steamed tableside. Eager and adventurous foodies are rewarded with items like marinated duck tongue; jellyfish in chili bean sauce; or cold chicken feet. Look for servers in pink jackets if you don't speak Cantonese.

Iberia

Spanish 🍴🍴

C4

1026 Alma St. (at Ravenswood St.), Menlo Park

Phone: 650-325-8981
Web: www.iberiarestaurant.com
Prices: $$

Lunch Mon – Sat
Dinner nightly

Charmingly housed in a cozy bungalow on a quiet street across from the train station, Iberia celebrates the best of bold Spanish cuisine. From the avocado relleno stuffed with bay shrimp to crab *buñuelos* in a roasted pepper-hazelnut sauce, offerings showcase a large selection of tapas, ever-changing specials, and more ambitious seafood entrées. Once you're comfortably seated, look forward to an array of delightful delicacies like *paella típica*, espalda *de cerdo* (pork shoulder), or *tarta de Santiago* (orange-almond torte).

The tree-shaded patio makes a perfect spot to sip a glass of the house sangria on a warm day. Next door, The Rock of Gibraltar Comestibles sells quality Spanish ingredients, as well as a sampling of dishes to go.

John Bentley's

Contemporary 🍴🍴

C3

2915 El Camino Real (bet. Berkshire Ave. & E. Selby Ln.), Redwood City

Phone: 650-365-7777
Web: www.johnbentleys.com
Prices: $$$

Lunch Mon – Fri
Dinner Mon – Sat

There's no mistaking a genuine local favorite, and John Bentley's is one such place. Find all the elements necessary to convert patrons into regulars: a trellised entrance entangled with vines; laid-back ambience; comfortable booths; rustic design; and American fare that is consistently good. Expect a working crowd at lunch and a mix of residents for dinner.

To start, John Bentley's serves an ample selection of California-fresh salads and Dungeness crab, in season. Eggplant and portobello mushroom ravioli, cooked al dente with balsamic reduction, is also an exciting first course. Hungrier guests can sink their teeth into a double-cut pork chop, flavorful though perhaps a touch dry, served with a rustic mash of Yukon gold potatoes and haricots verts.

Kabul

Afghan

B2

1101 Burlingame Ave. (at California Dr.), Burlingame

Phone: 650-343-2075 — Lunch & dinner daily
Web: www.kabulcuisine.com
Prices: $$

Sister to the original location in San Carlos, this pleasant Burlingame favorite offers a true taste of Afghanistan amid dark wood furnishings, colorful tapestries, and windowed walls that stream in sunlight. The décor is simple and the service informal, but this local spot is filled with surprises.

The home-style menu may include dishes of *sambosa-e-ghoushti*—fried pastries stuffed with a tender mix of ground lamb and chickpeas infused with garlic and spices. Topped with garlic yogurt, the large, sweet, and silky chunks of pumpkin in *challaw kadu* may actually melt in your mouth. The *kabal-e-gousfand*, skewers of tender marinated lamb, is charbroiled and perfectly completed with fragrant basmati rice and fluffy flatbread sprinkled with poppy seeds.

Kaygetsu

Japanese

B C4

325 Sharon Park Dr. (at Sand Hill Rd.), Menlo Park

Phone: 650-234-1084 — Lunch Tue – Fri
Web: www.kaygetsu.com — Dinner Tue – Sun
Prices: $$$

Owned by sushi Chef Toshio Sakuma and his wife, Keiko, this "beautiful moon" (as the name translates from Japanese) hangs on the corner of the Sharon Heights shopping center in Menlo Park. Here, the kaiseki menu shines amid the variety of sushi, nigiri, and maki. Harmonious balance of flavors, skillful preparations, and artistry characterize this traditional meal, which has origins in the Zen tea ceremony.

Those who indulge in this option should plan to spend two to three hours feasting on a series of small sensuous courses; though a new abbreviated menu is available for their ever-popular lunch. Delicate items range from fresh tuna sashimi to stewed Japanese turnip and pumpkin in dashi, and arrive in an array of pretty platters, baskets, and plates.

Peninsula

The Kitchen

Chinese XX

B2

279 El Camino Real (at La Cruz Ave.), Millbrae

Phone: 650-692-9688
Web: N/A
Prices: 💰

Lunch & dinner daily

Parked in a largely Asian locale, The Kitchen unfolds top-notch dim sum and delicacy-laden Cantonese specialties to a knowledgeable Asian crowd. Step into their professionally-run dining room freckled with large tables and fish tanks, then merely take a whiff. Rest assured, you will want to return with many friends and family to sample their abounding offerings.

Let the Cantonese chronicles at lunch begin with a tasting from the well-versed chef's classic or inventive dim sum such as chive dumplings; a cilantro bean curd salad; and a giant shark fin soup dumpling. Or turn a leaf to the sizeable dinner menu—think of wasabi-tossed chicken with pork belly or sautéed squab with foie gras and shredded lettuce—and let your palate absorb the rest.

Koi Palace

Chinese X

B1

365 Gellert Blvd. (bet. Hickey & Serramonte Blvds.), Daly City

Phone: 650-992-9000
Web: www.koipalace.com
Prices: 💰

Lunch & dinner daily

Koi Palace can seat 400 guests, and the ample parking lot often overflows with cars having to be stationed on the surrounding streets. This phenomenon bespeaks the restaurant's popularity—mostly with a local Chinese clientele who flock here for dim sum at appealing prices.

Walk through the moon gate to spot aquarium tanks swimming with the day's catch; koi ponds in the dining room add aesthetic appeal for grown-ups and provide little ones with entertainment. Try to snag a seat on an aisle for the best service. From here, you can more easily hail the servers who hurry by with a staggering array of items. Offerings include everything from familiar *siu mai* with diced mushrooms or barbecued pork, to exotic fare like poached queen's clam and soya duck tongue.

La Costanera

A2

8150 Cabrillo Hwy. (bet. 1st & 2nd Sts.), Montara

Phone: 650-728-1600   Dinner Tue – Sun
Web: www.lacostanerarestaurant.com
Prices: $$$

Without taking a chilly plunge into the crashing tide, La Costanera is as close as you can come to the picturesque Pacific Ocean. This beachcomber's paradise has panoramic views of the sea and nods to its coastal digs with a natty nautical motif. Seashells encrust low-lit sconces and boat sails billow on the walls. But where the thematic effect is discreet, contemporary serenity prevails.

La Costanera's wall of windows allows moonlight to shine on Peruvian surf-and-turf dinners. Look forward to fresh ceviche of calamari, octopus, and prawns that may be doused in a pool of spicy aji and studded with crisp corn; tender lamb chops made delicious with herbaceous *huacatay* sauce; and exotic pisco cocktails that refreshingly wash it all down.

Little Sheep Mongolian Hot Pot

B2

215 S. Ellsworth Ave. (bet. 2nd & 3rd Sts.), San Mateo

Phone: 650-343-2566   Lunch & dinner daily
Web: www.littlesheephotpot.com
Prices: $$

You could hop a flight to China, where Little Sheep Mongolian Hot Pot's parent company is based. Or, you could jaunt to San Mateo for lunch and be back in the city for afternoon tea. While quite contemporary, Little Sheep is also reminiscent of its home country with a trickling water fountain, stalks of bamboo, and grassy swaths of paint.

Piquant spices waft from each table where a cauldron of simmering broth sits on a small warming burner: dining here is a do-it-yourself affair. The adventure begins with a high-quality aromatic broth, either original or spicy, but gets exciting when bountiful platters of ingredients arrive. Choose from sliced raw meats, assorted fresh vegetables, and herbs, then toss it all in for a fragrant, group-friendly feast.

Madera

Contemporary XXX

B4

2825 Sand Hill Rd. (at I-280), Menlo Park

Phone: 650-561-1540   Lunch & dinner daily
Web: www.maderasandhill.com
Prices: $$$

Rosewood Hotels & Resorts

Nestled into the sprawling grounds of Rosewood Sand Hill resort in Menlo Park, Madera transports you into a relaxed otherworld from the minute you turn into the beautiful property.

Once inside, you'll find an airy, elegant dining room fitted out in earthy shades, replete with a soaring vaulted ceiling; a pleasantly humming open kitchen; and an outside dining area with handsome wood tables and pretty yellow awnings that retract to catch those wicked sunsets over the Santa Cruz Mountains.

Chef Peter Rudolph's Californian menu is a seasonal affair, though his devotion to small, local farms and clever use of his wood-fired grill (Madera means "fire" in Spanish) is worth extra mention. Embark with a plate of pristine Steelhead trout *crudo*, lovingly wrapped around asparagus tips and paired with shaved Delta asparagus, sorrel leaves, creamy avocado purée, crunchy watermelon radish, and sauce gribiche; and then move on to tender, butter-poached lobster tail paired with subtly sweet sunchoke purée, crispy pan-fried veal sweetbreads, and wild mushroom salad; or succulent, pan-roasted duck breast fanned over wilted black kale, braised pine nuts, and candied kumquat slices.

Marché

Contemporary

898 Santa Cruz Ave. (at University Dr.), Menlo Park

Phone: 650-324-9092   Dinner Tue – Sat
Web: www.restaurantmarche.com
Prices: $$$

This spot continues to be a good choice for fine dining in downtown Menlo Park. Fresh products from local farms harmonize with interesting flavor combinations on Marché's seasonal menu. Mediterranean elements spark the contemporary fare in homemade ricotta gnocchi with blue prawns, and an organic chicken breast plated with braised leg cannelloni and pipérade. Attention to detail pops out in a pancetta-wrapped pork loin and fresh sausage served atop a bed of sweet corn and caramelized onion salsa, with a purée of ginger-infused peaches.

Service is discreet and professional in the dining room, sleek in shades of chocolate brown, with smoked mirrors lining one wall. On the opposite side of the room, large windows provide great views into the kitchen.

Martins West

Gastropub

831 Main St. (bet. Broadway & Stambaugh Sts.), Redwood City

Phone: 650-366-4366   Lunch Tue – Sat
Web: www.martinswestgp.com   Dinner Mon – Sat
Prices: $$

Turn of the century columns and exposed brick walls hint at the history of this Redwood City locale. Built in 1896, the Alhambra saw rowdier days as a theater and saloon frequented by outlaw Wyatt Earp. Today, the dove grey dining room and sophisticated art, befit its status as a stylish gastropub. Still, Martins West tips a hat to the venue's merrymaking tradition with Scottish fare and an array of Scotch worthy of its name and history.

Sample traditional tastes in dishes such as tiny Scotch-style quail eggs with a zesty sausage-breadcrumb crust; rich terrines of pheasant; or flaky, ale-battered fish and chips doused in malt vinegar. Then, consider drinking your dessert—the spiked apple cider with Drambuie cream tops the seasonal offerings.

Peninsula

Mingalaba

Asian

B2

1213 Burlingame Ave. (bet. Lorton Ave. & Park Rd.), Burlingame

Phone: 650-343-3228

Lunch & dinner daily

Web: www.mingalabarestaurant.com

Prices: 💰💰

Bamboo wainscoting, modern lighting, and red-gold walls dotted with Asian artifacts add a touch of pretty to this quick-service hot spot in the center of Burlingame. Popular among local business types and afternoon shoppers, a table at Mingalaba is well worth the wait—provided you opt for the bold Burmese fare in lieu of forgettable Mandarin menu options.

Begin with light and crispy vegetarian *samusa* stuffed with potatoes and onion, or an interesting tea leaf salad—mounds of fresh ingredients are mixed at the table to an earthy, crunchy finish. Burmese-style curries are vividly flavored and the black pepper soup with a fresh fish fillet is an unusual delight. Cool down at dessert with a mildly sweet mango pudding served in a leaf-shaped bowl.

Naomi Sushi

Japanese

C3

1328 El Camino Real (bet. Glenwood & Oak Grove Aves.), Menlo Park

Phone: 650-321-6902

Lunch Tue – Fri

Web: www.naomisushi.com

Dinner Tue – Sun

Prices: $$

Set on bustling El Camino Real, this modest Menlo Park sushi grill may have an unassuming façade, but duck inside for very well-prepared sushi and sashimi of true quality. The sushi bar, which welcomes patrons as they enter, is the place to park yourself and to enjoy the traditional, reasonably priced omakase offerings. Elsewhere on the menu, Japanese entrées exhibit a clear Californian twist, as in the poached pork loin with shiitake mushrooms, or grilled sea bream with fresh vegetables. Daily specials are worth investigating, as are the sake tastings that change each week.

Two dining rooms recall a rustic seaside tavern, decorated with fishing paraphernalia, a mounted game fish, and murals of the sea. Restaurant guests enjoy private parking.

Navio

Californian

A3

1 Miramontes Point Rd. (at Hwy. 1), Half Moon Bay

Phone: 650-712-7040
Web: www.ritzcarlton.com
Prices: $$$$

Lunch Sat – Sun
Dinner nightly

From its stunning bluff above the crashing Pacific surf, this sleek restaurant (in the Ritz-Carlton Half Moon Bay) takes every advantage of its breathtaking location. Although its space is well-designed with vaulted ceilings and abundant windows, watching the waves roll in over the rocky coast clearly trumps all—especially at sunset.

Such natural splendor makes it difficult to focus on the food, but this contemporary fare is worthy of its setting. The concise, widely appealing seafood and meat preparations may include pan-roasted Grimaud duck breast with black forbidden rice and Asian pear, or short ribs braised for 48 hours on a mascarpone polenta with trumpet mushrooms and Medjool dates.

The international wine list focuses on Californian varietals.

New Kapadokia

Turkish

C3

2399 Broadway St. (at Winslow St.), Redwood City

Phone: 650-368-5500
Web: www.newkapadokia.com
Prices:

Lunch Tue – Fri
Dinner Tue – Sun

Named for Turkey's region known for ancient underground cities, New Kapadokia is perhaps the most genuine culinary experience this side of the Aegean Sea. Unlike the average Turkish eatery, this family-run restaurant is proud of its heritage and serves only authentic recipes, many of which were handed down from the chef's mother and grandmother. The uninitiated should rely on the knowledgeable staff and the trays of starters or desserts they bring to you to assist with ordering. Kebabs are wrapped in *lavash* and served with garlicky yogurt, sumac, and spicy sauce, while platters teem with lamb and vegetable stew.

Say hello to gracious owner Celal Alpay, and don't miss the spinning Turkish coffee—its service here is quite the performance!

Pasta Moon

 Italian

A3

315 Main St. (at Mill St.), Half Moon Bay

Phone: 650-726-5125
Web: www.pastamoon.com
Prices: $$

Lunch & dinner daily

 Pasta Moon offers a taste of Italy to the fog-shrouded hamlet of Half Moon Bay, which feels one part Mayberry, one part Beachtown, USA. Regulars have been flocking here for some 20 years for house-made, hand-cut pasta and an exclusively Italian wine list, with many available by the glass. Tourists are learning that both the food and the town—with its quaint tapestry of Southwestern adobe and New England-style façades—merit the winding, half-hour drive down Highway 1 from San Francisco.

Inside Pasta Moon, find cocoa-colored walls, packed tables, and heady aromas of garlic and spices in the air. Frequently changing offerings like lace-battered local pumpkin with spiced apple butter and pumpkin seed pesto capture the essence of each season.

Quattro

 Italian

C4

2050 University Ave. (at I-101), East Palo Alto

Phone: 650-566-1200
Web: www.fourseasons.com/siliconvalley
Prices: $$$

Lunch & dinner daily

 Inside the Four Seasons Silicon Valley, Quattro is inspired by the constant revolution of nature. A garden patio is ideal for warmer months while a roaring fireplace in the lounge wards off a winter chill. In the main dining room, high ceilings embrace glowing natural light while plush chairs invite business travelers and posh couples to get cozy—frosted glass panels lend extra privacy to the banquettes.

A casually refined clientele nibbles focaccia with truffled ricotta while perusing the seasonal menu. Expect such contemporary Italian fare as prosciutto-wrapped quail with saffron-poached kumquats in foie gras sauce; *pizzocheri*, flat buckwheat pasta with Taleggio and earthy mushrooms; and expertly roasted duck breast with apples and parsnip purée.

Peninsula

Red Lantern

 C3

808 Winslow St. (at Broadway St.), Redwood City

Phone: 650-369-5483
Web: www.redlanternrwc.com
Prices: $$

Lunch Mon – Fri
Dinner nightly

 Housed in the heart of Redwood City, homey Red Lantern is a stylish melting pot of Asian and Southeast Asian art and cuisine. Inside, soaring ceilings are adorned with dramatic red silk lanterns, and carved wooden artifacts decorate the main dining room where the aura is casual and service informal. Art aside, it is their unique, home-style cooking that draws a medley of business folk, families, and locals who know the food is as consistent as it is delicious.

The pan-Asian menu offers something for everyone. Pork and shrimp dumplings with spicy Sichuan sauce are the perfect prelude to a refreshingly cool salad of green papaya and prawns tossed in mild fish sauce vinaigrette, or perhaps cambogee beef (cubes of beef with lemongrass and galangal).

Sakae

 B2

243 California Dr. (at Highland Ave.), Burlingame

Phone: 650-348-4064
Web: www.sakaesushi.com
Prices: $$

Lunch & dinner daily

Get to know this sushi-ya and Japanese grill, and you will fall in love with it. The contemporary, popular dining room offers plentiful wood tables and sits amid numerous car dealerships, with abundant parking. There are additional seats at the (exclusively) sushi counter, but beware of a $20 minimum and ordering cooked items (like the superb egg custard, *chawan mushi*) from the broad menu is forbidden.

The real lure of Sakae is fresh, top quality fish sourced from the U.S. and Japan. Expect deep red and silky tuna, or sweet, buttery salmon among the offerings. While some maki seem bulky, the seven-course sushi omakase best highlights the seafood, which might include seared fluke fin and amberjack. This may help forgive their uneven service.

Shanghai Dumpling Shop

Chinese

 B2

455 Broadway (bet. Hillcrest & Taylor Blvds.), Millbrae

Phone: 650-697-0682
Web: N/A
Prices: 💰💰

Lunch & dinner daily

Neat red lettering on a tall pale façade spells out the name in both Chinese and English, while inside white tiled floors topped with plain wooden tables set up a no frills vibe. Plumb in the heart of Millbrae amidst a quaint street of shops and businesses, Shanghai Dumpling Shop is a must stop for authentic Shanghainese cuisine. It won't take much persuasion to start with a bowl of savory steamed soup dumplings—*xiao long bao*—just check out the selections of your fellow diners for evidence of the dish's popularity. Move on to one of the tasty Shanghai-style braises—"lion head" meatball, pork rump, fish tail, or gluten puff perhaps?

For a fantastic finale, the sesame rice dumplings with rice wine soup are a lovely sweet and sticky creation.

Sirayvah

Thai

B3

366 El Camino Real (bet. Bush & Oak Sts.), San Carlos

Phone: 650-637-1500
Web: www.sirayvahorganicthaicuisine.com
Prices: $$

Lunch Mon – Fri
Dinner nightly

Sirayvah is a vibrant departure from the ho-hum Thai joints where sauces and spices overwhelm. In this tiny bungalow, homegrown organic herbs and vegetables, free-range and hormone-free meats, and wild-caught fish are allowed to shine in fresh, light, and buoyant preparations. Dishes may be spicy upon request.

The understated, contemporary dining room dressed in dark wood and tan is a relaxed environment for lunch or dinner. If you judge a restaurant by its soup, Sirayvah's inspired interpretation does not disappoint: a *kabocha* pumpkin purée with bits of mixed vegetables and sweet coconut milk is velvety and delicious. Crunchy green beans and bell peppers, as well as delightfully nutty rice, are a surprising highlight of tender *prik khing* chicken.

247

Peninsula

Sushi Sam's

Japanese ✗

B2

218 E. 3rd Ave. (bet. B St. & Ellsworth Ave.), San Mateo

Phone: 650-344-0888   Lunch & dinner Tue – Sat
Web: www.sushisams.com
Prices: $$

Do not be fooled by the no-frills dining space and nondescript exterior—this San Mateo sushi spot is a treasure. Forget the lunchtime bento box and opt for the luscious omakase, which promises that this very good little sushi-ya understands excellence.

On this menu, the chef prepares generous slices of their freshest fish, with garnishes that enhance natural flavors. Expect succulent, sweet blue shrimp; silky butterfish topped with tangy pickled daikon and scallions; ponzu-topped wild Japanese yellowtail; or sweet lobster nigiri with creamy tobiko mayo and toasted, sliced almonds. Dessert may include mild and creamy *teh kuan yin* panna cotta, delicately embellished with chrysanthemum syrup, poached goji berries, crispy puffed brown rice, and *mochi*.

Sweet Basil

Thai ✗

C2

1473 Beach Park Blvd. (at Marlin Ave.), Foster City

Phone: 650-212-5788   Lunch & dinner daily
Web: www.sweetbasilfoster.com
Prices:

While veggie lovers may head to Basil Cha Cha, the vegetarian sister restaurant in Sweet Basil's former neighboring locale, this new address for the Foster City favorite is now serving the same (often meaty) fare in a refreshed and spruced up space. Mod red light fixtures, Thai artefacts, and lacquered chairs dress the interior and may be new, but rest assured as the bamboo tabletops will still be heaped with Sweet Basil's beautifully plated, authentic Thai food.

Expect a wait at lunch for tamarind-glazed duck served with fried, crispy shallots, as well as yellow curry with lamb and honey-glazed ginger fish. A plethora of vegetarian options are on hand, of course, including fried basil tofu with bell peppers. Cool your palate with a sweet Thai iced tea.

231 Ellsworth

 B2

Contemporary XX

231 S. Ellsworth Ave. (bet. 2nd & 3rd Aves.), San Mateo

Phone: 650-347-7231
Web: www.231ellsworth.com
Prices: $$$

Lunch Tue – Fri
Dinner Mon – Sat

231 Ellsworth remains slightly off the radar, though it may be San Mateo's most seductive fine dining destination. Perhaps it is the dramatic, barrel-vaulted azure ceiling or the spacious curving booths that lend plenty of privacy for business or pleasure. Or, perhaps credit is due to the elegant place settings and sophisticated contemporary cuisine, which is consistent and skillfully prepared.

At lunch, a well-tailored business set talks shop over pillowy potato gnocchi with a subtle hint of curry; moist hanger steak with crème fraîche potatoes and red wine demi-glace; and strawberry shortcake with a touch of floral lavender. The subdued dining room is typically quiet, but the restaurant's bar, with its extensive wine list, does awaken after dark.

Viognier

 B2

Contemporary XXX

222 E. 4th Ave. (at B St.), San Mateo

Phone: 650-685-3727
Web: www.viognierrestaurant.com
Prices: $$$

Dinner nightly

 Like fine wine, some restaurants improve with age. Such is the case with Viognier, the Draeger's Market mainstay that now stands on solid terroir thanks to a new toque in the open kitchen. The chef is taking aim at consistency and creative flavor combinations in contemporary American fare made from largely local and sustainable ingredients. Menu highlights may include the creamy bed of bourbon-whipped sweet potatoes, with a crispy-skin duck breast and persimmon *brunoise*.

Despite a fresh face at the stoves, the second-floor dining room is filled with the same San Mateo suit-and-tie crowd who blend well into the atmosphere, which is refined but a touch corporate. Opt for a warmer seat in a booth by the central fireplace with views of the pizza oven.

The Village Pub

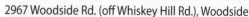

B3·4

2967 Woodside Rd. (off Whiskey Hill Rd.), Woodside

Phone: 650-851-9888
Web: www.thevillagepub.net
Prices: $$$

Lunch Mon – Fri
Dinner nightly

Frankie Frankeny

Closely spaced tables, a wood-burning oven, and a clubby, old-school bar lined in glossy mahogany might give this gorgeous restaurant some pub cred. But the always packed Village Pub—tucked into the adorable mountain town of Woodside, just south of San Francisco—is pure upscale elegance, from the pristine table settings to the handsomely-suited staff to the plush red velvet banquettes.

Chef Mark Sullivan's rustic menu is decidedly seasonal but might include crispy, pan-sautéed sweetbreads sporting silky, tender middles, puddled in fragrant black truffle jus, and topped with a slow poached egg and a frothy celery cream; or a sinfully moist grilled rack of pork, infused with the scent of smoked almond wood and served with caramelized quince and braised endive wrapped with speck.

Arrive early for a pre-dinner cocktail, and you'll find a great neighborhood bar scene—with regulars pouring in by early evening to relax by the crackling fireplace and soak up the irresistible buzz of the room. Over in the dining room, the service staff hums quietly to and fro—always informed and polished, but never overly fussy. If only everyone's neighborhood pub were so cozy and lovely.

Wakuriya

Japanese ✗

B3

115 De Anza Blvd. (at Parrot Dr.), San Mateo

Phone: 650-286-0410
Web: www.wakuriya.com
Prices: $$$$

Dinner Tue – Sun

Wakuriya

Don't let the neighboring Safeway in the Crystal Springs shopping center fool you: Wakuriya may require a reservation at least a month in advance for a seat at one of its few coveted tables. Run by husband-wife team Katsuhiro and Mayumi Yamasaki, Wakuriya is as intimate and authentic as Japanese dining gets.

The narrow space hosts just a handful of tables, with much of its casual clientele preferring to sit at the long wood counter facing a broad open kitchen. Because of Wakuriya's minimalist ambience, action takes the place of décor as Katsuhiro puts on a show in his stainless steel–clad stage.

The chef's *kaiseki* menu is deliberately paced for maximum enjoyment (read: a little bit slow), but the leisurely schedule is all part of the experience. Sit back with a glass of sake, served in beautiful handmade glasses, as dish after dish is served in delicate Japanese earthenware and crocks that steam with rich aromas. The tasting menu is served in either six or nine course with recipes ranging from seared *washugyu* beef with fresh octopus salad, plum dressing, and pickled mushrooms to precisely cut sashimi and tempura-fried yuba roll with snow crab, *jidori* egg, and shiitake mushrooms.

Zen Peninsula

Chinese Chinese 𝕏

B2

1180 El Camino Real (at Center St.), Millbrae

Phone: 650-616-9388
Web: www.zenpeninsula.com
Prices: **$$**

Lunch & dinner daily

A much frequented spot for dim sum and banquet dining in Millbrae, Zen Peninsula is regularly jammed with hungry Chinese families. There's not enough space between the closely packed tables in the elegant room for dim sum carts to maneuver, so waitresses carry platters laden with steaming baskets of dumplings and other delicacies from table to table.

Quality ingredients are evident in rich morsels of barbecued pork, their skins crusted with a satisfying five-spice coating; and crispy fried packets of tofu skin that hold small shrimp, ground pork, ginger, and garlic. Beyond dim sum, the extensive à la carte menu runs from noodles dishes to clay pot creations, and incorporates specialties such as abalone in oyster sauce and braised bird's nest soup.

Couverts (𝕏 ... 𝕏𝕏𝕏𝕏) indicate the level of comfort found at a restaurant. The more 𝕏's, the more upscale a restaurant will be.

South Bay

South Bay

Tech geeks the world over know the way to San Jose, but foodies typically get lost in San Francisco. It's a shame: Tech money plus an international population equals a dynamic culinary scene. Not to mention the rich wine culture descending from the Santa Cruz Mountains, where a burgeoning vintner community takes great pride in its work. In May, sample all 70 area wines at the **Santa Cruz Mountains Wine Express**, at Roaring Camp Railroad in Felton.

Festive Foods

The Valley may have a nerdy rep, but South Bay locals know how to party. In San Jose, festival season kicks off in May with music, dancing, and eats at the wildly adored **Greek Festival**. Then in June, buckets of corn husks wait to be stuffed and sold at the **Story Road Tamale Festival**, in the fruit orchards of Emma Prusch Farm Park. In July, Japantown comes alive for the two-day **Obon/Bazaar** and, in August, the Italian American Heritage Foundation celebrates its yearly **Family Festa**.

Santana Row also keeps the party going yearround: The sleek shopping village is home to numerous upscale restaurants and its very own farmers market. Opened in August 2010, San Jose's newest foodie destination is **San Pedro Square Market**, which houses artisan merchants at the historic Peralta Adobe downtown. Farmers and specialty markets are a way of life for South Bay locals: Each city has one or more throughout the week.

A Morsel of Vietnam

San Jose is also a melting pot for global culinary influences. Neighborhood *pho* shops and *banh mi* delis sate the growing Vietnamese community, which also heads to **Grand Century Mall** for hard-to-find traditional snacks.

The intersection of King and Tully Streets, meanwhile, is home to some of the area's best Vietnamese flavors: Try **Huong Lan** for delicious *bahn mi* sandwiches; **Vua Kho Bo & O Mai** for heaping bins of exotic candies, dried fruits, and jerky; cream puffs at **Hong-Van Bakery**; and green waffles flavored with *pandan* paste at **Century Bakery**, just a few blocks away. But that's not all! **Lion Plaza** is another hub for Vietnamese bakeries, markets, and eateries.

Mouthwatering for Mexican food? Devotees of South-of-the-Border cuisine pick up still-warm fresh tortillas at **Tropicana** and surprisingly good tacos from one of the area's 18 **Mi Pueblo Food Centers**. If Cambodian noodle soup is more your cup of tea, look no further than **Nam Vang Restaurant** or **F&D Yummy**. The lofty **Dynasty Chinese Seafood Restaurant**, on Story Road, is popular for large parties and is also the local dim sum favorite.

A SPREAD FOR STUDENTS

There is more to the South Bay than just San Jose. Los Gatos is home to the sweet patisserie **Fleur de Cocoa** as well as **Testarossa Winery**, the Bay Area's oldest, continually operating winery. Meanwhile, Palo Alto is a casual homebase for the students and faculty of Stanford University. Here, locals line up for organic artisanal yogurts at **Fraîche** and delish double-decker sandwiches at **Village Cheese House**.

If you're hungering for Korean fare, head to Santa Clara where the Korean community enjoys authentic nibbles and scrumptious treats at **Lawrence Plaza** food court; and if in urgent need of groceries, shopping along El Camino Real near the Lawrence Expressway intersection is a feast for the eyes. Local foodies favor the caramelized, roasted sweet potatoes at **Sweet Potato Stall**, just outside the Galleria, and **SGD Tofu House** for *bibimbop* or *soondubu jjigae*.

Despite the fast pace of technology in Silicon Valley, **Slow Food**—the grassroots movement dedicated to local food traditions—has a thriving South Bay chapter. Even Google, in Mountain View, feeds its staff three organic squares a day.

AND TO FINISH...

For a selection of delicacies, **Charlie's Place** dishes gourmet goods and ethnic eats but sorry, Google employees only. The rest of us can visit nearby **Milk Pail Market**, known for more than 300 varieties of cheese, or **Dittmer's Gourmet Meats & Wurst-Haus**, a beloved family-owned butcher shop and deli since 1978. Pair your charcuterie and cheese with a bottle from Mountain View's new **Savvy Seller Wine Bar & Wine Shop**—it's a picnic in the making!

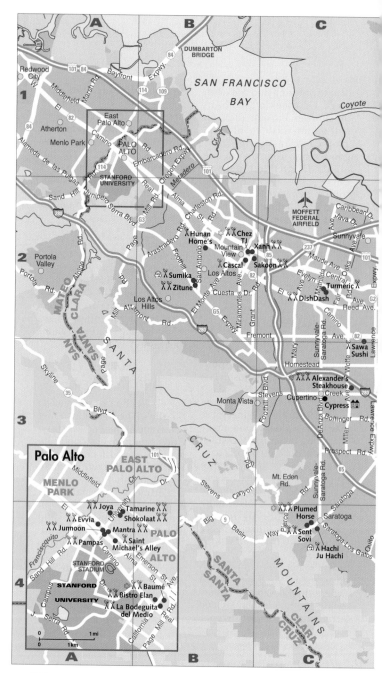

258

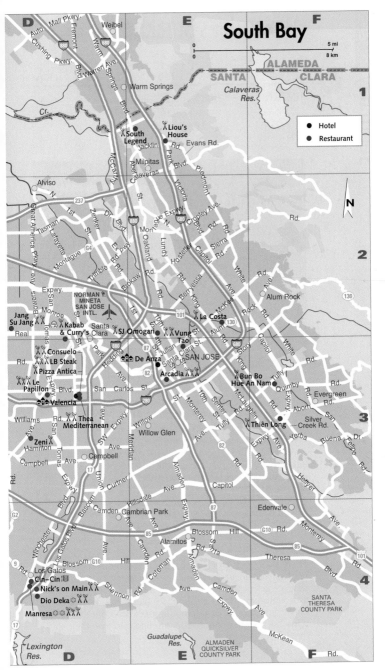

South Bay

0   5 mi
0   8 km

ALAMEDA
SANTA   CLARA

● Hotel
● Restaurant

N

D

Auto Mall Pkwy.
Fremont
Weibel
Cushing Pkwy.
680
Warm Springs Blvd.
Warren Ave.
Cr.
Warm Springs

E

F

Calaveras Res.

South Legend
Liou's House
Jacklin
Rd.
Evans Rd.
Milpitas
Abel
Calaveras
Park
McCarthy
Piedmont

1

Alviso
237
Tasman
Great America Pkwy.
1st
Zanker
Dr.
Lafayette
Montague
Trimble
Rd.
G4
E. Expwy.
Bowers
Monroe
Santa Clara
San Tomas
Expwy.
Lick
Mill
Park
Rd.
Brokaw
Oakland
Rd.
Montecito Expwy.
680
Lundy
Hostetter
Berryessa
Rd.
King
Capitol
Sierra
Rd.
Copley Ave.
Victoria
White
Rd.
Ave.
Rock

2

130

Jang Su Jang
Real
Kabab & Curry's
NORMAN Y. MINETA SAN JOSE INTL.
Santa
Clara
1st
101
SJ Omogari
Vung Tau
La Costa
McKee
Alum
Rock
130
Alum Rock
Rock
Ave.
White
Rd.
Story

Consuelo
LB Steak
Pizza Antica
Le Papillon
Valencia
Rd.
880
87
Hedding
Julian
Santa Clara St.
SAN JOSE
680
De Anza
Arcadia
St.
San Carlos St.
280
10th
St.
San
Senter
McLaughlin
King
Story
Capitol
Tully
Bun Bo Hue An Nam
Quimby
Aborn
Evergreen
Rd.
Buena
Felipe

3

Williams
Rd.
Thea Mediterranean
Zeni
Hamilton
Campbell
San Tomas Expwy.
Blvd.
San
Willow
Willow Glen
Meridian
Almaden
Monterey
Rd.
82
Senter
Tully
Rd.
Yerba
Thiên Long
Silver Creek Rd.
San
Hellyer
Dr.

Campbell
Ave.
17
Union
Curtner
Ave.
Capitol
Bascom

G2
Rd.
Winchester
Los Gatos Blvd.
Camden
Ave.
Hillsdale
Ave.
Cambrian Park
85
Blossom
G10
Blossom Hill
Alamitos
Santa
Rd.
Teresa
85
Edenvale
Monterey
Rd.
G10
Rd.
101
Blvd.

4

9
Rd.
Los Gatos
Cin–Cin
Nick's on Main
Dio Deka
Manresa
Blossom
G10
Hill
Rd.
Shannon
Camden
Coleman
Ave.
Almaden
Camden
Expwy.
Ave.
McKean
SANTA THERESA COUNTY PARK

17
Lexington Res.
Guadalupe Res.
ALMADEN QUICKSILVER COUNTY PARK
McKean
Rd.

D   **E**   **F**

Alexander's Steakhouse

C3

Steakhouse XXX

10330 N. Wolfe Rd. (at I-280), Cupertino

Phone: 408-446-2222
Web: www.alexanderssteakhouse.com
Prices: $$$$

Dinner nightly

Kingmond Young Photography

Far from your average meat-and-potatoes joint, the ambitious Alexander's Steakhouse is an oasis for South Bay beefhounds—taking this American standard to new heights by giving top quality cuts a creative Asian twist.

You can thank Chef Jeffrey Stout, who makes wide use of his Japanese background in the globe-trotting menu, which features an impressive selection of beef from different Japanese prefectures, along with a gorgeous, ever-rotating roster of seasonal accompaniments (this is California, after all). A gleaming red tuna tartare gets paired with crispy noodles, Kalamata olive foam, smoked tomato gelée, Toy Box tomatoes, quail egg yolk, and anchovy; while an enormous Porterhouse is cooked to rosy pink perfection and may arrive with bright pesto, black garlic demi-glace, and roasted black garlic cloves.

There's a few different rooms in the enormous space to find yourself seated in, and couples may want to try to snag a seat at one of the smaller, more intimate alcoves scattered thorough the bi-level steakhouse. Don't miss a stop by the beef aging rooms, or a tempting peek into the extravagant wine list, where connoisseurs are liable to lose their shirt if they're not careful.

Arcadia

Steakhouse 🍴🍴🍴

E3

100 W. San Carlos St. (at Market St.), San Jose

Phone: 408-278-4555
Web: www.michaelmina.net
Prices: $$$

Dinner nightly

Spacious Arcadia—Michael Mina's take on the modern American steakhouse—is pleasantly situated in the San Jose Marriott, where natural light floods through glass walls that peer onto the neighboring park. This corner spot features an open kitchen with views of a glowing pizza oven and raw bar, overlooking an earth-toned dining room with mocha carpeting and dark wood tables set with woven fiber placemats.

The menu follows suit with its contemporary approach to meat and seafood dishes. While some may opt for chilled shellfish and charcuterie, snacks like foie gras sliders, mini crab Po'boys, and lobster corn dogs offer deliciously whimsical takes on American classics.

Keeping with the theme, nostalgia inspires a root beer float for dessert.

Bistro Elan

Californian 🍴🍴

B4

448 California Ave. (near El Camino Real), Palo Alto

Phone: 650-327-0284
Web: www.bistroelan.com
Prices: $$

Lunch Tue – Fri
Dinner Tue – Sat

It doesn't take a rocket scientist to know that Bistro Elan is a terrific destination. Located on California street in the heart of Palo Alto, this charming little sanctum crafts its whole world around ingredients, many of which are grown in the lovely back garden. Citrus trees, olive trees, and beds full of herbs, climbing rosemary, and other edible plants aren't just for looks—they are the inspiration behind most of the meals. What isn't grown in the back is typically sourced from the farmers market down the street.

From house-cured gravlax with Chioggia beef carpaccio to roasted Niman Ranch rack pork chop, everything is fresh and flavorful.

The casual setting is ideal for business lunches and intimate dinners alike.

Baumé ❀

B4

201 S. California Ave. (at Park Blvd.), Palo Alto

Phone: 650-328-8899
Web: www.baumerestaurant.com
Prices: $$$$

Lunch Thu – Fri
Dinner Thu – Sun

Peter Giles

Modern French cuisine with a zen touch is how Bruno Chemel's new Palo Alto restaurant bills itself; its name is derived from an 18th century chemist, Antoine Baumé, who (according to the restaurant's menu) "pioneered the marriage of science and gastronomy."

Chemel, fresh from Mountain View's esteemed Chez TJ, is quite deft at the clean lines of molecular gastronomy, and here he's built an elegant temple to enjoy it in, with inlayed marble floors, burnt orange walls, and minimalist décor. Dinner begins with a list of ingredients to be used over the course of the evening, and the set menus are available in a varying number of courses.

Though dinner spins with the season, one menu may include a single stalk of perfectly poached asparagus over a vibrant asparagus purée with shaved Parmesan, hollandaise pearls, and tangy shallot-rosemary vinaigrette; perfectly seared foie gras with sweet apricot sauce and an airy miso sponge cake; impeccably tender grass-fed beef with Earl Grey tea and black truffle jus; or an ambitious, but brilliant, chocolate-tarragon tranche with bitter almond-liquid nitrogen ice cream, deconstructed berries, chocolate powder, and raspberry-strawberry sorbet.

Bun Bo Hue An Nam

Vietnamese ✕

F3

2060 Tully Rd. (at Quimby Rd.), San Jose

Phone: 408-270-7100   Lunch & dinner Tue – Sun
Web: N/A
Prices: 🍜

Take a cue from Vietnamese locals and march into this popular San Jose joint for steaming bowls of fantastic *pho*. Soups and stews are the name of the game here, many of which are jazzed up with ingredients like shrimp cake, soft tendon, fat brisket, and tripe. Slurp down the *bún bò hue*—spicy beef soup with tender chunks of flank steak, pork knuckles, shrimp cake, and rice noodles in a fragrant lemongrass broth, presented with a pile of fresh bean sprouts, mint, cilantro, lemon wedges, and green chilis. Or sample the *pho bò áp chao*—piquant pan fried beef dressed in a garlic-lemongrass chili sauce, tossed over rice noodles with peppers, onions, basil, cilantro, and mint.

This is the second of two locations—the first is also in San Jose—on Story Road.

Cascal

Spanish ✕

B2

400 Castro St. (at California St.), Mountain View

Phone: 650-940-9500   Lunch & dinner daily
Web: www.cascalrestaurant.com
Prices: $$

It's no mystery why Mountain View locals adore Cascal: this vibrant eatery shakes infinite and wickedly tempting variations on the mojito, margarita, and caipirinha for a festive after work crowd enjoying the extensive selection of rum.

Splashy Latin American hues and dressed up Spanish architectural elements, such as wrought iron fixtures and polished wood tables, hint at the pan-Latin, tapas-style fare. Flavorful dishes include Mexican *sopes* with tender chicken *picadillo* or Cuban roast pork atop crisp masa cakes; lamb *albondigas* with spicy piquillo pepper purée; and wraps stuffed with adobo marinated pork, cilantro, watercress, and lime. At lunch, Cascal is a popular escape among the cubicle crowd, while dog lovers enjoy family meals on the patio.

Chez TJ ✿

Contemporary ✕✕

938 Villa St. (bet. Bryant & Franklin Sts.), Mountain View

Phone: 650-964-7466
Web: www.cheztj.com
Prices: **$$$$**

Dinner Tue – Sat

Mark Leet

Set in a stunning 19th century Victorian house along a quaint street in downtown Mountain View, Chez TJ oozes old-world charm—rooms lined in antiqued mirrors and fabric wallpapers give way to bay windows overlooking manicured greens; intimate tables flicker with romance and bubble with celebration.

It harkens back to a different era—farther back, of course, then when this revered fine dining institution opened its doors in 1982—one where waiters, donned in formal vests and ties, still called you "sir" and a sense of formality graced a meal of such caliber.

Chef Scott Nishiyama lays out two delicious menus nightly—a four-course menu (which holds a few choices for each course) and an eight-course tasting menu. Dinner is ever changing, but one can await a tender square of Moulard duck foie gras garnished with strawberries, *fleur de sel*, and nasturtium leaves; slow baked New Zealand *tai* (snapper) topped with silky mounds of Mendocino uni, shaved toy box radish, and wilted romaine hearts; or a decadent confit of chicken wing humming with a Moroccan-spiced chicken jus and paired with roasted artichoke hearts, caramelized Applewood-smoked bacon, red pepper purée, and fresh yogurt.

Cin-Cin

International

D4

368 Village Ln. (at Saratoga Los Gatos Rd.), Los Gatos

Phone: 408-354-8006
Web: www.cincinwinebar.com
Prices: $$

Dinner Tue – Sun

Tucked down a tiny lane in downtown Los Gatos, this bungalow hides a neighborhood hot spot for the local happy hour set. Though it bills itself as a wine bar, Cin-Cin boasts a large dining room incorporating recycled items amid the green walls and wine-themed artwork that sets the scene for shareable small plates.

Flavors from many nations influence the menu. Peppercorn ahi tuna *crudo* roams to Asia, while duck confit served over a bed of creamy cannelini beans pays homage to the cuisine of France. Addictive *tostaditos* topped with shredded lamb and striped with a smoky chipotle sauce, avocado crème fraîche, and tangy tomatillo salsa salute Mexican flavors. Featured wine flights make it easy to sample your way through the international list.

Consuelo

Mexican

D3

377 Santana Row (bet. Olin Ave. & Olsen Dr.), San Jose

Phone: 408-260-7082
Web: www.consuelomexicanbistro.com
Prices: $$

Lunch & dinner daily

In a lively yet professional atmosphere, hospitality rules the attentive and efficient staff at this authentic Mexican spot, located in the upscale Santana Row shopping center.

From *pipián* to a filling *torta de elote*, this reasonably priced menu is ambitious and unapologetically traditional—without any nods to the nachos set. Layers of flavor stand out in each regional Mexican dish, and there's no holding back on the heat. A meal here begins with warm house-made tortillas, accented by mango, tomatillo, and toasted chile salsas.

A festive mood prevails in the evening, when friends gather for margaritas, or to enjoy the impressive tequila list. For those who prefer their drinks non-alcoholic, Consuelo features a different *agua fresca* daily.

265

Dio Deka ✿

D4

Greek ✗✗

210 E. Main St. (near Fiesta Way), Los Gatos

Phone: 408-354-7700   Dinner nightly
Web: www.diodeka.com
Prices: $$$

Dio Deka

A day trip to the quaint and upscale town of Los Gatos ends on a pitch-perfect note at this fantastic Greek tavern, housed in the Hotel Los Gatos on Main Street. Chef Salvatore Calisi has fun with the menu, lending it some Mediterranean touches and infusing it with a contemporary sensibility that utilizes both local California products as well as global accents.

With a big, open kitchen; a roaring fireplace; softly flickering oil votives; and a whole lot of Greek hospitality to indulge in, you might want to kick things off with a drink plucked off the extensive 1,200-label wine list, which features a wide selection of Greek, French, Italian, and Californian varietals, as well as an ace Ouzo selection.

When you're ready for dinner, you'll find the traditional Greek spreads alongside a creative lineup that might feature tender, fall-off-the-bone baby back pork riblets, mesquite-grilled and infused with nutmeg and Ouzo, then served with quince and pistachio relish; or a wildly fresh fillet of Japanese *mero* dressed in a lemon, dill, and white wine sauce, then paired with an irresistible spring pea risotto cake, plump rock shrimp, and a silky mound of wilted spinach.

DishDash

Middle Eastern ✕✕

C2

190 S. Murphy St. (bet. Evelyn & Washington Aves.), Sunnyvale

Phone: 408-774-1889
Web: www.dishdash.net
Prices: $$

Lunch & dinner Mon – Sat

Named after a traditional, cozy piece of Middle Eastern garb, this hoppin' Murphy Street spot captures just that kind of spirit. Notes of sumac and saffron drift through the air, dark wood tables sit against exposed brick walls, and cultural knick knacks dot the dining space. Bold flavors rock a vibrant, pan-Middle Eastern menu, with offerings from tangy chicken *shawarma* salad (spit-roasted chicken atop Romaine, cucumber, tomato, onions, and parsley drizzled with garlicky yogurt) to tasty *beriani dajaj* (potatoes, golden raisins, slivered almonds, and garbanzo beans touched with aged yogurt, alongside saffron rice and garlic-herbed chicken breast).

Sugar craving? Work your sweet way through assorted baklavas: six syrupy choices from cashew to walnut.

Evvia

Greek ✕✕

A4

420 Emerson St. (bet. Lytton & University Aves.), Palo Alto

Phone: 650-326-0983
Web: www.evvia.net
Prices: $$

Lunch Mon – Fri
Dinner nightly

Briefly closed to renovate after a small kitchen fire, Evvia is back in business and better than ever. The warmly lit dining room has the rustic coziness of a Greek estiatorio, with a roaring stone fireplace, close tables, and open kitchen adorned with hanging copper pots and pans. A lovely backlit wall of shelves illuminates a colorful array of glass bottles of oils, vinegars, and grains.

Frequently packed, the place is popular among the business crowds at lunch and Palo Alto residents at dinner (reservations are recommended). Fresh, flavorful Greek favorites may include roasted artichoke and eggplant souvlaki, served with fresh strained yogurt and house-made pita; or the tender, perfectly seasoned, herb-roasted lamb with dill-flavored *tzatziki*.

267

Hachi Ju Hachi

Japanese 🍴

14480 Big Basin Way (bet. Saratoga Los Gatos Rd. & 3rd St.), Saratoga

Phone: 408-674-2258

Dinner Tue – Sun

Web: www.hachijuhachi88.com

Prices: $$

On the hunt for Americanized Japanese fare? You'll change your mind in a flash once you set foot in this sublime little spot, where true and traditional Japanese dishes reign. Outfitted in blonde woods and soft lighting, the minimal space offers a few tables and a long, angled counter for seating. The slow paced service and exquisite menu is as authentic as it gets.

Heavenly bites like luscious grilled pork belly, sliced and coated with caramelized white miso marinade; tender duckling stewed in rice wine and soy sauce, swimming in maitake mushroom broth; delicate seafood and egg custard flavored with dashi and sweet mirin, astound the senses. Young offspring visiting? Drop them off in the delightful playroom at the back of the restaurant.

Hunan Home's

B2

Chinese 🍴

4880 El Camino Real (bet. Jordan Ave. & Los Altos Sq.), Los Altos

Phone: 650-965-8888

Lunch & dinner daily

Web: www.hunanhomes.com

Prices: 💰

If home is where the heart is, then follow yours to Hunan Home's. Chinese may be the cuisine craze in this city, and this restaurant's name may be lost in translation, yet it continues to seduce business and family circles with its wonderfully authentic food. Set in a bungalow beset with shopping stalls, the elevated dining room is cheery with smiling service.

Groups of all sizes gather to ogle the gamut of Chinese delights—from *kung pao* prawns dressed in silky, spicy oyster sauce, to the house specialty of deeply caramelized Peking duck sandwiched in steamed pancakes with scallions and hoisin, to soft tofu cubes sautéed with chili and fermented black bean paste. The same in any language, a dizzying array of complimentary dishes adds incredible value.

Jang Su Jang

D2

Korean ✗✗

3561 El Camino Real #10 (bet. Flora Vista Ave. & Lawrence Expwy.), Santa Clara

Phone: 408-246-1212
Web: N/A
Prices: $$

Lunch & dinner daily

You may as well call this stretch of El Camino in Santa Clara "Little Korea": the plaza brims with Korean-owned businesses whose owners and families congregate at nearby tofu shops and groceries. Jang Su Jang is among the local haunts, serving such authentic recipes as crisp Korean pancakes, filled with vegetables and flavored with sesame oil; and spicy beef stew with hand-cut noodles and scrambled egg in bright red broth.

Screens offer a bit of privacy between tables, which are equipped with call buttons to summon your server. Cushioned banquettes are comfortable for intimate groups, while scattered private dining areas accommodate large family gatherings and special occasions. DIY-ers should request a grill table to savor homemade barbecue meats.

Joya

A4

Latin American ✗✗

339 University Ave. (at Florence St.), Palo Alto

Phone: 650-853-9800
Web: www.joyarestaurant.com
Prices: $$

Lunch & dinner daily

Cheerfully occupying the corner of University and Florence in Palo Alto, Joya is filled with natural light and a sunshiney vibe—from its yuppy clientele. Happy hours truly are, with the cocktail crowd sipping guava mojitos at the central bar and lounge. As the rum flows, the noise continues to crank—but nobody here minds a bit.

Tile floors and leather chairs accent the vivacious space where colorful Latin American small plates and entrées are served in the dining room. Joya is best enjoyed with a group of friends, so grab your pals and share plates of corn *croquetas* deep-fried with English peas and pasilla peppers; roasted chicken *sopes* with chipotle-tomato sauce; and boldly flavored short rib tacos with jicama salsa and horseradish cream.

Junnoon

Indian

150 University Ave. (at High St.), Palo Alto

Phone: 650-329-9644
Web: www.junnoon.com
Prices: $$

Lunch Mon – Fri
Dinner nightly

With a sultry dark wood interior, creative cocktails, and patio conducive to warm weather carousal, Junnoon is a perennial favorite among denizens of Palo Alto and Stanford University.

Despite rave reviews from national press, this Indian cuisine can be hit-and-miss. While the Darjeeling-steamed dumplings may be dry, they are beautifully brightened by fantastic, über spicy chili-garlic chutney. In fact, some dishes are downright exciting: the chewy roasted garlic naan has rich buttery flavor and arrives piping hot; and tandoori lamb chops, flavored with cardamom and accompanied by vibrant mint sauce, are expertly cooked.

Rather than stay for dessert, arrive early to indulge in exotic libations during happy hour—an undeniable hit.

Kabab & Curry's

Indian

1498 Isabella St. (at Clay St.), Santa Clara

Phone: 408-247-0745
Web: www.kababandcurrys.com
Prices: ⊜⊜

Lunch & dinner Tue – Sun

If you're hanging around the South Bay at lunchtime and wondering where the area's large Indian and Pakistani population goes to eat, follow the crowd of engineers from Intel and Google to Kabab & Curry's, an authentic eatery that literally serves all you can eat.

Expect a line at the door—this place is a zoo at lunch—but be patient: The $10 buffet is worth the wait at Kabab & Curry's. Here, plates are laden with tender lamb cubes in spicy *vindaloo*; tandoori chicken so moist it's falling off the bone; and velvety chicken *tikka masala*. Every dish is hearty and delicious, the atmosphere is easygoing with plain wood furniture and tiled floors, and the naan is warm, bountiful, and always served with a smile. Come hungry, and leave stuffed!

La Bodeguita del Medio

B4

Cuban 🍴

463 S. California Ave. (bet. Ash St. & El Camino Real), Palo Alto

Phone: 650-326-7762
Web: www.labodeguita.com
Prices: $$

Lunch Mon – Fri
Dinner Mon – Sat

Palo Alto cigar aficionados head to La Bodeguita del Medio for its adjacent Cigar Divan, a cozy retail space with a walk-in humidor. Connoisseurs should try the house's private label Nicaraguan cigar—pair it with a Hemingway rum cocktail to get the full experience. Non-smokers love La Bodeguita for tasty Cuban cuisine that hails from the restaurant's original Havana locale.

The casual, friendly spot is conducive to sharing fun small plates. Start with a house-cured shrimp ceviche in tangy key lime juice flavored with coconut milk, and don't miss tender *picadillo* pork empanadas with roasted chiles and cabbage slaw. Still hungry? Sink your teeth into moist *masitas*, a roasted pork shoulder with black beans and Rioja-caramelized red onions.

La Costa

E2

Mexican 🍴

1805 Alum Rock Ave. (bet. Jackson Ave. & King Rd.), San Jose

Phone: 408-937-1010
Web: N/A
Prices: 💰

Lunch & dinner daily

Is it a taqueria, or is it a taco stand? You be the judge at La Costa, a San Jose hot spot where the décor is, well, the great outdoors. Inside, La Costa 's space features a kitchen with red, green, and white tile floors. But never mind that, because you're not going inside.

Belly up to the cashier's window and order your heart's content: perhaps a tender taco *asado* seasoned with spices and chiles and topped with crunchy salsa? Or maybe a burrito stuffed with strips of grilled chicken, avocado, cheese, and spicy condiments. Whatever you order, expect it to come fast and come outside—the only seating at La Costa is on the covered patio. But the food is cheap, tasty, and enjoys a motley following; regulars include foodies and working class folk alike.

LB Steak

D3

Steakhouse

334 Santana Row, Ste. 1000 (bet. Olin Ave. & Stevens Creek Blvd.), San Jose

Phone: 408-244-1180
Web: www.lbsteak.com
Prices: $$$

Lunch & dinner daily

Sister to the Left Bank Brasserie located at the opposite end of Santana Row, LB Steak is a good fit for this tony mixed-use complex. At lunchtime, the patio is the place to be for local business folks to sink their teeth into gourmet burgers and steak sandwiches. In the evening, couples and shoppers stop by for brawny USDA prime steaks and elegant seafood. Dishes get a soupçon of French sophistication courtesy of Chef/proprietor Roland Passot.

When it's time for dessert, look to the pastry cart for more refined offerings than the usual steakhouse sweets. Among the cookies, financiers, and fruit tarts, a raspberry *macaron* filled with vanilla pastry cream and scattered with plump, sweet raspberries does justice to the restaurant's French legacy.

Le Papillon

D3

French

410 Saratoga Ave. (at Kiely Blvd.), San Jose

Phone: 408-296-3730
Web: www.lepapillon.com
Prices: $$$$

Lunch Fri
Dinner nightly

In San Jose, Le Papillon is at once dated but charming in an old-fashioned way: just a glance through its plantation shutters to the luxury cars parked out front indicates a deep-pocketed clientele who finds comfort in massive florals (both in vases and upholstery), white linens, wallpapered wainscoting, and shaded tabletop lamps. Another perk of Le Papillon's old-school manner is its attentive and professional service. Here, the staff is well equipped to please both the corporate crowd at lunch and couples craving a romantic dinner.

French preparations and primo ingredients define the solid cuisine, which might feature ricotta gnocchi with artichokes and morels; pinot noir-braised duck breast with sour cherry sauce; and an airy Grand Marnier soufflé.

Liou's House

E1

Chinese ✗

1245 Jacklin Rd. (at Park Victoria Dr.), Milpitas

Phone: 408-263-9888
Web: N/A
Prices: 💰💰

Lunch & dinner Tue – Sun

Looking for authentically fiery Hunan cuisine? Drop by Chef Liou's House, near the Summitpointe Golf Club in Milpitas. This cushy family run restaurant features a large selection of expertly prepared Hunan fare, as well as a zesty sampling of regional Chinese dishes.

The cognoscenti—a sizeable contingent of Chinese residents among them—know to order from the chef's specialties list, which is an insert in the main menu. These dishes are where the talent of noted Taiwanese chef, James Liou really dazzles. "Addictive" best describes the blisteringly hot—as in spicy—nuggets of chicken coated in ground dried red chilis.

Top off such delicious food with warm, friendly service and you've got a go-to restaurant that's worth the trip to the South Bay area.

Mantra

A4

Indian ✗✗

632 Emerson St. (bet. Forest & Hamilton Aves.), Palo Alto

Phone: 650-322-3500
Web: www.mantrapaloalto.com
Prices: $$

Lunch Tue – Fri
Dinner nightly

Expect the unexpected in this urban-chic dining room serving exciting East Indian fare with Californian accents. Elegance and harmony permeate the space, where black stone floors echo the high, open-grid black ceiling, and the walls showcase contemporary Indian artwork.

From the kitchen come quirky dishes such as cinnamon-shrimp lollipops, and smoked cumin and pomegranate short ribs. In other preparations, the menu shines with well-balanced classics like chicken curry and Madras shrimp. Naan might come simply flavored with garlic, or innovatively with rosemary pesto or spicy jack cheese. Sophisticated cocktails and a good selection of international wines pair with exotic small plates in the swanky Daru Lounge, which claims Palo Alto's longest bar.

Manresa ✿ ✿

Contemporary 🍴🍴🍴

320 Village Ln. (bet. Santa Cruz & University Aves.), Los Gatos

Phone: 408-354-4330 Dinner Wed – Sun
Web: www.manresarestaurant.com
Prices: $$$$

South Bay

Pim Techamuanvivit

Tucked away in a teeny yellow house down a narrow street in the trendy shopping area of Los Gatos, Manresa possesses the kind of lovable ranch house charm northern California is known for, with a sunny dining room framed in silk drapes, exposed wood, oriental rugs, and a glorious outdoor terrace that fills up when the weather's right.

It's the kind of place you might visit just to soak in the ambience, but Chef David Kinch's food is the real draw here. The innovative master established a partnership with biodynamic farmer Cynthia Sandberg (of Love Apple Farm) to create their own fresh produce for special use at the restaurant, and their search for superior ingredients (in combination with his incredible artistry) has won him as many critical accolades as devoted locals.

The nightly 4-course or chef's tasting menu dances to the season, but look forward to a warm salad of heartbreakingly fresh Delta asparagus, shaved into ribbons and spears and bathed in a salt cod emulsion pocked with plump, crispy mussels; delicately poached Blue Nose bass over chopped oysters, fennel fronds, and Meyer lemon zest; or perfectly roasted duck with heirloom beets, zesty orange purée, and beet greens.

Nick's on Main

D4

American

35 E. Main St. (bet. College Ave. & Pageant Way), Los Gatos

Phone: 408-399-6457 — Lunch & dinner Tue – Sat
Web: www.nicksonmainst.com
Prices: $$$

Size has little to do with sophistication as this shoebox of a bistro attests. As chic as it is tiny, Nick's packs patrons elbow-to-elbow at closely spaced tables. The ladies who lunch don't seem to mind; they keep up a steady flow of chatter as they choose among zippy offerings—such as Chinese chicken salad, mushroom ravioli, and a Dungeness crab melt—on the reasonably priced midday menu. Lucky for everyone, the room's high ceilings help minimize the din of conversations.

The lighting turns down and prices for entrées jump up at dinnertime, when chef and owner Nick Difu concocts comforting dishes like pan-roasted pork filet. A playful touch comes at the end of the meal, when the bill is presented in a worn copy of *The New Food Lover's Companion*.

Pampas

A4

Brazilian

529 Alma St. (bet. Hamilton & University Aves.), Palo Alto

Phone: 650-327-1323 — Lunch Mon – Fri
Web: www.pampaspaloalto.com — Dinner nightly
Prices: $$$

With low slung banquettes, cool earth tones, and chic industrial accents, Pampas' urbane, bi-level interior defies common expectations of an all-you-can-eat affair (as do the sophisticated clientele sipping a full-bodied malbec). The sexy décor befits this Brazilian *churrascaria*, which specializes in authentic *rodízio* meals with limitless roasted meats stealing the scene.

Served on skewers by circulating *passadors*, flavorful highlights include pork loin seasoned with coriander adobo; sirloin filet with garlic and herbs; and spicy linguiça. Try to save room for a trip to the sidebar—not for the faint of appetite—with its heaps of cheese, charcuterie, gazpacho, salads, smoked fish, and hot sides of coconut whipped sweet potatoes or zucchini fritters.

Pizza Antica

Pizza 🍴

D3

334 Santana Row, Ste. 1065 (bet. Stevens Creek Blvd. & Tatum Ln.), San Jose

Phone:	408-557-8373	Lunch & dinner daily
Web:	www.pizzaantica.com	
Prices:	$$	

Shoppers and others consistently line up at this bistro-style pizza parlor at lunchtime, eager for a taste of the restaurant's thin crust pies. Dough proofs for three days before being rolled out cracker-thin, topped with a wide range of artisanal ingredients, and baked in the gas oven. "Our Pizza" features set combinations, while "Your Pizza" allows guests to customize their toppings—from pesto to pepperoni. It is equally worthwhile to explore the full menu of fresh salads, pasta, and entrées like herb-roasted breast of chicken and zinfandel-braised boneless short ribs.

High chairs and a kids menu that doubles as a coloring book make wee diners welcome. On sunny days, everyone clamors for the sidewalk seating in this heart of Santana Row.

Saint Michael's Alley

Contemporary 🍴

A4

140 Homer Ave. (at High St.), Palo Alto

Phone:	650-326-2530	Lunch Tue – Sun
Web:	www.stmikes.com	Dinner Tue – Sat
Prices:	$$	

What's old is new again, as this Palo Alto fixture recently moved to new digs at the corner of High Street and Homer Avenue, though the original Emerson Street location remains open for weekend brunch. The new restaurant packs in a business crowd at lunch, and a cadre of loyal locals for dinner.

An inviting front patio and a series of small rooms weave through the space. Cheery terra-cotta-colored walls, fresh wildflowers, and soft lighting create a charming atmosphere in which to enjoy light, flavorful, and well-prepared dishes. Straightforward describes the fluffy potato gnocchi served in a rich, basil-scented tomato sauce. A bit more modern are ginger prawn lollipops, deep-fried in egg roll wrappers and paired with a piquant dipping sauce.

Plumed Horse

Contemporary XXX

C4

14555 Big Basin Way (bet. 4th & 5th Sts.), Saratoga

Phone:	408-867-4711
Web:	www.plumedhorse.com
Prices:	$$$$

Dinner Mon – Sat

James Fong

Plumed Horse takes its moniker from the 19th century stable that once claimed its land. But aside from the name, this charming Saratoga locale, set on a tree-lined street among quaint artisan shops, has little to do with its country roots. Plumed Horse is decidedly sleek with neon fiber-optic light fixtures, a chic lounge for cocktails and more casual meals, and an illuminated glass wine cellar stocked with a dizzying 24,000 bottles.

Fancy folks may request a seat at the chef's table, which overlooks the polished kitchen. But rest assured, Plumed Horse's linen-clad tables are all elegantly set with contemporary whiteware and crystal stemware waiting to be filled with bubbly from the Champagne cart.

Chef Peter Armellino's seasonal Californian cuisine is decadently modern. Offerings include such delicious canapés as a deviled quail egg with black truffle; smoked chicken and Gruyère dumplings with a splash of mushroom bouillon; and black pepper and Parmesan soufflé with a rich fondue of Dungeness crab and melting uni. Don't forget to save room for dessert: Light and fluffy cardamom dusted raspberry beignets are served with poached rhubarb and vanilla ice cream.

Sakoon

Indian

B2

357 Castro St. (bet. California & Dana Sts.), Mountain View

Phone: 650-965-2000

Web: www.sakoonrestaurant.com

Prices: $$

Lunch & dinner daily

This may just be one of your most contemporary Indian meals yet. Transcending all notions of traditional and typical, Sakoon unveils a blingee, avant-garde arena filled with buoyant booths and a blithe bar. Dining dens dotted with tables feel preciously private. Dizzying up your senses are colorful fixtures, gleaming mirrors, and the hypnotic feat of techno beats. Waiting on gaggles from Google, the service straddles between crowning and colloquial.

The kitchen is solid and globally gifted. Traditional tastes kissed with top technique include cauliflower in a pungent *masala*, and *paneer* fired in fennel. Illustrating an intricacy of ingredients is calamari *kalimirch* with spring onion and curry leaf, and veggie patties puddled in a fiercely flavorful curry.

Sawa Sushi

Japanese

C2·3

1042 E. El Camino Real (at Henderson Ave.), Sunnyvale

Phone: 408-124-1125

Web: www.sawasushi.net

Prices: $$$$

Lunch & dinner Mon – Sat

At Sawa Sushi, Chef/owner/server Steve Sawa will craft your multi-course omakase and then deliver it to you at the sushi bar. Chef Sawa may be deeply dry and his restaurant borders on dingy—the fish cases are empty and plates may be chipped—but you've got to hand it to him: he's made plenty from nothing for 13 years running.

Without a reservation, the chef may question your motives. He may also mention that his super secret recipes come at a premium and are served omakase only. Take a cue from the full house and go with the flow. You'll be treated to the freshest fish even if his sometimes sloppy knife skills leave something to be desired. Expect unique items like slow-poached tuna belly in ponzu, and fresh shrimp topped with creamy uni and sea salt.

Sent Sovi

C4

Californian

14583 Big Basin Way (at 5th St.), Saratoga

Phone: 408-867-3110
Web: www.sentsovi.com
Prices: **$$$**

Dinner Tue – Sun

In the historic village of Saratoga on a lane shaded by overhanging trees, this petite cottage with sweeping windows and copper wainscoting is the very definition of charming. A honeyed glow fills the space and sets the tone for romantic meals, wherein Chef/owner Josiah Slone showcases sustainable ingredients sourced from local farms and ranches.

The ever-changing seasonal offering includes both à la carte items and various tasting menus, which might feature a vegetarian sampling. Highlights may include a smoked trout "martini" with fried capers; gnocchi with cardamom and wild mushroom ragù; or a torchon of creamy foie gras with a bruléed crust and sherry-maple mousse. The concise list of wines and flights is designed for perfect pairing.

Shokolaat

A4

Contemporary

516 University Ave. (bet. Cowper & Webster Sts.), Palo Alto

Phone: 650-289-0719
Web: www.shokolaat.com
Prices: **$$**

Lunch Mon – Fri
Dinner Mon – Sat

To say that Shokolaat is a fantastic patisserie would be to underestimate the scope of this Palo Alto culinary lounge dedicated to European decadence in many mouthwatering forms. True, a glass pastry case brims with chic little chocolates and elaborate confections, beckoning passersby on the go. But those who take the time to sit down in this sleek former art gallery with a Scandinavian aesthetic receive their just deserts: a surprising menu of ambitious savories ranging from light plates at lunch to heartier Gallic suppers.

Expect such palate-pleasers as tuna tartare with chopped black truffles, shallots, and toasted brioche; gratin of escargots with bone marrow; and duck confit *crépinette*. Ethereal soufflés are a sweet reward for those who wait.

South Bay

SJ Omogari

E2   Korean

154 E. Jackson St. (at 4th St.), San Jose

Phone: 408-288-8134   Lunch & dinner Mon – Sat
Web: www.omogari.biz
Prices:

This homespun, family-owned Korean eatery in San Jose is one to rival any of the cuisine's authentic go-tos in Santa Clara. The traditional *banchan* may be lackluster, but area foodies come anyway for terrific *bi bim bap*, a piping hot stone pot that may be loaded with tender spicy pork, shredded carrot and daikon radish salad, and scallions with an egg on top.

SJ Omogari is a small, simple space with just a few wood tables and little art. And while you won't find the ubiquitous grill-topped tables, you will find most memorable *galbi*—smoky, grilled, and caramelized beef short ribs—from the kitchen. Soft tofu stews arrive with mushrooms or kimchi for vegetable lovers, and all meals are complete with a complimentary scoop of green tea ice cream.

South Legend

E1   Chinese

1720 N. Milpitas Blvd. (bet. Dixon Landing Rd. & Sunnyhills Ct.), Milpitas

Phone: 408-934-3970   Lunch & dinner daily
Web: www.southlegend.com
Prices:

 Ring the alarm—South Legend's bold menu promises "all Szechuan, all the time" and is comprised of bold specialties from China's extra spicy province. The likes of *ma-po* tofu pocked with ground pork, scallions, and fermented black beans; boiled fish in fiery sauce; and twice cooked pork are not for the faint of heart. This is cuisine that will leave you blushing from a flavor-packed smackdown of chili paste, peppercorns, and red chili oil.

A listing of cooling sides like slices of winter melon seasoned with dried shrimp and a selection of dim sum that includes fried yam cakes filled with sweet red bean paste round out the offerings served at this unassuming local favorite found in a busy shopping center occupied by markets and small businesses.

Sumika

Japanese ✗

 B2

236 Plaza Central (bet. 2nd & 3rd Sts.), Los Altos

Phone:	650-917-1822	Lunch Tue – Sat
Web:	www.sumikagrill.com	Dinner Tue – Sun
Prices:	**$$**	

For a gratifying yakitori experience, venture off the beaten path and behold this authentic *izakaya*. A South Bay haven for the local Japanese folk, Sumika's crowning glory is its glass enclosed *binchotan* charcoal grill. However, *izakaya* faithfuls like dark wood floors and furnishings, soft lighting, and shelves of sake bottles adorn the rest of the space.

A field of families and couples flock to the tables, while the trendier set hovers over a long wood counter for delicious yakitori like *tsukune* (chicken meatballs), *mune* (chicken breasts), and *momo* (chicken thighs). Other grill thrills include juicy Kobe beef skewers freckled with *shichimi togarashi*; fried chicken *karaage* drizzled with lemon; and bacon-wrapped *unagi* glazed with a smoky eel sauce.

Tamarine

Vietnamese

A4

546 University Ave. (bet. Cowper & Webster Sts.), Palo Alto

Phone:	650-325-8500	Lunch Mon – Fri
Web:	www.tamarinerestaurant.com	Dinner nightly
Prices:	**$$**	

Traditional flavors get a modern makeover at Tamarine, the perennial Palo Alto hot spot serving elegant and contemporary Vietnamese cuisine to cosmopolitan crowds.

By day, the sleek dining room, dressed with modern furniture and Vietnamese art, hosts a business clientele. During evenings, the central bar buzzes with locals who come for innovative cocktails and wines by the glass, while chic couples linger over the Tamarine Taste—a delicious sampling of four appetizers that might include shrimp spring rolls, papaya salad, taro root rolls, and tea leaf beef. The menu may go on to include whole fillets of pan-fried snapper, lacquered in a sweet and tangy tamarind, kaffir lime, and lemongrass sauce–a perfect match for their crisp *grüner veltliner*.

Thea Mediterranean

 D3

Mediterranean ✗✗

3090 Olsen Dr. (at Winchester Blvd.), San Jose

Phone: 408-260-1444   Lunch & dinner daily
Web: www.thearestaurant.com
Prices: $$

Named for the mythical mother of the sun and moon, Thea shines its light on traditional Greek and Turkish specialties at reasonable prices. The 20-foot-tall olive tree in the center of the soaring dining room sets the stage for a delightful culinary journey through the Mediterranean.

Begin your trip with an authentic meze sampler that includes hummus, *tzatziki*, *htipiti*, and *melitzanosalata*, served with homemade pita bread and fruity olive oil. Then explore the region more intimately in entrées such as moussaka, chicken souvlaki, and *garides* (grilled prawns in Greek spices, served over a zucchini cake).

The young, polite staff is swift and efficient—a fact that the corporate Silicon Valley crowd who lunches here no doubt appreciates.

Thiên Long

 F3

Vietnamese ✗

3005 Silver Creek Rd. #138 (bet. Aborn Rd. & Lexann Ave.), San Jose

Phone: 408-223-6188   Lunch & dinner daily
Web: N/A
Prices:

No need to stop at the ATM on your way to this cash-only San Jose favorite: Thiên Long's cheap Vietnamese eats are easy on the pockets. It's located in a shopping center that brims with Asian storefronts and is popular among the area's burgeoning Vietnamese community.

With tile floors and wooden chairs, the interior isn't much. But it doesn't need to be: food is fresh and light, and service is friendly. On chilly days, sop up your *bánh mì bò kho*, a chunky beef stew with jalapeño and Thai basil, with a crusty baguette. Or, opt for a noodle bowl laden with barbecue pork and prawns for the perfect flavor combination of smoky, salty, and sweet. Don't miss the tapioca pearl smoothies, including a coffee rendition or exotic durian, jackfruit, and taro.

Turmeric

C2

Indian ✗

141 S. Murphy Ave. (bet. Evelyn & Washington Aves.), Sunnyvale

Phone: 408-617-9100
Web: N/A
Prices:

Dinner nightly

Located on Sunnyvale's historic and quaint Murphy Avenue, where boutiques and restaurants cram the sidewalks, Turmeric might not be as cute as its neighbors but don't judge this place by its cover. It may not offer much in the way of design and aesthetics, but with delectable Indian food at great prices, who needs fancy digs?

The buffet is well-known and draws droves, but forget traipsing upstairs and take a seat in the dining room for à la carte specialties. Instead of focusing on the typical, the menu gives equal treatment to traditional, regional dishes. Favorites such as chicken *makhani* from Delhi, *murg ka mukul* from Rajasthan, lamb *vindaloo* from Goa, and Malabar fish curry from Kerala—take you on a culinary trip around India without the jet lag.

Vung Tau

E3

Vietnamese ✗✗

535 E. Santa Clara St. (at 12th St.), San Jose

Phone: 408-288-9055
Web: www.vungtaurestaurant.com
Prices:

Lunch & dinner daily

Vung Tau's ample space is simply filled with tables for their hordes of loyal Vietnamese patrons. Despite their rather chaste décor and basic service, the gamut of food offerings keeps them riveted. While the hefty menu can stupefy, rest assured that the home-style food is as authentic as it is tasty. Imagine a plethora of both unique and classic delights from steaming noodle bowls to seafood and meat dishes. Watch as the faithful order the likes of *bo bia* (soft rolls filled with Chinese sausage and egg); or *tam bi tom cha* (broken rice cloaked with shredded pork and succulent prawns). *Banh khot* cupcakes are enticingly redefined here as savory confections, crisp at the edges, depressed at the center to hold a filling of sweet shrimp and minced scallions.

Xanh

B2

Vietnamese

110 Castro St. (bet. Evelyn Ave. & Villa St.), Mountain View

Phone: 650-964-1888
Web: www.xanhrestaurant.com
Prices: $$

Lunch Mon – Fri
Dinner nightly

Long a favorite for outstanding Vietnamese fare in Mountain View, Xanh has maintained its mod image over the years. Today, Xanh's über-contemporary design features mesh curtains and bright neon lights, and the 12,500 square-foot space seems deeply devoted to drinks, with a new bar and lounge that starts groovin' to DJ beats on weekends.

For those who like a little nosh with their nightlife, Xanh's Vietnamese food is still good, even if not quite what it once was. Dishes may unveil a roasted duck roll wrapped imperial-style in thin rice paper; bold peppercorn beef sautéed with bell peppers and onion; and fried, shell-on shrimp with sliced hot jalapeños—they're difficult to peel but always worth it. Don't forget a scoop of the lightly sweet coconut rice.

Zeni

D3

Ethiopian

1320 Saratoga Ave. (1320 Saratoga Ave.), San Jose

Phone: 408-615-8282
Web: www.zenirestaurant.com
Prices: $$

Lunch & dinner Tue – Sun

Ethiopia's cuisine—while roaming the globe—has cultivated a global following. Zeni is a cultural delight luring natives with a deliciously authentic menu and proper set featuring a thatched bar, exotic artwork, and classic furnishings. Amicability reigns as diners dispel with cutlery and chow in communion. With no utensil in sight, visit the wash basin before diving in...fingers first.

Embodying simple food is the *injera*—a fluffy flatbread used to scoop up flavorful meats and sauces. Chatty servers indulge locals with dreamy collard greens; tangy, spiced lentils; split peas with turmeric; and veggies gilded with garlic 'n ginger. *Kitfo* (ground steak with herb butter and chili powder) is quickly quenched by black tea swirled with honey-spice syrup.

Zitune

Moroccan XX

B2

325 Main St. (bet. 1st & 2nd Sts.), Los Altos

Phone: 650-947-0247
Web: www.zitune.com
Prices: $$

Lunch Mon – Fri
Dinner Tue – Sun

Rather than a Moroccan restaurant, Zitune is more of a Mediterranean fantasy marrying culinary skill, contemporary flair, and generous taste of *chermoula*. Menu offerings may include *merguez* tagine, with links of lamb sausage and fluffy, spice-infused couscous. Bright Mediterranean influences are showcased in such dishes as pan-seared *bronzini* served over a fine *brunoise* of ratatouille Provençale. Desserts may include a sticky-sweet almond pastille with lavender ice cream.

The interior stylishly evokes northern Africa without feeling over the top: barrel-vaulted ceilings slope gently toward simple iron wall hangings, artwork, wood furnishings, and plank floors.

With a well-to-do feel, Zitune is popular for business lunches as well as after-work drinks.

Bib Gourmand 😋
indicates our inspectors'
favorites for good value.

Peter L. Wrenn/MICHELIN

Wine Country

Wine Country
Napa Valley & Sonoma County

Picnicking on artisan-made cheeses and fresh crusty bread amid acres of gnarled grapevines; sipping wine on a terrace above a hillside of silvery olive trees; touring caves heady with the sweet smell of fermenting grapes: this is northern California's wine country. Lying within an hour's drive north and northeast of San Francisco, the hills and vales of Sonoma County and Napa Valley thrive on the abundant sunshine and fertile soil that produce grapes for some of North America's finest wines.

Fruit of the Vine

Cuttings of Criollas grapevines traveled north with Franciscan padres from the Baja Peninsula during the late 17th century. Wines made from these "mission" grapes were used primarily for trade and for sacramental purposes. In the early 1830s, a French immigrant propitiously named Jean-Louis Vignes (vigne is French for "vine") established a large vineyard near Los Angeles using cuttings of European grapevines (Vitis vinifera), and by the mid-19th century, winemaking had become one of southern California's principal industries.

In 1857 Hungarian immigrant Agoston Haraszthy purchased a 400-acre estate in Sonoma County, named it Buena Vista, and cultivated Tokay vine cuttings imported from his homeland. In 1861, bolstered by promises of state funding, Haraszthy went to Europe to gather assorted vinifera cuttings to plant in California soil. Upon his return, however, the state legislature reneged on their commitment. Undeterred, Haraszthy persisted in distributing (at his own expense) some 100,000 cuttings and testing varieties in different soil types. Successful application of his discoveries created a boom in the local wine industry in the late 19th century.

The Tide Turns

As the 1800s drew to a close, northern California grapevines fell prey to phylloxera, a root louse that attacks susceptible vinifera plants. Entire vineyards were decimated. Eventually researchers discovered they could combat phylloxera by replanting vineyards with disease-resistant wild grape rootstocks, onto which vinifera cuttings could be grafted. The wine industry had achieved a modicum of recovery by the early 20th century, only to be slapped with the 18th Amendment to the Constitution, prohibiting the manufacture, sale, importation, and transportation of intoxicating liquors in the US.

California's winemaking industry remained at a near-standstill until 1933, when Prohibition was repealed. The Great Depression slowed the reclamation of vineyards and it wasn't until the early 1970s that California's wine industry was fully re-established. In 1976, California wines took top honors in a blind taste testing by French judges in Paris. The results helped open up a whole new world of respectability for Californian vineyards.

COMING OF AGE

As Napa and Sonoma wines have established their reputations, the importance of individual growing regions has increased. Many sub-regions have sought and acquired Federal regulation of the place names as American Viticultural Areas, or AVAs, in order to set the boundaries of wine-growing areas that are distinctive for their soil, microclimate, and wine styles. Although this system is subject to debate, there is no doubt that an AVA such as Russian River Valley, Carneros, or Spring Mountain can be very meaningful. The precise location of a vineyard relative to the Pacific Ocean or San Pablo Bay; the elevation and slope of a vineyard; the soil type and moisture content; and even the proximity to a mountain gap can make essential differences.

Together, Sonoma and Napa have almost 30 registered appellations, which vary in size and sometimes overlap. Specific place names are becoming increasingly important as growers learn what to plant where and how to care for vines in each unique circumstance. The fact that more and more wines go to market with a specific AVA flies in the face of the worldwide trend to ever larger and less specific "branded" wines. Individual wineries and associations are working to promote the individuality of North Coast appellations and to preserve their integrity and viability as sustainable agriculture.

DESTINATION WINE COUNTRY

In recent decades the Napa and Sonoma valleys have experienced tremendous development. Besides significant increases in vineyard acreage, the late 20th century witnessed an explosion of small-scale operations, some housed in old wineries updated with state-of-the-art equipment. Meanwhile, the Russian River Valley remains less developed, retaining its rural feel with country roads winding past picturesque wineries, rolling hills of grapevines, and stands of redwood trees.

With easy access to world-class wines, and organic produce and cheeses from local farms, residents of northern California's wine country enjoy an enviable quality of life. Happily for visitors, those same products supply the area's burgeoning number of restaurants, creating a culture of gourmet dining that stretches from the city of Napa north to Healdsburg and beyond.

Note that if you elect to bring your own wine, most restaurants charge a corkage fee (which can vary from $10 to as much as $50 per bottle). Many restaurants waive this fee on one particular day, or if you purchase an additional bottle from their list.

Which Food?	Which Wine?	Some Examples
Shellfish	Semi-dry White	Early harvest Riesling, Chenin Blanc, early harvest Gewürztraminer, Viognier
	Dry White	Lighter Chardonnay (less oak), Pinot Blanc, Sauvignon Blanc, dry Riesling, dry Chenin Blanc
	Sparkling Wine	Brut, Extra Dry, Brut Rosé
	Dry Rosé	Pinot Noir, Syrah, Cabernet
Fish	Dry White	Chardonnay (oaky or not) Sauvignon Blanc, dry Riesling, dry Chenin Blanc, Pinot Blanc
	Sparkling Wine	Brut, Blanc de Blancs, Brut Rosé
	Light Red	Pinot Noir, Pinot Meunier, light-bodied Zinfandel
	Dry Rosé	Pinot Noir, Syrah, Cabernet
Cured Meats/ Picnic Fare	Semi-dry White	Early harvest Riesling or early harvest Gewürztraminer
	Dry White	Chardonnay (less oak), Sauvignon Blanc, dry Riesling
	Sparkling Wine	Brut, Blanc de Blancs, Brut Rosé
	Light Red	Gamay, Pinot Noir, Zinfandel, Sangiovese
	Young Heavy Red	Syrah, Cabernet Sauvignon, Zinfandel, Cabernet Franc, Merlot
	Rosé	Any light Rosé
Red Meat	Dry Rosé	Pinot Noir, Cabernet, Syrah, Blends
	Light Red	Pinot Noir, Zinfandel, Gamay, Pinot Meunier
	Young Heavy Red	Cabernet Sauvignon, Cabernet Franc, Syrah, Grenache, Petite Sirah, Merlot, Blends, Pinot Noir, Cabernet Sauvignon
	Mature Red	Merlot, Syrah, Zinfandel, Meritage, Blends
Fowl	Semi-dry White	Early harvest Riesling, Chenin Blanc, Viognier
	Dry White	Sauvignon Blanc, Chardonnay, Pinot Blanc, dry Riesling
	Sparkling Wine	Extra Dry, Brut, Brut Rosé
	Rosé	Any light Rosé
	Light Red	Pinot Noir, Zinfandel, Blends, Gamay
	Mature Red	Pinot Noir, Cabernet Sauvignon, Merlot, Syrah, Zinfandel, Meritage, Blends
Cheese	Semi-dry White	Riesling, Gewürztraminer, Chenin Blanc
	Dry White	Sauvignon Blanc, Chardonnay, Pinot Blanc, dry Riesling
	Sparkling Wine	Extra Dry, Brut
	Rosé	Pinot Noir, Cabernet, Grenache
	Light Red	Pinot Noir, Zinfandel, Blends, Gamay
	Young Heavy Red	Cabernet Sauvignon, Cabernet Franc, Syrah, Grenache, Petite Sirah, Merlot, Blends
Dessert	Sweet White	Any late harvest White
	Semi-dry White	Riesling, Gewürztraminer, Chenin Blanc, Muscat
	Sparkling Wine	Extra Dry, Brut, Rosé, Rouge
	Dessert Reds	Late harvest Zinfandel, Port

Vintage	2007	2006	2005	2004	2003	2002	2001	2000	1999	1998	1997	1996	1995
Chardonnay **Carneros**	🍇	🍇	🍇	🍇	🍇	🍇	🍇	🍇	🍇	🍇	🍇	🍇	🍇
Chardonnay **Russian River**	🍇	🍇	🍇	🍇	🍇	🍇	🍇	🍇	🍇	🍇	🍇	🍇	🍇
Chardonnay **Napa Valley**	🍇	🍇	🍇	🍇	🍇	🍇	🍇	🍇	🍇	🍇	🍇	🍇	🍇
Sauvignon Blanc **Napa Valley**	🍇	🍇	🍇	🍇	🍇	🍇	🍇	🍇	🍇	🍇	🍇	🍇	🍇
Sauvignon Blanc **Sonoma County**	🍇	🍇	🍇	🍇	🍇	🍇	🍇	🍇	🍇	🍇	🍇	🍇	🍇
Pinot Noir **Carneros**	🍇	🍇	🍇	🍇	🍇	🍇	🍇	🍇	🍇	🍇	🍇	🍇	🍇
Pinot Noir **Russian River**	🍇	🍇	🍇	🍇	🍇	🍇	🍇	🍇	🍇	🍇	🍇	🍇	🍇
Merlot **Napa Valley**	🍇	🍇	🍇	🍇	🍇	🍇	🍇	🍇	🍇	🍇	🍇	🍇	🍇
Merlot **Sonoma County**	🍇	🍇	🍇	🍇	🍇	🍇	🍇	🍇	🍇	🍇	🍇	🍇	🍇
Cabernet Sauvignon **Napa Valley**	🍇	🍇	🍇	🍇	🍇	🍇	🍇	🍇	🍇	🍇	🍇	🍇	🍇
Cabernet Sauvignon **Southern Sonoma**	🍇	🍇	🍇	🍇	🍇	🍇	🍇	🍇	🍇	🍇	🍇	🍇	🍇
Cabernet Sauvignon **Northern Sonoma**	🍇	🍇	🍇	🍇	🍇	🍇	🍇	🍇	🍇	🍇	🍇	🍇	🍇
Zinfandel **Napa Valley**	🍇	🍇	🍇	🍇	🍇	🍇	🍇	🍇	🍇	🍇	🍇	🍇	🍇
Zinfandel **Southern Sonoma**	🍇	🍇	🍇	🍇	🍇	🍇	🍇	🍇	🍇	🍇	🍇	🍇	🍇
Zinfandel **Northern Sonoma**	🍇	🍇	🍇	🍇	🍇	🍇	🍇	🍇	🍇	🍇	🍇	🍇	🍇

🍇 = Outstanding   🍇 = Above Average   🍇 = Average

Peter L. Wrenn/MICHELIN

Napa Valley

Wine is the watchword in this 35-mile-long valley, which extends in a northerly direction from the San Pablo Bay to Mount St. Helena. Cradled between the Mayacama and the Vaca mountain ranges, the area boasts some of California's most prestigious wineries, along with a host of restaurants that are destinations in themselves.

Reclaimed 19th century stone wineries and Victorian houses punctuate the valley's landscape, reminding the traveler that there were some 140 wineries here prior to 1890. Today, Napa Valley has 325 producing wineries (and more than 400 brands), up from a post-Prohibition low of perhaps a dozen. They are all clustered along Route 29, the valley's main artery, which runs up the western side of the mountains, passing through the commercial hub of Napa and continuing north through the charming little wine burgs of Yountville, Oakville, Rutherford, St. Helena, and Calistoga. More wineries dot the tranquil Silverado Trail, which hugs the foothills of the eastern range and gives a more pastoral perspective on this rural farm county. Along both routes, picturesque spots for alfresco dining abound. So pick up some picnic supplies at the **Oakville Grocery** (on Route 29), or stop by either the **Model Bakery** in St. Helena or **Bouchon Bakery** in Yountville

for fresh-baked bread and delectable pastries.

Throughout the valley you'll spot knolls, canyons, dry creek beds, stretches of valley floor, and glorious mountain vistas, all of which afford varying

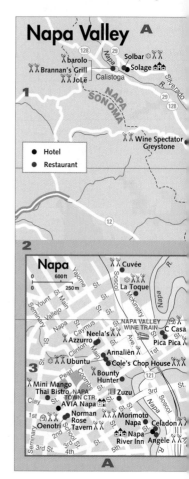

microclimates and soil types for growing wine. San Pablo Bay has a moderating effect on the valley's temperatures, while the influence of the Pacific Ocean is lessened by the mountains. In the valley, powerfully hot summer days and still cool nights provide the ideal climate for cabernet sauvignon grapes, a varietal for which Napa is justifiably famous.

Among the region's many winemakers are well-known names like Robert Mondavi, Francis Ford Coppola, and the Miljenko "Mike" Grgich. Originally from Croatia, Grgich rose to fame as the winemaker at **Chateau Montelena** when his 1973 chardonnay took the top prize at the Judgment of Paris in 1976, outshining one of France's best white Burgundies. This feat turned the wine world

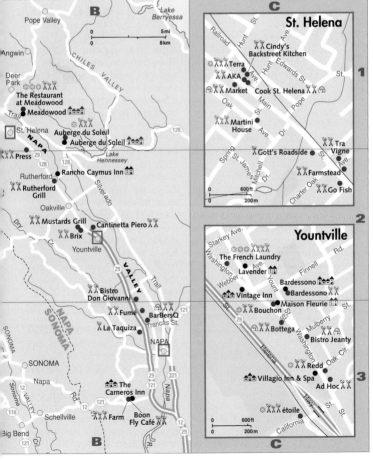

on its ear, and put California on the map as a bona fide producer of fine wine. Since then, Napa's success with premium wine has fostered a special pride of place. Fourteen American Viticultural Areas (AVAs) currently regulate the boundaries for sub-regions such as Carneros, Stags Leap, Rutherford, and Los Carneros.

The boom in wine production has spawned a special kind of food-and-wine tourism: Today tasting rooms, tours, and farm-fresh cuisine are de rigueur here. Along Washington Street, acclaimed chefs such as Thomas Keller, Richard Reddington, Michael Chiarello, and Philippe Jeanty rub elbows. Many other well-known chefs hail from the Napa Valley—Cindy Pawlcyn, Jeremy Fox, and Hiro Sone, to name a few—and have successfully raised their local-legend status to the national level.

Those touring the valley will spot fields of wild fennel, silvery olive trees, and rows of wild mustard that bloom between the grapevines in February and March. The mustard season kicks off each year with the Napa Valley Mustard Festival, which celebrates the food, wine, art, and rich agricultural bounty of the area. Several towns host seasonal farmers' markets, generally held from May through October. These include Napa (held in the Wine Train parking lot Tuesdays and Saturdays); St. Helena (Fridays in Crane Park); and Calistoga (Saturdays on Washington Street). On Thursday nights in the summer, there's a **Chef's Market** in Napa Town Center. Opened in early 2008, **Oxbow Public Market** is a block-long 40,000-square-foot facility that is meant to vie with the Ferry Building Marketplace across the bay. Oxbow brims with local food artisans and wine vendors, all from within a 100-mile radius of the market. Within this barn-like building you'll find cheeses and charcuterie; spices and specialty teas; olive oils and organic ice cream; and, of course, stands of farm-fresh produce. And there are plenty of snacks available after you work up an appetite shopping. Elsewhere around the valley, regional products such as St. Helena Olive Oil, Woodhouse Chocolates, and Rancho Gordo heirloom beans are gaining a national following.

Just north of downtown St. Helena, the massive stone building that was erected in 1889 as Greystone Cellars now houses the West Coast campus of the renowned Culinary Institute of America (CIA). The Culinary Institute has a restaurant and visitors here are welcome to view the several unique cooking demonstrations—reservations are recommended.

With all this going for the Napa Valley, one thing is for sure: From the city of Napa, the region's largest population center, north to the town of Calistoga—known for its mineral mud baths and spa cuisine—this narrow valley represents paradise for lovers of good food and fine wine.

Ad Hoc

American ✗✗

C3

6476 Washington St. (bet. California Dr. & Oak Circle), Yountville

Phone: 707-944-2487
Web: www.adhocrestaurant.com
Prices: $$$

Lunch Sun
Dinner Thu – Mon

A lovely weathered farm table is the centerpiece at bustling Ad Hoc, the third in Chef/owner Thomas Keller's Yountville family. The kind of hangout that Keller himself might frequent at the end of a long night, low-key Ad Hoc epitomizes wine country with a rustic aura, warm hospitality, and plain good food crafted from the most exquisite ingredients.

In keeping with the ease of Napa Valley, Ad Hoc makes the tough decisions for you, serving a nightly four-course prix-fixe. What you see—perhaps smoky Kansas City barbecue or fried chicken—is what you get. Family-style meals begin with a salad such as romaine hearts rich with the flavor of anchovy, and finish with a simple cheese course and a dessert that showcases Keller's heralded knack for pastry.

AKA

American ✗✗

C1

1320 Main St. (bet. Adam St. & Hunt Ave.), St. Helena

Phone: 707-967-8111
Web: www.akabistro.com
Prices: $$

Lunch Wed – Sat
Dinner Tue – Sun

Look for the vintage neon sign reading "Keller's Meat Market" to find AKA, a casual bistro and wine bar. Inside, pressed-tin ceilings, polished concrete floors, and grapevine-wrapped pendant lamps provide a comfy setting for dinners of build-your-own-burgers. More upscale entrées may include tender grilled pork chops with crispy oven potatoes and a deliciously eclectic medley of accompaniments.

Owner Robert Simon is a fixture in the dining room, though service can be hit or miss. Perhaps AKA's best draw is the California-centric wine list. An electronic wine dispensing system has 20 varietals to taste, while a rustic wood tower showcases nearly 600 vintages from mostly local labels. Cured meats and cheese plates are perfect for pairing.

Angèle

A3

540 Main St. (at 5th St.), Napa

Lunch & dinner daily

Phone: 707-252-8115
Web: www.angelerestaurant.com
Prices: $$$

Located south of the new Napa Riverfront, all traces of the modern age disappear at this winning hideaway inside an historic boathouse overlooking the Napa River. Take advantage of the elements from the breezy covered patio, or relish the friendly interior where a pitched timber ceiling, bistro furnishings, and blue and yellow accents suggest a French Country aspect. Savvy, good-natured service extends from dining room to bar—a recommended stop for those without reservations.

Californian sensibilities enliven this traditional brasserie fare. Watercress and shaved fennel garnish crispy sweetbreads and a caramelized onion tart, while chorizo and peppers spice a pan-seared grouper. Classic renditions include onion soup and *coquilles Saint-Jacques*.

Annaliên

A3

1142 Main St. (bet. 1st & Pearl Sts.), Napa

Lunch & Dinner Tue – Sat

Phone: 707-224-8319
Web: N/A
Prices: $$

Asiaphiles in Napa Valley are thankful for the precious Annalien, since quality Far Eastern cuisine is a rarity in these parts. Here, contemporary Vietnamese flavors marry Californian influences with such ease, creativity, and success that a blithe and buzzing scene is expected. The Spartan décor features skylights and shaded sconces alongside a flower-topped black granite bar.

Under the guidance of Chef/owner Annaliên "Anna" Shepley, the kitchen may prepare an enticing spread from pot stickers, filled with minced chicken and spices, to shaking beef—rib eye cubes wok-fried with peppers and onions—served atop crunchy romaine. The popular lemongrass chicken and lavender sea salt-crusted rack of lamb are as pleasing as the informed and affable staff.

Auberge du Soleil ✿

Californian 🍴🍴🍴

B1

180 Rutherford Hill Rd. (off the Silverado Trail), Rutherford

Phone: 707-963-1211 — Lunch & dinner daily
Web: www.aubergedusoleil.com
Prices: $$$$

Auberge du Soleil

This gorgeous little hideaway, nestled into a picturesque hill just off the Silverado Trail, will knock the socks off anyone you bring to its door—guaranteed. Reserve them a room at the gorgeous luxury inn of the same name (which opened after the restaurant, likely because no one wanted to leave) and they just might marry you.

By day, Auberge Du Soleil's dining room is drenched in sunlight, with an easy country chic dressed in earth tones, exposed beams, and rustic furnishings. As night falls, it simply doesn't get more beautiful than the view from this restaurant's terrace, where a lingering meal overlooking Napa Valley is positively transformative.

And yet the prettiest scenes lie in Chef Robert Curry's beautifully designed dishes—a seasonal, farm-fresh affair that might include tender grilled octopus over a warm mound of fried fingerling potatoes, feta cheese, chorizo, fried capers, and sautéed leeks surrounded by lemon aïoli; perfectly seared Wolfe farm quail, served with savory black garlic *croutes* and quartered romaine hearts laced with warm bacon dressing and balsamic red onions; or ethereally light *galette au sucre* with lemon-vanilla foam, apple sorbet, and candied quince.

Azzurro

Pizza ✗

A3

1260 Main St. (at Clinton St.), Napa

Phone: 707-255-5552
Web: www.azzurropizzeria.com
Prices: $$

Lunch & dinner daily

A blue and white tiled gas-fired pizza oven gleams in the center of the sleek open kitchen, where a marble bar at the chef's station offers views of the action. The airy dining space features a long wooden banquette, zinc-topped tables, and glossy black chairs.

Ten tasty varieties of thin crust pizza—with combinations for both purists and gourmands—are the specialty at Azzuro. Try the *funghi*, with roasted crimini and wild mushrooms, Taleggio, and thyme; or the *salsiccia*, with fennel sausage, red onion, and mozzarella. Anyone torn between a salad and a slice can go for the *manciata*—baked pizza dough topped with a choice of salads. Rustic pasta and antipasti dishes like Gamberi (grilled shrimp, white beans, sausage and arugula) complete the menu.

BarBersQ 😊

Barbecue ✗✗

B3

3900 D, Bel Aire Plaza (at Trancas St.), Napa

Phone: 707-224-6600
Web: www.barbersq.com
Prices: $$

Lunch & dinner daily

What could be better than good, old-fashioned American classics whipped up outta the fresh bounty of local gardens and farms? Not a whole lot. Here at the ever-popular BarBersQ, Memphis-style BBQ gets a conscientious kick in the pants—sustainable ingredients from grass-fed beef and free-range chicken to organic fruits, veggies, and herbs (much of which come to the kitchen the same day they're picked), command the hearty menu.

Lip-smackers like wild Atlantic fried shrimp with zingy tartar sauce, or the Q-combo (go for tender brisket and baby back ribs) are sure to satiate. Delish meat sandwiches and sides like warm cornbread with honey butter make it all the more irresistible. The small interior, styled in stainless steel and marble, crowds up quickly.

Bardessono

Californian 🍴🍴

C2

6526 Yount St. (at Finnell Rd.), Yountville

Phone: 707-204-6030   Lunch & dinner daily
Web: www.bardessono.com
Prices: $$$

A stone's throw from the kitschy decadence of Yountville's main drag, Bardessono is an unexpected, contemporary retreat touted as the country's greenest resort. The restaurant is an example of recycled design, with repurposed California cypress and walnut composing much of the space. A recycled glass leaf chandelier is a whimsical evocation of the natural surrounds while a massive mural spells it out in a bucolic watercolor view.

The Californian menu is local and seasonal, organized into the categories Field & Forest, Ocean, Pasture & Range. Dishes like gnocchi with plump morels are available in half portions; entrées may include a pan-roasted lamb loin with spicy vermicelli *laksa*. Don't miss the wine list of mostly local and biodynamic producers.

barolo

Italian 🍴

A1

1457 Lincoln Ave. (bet. Fair Way & Washington St.), Calistoga

Phone: 707-942-9900   Dinner Wed – Sun
Web: www.barolocalistoga.com
Prices: $$

Wine bar-cum-full-scale restaurant, barolo might have formerly been known as barVino, but there's so much more to this wine country restaurant than just the local grape juice. After a day of lolling in the mud, or yes, tasting wine at local vineyards, visit this lounge-like spot for a little city chic in the heart of sleepy Calistoga. As might be expected, the wine list has some unique local and small production labels that blend perfectly with the Italian dishes (gourmet thin-crust pizzas, perfect al dente pastas) hailing from the kitchen.

This is Italian in that cool, metropolitan way. Not a checkered table cloth or red sauce joint, this place is all about red leather booths, metallic fixtures, and a candy apple red Vespa perched on the wall.

299

Bistro Don Giovanni

Italian ✕✕

B2

4110 Howard Ln. (at Hwy. 29), Napa

Phone: 707-224-3300
Web: www.bistrodongiovanni.com
Prices: $$

Lunch & dinner daily

The stars in Galileo's sky aligned in the making of Don Giovanni, the Napa mainstay that owes its success equally to location, ambience, and consistent cuisine. Perched conveniently on Highway 29, the restaurant remains true to rustic Italian form with terra-cotta floors, country-style rattan chairs, and gleaming copper cookware dangling above the *pizzaiolo's* wood-burning oven.

From the kitchen, a bounty of antipasti, seasonal risottos, and house-made pastas refuel locals and wine tasters alike, while savory fried green olives with Marcona almonds or *fettuccine alla lina*, tossed with porcini and sausage ragù, make for a cocktail-friendly start. High ceilings can't contain the din of the constant crowd but, on sunny days, the real party is on the patio.

Bistro Jeanty

French ✕✕

C3

6510 Washington St. (at Mulberry St.), Yountville

Phone: 707-944-0103
Web: www.bistrojeanty.com
Prices: $$

Lunch & dinner daily

There is no culinary destination quite like Yountville, where boldface names like Thomas Keller and Michael Chiarello rule a notable restaurant row. Chef Philippe Jeanty may be less recognizable to the Food Network set, but his Bistro Jeanty is still a Washington Street star.

Housed behind a red brick façade with a striped awning and window boxes abloom with roses and geraniums, Bistro Jeanty has all the trappings of a wine country favorite—French antiques inside and woven café chairs and mismatched tables, set with peppermills and cruets of Dijon mustard, on the heated terrace. With a respectful approach to classical fare, the kitchen sends out excellent renditions of pig's foot salad, with al dente haricots verts, and Petrale sole meunière.

Boon Fly Café

Californian

B3

4048 Sonoma Hwy. (at Los Carneros Ave.), Napa

Phone: 707-299-4870   Lunch & dinner daily
Web: www.thecarnerosinn.com
Prices: $$

Straddling the wine growing areas of Napa and Sonoma, the Carneros region maintains a pastoral aspect, echoed in the rustic red barn-style of the Boon Fly Café. Part of the Carneros Inn, amid 27 bucolic acres off the Old Sonoma Highway, the café serves breakfast, lunch, and dinner to visitors and locals alike. With corrugated aluminum walls and porch swings to ease the brunchtime waits, this is a decidedly upscale roadhouse eatery.

Sandwiches like the Reuben; Kobe beef burger; or flatbreads decked with blue cheese, caramelized onions, bacon, mushrooms, and thyme may be on both lunch and dinner menus. Heartier appetites will savor homier dishes such as ribs with orange-habanero barbecue sauce or fried chicken with torpedo onion and snap pea salad.

Bottega

Italian

C3

6525 Washington St. (near Yount St.), Yountville

Phone: 707-945-1050   Lunch Tue – Sun
Web: www.botteganapavalley.com   Dinner nightly
Prices: $$

In Italian, a *bottega* is a master artisan's atelier. In Yountville, Bottega is both workplace and showplace for maestro Michael Chiarello who, despite his small screen fame, isn't kicking back on his laurels. He leaves that to his jovial guests, who sink into plush couches on the flagstone terrace warmed by roaring fires.

Terra-cotta and leather add richness to the interior, where Chef/owner Chiarello makes his presence known. When he isn't charming the dining room with shots of *amaro* and jokes on the house, Chiarello is orchestrating the kitchen. His impeccable Californian touch can be tasted in every Italian bite, with such dishes as warm polenta "under glass"; sole with grapes and rosemary brown butter; and perfectly al dente handmade pastas.

Bouchon ✿

French 🍴

C3

6534 Washington St. (at Yount St.), Yountville

Phone: 707-944-8037
Web: www.bouchonbistro.com
Prices: $$$

Lunch & dinner daily

Bouchon

Chef Thomas Keller might be internationally lauded for the intricate dishes he concocts at The French Laundry, but his decidedly casual Bouchon—a hopping little bistro named for a traditionally meat-heavy café found in Lyon—proves that the man many consider to be the world's greatest chef knows how to throw down simple country fare with the best of them.

The dining room is intimate and fun, with specials scratched out on a chalkboard and waiters happily buzzing to and fro. Come summer, the outdoor terrace fills up with regulars lingering over fresh shucked oysters and bubbly. Put together, the whole place oozes a kind of haphazard, cozy-sweater Parisian charm, but a closer inspection of the menu reveals Keller's trademark perfectionism: a goldmine of rustic French offerings, refined to sublime perfection by the master chef.

Dinner kicks off with the house's legendary epi baguette, and just gets more delicious from there. A light, perfectly crispy trio of brandade beignets arrives topped with fried sage leaf and set atop a wedge of sun-dried tomato; while a plump, mouthwatering boudin noir is paired with smooth, buttery pomme purée and soft caramelized apples.

Bounty Hunter

A m e r i c a n

 A3

975 First St. (at Main St.), Napa

Phone: 707-226-3976
Web: www.bountyhunterwinebar.com
Prices: $$

Lunch & dinner daily

Deep in the heart of Napa, a landmark 1888 brick building with worn wood floors and pressed-copper ceilings is just the place for a wine bar-meets-barbecue joint that feels worlds away from the honkytonks of yore. Designer tasting flights and private label wines fit the oenophile locale, but those juicy meats from the grill out back make the Bounty Hunter a real prize.

Majestic mounted game presides over the saloon-style space where locals pair their wines with shredded crab and red pepper bisque; bone-in rib eyes; and hearty barbecue sandwiches. The beer can chicken is a must, even if it does elicit a sophomoric chuckle—the crispy Cajun-skinned fowl stands upright on a Tecate can. The job of carving the bird is all yours, but so is the reward.

Brannan's Grill

A m e r i c a n

 A1

1374 Lincoln Ave. (at Washington St.), Calistoga

Phone: 707-942-2233
Web: www.brannansgrill.com
Prices: $$

Lunch & dinner daily

After a soothing mud bath or a healing dip in one of Calistoga's famous mineral springs, a mountain breeze pouring through large screen windows and a blazing fire in the stone hearth could be just what the doctor ordered. And with genuine service and a richly decorated mahogany-paneled dining room that dates to the 19th century, Brannan's Grill is the right prescription for a cushy night out. Live piano or jazz sets the mood for casual American suppers on weekends.

Dishes might include puréed butternut squash soup garnished with blue cheese beignets, or chipotle-glazed pork loin with crispy straw onions. You can't go wrong, however, with a straightforward burger. Cap the night with a glass of pinot noir at the romantic Victorian bar.

Brix

B2

7377 St. Helena Hwy. (at Washington St.), Yountville

Phone: 707-944-2749 — Lunch & dinner daily
Web: www.brix.com
Prices: $$$

With prolific vegetable gardens, a burgeoning orchard, and an award-winning vineyard, Brix gives new meaning to fresh, local food. Peek out the floor-to-ceiling windows and spot Chef Anne Gingrass-Paik with an armful of produce on its way to your plate. Their garden patio may be the wine country's most picturesque locale for sipping and savoring Californian cuisine. At the restaurant's center, wrought-iron chandeliers preside over a glass-encased wine cellar, which doubles as a dramatic venue for private parties.

The menu is presented in straightforward categories: the "Wood Oven" may tempt with a fig and candied bacon pizza; the "Charcoal Grill" may feature swordfish with Tuscan bean stew; and the "Range" may offer lamb osso buco over polenta.

Cantinetta Piero

B2

6774 Washington St. (at Madison St.), Yountville

Phone: 707-299-5015 — Lunch & dinner daily
Web: www.cantinettapiero.com
Prices: $$

On the west end of Washington Street, inside the new Hotel Luca, Cantinetta Piero is redolent of Tuscany with exposed timber beams, electric candle fixtures hanging from vaulted brick, and old Italian tins lining the main dining room. In northern Californian custom, recycled design also plays a part here: an antique wine barrel acts as an ice chest to chill bottles of water and wine.

Named for legendary winemaker Piero Antinori, Cantinetta Piero pours only Italian and Napa varietals. The selection complements Northern Italian antipasti, such as house-made *salumi* or wild mushrooms with bubbly fonduta cheese; wood-fired (and pricey) artisanal pizzas; handmade pastas; and seasonal entrées such as crispy salmon with blood orange and fennel salad.

C Casa

Mexican ✗

A3

610 1st St. #6 (at McKinstry St.), Napa

Phone: 707-226-7700
Web: www.myccasa.com
Prices:

Lunch & dinner daily

Bay Area foodies will instantly recognize the Oxbow Public Market, Napa's answer to SF's Ferry Building bursting with kitchen shops and international foodstuffs. Relatively new to the culinary destination, co-owner Catherine Bergen—also former owner of Made in Napa's all-natural pantry products—is translating her taste for healthy gourmet eats to this innovative taqueria.

C Casa is an order-at-the-counter affair, but don't let the casual setting fool you. The market kitchen beats any upscale taqueria with its made-to-order tortillas topped with spiced lamb and grilled mahi mahi. Dig your compostable fork into a lean ground buffalo taco with goat cheese and chipotle aïoli, or try a grilled shrimp cocktail with tomato and cucumber relish.

Celadon

International ✗✗

A3

500 Main St., Ste. G (at 5th St.), Napa

Phone: 707-254-9690
Web: www.celadonnapa.com
Prices: $$

Lunch Mon – Fri
Dinner nightly

Chef/owner Greg Cole must be raising a glass to his loyal clientele who, for years, has dodged the detritus of nearby construction to dine on his riverfront restaurant's global cuisine. With the Napa Riverfront finally completed, Celadon is again as amicable and tranquil as it is accessible.

A brick fireplace warms the large covered atrium with an aluminum cathedral ceiling and whitewashed brick walls. Cool gray-green coats the interior, where butcher paper and white linens dress the small tables and a quaint bar is ideal for a glass. The menu is as worldly as its wine country patronage, wandering the globe from sweet coconut-fried prawns to a crisp-skinned duck breast perched on roasted spaghetti squash, cranberries, and chestnuts.

Cindy's Backstreet Kitchen

International ✗✗

C1

1327 Railroad Ave. (bet. Adams St. & Hunt Ave.), St. Helena

Phone: 707-963-1200
Web: www.cindysbackstreetkitchen.com
Prices: $$

Lunch & dinner daily

You can almost catch a whiff of fresh-baked pie cooling above the blooming window boxes at Cindy's Backstreet Kitchen, an 1829 country home with swaying arbors and a small stone hearth on the patio. A zinc bar and black-and-white wallpaper depicting fruits and vegetables keep with a modern rural theme, as do the shakes and floats to pair with classic American cuisine.

Chef/owner Cindy Pawlcyn wouldn't be content to remain in Americana alone. Her global palate can be seen in Vietnamese lettuce wraps or *pollo loco* chicken with avocado salsa and stuffed green chile. Pawlcyn brings it back home for dessert with a s'more-sational campfire pie. On Wednesdays, stop by Cindy's Supper Club for a three-course prix-fixe with globetrotting international roots.

Cole's Chop House

Steakhouse ✗✗✗

A3

1122 Main St. (bet. 1st & Pearl Sts.), Napa

Phone: 707-224-6328
Web: www.coleschophouse.com
Prices: $$$$

Dinner nightly

An original open truss ceiling and Douglas fir floors attest to the history of the 1886 hand-hewn stone building now home to Cole's Chop House, a classic meat-and-potatoes destination with clubby ambience and spendy cuisine: entrées top out at $69 for a 21-day dry-aged porterhouse. But don't fret, as there are 20 plus pages of wines, including several luscious Napa Cabs, or classic and seasonal cocktails to take your mind off the bill.

Boozier pleasures aside, Greg Cole's Chop House serves an American-style menu that is dizzying for omnivores. Look for succulent Iowa pork, New Zealand lamb, and sustainable seafood in addition to such classics as oysters Rockefeller and a chophouse Caesar. Herbivores can wait at Ubuntu, the vegetarian mecca, next door.

Cook St. Helena

 Italian ✗✗

C1

1310 Main St. (bet. Adams St. & Hunt Ave.), St. Helena

Phone: 707-963-7088
Web: www.cooksthelena.com
Prices: $$

Lunch Mon – Sat
Dinner nightly

In this wine country hamlet lined with posh boutiques, locals come to Cook's for friendly hospitality and satisfying Italian fare at a great value. The small, modern eatery is narrow and intimate yet comfortable, with antiques, prints of black-and-white vegetables, and a whimsically bovine paper lamp. The Carrera marble wine counter, which pours a concise list of Napa and Italian varietals, is perfect for walk-ins and solo diners.

In the kitchen, the fresh produce is vibrantly showcased with Californian sensibility in Chef/owner Jude Wilmouth's all-day menu. Highlights may include fluffy gnocchi with sage brown-butter, marinara, or gorgonzola cream; or a whole-roasted red trout with fingerling potatoes, sun-dried tomatoes, and artichokes.

Cuvée

American ✗✗

A2

1650 Soscol Ave. (at River Terrace Dr.), Napa

Phone: 707-224-2330
Web: www.cuveenapa.com
Prices: $$

Dinner nightly

What would a trip to Napa Valley be without dinner on a tree-lined courtyard to the tune of live music and Old World-style barrel tastings of Californian wines? In this sense, Cuvée, at the River Terrace Inn, answers the call. Despite its location in Napa's business district, Cuvée's contemporary dining room, with wall hangings composed of vineyard clippings, provides a charming backdrop for American dishes with a local twist, such as grilled prawns with sweet corn salad, or salmon and rock shrimp potpie. For dessert, a gingered pear crisp arrives hot from the oven. Wednesday evenings bring one of the Valley's best values: three courses for $33.

The restaurant also waives its corkage fee—for wine country tourists fresh from Route 29.

étoile ✿

Contemporary ✗✗✗

1 California Dr. (off Hwy. 29), Yountville

Phone: 707-204-7529   Lunch & dinner Thu – Mon
Web: www.chandon.com
Prices: $$$$

John Benson

This book should be judged by its gorgeous cover, a cliché-of-sorts so fitting especially considering the long, lovely drive leading to étoile. Get a head start: you'll want to take a bit of time to savor the lovely ponds, rock sculpture gardens, and arched bridge at Domaine Chandon—the winery estate where étoile is housed—not to mention the requisite duck into the winery's gift shop or tasting room.

At étoile, you'll find a magnificent, multi-tiered room rich with olive, gold, and mocha tones broken up by splashes of white and barrel vaulted wood ceilings. Service is reserved, well-informed, and personable, and guests are encouraged to relax. This is a destination restaurant, after all.

Chef Perry Hoffman heads the kitchen, which turns out seasonally inspired tasting menus that may rotate but usually include a soft, perfectly cooked crêpe filled with sweet chunks of lobster and béchamel floating with smoked mussels, then topped with a cloud of yellow curry foam, and garnished with wilted fava bean leaves; or Jones Farm rabbit leg, well-browned and sprinkled with fennel pollen, paired with a strip of rich pork belly, a sliver of pickled rhubarb, and a silky pile of glazed turnips.

Farm

Californian ✗✗✗

B3

4048 Sonoma Hwy. (at Old Sonoma Rd.), Napa

Phone: 707-299-4882   Dinner nightly
Web: www.thecarnerosinn.com
Prices: $$$

Winding your way down the vine-lined Highway 121, you might expect a restaurant named Farm to have an earthy vibe with all the artistic sophistication of wine country. And you'd be right: The Carneros Inn's fine dining restaurant is a picture of bucolic elegance with large firepits warming the barn-like exterior, and trussed cathedral ceilings that indicate a place of culinary worship.

The praise is justified: Farm's contemporary cuisine centers on organic, sustainable ingredients sourced within 150 miles, of course. Begin with a perfectly al dente Carnaroli risotto with golden brown sea scallops and crispy sunchokes; then, indulge in moist roast chicken with artichokes and pearl onions. Pair with a glass of boutique wine from the Napa Valley.

Farmstead

Californian ✗✗

C2

738 Main St. (at Charter Oak Ave.), St. Helena

Phone: 707-963-9181   Lunch & dinner daily
Web: www.thefarmsteadnapa.com
Prices: $$

Simply stated, Farmstead is darn quaint. Located in St. Helena's Long Meadow Ranch, this unique solar powered, barn-turned-restaurant with its own farm stand, organic gardens, nursery, tasting room, and toasty fireplace, is a sight for sore eyes.

Recycled redwood and polished granite clothe the rustic interior where light fixtures are made from poultry feeders, and glass milk bottles—in old metal carriers—are filled with wild flowers. The menu is, of course, wholly organic and sustainable with such options as "potted pig"—pork rillettes stuffed in a mason jar and served with horseradish mustard; spring vegetable dumplings; and cornmeal griddle cake with fig preserve and olive oil ice cream. Farmstead also donates its $2 corkage fee to charity.

The French Laundry

C2

Contemporary XXXX

6640 Washington St. (at Creek St.), Yountville

Phone: 707-944-2380	Lunch Fri – Sun
Web: www.frenchlaundry.com	Dinner nightly
Prices: $$$$	

Deborah Jones

There's not a lot to say about Thomas Keller's legendary restaurant that hasn't been said before, but let's give it a go: it is ubiquitously regarded as one of the best restaurants in the world; it has pocketed enough awards to line a football field; and if you're lucky enough to enter its hallowed, century-old stone walls, you may never look at food the same way again.

Sound a bit overblown? With a bit of careful planning (reservations need to be made two months in advance; and men must wear jackets), you can see for yourself. Every dinner is a new adventure: the two multi-course tasting menus (one is vegetarian), explained in detail by the graceful staff, are highly seasonal and vary each night.

Yours might divulge exquisite, pale peach shad roe, delicately wrapped in bacon and garnished with pommes purée, Swiss chard, and a drizzle of maple syrup; tender, milk-fed poularde topped with a layer of golden bread crumbs and served alongside softened green garlic, Nantes carrots, *cipollini* onion, and a gorgeous baby turnip; or a tiny, pristine section of Snake River Farms ribeye plated with moist cubes of pain perdu, a smooth Dijon mustard emulsion, and fresh, woodsy asparagus tips.

Fumé

International ✕✕

B3

4050 Byway East (bet. Avalon Ct. & Wise Dr.), Napa

Phone: 707-257-1999   Lunch & dinner daily
Web: www.fumebistro.com
Prices: $$

Those who seek an unpretentious, friendly atmosphere and comfortable neighborhood vibe head to Fumé, where family-style hospitality and a blaze in the wood-burning pizza oven keep things cozy.

The mood is as jovial as the menu is eclectic in the broad, golden dining room where chatter rises to the exposed rafters and a long bar allows for overflow. The semi-open kitchen dedicates weekday specials to casual themes such as "local" and "little Italy," while Sunday nights bring old-fashioned beef stew. Some of the more wide-ranging dishes might include panko-crusted ahi tuna with tangy Asian slaw or a signature pork chop wrapped in applewood smoked bacon with whole grain mustard sauce. The respectable list of wines hails from (of course) Napa.

Go Fish

Seafood ✕✕

C2

641 Main St. (bet. Charter Oak Ave. & Mills Ln.), St. Helena

Phone: 707-963-0700   Lunch & dinner daily
Web: www.gofishrestaurant.net
Prices: $$$

A sleek adieu to wine country's prevailing Cal-French quaintness, Chef Cindy Pawlcyn's Go Fish is a gleaming ode to contemporary seafood. Designed by architect Howard Backen, the St. Helena space looks chic in minimalist dress with a few earth tones and a mammoth, vibrant chalk drawing to warm the white interior.

Cosmopolitan weekenders and wealthy retirees flock to the long Carrara marble sushi bar loaded with fresh oysters, clams, lobsters, and combination platters. Prices are a tad high but, with little competition in the area, so is the demand. Cooked options include plump steamed mussels with curried coconut broth and, for meat eaters, Cabernet-braised beef short ribs. The garden patio and extensive wine selection are consummate crowd pleasers.

Gott's Roadside

C2

933 Main St. (at Charter Oak Ave.), St. Helena

Phone: 707-963-3486

Lunch & dinner daily

Web: www.gottsroadside.com

Prices: 🅑🅑

For a quick burger in wine country, look no farther than this roadside icon that opened in 1949, long before Napa was renowned for wine. A bit of a naming feud led to the hamburger haven's (formerly known as Taylor's) name change. At Gott's Roadside Tray Gourmet, while the prices seem high, so is the quality—know that juicy Niman Ranch beef lies between buns, beneath toppings like grilled mushrooms or guacamole. The restaurant also churns out hot dogs topped with hearty homemade chile and sides of sweet potato fries. Gott's refreshes with milk shakes, draft beers, and local wines by the glass, half-bottle, or bottle.

All three locations (San Francisco's Ferry Building and Napa's Oxbow Public Market) have picnic tables perfect for alfresco dining.

JoLē

A1

1457 Lincoln Ave. (bet. Fair Way & Washington St.), Calistoga

Phone: 707-942-5938

Dinner Tue – Sun

Web: www.jolerestaurant.com

Prices: $$

It's ok to be married to your work when you're married to each other, right? It seems to work for husband-and-wife team Matt and Sonjia Spector, the dynamic duo behind JoLē?, named for the other fruit of their labor—their two sons.

The sleek, contemporary décor, set with dark wood tables and a marble bar, belies the food. It's wholeheartedly farm-to-table and the food bears a Mediterranean twist. Sample a plate or two of meals ranging from light to heavy, but for a true test of the kitchen's talents, customize a 4, 5, or 6 course prix-fixe menu from the à la carte selections. Pork belly and heavenly coconut cream pie are among many stand outs. Didn't leave room for dessert? Ask about The Bakeshop to bring home some sweet goodness.

La Taquiza

Mexican 🗡

B3

2007 Redwood Rd. (at Solano Rd.), Napa

Phone: 707-224-2320 Lunch & dinner Mon – Sat
Web: www.lataquizanapa.com
Prices: 😊😊

&

Wine country palates on burrito budgets find salvation *con salsa* at La Taquiza, a taqueria with cool local art and Baja-style fresh Mex that defies its Redwood Plaza locale (where taco truck-loving patrons indulge in hefty if average burritos). This chef/owner, a Bouchon Bakery alum, is partial to lighter, more inventive, seafood-driven fare.

Whether fried or grilled, signature fish tacos are a delicious starting point, but the menu's more exotic options whet adventurous appetites. Don't hesitate to sample fresh ceviches, beer-battered oysters, and *pulpo*—grilled, tender octopus ideal for a unique taco—as well as chilled seafood *coctels* and bowls known as *tazones*. Swing by the salsa bar for varying degrees of heat and smokiness to satisfy all tastes.

Market 😊

American 🗡🗡

C1

1347 Main St. (bet. Adams & Spring Sts.), St. Helena

Phone: 707-963-3799 Lunch & dinner daily
Web: www.marketsthelena.com
Prices: $$

&

At this friendly local favorite along St. Helena's rather elegant Main Street, Chef/owner Eduardo Martinez never skips a beat in preparing food as delicious, comforting, and market-fresh as ever. Amid exposed stone walls, impeccably dressed tables, and a massive wooden bar, humble cult favorites abound in macaroni and cheese with aged *Fiscalini* cheddar or champagne-battered fish and chips. The clipboard menu also includes dishes like smoked chicken empanadas and fried Green Zebra tomatoes with Romesco sauce. A blissfully old-fashioned butterscotch pudding—boldly made with real Scotch—is worth the trip in itself.

An anomaly in these parts, Market charges no corkage fee; feel free to bring your latest prize after wine tasting in the valley.

La Toque ✿

Contemporary 🍴🍴🍴

1314 McKinstry St. (at Soscol Ave.), Napa

Phone: 707-257-5157
Web: www.latoque.com
Prices: $$$

Dinner nightly

Melissa Werner, CCS Architecture

A big, illuminated chef's hat and pretty timber awning welcome you into Chef Ken Frank's critically acclaimed La Toque, housed in the Westin Verasa Napa.

After a decade-long stint in nearby Rutherford, the newer Napa digs are lovely—with a polished, contemporary dining room soaked in soothing earth tones broken up by the occasional bright dot of fresh flowers. And though La Toque's impressive wine inventory has slimmed down since the move, the list is still wildly precise, as is the wine service—in fact, many would argue that Scott Tracy, who usually weaves an engaging story around each selection, is the best sommelier in town. The waitstaff is equally on point, the whole room functioning, it would seem, as one perfectly orchestrated ensemble meant to cater to your every whim.

All the better to enjoy Frank's killer contemporary fare, which changes often but might include a warm salad of fresh lobster and tender sweet potato; juicy, perfectly seared quail puddled in a rich demi-glace with chanterelles and braised winter root vegetables; or roasted bison loin served with a terrine of fork-tender bison, wilted Swiss chard, aged cheese, roasted potatoes, and carrots.

Martini House

Contemporary

C1

1245 Spring St. (bet. Main & Oak Sts.), St. Helena

Phone: 707-963-2233
Web: www.martinihouse.com
Prices: $$$

Lunch Fri – Sun
Dinner nightly

Don't be confused by the name, this wine country winner isn't named for the cocktail. Instead, this restaurant tucked inside a charming 1920s bungalow was once the private home of opera singer Walter Martini. The craftsman-style building is just off the main street of St. Helena. Inside, it's mountain cabin-meets-tepee with its blend of rustic lodge style and Native American flair.

Chef Todd Humphries loves mushrooms and he is an avid forager. They pop up all over the menu and he even dedicates an entire tasting menu to mushrooms. Don't worry if fungi aren't your friend, since there are plenty of fish, meat, and poultry selections. Go for the no brainer three- and four-course prix-fixe tasting menus for a sure thing.

Mini Mango Thai Bistro

Thai

A3

1408 W. Clay St. (bet. Franklin and Seminary Sts.), Napa

Phone: 707-226-8884
Web: N/A
Prices: ⛁⛁

Lunch & dinner daily

This tiny Napa nook has certainly seen more dismal times considering the location has proved a challenge to previous inhabitants. But there is no stopping Mini Mango, a promising Thai bistro that's low on tables but big on flavor. The space does double in pretty weather however, with a roomy front patio ringed in olive trees that bustles when beautiful outside.

Thanks to owners Pornchai and Cherry Pengchareon, Mini Mango is a small slice of Thailand in the wine country with a hint of a Californian accent. Pleasant servers overcome the challenges of cramped quarters to deliver such classics as pad Thai along with more audacious options—think Indochine corn fritters with tangy plum sauce; spicy grilled calamari; and tiger prawns preening in tomato curry.

315

Morimoto Napa

A3

J a p a n e s e ✕✕✕

610 Main St. (at 5th St.), Napa

Phone: 707-252-1600
Web: www.morimotonapa.com
Prices: **$$$**

Dinner nightly

You may not spot celebrity chef, Masaharu Morimoto wielding his knives behind the sushi bar, but your reservation at Morimoto's Napa outpost will be nonetheless worthwhile. In summer, riverfront tables are among the most sought-after in the Valley, and it's a safe bet that you won't find sushi like this elsewhere in wine country.

A massive staff sees to the curious clientele, answering queries on the seven page seafood menu. Here, local ingredients mingle with delicacies from Tokyo's Tsukiji fish market, flown in daily, and Wagyu beef for land lovers. Diehard sushi fans will enjoy the multi-course omakase, while the pricey à la carte menu features beautiful sashimi, foie gras in a creamy *chawan mushi*, and a whole branzino (head-to-tail) tempura.

Mustards Grill

B2

A m e r i c a n ✕✕

7399 St. Helena Hwy. (at Hwy. 29), Yountville

Phone: 707-944-2424
Web: www.mustardsgrill.com
Prices: **$$**

Lunch & dinner daily

Napa Valley foodies had a scare in early 2009, when a kitchen fire forced Mustards Grill to close. All's well that ends well, though, and owner Cindy Pawlcyn took this opportunity to spruce the place up a bit. Nothing has been drastically altered, but the staff now operates in a remodeled kitchen.

Despite a chef change, the menu sticks to favorites such as the ever popular seafood tostada (the main ingredient of which varies daily); sweet corn tamales; and the Truckstop Deluxe ("always meat, usually potatoes, rarely vegetables").

Long before it was trendy for chefs to farm, Pawlcyn created an organic garden adjacent to the restaurant. That plot is now bigger and more bountiful than ever, supplying Mustards with a cornucopia of just-picked produce.

Neela's

 Indian

975 Clinton St. (at Main St.), Napa

Phone: 707-226-9988
Web: www.neelasindianrestaurant.com
Prices: $$

Lunch Tue – Fri
Dinner Tue – Sun

With a jewel-toned interior and bar streaming Bollywood music videos, this is as close to Mumbai as wine country gets. Raised in old Bombay, Chef/owner Neela Paniz moved from L.A. to Napa to share her native flavors with a town that lacked an Indian eatery. Now, the scent of fresh ground spices can be traced to Neela's, serving contemporary fare reflective of India's many culinary styles.

Offerings range from *chaat* to such sophisticated dishes as a "Niçoise" salad with garam masala-crusted ahi; or *sev puri*, wheat crackers topped with potatoes, onions, contrasting chutneys, and crisp chick pea noodles. Super fresh ingredients guarantee outstanding chicken *tikka masala*; Thursday "bread nights" are carbo-licious with melty pepperjack naan.

Norman Rose Tavern

 Gastropub

1401 1st St. (at Franklin St.), Napa

Phone: 707-258-1516
Web: www.normanrosenapa.com
Prices:

Lunch & dinner daily

Chef/owner Michael Gyetvan has sharpened his skills at Lark Creek Inn, Tra Vigne, Azzurro down the street, and now in this family-friendly pub in downtown Napa. It seems the chef wasn't the only one in town craving affordable, approachable bites—locals are lining up for a taste of bubbling crab and artichoke dip and sliders with a secret ingredient (crushed Fritos in the beef!).

With weathered barn planks siding the walls and ceilings lined with empty beer bottles, the atmosphere is equally comfortable. Plenty of bar seating allows for jovial conversations over one of many micro-brewed beers that pair well with this elevated gastropub fare. Expect buttermilk-fried chicken on a toasted brioche bun; organic hot dogs; and truffled fries.

Oenotri

A3

1425 1st St. (bet. Franklin & School Sts.), Napa

Phone: 707-252-1022
Web: www.oenotri.com
Prices: $$

Dinner nightly

Part of the downtown Napa revival, Oenotri is quick and fuss-free, but continues to dazzle with its mod design and fab food. Chefs Curtis Di Fede and Tyler Rodde, veterans from acclaimed Oliveto, run the show and hone in on specialties from the Southern Italian regions of Campagnia, Calabria, and Puglia. Details are key here—they even imported a wood-burning oven from Naples to Napa for quality.

These professionals certainly get it, since the pizza is a standout. It may only spend a minute and a half in the oven, but the smoky flavor, perfect crust, and top-notch ingredients all pack a serious punch. House-made *salumi* and fresh pastas run a close second and desserts are divine, so make reservations and arrive hungry because you'll want to sample it all.

Pica Pica

A3

610 First St. (at McKinstry St.), Napa

Phone: 707-205-6187
Web: www.picapicakitchen.com
Prices:

Lunch & dinner daily

Fast, fresh, and flavorful Venezuelan cuisine highlights this casual eatery in the Oxbow Public Market, which cannot be navigated on an empty stomach. Among these shops selling local produce, seafood, and wine, is Pica Pica—a standout for its delicious food but also one of the building's few fast and easy dining options.

Catering largely to a take-out crowd, this "corn-centric kitchen" centers on the *arepa*, a grilled white corn flatbread, stuffed with chicken salad and avocado, or shredded skirt steak with fried plantains and black bean paste. Heartier fare includes *cachapas*, a large yellow corn pancake wrapped around a choice of fillings.

A new beverage bar across the way and newer stand-alone restaurant in the Mission are broadening palates even more.

Press

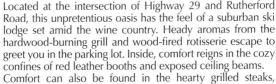

Steakhouse

B1·2

587 St. Helena Hwy. South, St. Helena

Phone: 707-967-0550   Dinner Wed – Mon
Web: www.pressthelena.com
Prices: $$$$

Demanding bosses, impending deadlines, buzzing Blackberries. Step inside this lovely modern American steakhouse and the one thing you won't be hard-pressed to do is relax. The setting, backed up against the mountains in St. Helena, is glorious. From its black walnut floors and reclaimed wood panels from a Midwestern mill, to its bar crafted from three walnut trees, it's clear that the pastoral setting isn't just a gimmick.

Neither is the food, which is top-notch. The menu features the stuff of classic steakhouses, with raw bar selections and a few poultry and pork dishes sprinkled in for good measure; but it's all about the sensational grass-fed, wood-grilled steaks that melt in your mouth. Got deep pockets? Go for the Kobe Wagyu from Idaho.

Rutherford Grill

American

B2

1180 Rutherford Rd. (at Hwy. 29), Rutherford

Phone: 707-963-1792   Lunch & dinner daily
Web: www.hillstone.com
Prices: $$

Located at the intersection of Highway 29 and Rutherford Road, this unpretentious oasis has the feel of a suburban ski lodge set amid the wine country. Heady aromas from the hardwood-burning grill and wood-fired rotisserie escape to greet you in the parking lot. Inside, comfort reigns in the cozy confines of red leather booths and exposed ceiling beams.

Comfort can also be found in the hearty grilled steaks, barbecued ribs, fish, and rotisserie chicken with sides of mashed potatoes colcannon and creamy coleslaw. Starters such as grilled jumbo artichokes play second fiddle to the sweet and buttery skillet corn bread, studded with jalapeños and kernels of fresh corn.

Popular with locals as well as wine tasting tourists, the Grill usually has a wait.

319

Redd ✿

Contemporary ✕✕

C3

6480 Washington St. (at Oak Circle), Yountville

Phone: 707-944-2222   Lunch & dinner daily
Web: www.reddnapavalley.com
Prices: **$$$$**

Andy Katz

Located along Yountville's restaurant row, at the south end of Washington Street, striking Redd is just as pretty to look at as it is to eat in. You can thank New York's Asfour Guzy Architects for the gorgeous, sun-soaked dining room, washed in minimalist white walls and pale wood; and Mother Nature for the breathtaking courtyard dining area, where stylish guests sip wine by a gently lapping fountain.

Oh and then there's the food, where no tiny detail goes unnoticed under the watchful eye of Chef/owner Richard Reddington, who once spun his magic up the road at Napa Valley's esteemed Auberge du Soleil. The highly seasonal cuisine does a bit of studied globe-trotting, with playful Asian touches making their way into Reddington's contemporary American menu.

Kick things off with a bright starter of yellowfin tuna tartare pocked with sweet, crunchy Asian pear and scallion, laced with chili oil and topped with crispy flash fried rice and zesty cilantro shoots; then move on to meltingly good crispy duck confit paired with Savoy cabbage, tender foie gras meatballs, and crispy spätzle; and finish with a decadent peanut butter and milk chocolate *gianduja* with peanut honeycomb parfait.

The Restaurant at Meadowood ✿ ✿ ✿

Contemporary XXX

B1

900 Meadowood Ln. (off Silverado Trail), St. Helena

Phone: 707-967-1205   Dinner Mon – Sat
Web: www.meadowood.com
Prices: $$$$

Meadowood

A mile or so outside of St. Helena, off the Silverado Trail and buried into the mountain perch that holds the secluded, luxurious Meadowood resort, sits a beautiful cottage devoted to culinary magic.

In the winter, a cozy bar dressed with a roaring fireplace greets customers who proceed to sink into the plush dining room, decked out in hues of rich chocolate and milky white. In the summer, patrons follow the host to a patio overlooking the hotel's rolling golf course to soak in the luscious landscape. A reserved service staff is polished and discreet, reading customers' minds with minimal fuss and attending to their every need.

At the center of the delightfully orchestrated operation, diners set their sights on Chef Christopher Kostow's meticulously crafted cuisine, where inventive dishes showcase the local Californian bounty in unique ways. The multi-course and tasting menus rotate often, but might uncover bright red Wagyu beef cured in Meadowood pine; crispy, pan-fried sweetbreads in black truffle broth; wildly fresh scallop and Dungeness crab paired with grapefruit, tapioca pearls, and Osetra caviar; or white chocolate and foie gras ganache topped with brûleéd ripe banana.

Solbar ✿

Californian 🍴

A1

755 Silverado Trail (at Rosedale Rd.), Calistoga

Phone: 707-226-0850
Lunch & dinner daily

Web: www.solagecalistoga.com

Prices: $$$

Solage Calistoga

Solbar is hip and knows it—tucked inside the gorgeous Solage Calistoga, an upscale resort at the base of the Silverado Trail, this Auberge family restaurant couldn't have asked for better real estate. Between the slick, leather-clad lounge and haute barnyard dining room (think polished wood communal tables and vaulted tin ceilings), there's no shortage of places to see and be seen at Solbar. You can even take your meal poolside, a fire pit roaring off to one side and a cool cocktail in your palm.

By lunch, the kitchen pushes out relaxed gourmet sandwiches utilizing pristine ingredients; by night, things get turned up a few notches with a seasonal menu that dances between lighter spa fare and heartier dishes.

Kick things off with a fresh pile of ricotta-filled *agnolotti* bathed in a chive butter sauce and topped with three types of roasted mushrooms; then move on to succulent lemon-thyme roasted Sonoma chicken paired with silky Yukon Gold whipped potatoes and roasted Brussels sprouts with whole grain mustard jus. For all its stylishness, Solbar still knows how to keep it real: the restaurant does a family-style fried chicken night every Tuesday that's an especially good value.

Terra 🕸

Contemporary 🍴🍴🍴

C1

1345 Railroad Ave. (bet. Adams St. & Hunt Ave.), St. Helena

Phone: 707-963-8931

Web: www.terrarestaurant.com

Prices: $$$

Dinner Wed – Mon

&

Hiro Sone

What's not to love about this pair? He whips up cutting-edge fare like foie gras tortellini at the drop of a hat; she oversees production of pastries so fresh it seems a sin to eat them. When husband-and-wife restaurateurs Hiro Sone and Lissa Doumani get together, there's magic in the kitchen. Napa's just happy they let the lay folk join the party.

It's a pretty party at that. Housed in a late 19th century historical foundry tucked behind downtown St. Helena's main drag, Terra's arched windows and old stone walls lead to a romantic interior outfitted with lofty, wood-beamed ceilings, rustic terra-cotta floor tiles, and cozy little tables built for lingering. The ample wine list, which pays homage to the local artisanal scene from Dry Creek, Alexander Valley, and the Russian River Valley, offers even more reason to loiter.

Sone's menu rotates with the season, but may unveil smoky Monterey squid, perfectly grilled and paired with succulent pork belly, English peas, and mint; tender lamb loin chops over Anson Mills polenta with grilled artichoke hearts and an irresistible black olive lamb jus; or melt-in-your-mouth strawberry shortcake, served with a tangy scoop of buttermilk ice cream.

Tra Vigne

Italian   XX

C2

1050 Charter Oak Ave. (off Hwy. 29), St. Helena

Phone: 707-963-4444   Lunch & dinner daily
Web: www.travignerestaurant.com
Prices: $$$

Few *ristorantes* leave a first impression quite like Tra Vigne. Majestic olive trees twinkle with lights above a Tuscan-style courtyard patio, surrounded by vineyards and heated to ward off the evening chill. A grand neo-Italian dining room boasts a beautifully hand carved bar and reflects the ambitious Italian menu.

Begin with the house's signature dish—mozzarella *"al minuto"* with fresh ground pepper, olive oil, and grilled country bread—then settle in for a rich and savory Liberty Farms duck risotto, slow cooked with green apple, fresh thyme, and quince-scented *saba*. The prolific wine list features both high-end Italian and Californian labels.

For more casual nibbles among local vintners, order a seasonal pie at adjacent Pizzeria Tra Vigne.

Wine Spectator Greystone

California   XX

A1

2555 Main St. (at Deer Park Rd.), St. Helena

Phone: 707-967-1010   Lunch & dinner daily
Web: www.ciachef.edu
Prices: $$$

Try to conjure the most idyllic wine country setting imaginable, but know your arrival at Greystone will exceed expectations. This historic hilltop chateau is surrounded by grapevines intertwining like lace through the grounds, as olive trees, rosemary, and lavender pave the way toward a sunny terrace with a trickling fountain.

Inside, the Wine Spectator dining room is massive, with stone walls rising to soaring ceilings and a fireplace in the cozy lounge. Since Greystone houses the Culinary Institute of America's California campus, the three exhibition kitchens provide a veritable dinner theater. On stage: seasonal Californian acts with Mediterranean flair, as in sweetbread vol-au-vent and crispy pork belly with perfectly seared day boat scallops.

Ubuntu ✿

1140 Main St. (bet. 1st & Pearl Sts.), Napa

Phone: 707-251-5656
Web: www.ubuntunapa.com
Prices: $$

Lunch Fri – Sun
Dinner nightly

Elijah Woolery

Nowhere else can you catch a candlelight yoga class and then slip downstairs, still in workout gear, for a truly inspired vegetarian dinner. Ubuntu, whose name means "humanity toward others," is a divine new mainstay in downtown Napa. Good energy prevails inside the airy restaurant, where a lively redwood communal table takes center stage and stone walls are adorned with uplifting art.

At the helm of the kitchen is top chef, Aaron London, whose mastery includes the humble vegetable, many of which are harvested daily from the restaurant's biodynamic garden. As you would expect from a yoga studio cum culinary nirvana, Ubuntu takes great care in its artistic presentations.

Dishes are designed to share, but if you prefer to keep the poached Rhode Island Red egg—atop arugula, smoked yams, and leeks—all to yourself, the casual staff won't mind. There's no shortage of cheese and butter to liven up the veggies: Horseradish gnocchi with turnip confit and fava leaves gets a boost from Midnight Moon Gouda, and the thin white chocolate bar with pickled rhubarb and creamy white chocolate custard is the reason you went to yoga in the first place.

Zuzu

Wine Country ▶ Napa Valley

829 Main St. (bet. 2nd & 3rd Sts.), Napa

Phone: 707-224-8555
Web: www.zuzunapa.com
Prices: $$

Lunch Mon – Fri
Dinner nightly

Faded tile floors, exposed wood beams, and a weathered tin ceiling salvaged from Mexico set an old-world stage for Spanish and Mediterranean tapas at Zuzu, a self-proclaimed celebration of food, wine, and art. Latin beats are a groovy backdrop for paintings and metalwork by area artisans, while more than 20 off-the-beaten-path wines are poured by the glass at the recycled pine bar.

Feast on crisp fried Manchego cheese with tangy *guajilo* salsa; tender Niman Ranch meatballs with tangy sweet wine and spicy piquillo pepper sauce; or *harissa*-spiked lamb burgers cooled with goat cheese *tzatziki*. Ceviche and paella specials change daily. With few late night spots in Napa, Zuzu is ideal for a bite before or after a Napa Valley Opera House performance.

Couverts (✕ ... ✕✕✕✕✕) indicate the level of comfort found at a restaurant. The more ✕'s, the more upscale a restaurant will be.

Sonoma County

Often eclipsed as a wine region by neighboring Napa Valley, the county that borders Marin County claims 76 miles of Pacific coastline, as well as 250 wineries that take advantage of some of the best grape-growing conditions in California. Northern California's first premium winery, **Buena Vista**, was established just outside the town of Sonoma in 1857 by Agoston Haraszthy. Today thirteen distinct wine appellations (AVAs) have been assigned in Sonoma County, where vintners produce a dizzying array of wines in an area slightly larger than the State of Rhode Island. Along

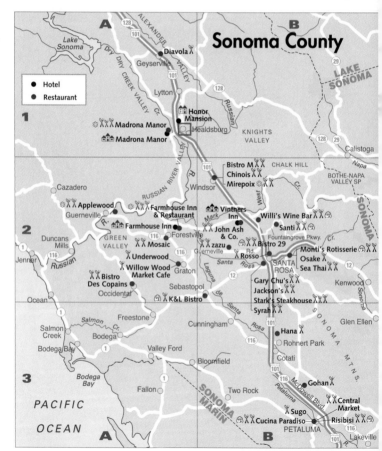

Sonoma County

- Hotel
- Restaurant

Lake Sonoma
ALEXANDER VALLEY
128
101
Diavola
Geyserville
DRY CREEK VALLEY CR.
Lytton
128
Russian
RUSSIAN RIVER VALLEY
Honor Mansion
Madrona Manor
Madrona Manor
Healdsburg
KNIGHTS VALLEY
Calistoga
LAKE SONOMA
29
128
29
Bistro M
Chinois
Mirepoix
CHALK HILL
West
Napa
BOTHE-NAPA VALLEY SP
Cazadero
Windsor
Applewood
Guerneville
Farmhouse Inn & Restaurant
Farmhouse Inn
Vintners Inn
Willi's Wine Bar
Mark
John Ash & Co.
Santi
Duncans Mills
GREEN VALLEY
116
Forestville
Mosaic
zazu
Bistro 29
Fountaingrove Pkwy.
Cr.
Monti's Rotisserie
Jenner
116
Russian
Underwood
Guerneville Rd.
Rosso
SANTA ROSA
Osake
Sea Thai
12
1
Willow Wood Market Cafe
Graton
Santa
Laguna
12
Gary Chu's
Jackson's
Stark's Steakhouse
Syrah
Kenwood
Bistro Des Copains
Occidental
Sebastopol
de
Santa
SONOMA MTNS.
Ocean
K&L Bistro
Rosa
Freestone
Cunningham
Hana
Glen Ellen
Salmon
Cr.
101
116
Salmon Creek
Bodega
Rohnert Park
Bodega Bay
1
Valley Ford
Cotati
Sonoma
Bodega Bay
Bloomfield
101
116
Gohan
McDowell Blvd.
Fallon
Two Rock
SONOMA
MARIN
Petaluma
Sugo
Central Market
PACIFIC OCEAN
Cucina Paradiso
PETALUMA
Risibisi
116
Lakeville
101

Highway 12 heading north, byroads lead to out-of-the-way wineries, each of which puts its own unique stamp on the business of winemaking.

The Russian River Valley edges the river named for the early Russian trading outposts that were set up along the coast. This is one of the coolest growing regions in Sonoma, thanks to the river basin that offers a conduit for cool coastal air. Elegant pinot noir and chardonnay headline here, but syrah is quickly catching up.

At the upper end of the Russian River, the Dry Creek Valley yields excellent sauvignon blanc, chardonnay, and pinot noir. This region is also justly famous for its zinfandel, a grape that does especially well in the valley's rock-strewn soil. Winery visits in Dry Creek are a study in contrasts. Palatial modern wineries rise up along the same rural roads that have

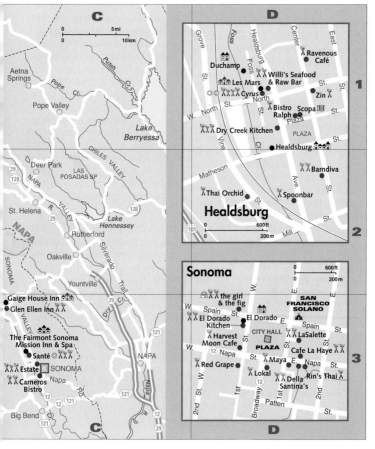

been home to independents for generations, and young grapevines trained into laser-straightened rows are broken up by the dark, gnarled fingers of old vines.

Sonoma County's inlandmost AVAs are Knights Valley and Alexander Valley. These two warm regions both highlight cabernet sauvignon. Nestled between the Mayacamas and Sonoma ranges, the 17-mile-long Sonoma Valley dominates the southern portion of the county. At its center is the town of Sonoma, site of California's northernmost and final mission: San Francisco Solano Mission, founded in 1823. The mission once included a thriving vineyard before secularization and incorporation into the Sonoma State Historic Park system 102 years ago, when the vines were uprooted and transplanted elsewhere in Sonoma. The town's eight-acre plaza is still surrounded by 19th century adobe buildings, most of them now occupied by shops, restaurants, and inns. Of epicurean note is the fact that building contractor Chuck Williams bought a hardware store in Sonoma in 1956. He gradually converted its stock from hardware to French cookware, kitchen tools, and novelty foods. Today **Williams-Sonoma** has more than 200 stores nationwide, and is a must-stop for foodies.

Just below Sonoma lies a portion of the Carneros district, named for the herds of sheep (*los carneros* in Spanish) that once roamed its hillsides. Carneros is best known for its cool-climate grapes, notably pinot noir and chardonnay.

Throughout this bucolic county—called SoCo by savvy locals—vineyards rub shoulders with orchards and farms that take advantage of the area's fertile soil to produce everything from apples and olives to artisan-crafted cheeses. Sustainable and organic are key words at local farmers' markets, which herald the spring (April or May) in Santa Rosa, Sebastopol, Sonoma, Healdsburg, and Petaluma. At these open-air smorgasbords, you can find everything from just-picked heirloom vegetables to sea urchins taken out of the water so recently that they are still wiggling. Artisanal olive oils, chocolates, baked goods, jams, and jellies count among the many homemade products available. In addition, ethnic food stands cover the globe with offerings that have their roots as far away as Mexico, India, and Afghanistan.

Thanks to the area's natural bounty, farm-to-table cuisine takes on new heights in many of the county's restaurants. Some chefs need go no farther than their own on-site gardens for fresh fruits, vegetables, and herbs. With easy access to local products such as Dungeness crab from Bodega Bay, poultry from Petaluma, and cheeses from the Sonoma Cheese Factory, it's no wonder that the Californian cuisine in this area has attracted national attention.

Applewood ✿

Californian 🍴🍴

13555 Hwy. 116, Guerneville

Phone: 707-869-9093
Web: www.applewoodinn.com
Prices: **$$$**

Dinner Tue – Sat

IntLight Marketing

Never has the old adage "getting there is half the fun" been so apt. Situated along beautiful, winding Hwy. 116, amongst the soaring redwoods and free-roaming deer that populate the area, a jaunt out to this Russian River Valley bed-and-breakfast is a wine country weekend in the making.

Mercifully, pancakes and down comforters aren't the only thing this inn knows how to do right. An elegant dinner in the hotel's lovely barn-styled restaurant, with its exposed wood beams, roaring fireplace, and enclosed sun porch, is a delight thanks to Chef Bruce Frieseke's seasonal Californian menu, which utilizes superior ingredients and pulls influence from France and Italy.

A five-course tasting menu offers dishes from the à la carte selection, and may involve miso-glazed white sablefish with fiddlehead ferns, chopped fava beans, pickled ramps, and a drizzle of hibiscus-orange vinaigrette; plump lamb chops coated with crushed cocoa nibs and paired with brown butter parsnips, sherry-braised chorizo, mint *chimichurri*, and a mash of spring peas and fava beans; or creamy panna cotta, surrounded by cubes of roasted pineapple in vanilla syrup, batons of green lime zest confit, and julienned mint.

Barndiva

D2

Californian ✗✗

231 Center St. (bet. Matheson & Mills Sts.), Healdsburg

Phone: 707-431-0100   Lunch & dinner Wed – Sun
Web: www.barndiva.com
Prices: $$

If wine country epitomizes fancy farming, then this barn is certainly fitting. Hip and hot, Barndiva (blocks from Healdsburg square) is exalted for its consummate cocktails, magnificent meals, and gorgeous gardens. Mod and charming, the décor is graced with mirrors, lofty ceilings, vivid artwork, and eclectic sculptures.

Just as delicious as the sun-drenched grounds is its dynamic menu. Strutting stuff from local purveyors and food artisans, dishes like asparagus tempura with tarragon aïoli and *fromage blanc* gnocchi sing the praises of the season. Starring Californian flavors are pastas with pristine condiments, and a red velvet cake whirled with creamy goodness. Nurse a local wine or classic cocktail on the thrilling terrace and realize nirvana!

Bistro Des Copains

A2

French ✗✗

3782 Bohemian Hwy. (at Occidental Rd.), Occidental

Phone: 707-874-2436   Dinner nightly
Web: www.bistrodescopains.com
Prices: $$

Don your vintage driving gloves, turn up "La Vie en Rose," and imagine yourself on the Côte d'Azur as you wind your way to Occidental, the out-the-way hamlet home to Bistro Des Copains. Delightfully located on Bohemian Highway, the petite green cottage with bright white trim transports you to Provence via the California wine country. Sonoma wines, as well as a few French labels, complement Southern Gallic fare like buckwheat crêpes stuffed with mushrooms and brie, scallops gratiné, and creamy chocolate *pot de crème*.

Reservations are a good idea, especially on Wednesdays when dollar oysters lure locals by the dozen.

The wine bar, warmed by a wood oven in the kitchen and adorned with photos of the owner's ancestral farm, is a cozy spot to wait.

Bistro M

French ✗✗

B2

610 McClelland Dr. (at Market St.), Windsor

Phone: 707-838-3118   Lunch & dinner daily
Web: www.thebistrom.com
Prices: $$

The itty-bitty Sonoma town of Windsor is an unsuspecting locale for one elegant French bistro—let alone two. *Petite sœur* to neighboring Mirepoix, Bistro M is a humble eatery dressed in simple wood furnishings and bucolic hues. But don't let the down-to-earth vibe fool you: Proximity to Mirepoix guarantees a watchful eye and strictly classical French technique in the kitchen.

Briny bites from the oyster bar and a large array of salads, including duck confit with roasted beets, make Bistro M a lovely spot for a light snack or lunch. Dinner, meanwhile, brings more substantial entrées like trout amandine with haricots verts and coq au vin *en croute*. Come dessert, calorie counters can feel righteous about skipping the all-too-common molten chocolate cake.

Bistro Ralph

Californian ✗

D1

109 Plaza St. (bet. Center St. & Healdsburg Ave.), Healdsburg

Phone: 707-433-1380   Lunch & dinner Mon – Sat
Web: www.bistroralph.com
Prices: $$

A pair of sidewalk tables marks the entrance to Chef/owner Ralph Tingle's eponymous bistro overlooking the boutiques of Healdsburg's central plaza. The whitewashed brick interior is studded with metal furnishings and a bar counter lends a view into the open kitchen, where each season's bounty inspires the concise menu.

Order a carefully selected local wine or martini from the respectable vodka and gin offerings, then sit back to enjoy a delightful, no fuss Cal-French meal. Lunch may bring a fully loaded Cobb salad or a tender chicken paillard with capers and shoestring fries. Ravenous appetites can opt for a juicy lamb burger or braised short rib ravioli with freshly grated horseradish. Finish with a cheese board or one of a few homemade sweets.

Bistro 29 🍽

French ✕✕

B2

620 Fifth St. (at Mendocino Ave.), Santa Rosa

Phone: 707-546-2929   Lunch Tue – Fri
Web: www.bistro29.com   Dinner Tue – Sat
Prices: $$

Named for the county of Finistère in Northwest France, Bistro 29 is a Breton gem in Santa Rosa. Best known for reasonably priced buckwheat crêpes—think homemade sausage with cave-aged gruyère and apples—the homey spot draws regulars for conversation and comforting Gallic fare. Dinner, can bring more sophisticated choices, including pan-roasted duck with mascarpone faro and chanterelles.

The ambience is equally lovely and familiar. Bask in rays of sunshine beaming from the sky light upon interior brick walls and mustard yellow accents. White linen tablecloths and dark wood accents perfect the classic bistro look. Tuesday through Thursday, a $29 three-course menu is an unbeatable value, while Fridays bring half-off crêpes and $10 bottles of *vin*.

Cafe La Haye

Californian ✕✕

D3

140 E. Napa St. (bet. 1st & 2nd Sts.), Sonoma

Phone: 707-935-5994   Dinner Tue – Sat
Web: www.cafelahaye.com
Prices: $$

This quaint and comfortable little café, opened by Saul Gropman, has a charming spirit and strong local following. A rotating selection of work by local artists hangs around the room, giving the place a gallery feel. In the bi-level dining room, butter-yellow walls reflect a soothing light under the exposed beams of the pitched roof. Art lovers and foodies alike flock here to sample items on the concise market-driven menu that focuses on cheeses, vegetables, and meats from nearby farms and ranches.

Complementary ingredients take center stage in chipotle glazed pork chop dated with red lentil purée and eggplant caponata. The daily risotto and fish specials always spotlight the freshest flavors of the season.

Carneros Bistro

Californian ✕✕

C3

1325 Broadway (at Napa Rd.), Sonoma

Phone: 707-931-2042
Web: www.thelodgeatsonoma.com
Prices: $$

Lunch & dinner daily

Cathedral ceilings over merlot and mustard hues set the scene at Carneros Bistro & Wine Bar, the Lodge at Sonoma restaurant that is almost a microcosm of the wine country. Not only can one purchase a piece of local art right from the walls, but the contemporary Cal-French cuisine adheres to a farm-to-table philosophy; much of the produce is plucked from the eatery's gardens.

Wine barrels teeter above the open kitchen where, despite some inconsistency, dishes are inventive and usually quite good. Dinner might include day boat scallops alongside tempura sweet potatoes or hearty sturgeon with cannellini beans and chanterelles. The wine list, meanwhile, boasts more than 400 bottles, many from Sonoma County. Sink into a banquette and savor a local flight.

Central Market

Mediterranean ✕✕

B3

42 Petaluma Blvd. N. (at Western Ave.), Petaluma

Phone: 707-778-9900
Web: www.centralmarketpetaluma.com
Prices: $$

Dinner nightly

The lofty 1920s Maclay Building may seem an unlikely spot for an intimate Mediterranean eatery, yet Central Market feels as welcoming as a private invitation to Chef/owner Tony Najiola's own home. Perhaps this is due to his convivial presence around the house.

Foodies take a front-row seat at the zinc counter for the performance in the open kitchen, where the specialty is Slow Food with flourishes from Italy and France. The menu shows passion, as if dishes are made with the hands of an artist. Take time to peruse the offerings over an aperitif and Castelvetrano olives. Then, sample house-made sausages like New Orleans–style seafood boudin; ground lamb cabbage rolls flavored with cumin and coriander; and spicy chorizo that gives zing to stuffed quail.

Chinois

Asian Asian ✗✗

B2

186 Windsor River Rd. (at Bell Rd.), Windsor

Phone: 707-838-4667
Web: N/A
Prices: $$

Lunch Mon – Fri
Dinner nightly

Chinois' owners have cornered the market on Asian cuisine in this neck of the woods (they also own Ume Japanese Bistro down the road), but in this case, monopolies aren't a bad thing. A delightful gem, delivering fresh flavors that are a welcome change from the sticky sweet sauces of other Asian spots, Chinois is Asian fusion without the confusion.

A little bit of this, a little bit of that, the menu proudly highlights curries from Thailand, dim sum from China, and noodle dishes from all over. It may seem like a tall order to blend so many different styles, but the kitchen executes this task flawlessly. Thanks to its wine country location, the Asian haven touts a respectable list of wines to accompany the beer selections.

Cucina Paradiso ☺

Italian ✗✗

B3

114 Petaluma Blvd. N. (bet. Washington St. & Western Ave.), Petaluma

Phone: 707-782-1130
Web: www.cucinaparadisopetaluma.com
Prices:

Lunch & dinner Mon – Sat

From the crusty focaccia to the pastas and sauces, everything at this homey Petaluma trattoria is made from scratch, which accounts in part for its devoted following. The other reason is the warm, family oriented vibe and gracious service that Chef/owner Dennis Hernandez and his wife, Malena cultivated, prior to moving this charming restaurant to Petaluma's main drag.

Evidence of the chef's culinary training in Italy is everywhere; the arias playing as background music seem perfectly suited to a satisfying and rustic plate of homemade roast duck ravioli with sun-dried tomato, pine nut, and basil sauce; or fluffy gnocchi in Gorgonzola-walnut sauce. Perhaps best of all, the price is a wonderful value for the high quality of the cuisine.

Cyrus ✿✿

D1

Contemporary ✗✗✗✗

29 North St. (bet. Foss St. & Healdsburg Ave.), Healdsburg

Phone: 707-433-3311 Dinner nightly
Web: www.cyrusrestaurant.com
Prices: $$$$

Andy Katz

Attached to Sonoma's tony Les Mars Hotel, Cyrus is so exquisitely sophisticated you'll think you've died and gone to Napa. You can thank Chef Douglas Keane, whose elegant nightly tasting menus—which come in five- and eight-course prix-fixe options (both available with vegetarian choices)—set the bar extraordinarily high, even for the increasingly posh town of Healdsburg.

As it turns out, the rest of the restaurant lives up to the food quite perfectly, with a pleasantly intimate interior featuring cloistered ceilings, curved banquettes, and wooden armoires; a masterful service staff that anticipates your every need; and wine service that's exceptional without being pretentious.

Keane's menu is a highly seasonal, seafood-strewn affair that often dances with Asian influences, and might include a bowl of pristine hamachi, perfectly seared and surrounded by radish, kombu, candied kumquats, and baby shiso in a chilled dashi; sweet butter poached lobster presented over braised ramps and caramelized spring onions carrying hints of fresh marjoram; or fork-tender short rib, glazed with a sweet, smoky hoisin sauce and served with wilted *tatsoi* and an otherworldly bone marrow-and-ginger flan.

Della Santina's

D3

133 E. Napa St. (bet. 1st & 2nd Sts.), Sonoma

Phone: 707-935-0576   Lunch & dinner daily
Web: www.dellasantinas.com
Prices: $$

Benvenuto to Della Santina's, the homespun *ristorante* where family portraits and framed lace napkins adorn the interior walls and a fountain on the trellised brick patio reinforces the rustic Tuscan appeal. Al fresco diners will feel especially comfortable here: the enclosed terrace is heated, spacious, and lovely year-round.

The dining room is a touch more cramped and service, though well meaning, is somewhat unrefined. Still, Della Santina's can credit 20 years in Sonoma to its genuine hospitality and solid Northern Italian cuisine. Feast on pastas such as lasagna Bolognese and cannelloni Florentine, stuffed with grilled chicken and veal, then drizzled with béchamel; spit-roasted meats including duck and rabbit; and daily veal and gnocchi specials.

Diavola

A1

21021 Geyserville Ave. (at Hwy. 128), Geyserville

Phone: 707-814-0111   Lunch & dinner daily
Web: www.diavolapizzeria.com
Prices: $$

Since sibling, Santi, relocated to Santa Rosa, Diavola is the only serious culinary contender for miles. At mealtime, cars jam the spaces on tiny Geyserville's main drag as their occupants anticipate the rustic fare hand-crafted by Chef Dino Bugica.

Artisanal cured meats, sausages, and wood-fired pizzas are the heart of the cuisine here. Bugica has a passion for all things porcine, which figure prominently on the menu—be it in the daily selection of salami; pizza Sonja with prosciutto, mascarpone, and arugula; or roasted asparagus salad tossed with pancetta and truffled pecorino.

A former brothel, the narrow dining space touts its genuine feeling of history with original wood floors, pressed-tin ceilings, exposed brick, and simply dressed tables.

Dry Creek Kitchen

Californian

 D1

317 Healdsburg Ave. (bet. Matheson & Plaza Sts.), Healdsburg

Phone: 707-431-0330   Lunch Fri – Sun
Web: www.charliepalmer.com   Dinner nightly
Prices: $$$

Just look for the lime green façade on Healdsburg's main square and you will have arrived at Dry Creek Kitchen, an airy space where vaulted ceilings hum with the melody of piano and cello. Seafoam walls and a spacious bar and patio supply an aura of relaxation.

A touch stiff, the informed waitstaff can also warm you with the intricacies of new American cuisine. While highlights abound throughout the menu, Charlie Palmer's rotating roster may lend to some inconsistencies. No detail is overlooked in delicacies like sweetbread and confit chicken *agnolotti*. Flaky halibut poached in olive oil is a dream, and the chocolate-peanut butter *marquis* is layered with flavor and sin.

Naturally, the winning wine selection hails from surrounding Sonoma.

El Dorado Kitchen

Californian

D3

405 1st St. W. (at Spain St.), Sonoma

Phone: 707-996-3030   Lunch & dinner daily
Web: www.eldoradosonoma.com
Prices: $$

A stone's throw from the grassy Sonoma town square, this casual kitchen is nestled inside the El Dorado Hotel. The urban-chic interior boasts white washed walls, dark woods, and sage green accents. In the center of the dining room, two long rectangular hanging lamps illuminate the communal table fashioned from a single plank of wood salvaged from a bridge in Vermont.

Sit at the far end of the room to view Chef Justin Everett in the open kitchen. From here come decidedly Californian preparations, like house-made charcuterie, herb-basted beef tenderloin, or Niman Ranch pork osso buco. The breezy, family-friendly stone courtyard makes a perfect perch for creative Sunday brunch dishes, especially when they feature bœuf Bourguignon hash or smoked salmon.

Estate

Italian

C3

400 W. Spain St. (at 4th St.), Sonoma

Phone: 707-933-3663

Web: www.estate-sonoma.com

Prices: $$

Lunch Sun
Dinner nightly

With sweeping grounds, masterfully cultivated gardens, a wraparound porch, and sumptuous interiors dressed in burgundy and gold, this former home of General Mariano Vallejo's daughter is worthy of its new name. The historic Victorian was taken over in 2008 by the proprietors of the successful the girl & the fig. Today, the mystical manor draws foodies into its art-filled dining rooms for delicious small plates evocative of Southern Italy, like sautéed foraged mushrooms and crisp semolina *gnocchetti* with tender pork, fried sage, and black pepper. Main dishes such as fresh arctic char and leg of lamb are skillfully prepared, and many infuse handpicked ingredients from Estate's edible gardens.

The outdoor fireplace is an alluring spot for a cocktail.

Gary Chu's

Chinese

B2

611 5th St. (at Riley St.), Santa Rosa

Phone: 707-526-5840

Web: www.garychus.com

Prices:

Lunch & dinner daily

Craving a savory plate of sautéed Champagne scallops or bowl of steaming crab and corn soup? You aren't the only one: locals flock to this popular Chinese haunt where the well-priced, creative menu draws everyone in droves. Dark floral banquettes line the apricot walls in this modest space, and a smaller tented area near the entry—intended for larger groups—faces a pristine aquarium of tropical fish.

Start with tasty Sichuan wontons, stuffed with tender ground pork and served with the house secret sauce. For a quick fix at midday, swing by for one of the executive lunch specials, most of which are less than ten bucks and include an entrée, soup, and salad. Sweeten any meal with crispy tempura banana served with caramel sauce and vanilla ice cream.

Farmhouse Inn & Restaurant ✿

Californian ⅋⅋⅋

A2

7871 River Rd. (at Wohler Rd.), Forestville

Phone: 707-887-3300   Dinner Thu – Mon
Web: www.farmhouseinn.com
Prices: $$$

Tai Power Seeff

Wind your way along the Russian River Valley's River Road, with its rolling green hills and meandering vineyards, and eventually you'll stumble upon the Farmhouse Inn & Restaurant, an adorable cluster of pale yellow clapboard buildings along gravel paths.

Inside, you'll find a charming, country-chic dining room fitted out with wine storage racks, a big fireplace, and soft overhead lamps. Behind it, a porch-like second dining room offers sweeping views of the gardens and pool. It's a hideaway to take your breath away—and yet, ambience is only half the charm at the Farmhouse.

Given the lovely setting, Chef Steve Litke could have mailed it in with the food, but quite the opposite is true—this acclaimed restaurant is one of the best in the area, with Litke drawing on local, market-fresh ingredients to fashion a seasonal menu that may reveal a Vietnamese-style Hawaiian tuna ceviche layered with bright watermelon, fresh tomato, and vibrant basil; or luscious little seared pillows of Bellweather Farms ricotta gnocchi in a silky beurre blanc, pocked with spring peas, fresh fava beans, earthy morels, and shaved truffle. Don't miss the excellent wine list, teeming with local varietals.

Glen Ellen Inn

C3

Californian

13670 Arnold Dr. (at Warm Springs Rd.), Glen Ellen

Phone: 707-996-6409

Web: www.glenelleninn.com

Prices: $$

Lunch Fri – Tue
Dinner nightly

Clandestine lovers would be wise to hide away at the Glen Ellen Inn, a martini bar and grill in the heavily wooded hamlet of Glen Ellen. On a warm afternoon, the patio is ideal for cocktails and oysters, while a fireplace on the porch is snuggle friendly in winter. "Secret" cottages are available for an overnight rendezvous.

Dressed in jewel tones and heavy textiles, the dining room reflects its romantic, rural surroundings. Oddly highfalutin presentation dates the Californian fare, but dishes are pleasant enough. By day, savor a halibut filet with black bean and corn salsa. At dinner, sink into a panko-crusted Sonoma duck breast with foie gras and cherry Port sauce. If martinis are a touch too 007 for your taste, choose from more than 500 local wines.

Gohan

B3

Japanese

1367 N. McDowell Blvd. (at Redwood Way), Petaluma

Phone: 707-789-9296

Web: www.gohanrestaurant.com

Prices: $$

Lunch Mon – Fri
Dinner nightly

Some good sushi lies tucked away in the Redwood Gateway strip mall, where Gohan operates under Chef Takeshige Yahiro. The untimely death of the original Chef/owner Steve Tam two years ago, has inspired the Gohan team to keep Tam's dream alive. And they've been doing a fine job of it. Among the many meticulously formed and plated makimono rolls, the menu now lists one in Chef Steve's honor: shrimp tempura and snow crab salad wrapped in *maguro* and avocado with a dusting of *togarashi* for extra color and kick. At lunch, the best bargains are in the bento boxes; new style sashimi (*hirame* with ponzu citrus; albacore with jalapeño) is a bit pricier.

Dinner specials may include a ribeye with zinfandel teriyaki—this is wine country after all.

Hana

Japanese 🍴

101 Golf Course Dr. (at Roberts Lake Rd.), Rohnert Park

Phone: 707-586-0270

Web: www.hanajapanese.com

Prices: $$

Lunch Mon – Sat
Dinner nightly

Despite its unexpected location in the Double Tree Plaza, Hana has been Chef/owner Kenichi (Ken) Tominaga's baby for 15 years. Here, Tominaga and his chefs are known to nurture patrons with their pleasant demeanor, as well as nourishing them with the freshest fish flown in from Japan and the east and west coasts of the U.S.

Feel free to ask questions to the chefs at the bar—they are glad to describe the characteristics of a particular fish, or even display the day's fresh whole catch. The staff's love of food jumps out in their knowledgeable technique; and their exquisite omakase is perfect for those seeking true adventure.

If you miss Chef Ken's smiling face here, he is probably at Go Fish, the restaurant he runs with partner Cindy Pawlcyn in St. Helena.

Harvest Moon Cafe

Californian 🍴

487 1st St. W. (bet. Napa & Spain Sts.), Sonoma

Phone: 707-933-8160

Web: www.harvestmooncafesonoma.com

Prices: $$

Lunch Sun
Dinner Thu – Tue

Harvest Moon is the culinary child of a husband-wife team with true foodie pedigree: Nick and Jen Demarest, the chef and pastry chef respectively, hail from Chez Panisse and La Toque. As expected, the Californian cuisine exhibits a love of local, seasonal produce with just a kiss from the Mediterranean. Begin with Gruyère bruschetta with pork ragù and a fresh fried egg; finish with a bubbly apple-cherry cobbler and tart buttermilk ice cream.

The interior, while relaxed, is narrow despite the large open kitchen. Instead of settling in the dining room, mosey out back where olive, rosemary, and lavender branches festoon a spacious garden patio. Red metal tables provide a charming spot for casual meals; weather permitting, Wednesday is movie night.

Wine Country ▶ Sonoma County

343

Jackson's

〢〢

B2

135 4th St. (at Davis St.), Santa Rosa

Phone: 707-545-6900   Lunch & dinner daily
Web: www.jacksonsbarandoven.com
Prices: $$

Jackson's Bar and Oven might be summed up in just one dish: "Dad's pizza." Topped with Italian sausage, green olives, and roasted fennel, the pie is named for Chef/owner Josh Silver, whose restaurant is named after his son, Jackson. "Mom" also resides on the menu (in the form of a pizza *margherita*), and kid-friendly options abound in bacon-wrapped hot dogs and oven-baked macaroni and cheese. More serious eaters may opt for wood oven-roasted squid or pan-seared Pacific bass. Happily, the interior at Jackson's is mostly grown up. A chic palette of crimson and charcoal gray echoes the flame from the candy-apple red pizza oven, while the smooth marble-top bar resembles nutty nougat. Mezzanine seating allows parent types to watch over the buzz below.

John Ash & Co.

〢〢

B2

4330 Barnes Rd. (off River Rd.), Santa Rosa

Phone: 707-527-7687   Dinner nightly
Web: www.vintnersinn.com
Prices: $$$

A trip to John Ash & Co. is the culinary equivalent of getting a massage. Set at the Vintner's Inn in Santa Rosa, the restaurant is surrounded by more than 90 acres of soothing vineyards and gardens and, miraculously, plentiful parking. A sun-soaked patio overlooks the terrain, but the romantic interior is equally plush with a toasty fireplace and terra-cotta hues. White linens set the stage for organic Californian meals with a slight German inflection. Accompaniments of sauerkraut, cabbage, and spätzle hint at the chef's heritage, but the cuisine is generally worldly. A tasting menu might include salmon and cream cheese canapés with dill and briny capers; Canadian lobster tail with celery root puree; and a moist, herbaceous rack of lamb.

K & L Bistro

B2

Californian ✗

119 S. Main St. (bet. Burnett St. and Hwy. 12), Sebastopol

Phone: 707-823-6614 Lunch & dinner Mon – Sat
Web: www.klbistro.com
Prices: $$

Husband-wife duo Karen and Lucas Martin steer the stoves at K&L, a quintessential bistro that takes great pride in its craft. The intimate neighborhood gem typically bursts with Sebastopol locals rubbing elbows at close-knit tables topped with butcher paper. Exposed brick walls and dark wood accents lend a homey polish, while the granite bar is a terrific spot to sit and swirl.

Rusticity reigns in the semi-open kitchen where a crackling mesquite grill turns out French bistro classics and Californian fare. Traditionalists might begin with warm rabbit *rillette*, while others may prefer grilled Monterey Bay sardines or braised pork belly buns. A thick-cut pork Porterhouse, simply seasoned with salt and pepper, is a juicy cap to a chilly night.

LaSalette

D3

Portuguese ✗✗

452-H 1st St. E. (bet. Napa & Spain Sts.), Sonoma

Phone: 707-938-1927 Lunch & dinner daily
Web: www.lasalette-restaurant.com
Prices: $$

Fashioned with burlap draperies, hand-painted Portuguese pottery, and tables crafted from Port wine crates, LaSalette, the family-run affair near the Sonoma town square, tips its hat to the vibrant docks of Lisbon. Self-taught Chef/owner Manuel Azevedo and his cuisine, however, hail from the Azores Islands 1,000 miles from the capital. LaSalette is named for the chef's mother; his wife, Kimberly, is ready with a smile at the door.

Inside, pumpkin-hued walls echo the heat of a wood-burning oven that cranks out much of the restaurant's fare, including a whole roasted fish. On the enchanting patio, heaters ward off the evening chill, as do rich seafood and slow-cooked meat stews. Finish with a creamy flan, fresh berries, and a tasting of top-notch Ports.

Lokal

D3

522 Broadway (bet. E Napa & Patten Sts.), Sonoma

Phone: 707-938-7373   Lunch daily
Web: www.lokalsonoma.com   Dinner Wed – Mon
Prices: $$

It's pilsners, not pinot noirs at Lokal. Hansel and Gretel would feel right at home at this charming spot. Bringing a bit of the old country to wine country is what Lokal does best (or wurst). The menu makes you want to don a dirndl and dig in to European soul food like goulash meatball subs, *paprikash*, schnitzel, and spaetzle. Old family recipes like warm potato salad with tangy brown mustard and crisp bacon, pop up all over the menu and if you're a sausage lover, there's plenty to keep you smiling.

The trellised patio is a perfect *biergarten*, where you can put down lagers, pilsners, stouts, and Trappists served in pints, chalices, and even big glass boot mugs. And yes, if you must, there are some local wines too, but when near Romania...

Maya

D3

101 E. Napa St. (at 1st St.), Sonoma

Phone: 707-935-3500   Lunch & dinner daily
Web: www.mayarestaurant.com
Prices: $$

A "temple of tequila" may be an unexpected find at the corner of historic Sonoma Plaza, but that doesn't make it any less intoxicating: the restaurant's central bar, designed to evoke a Mayan ruin, is stocked with the blue agave spirit and topped with the Mesoamerican statue, Chac-Mool. Colorful paintings, stone walls, and swaying hammocks further invoke a vibrant Mexican culture and conjure a festive mood.

Maya infuses the Californian seasonal ethos with culinary influence found south of the border. Dishes might include prawns wrapped in cilantro enchiladas and topped with tarragon cream; pan-seared snapper Veracruz; or a textbook-creamy flan refreshed with berries. All pairs well with a boozy margarita perked up with spicy, toasted pumpkin seeds.

Madrona Manor ✿

Contemporary ✕✕✕

A1

1001 Westside Rd. (at West Dry Creek Rd.), Healdsburg

Phone:	707-433-4231
Web:	www.madronamanor.com
Prices:	$$$

Dinner Wed – Sun

Andy Katz/Madrona Manor

Perched atop a wooded hill in beautiful Dry Creek Valley, Madrona Manor's romance hits you the second you pull into the rambling gardens (all 8 acres of them) that surround the sunny yellow 19th century Victorian house.

A date at this lovely restaurant could begin with a cool drink on the carriage house porch, and then move on to the dining room, where a roaring fireplace, dripping chandeliers and gilded frame mirrors will make you feel like you've landed in an old European guesthouse.

Locally-born chef, Jesse Mallgren, divvies up his seasonal menu into categories like clean and crisp, soft and delicate, smooth, meaty, and sweet—and the nightly tasting menus, available in 4, 5, or 6-course options, truly come alive when paired with the Sonoma County wine list. Dinner might begin with gorgeous slices of pale pink Japanese tuna placed atop a bundle of enoki mushrooms and matched with a soy and ponzu foam, a dash of Serrano chili and diced mountain potato studded with cypress seeds; soft pillows of potato gnocchi sporting fresh sweet peas, julienned mint, crème fraîche, and toasted pistachios; or flaky, pristine white halibut laced with tangy salsa verde and smooth aïoli.

Wine Country ▶ Sonoma County

Mirepoix ✿

French 🍴🍴

B2

275 Windsor River Rd. (at Honsa Ave.), Windsor

Phone: 707-838-0162
Web: www.restaurantmirepoix.com
Prices: $$

Lunch Tue – Fri
Dinner Tue – Sun

Rob Huebschmann/Mirepoix

It's impossible not to describe Mirepoix as quaint, or even cute: the modern bistro is housed in a converted home, with hanging plants on the front porch, overlooking the quiet old downtown of Windsor.

Warm lighting fills the room where small production wines rest on cast iron and wooden racks, fresh flowers top the blonde wood bar, and upholstered high-back chairs surround the linen-topped tables. The dining room is convivial with patrons mostly from the neighborhood—all seem well acquainted with the restaurant and Chef Matthew Bousquet—and the lovely terrace.

Mirepoix's contemporary cuisine is offered both à la carte (items read like an ingredients list) and in four-, five-, and six-course prix-fixe menus. As the restaurant's name suggests, all dishes are prepared with French technique. One might begin with a velvety almond bisque heaped with spring onions, baby asparagus, and artichoke hearts before dipping into a creamy risotto with Meyer lemon and English peas. Dessert may bring rustic grilled banana bread with peanut butter ice cream and chocolate sauce. For the best experience, ask for the half-pour wine pairings at just $35 for the five-course meal.

Monti's Rotisserie

American ✗✗

B2

714 Village Court (bet. Farmer's Ln. & Hardmand Dr.), Santa Rosa

Phone: 707-568-4404   Lunch & dinner daily
Web: www.montisroti.net
Prices: $$

Carnivores delight in Mark and Terri Stark's addition to Santa Rosa's open-air Montgomery Village mall. A large wood-burning rotisserie takes center stage in the dining room, where glistening chunks of meat are roasted over the coals with exceptional skill. The mouthwatering aromas of the nightly selections are hard to resist; apple-glazed turkey may be offered one evening, pomegranate-glazed baby back ribs the next.

A long wooden bar zig-zags through the front room, packed with hungry shoppers who nosh on pasta, the addictive homemade French fries tossed with Gorgonzola and rosemary, and wood-fired pizzas. In nice weather, the spacious trellis-covered patio is an ideal spot. The Starks also run three other popular Sonoma County restaurants.

Mosaic

Californian ✗✗

A2

6675 Front St. (at Mirabel Rd.), Forestville

Phone: 707-887-7503   Lunch & dinner daily
Web: www.mosaiceats.com
Prices: $$

The vibe is shabby-chic and the interior is warm and bucolic in cinnamon-hued Mosaic. A big draw in the heart of wine country, Chef Tai Olesky's ingredients travel straight from soil to stove, reflecting his Sonoma County roots and food philosophy. Happy to have him close to home, locals gather at this rustic hearth—complete with glazed concrete floors and sturdy furnishings—to savor his fine home-grown food and wine.

When sunny, head to the timber-lined garden patio and feast on consummate Californian chow like pan-seared scallops with fennel pollen; stuffed filo purses; and duck confit. Fresh salads; a grilled chicken sandwich with avocado aïoli, bacon, and peppers; and a sinful burger of ground sirloin and tenderloin are widely appealing.

349

Osake

B2

Japanese ✗

2446 Patio Ct. (at Farmer's Ln.), Santa Rosa

Phone: 707-542-8282

Web: www.garychus.com

Prices:

Lunch Mon – Fri

Dinner Mon – Sat

Sleek lines and minimalist modern décor lure shoppers into this spacious Japanese restaurant in Montgomery Village mall. Here, they come to enjoy sushi at the welcoming bar, where a full complement of nigiri, sashimi, and maki rounds out the raw offerings. For those not seeking sushi, a *robata* grill turns out tantalizing skewers of Black Angus beef, chicken, yellowtail, and giant calamari cooked on the open fire. In between these options, a generous list of kitchen dishes ranges from monkfish pâté to vegetable tempura. Fixed-price bento box lunches and dinners add a lot of bang for the buck.

The name, meaning "respect for sake," inspires an array of sake offerings, as well as a selection of Sonoma County wines, to pair with the dishes.

Ravenous Café

D1

Californian ✗

420 Center St. (bet. North & Piper Sts.), Healdsburg

Phone: 707-431-1302

Web: www.theravenous.com

Prices: $$

Lunch & dinner Wed – Sun

Apricot walls, worn plank floors, and a crackling fireplace lend a folksy feel to this quaint cottage, whetting appetites for a home-cooked meal. Passion resides behind the stoves of Chefs/owners John and Joyanne Pezzolo, who turn out a different roster of Californian dishes each day. Items may range from a more rustic grilled portobello sandwich topped with roasted peppers and fontina, to fish cakes accompanied with ginger, lemon, and mint-cilantro aïoli. Generous desserts are sure to squelch any plans to diet, with the likes of apple-apricot crêpes, raspberry pavlova, or—with luck and timing—a creamy pumpkin-mascarpone cheesecake.

Once the smattering of tables fills up, a line usually forms for the first-come, first-served seats at the bar.

Red Grape

Pizza ✗

D3

529 1st St. W. (at Napa St.), Sonoma

Phone: 707-996-4103
Web: www.theredgrape.com
Prices:

Lunch & dinner daily

While other types of grapes may demand the lion's share of attention in Sonoma County, the Red Grape holds its own as a wine country pizzeria. The name refers to the type of tomatoes used to make the sauce that tops the cracker-thin New Haven-style pizza that owner Sam Morphy and his family discovered during a year spent in Connecticut.

Comfortable and family-friendly, the roomy interior fills almost as fast as the inviting outdoor garden patio on a sunny day, serving a lunchtime menu that features an extensive selection of panini. Crispy pies come out of the fiery-hot, stone-lined oven in a multitude of varieties, divided simply on the menu into "red" and "white" in combinations like Buffalo chicken with jalapeños and applewood-smoked bacon.

Rin's Thai

Thai ✗

D3

139 E. Napa St. (bet. 1st & 2nd Sts.), Sonoma

Phone: 707-938-1462
Web: www.rinsthai.com
Prices:

Lunch & dinner Tue – Sun

Set in a charming Victorian cottage that resembles a bed & breakfast, Rin's Thai demonstrates that perfect marriage between Thailand's vivid flavors and its warm hospitality. The inside is clean and open with cheery yellow walls, soaring ceilings dotted with fans, and the near absence of kitsch. Make yourself at home and wait to be dazzled by their authentic cuisine.

The food and flavors have that lucid Californian sensibility evident in delicacies such as *nuer prig king*, where fresh vegetables and thinly sliced beef tenderloin combine in a pungent garlic-chili sauce. Simple prawns become glorious when bundled whole in egg roll wrappers and lightly fried; while classics like pad Thai and chicken satay are sure to satisfy the less adventurous.

351

Risibisi

Italian ✗✗

B3

154 Petaluma Blvd. N. (bet. Washington St. & Western Ave.), Petaluma

Phone: 707-766-7600
Web: www.risibisirestaurant.com
Prices: $$

Lunch Mon – Sat
Dinner nightly

Named for a favorite risotto in the region of Friuli-Venezia Giulia, Petaluma's Risibisi is a true taste of the Italian city of Trieste. Owner Marco Palmieri hails from the Adriatic seaport and mingles a Californian sensibility with the traditional cuisine of his youth. This Sonoma County charmer also embraces whimsy, with heavy ropes and brightly hued chairs suspended from the ceiling and art works adorning exposed brick walls.

The kitchen makes magic of such familiar fare as *fritto misto*, which here is delicate in texture, bite, and flavor; or spaghetti carbonara bountiful with pancetta and Parmesan. Even that old dessert standby, tiramisu, is more lovingly articulated with the distinct flavors of coffee, liqueur, and fluffy mascarpone cream.

Rosso

Pizza ✗

B2

53 Montgomery Dr. (at 3rd St.), Santa Rosa

Phone: 707-544-3221
Web: www.pizzeriarosso.com
Prices: $$

Lunch & dinner daily

For those who think that vino and *futbol* (read: soccer) don't pair well together, think again. At Rosso, Italian wines live in utter harmony with the flat screen TV. And while the sports channel may feel appropriate to the Creekside Center strip mall locale, the crisp pizza *Napoletana* is a divine departure abroad.

Owner John Franchetti did time at St. Helena's Tra Vigne before opening this pizzeria. Here, amidst an urbane vibe, you'll find crisp salads with smoked chicken and walnuts and, the highlight, chewy 12-inch pies with fresh ingredients that pay homage to the Slow Food Movement. Take a walk on the wild side and order the "goomba" pizza topped with spaghetti, meatballs, and saffron tomato sauce; or stay closer to home with a white pizza *funghi*.

Santé ✿

Californian 🍴🍴🍴

100 Boyes Blvd. (at Hwy. 12), Sonoma

Phone:	707-939-2415	Lunch & dinner daily
Web:	www.fairmont.com/sonoma	
Prices:	**$$$**	

Fairmont Sonoma Mission Inn

Wine Country ▶ Sonoma County

With its abundance of restaurants dishing out inventive cuisine, Sonoma Valley has always been synonymous with fine dining. Quaint homes, out-of-the-way spots, and places that people like to consider "finds" are all terrific, but one of the region's best is located in a spot some don't equate with cutting edge cuisine—a hotel. Santé is tucked inside the Fairmont Sonoma Mission Inn. You don't need to be a guest at this historic property to taste the artistry, but after tucking in to a satisfying meal and polishing off one of the several bottles of wine, you might just want to retire to a room.

Smiling staff set the tone at this laid back, yet luxurious restaurant. From John Dory pan-fried until golden brown yet moist and flaky on the inside, to tender pork cheeks over a bed of sharp white cheddar polenta, the dishes are simply perfect. Even the bread basket, which showcases the talents of a local bakery, is beyond compare. The menu features á la carte selections, though a tasting menu is available nightly for those who can get the group to agree.

The wine list is beyond comprehensive, offering 500 different types of domestic and Californian selections.

Santi 😊

Italian ✗✗

2097 Stagecoach Rd. (at Fountaingrove Pkwy.), Santa Rosa

Phone: 707-528-1549
Lunch & dinner daily
Web: www.santirestaurant.com
Prices: $$

This Geyserville transplant enjoyed a decade-long success there, and hasn't skipped a beat in its relocation to Santa Rosa. It fits right in at its new location within the Fountaingrove Village shops and is conveniently located next door to Traverso's gourmet Italian food market.

From its polished concrete floors and chunky farmhouse-style furnishings to its wood-burning oven, Santi is the very definition of rustic charm. The open kitchen shines a spotlight on the workings of the talented staff. Chef Liza Hinman takes a light and healthy approach and infuses Italian cooking with a Californian sensibility. A beat is never missed here; flavors are rich, and meats are juicy and tender. Both the dessert list and the wine list are short, but sweet.

Scopa

Italian ▤

109A Plaza St. (bet. Center St. & Healdsburg Ave.), Healdsburg

Phone: 707-433-5282
Dinner Tue – Sun
Web: www.scopahealdsburg.com
Prices: $$

Named for a raucous Italian card game, Scopa packs a lot of life in a bite-size space. A genuine family affair that prides itself on hospitality, Scopa sees Chef Ari Rosen and his wife, Dawnelise, mastering the kitchen and wine program respectively. (Mom does the books; Dad helps with the baking.)

Locals feel at home in the snug setting and are often inclined to chat with their neighbors. The concrete walls are bare, but the rustic Italian menu has plenty to feast on. Small plates such as spicy meatballs in a cast iron skillet, or prosciutto wrapped around oozing fontina encourage sharing. Handmade pastas and crusty artisanal pizzas complement the local wines.

On Wednesdays, area vintners hang around to talk shop with aspiring oenophiles.

Sea Thai

Thai

2323 Sonoma Ave. (at Farmer's Ln.), Santa Rosa

Phone:	707-528-8333	Lunch & dinner daily
Web:	www.seathaibistrosr.com	
Prices:	**$$**	

Parked on a cozy corner in the bustling Montgomery Village outdoor mall, Tony Ounpamornchai's authentic, upscale Thai-fusion bistro is more than a strip mall stop. Here, crimson walls crawl along a narrow dining space, and upscale Thai gets a Westernized spin in dishes like shrimp bruschetta, made with four squares of fresh, delicious bread topped with avocado, shrimp, cilantro, and spicy homemade Asian pesto. The lunch menu has plenty of goodies to choose from, though curry dishes are only served at dinner. For a fabulous finale, try the banana fritters with coconut ice cream—that should hush the aficionados complaining that prices here are higher than divier joints.

Folks in Petaluma enjoy the older sibling restaurant, SEA Modern Thai Cuisine.

Spoonbar

Mediterranean

219 Healdsburg Ave. (bet. Matheson & Mill Sts.), Healdsburg

Phone:	707-431-2202	Dinner nightly
Web:	www.spoonbar.com	
Prices:	**$$**	

If the Hotel Healdsburg's Dry Creek Kitchen caters to the silver spoons of culinary travelers, then little sister Spoonbar dishes it out for the "green" spoons in the new h2hotel. Raised on the Bay Area ethos "local, organic, sustainable," Spoonbar's patrons have a taste for the contemporary resto's recycled design and trickling fountain made of rocking spoons.

With master mixologist Scott Beattie helming the bar, Spoonbar is a booze hound's paradise with such deftly crafted concoctions as the Corpse Reviver #2. The extensive drinks list is best paired with food—particularly if you're driving home. Sample Mediterranean fare like Sicilian pinenut and raisin meatballs with cucumber salad, or a Moroccan lamb tagine with black chickpeas and mint.

Stark's Steakhouse

Steakhouse

521 Adam St. (at 7th St.), Santa Rosa

Phone: 707-546-5100
Web: www.starkrestaurants.com
Prices: $$$

Lunch Mon – Fri
Dinner nightly

Fourth in the brood of Mark and Terri Stark (of Willi's Wine Bar and Monti's), Stark's Steakhouse is at last grown up and hitting its stride. On Santa Rosa's historic Railroad Square, Stark's draws suitors with a baby grand piano, a pair of roaring fireplaces, and an ample selection of bourbon and Scotch in the snug bar and lounge, which serves an all day menu.

Unexpected starters like Dungeness crab tater tots or tamarind barbecue prawns show contemporary playfulness, while classics like chilled oysters hint at the experience to come. Stark's tome-lined dining room is best known for its traditional steakhouse dinners of grass-fed and dry-aged beef as well as storied American Kobe. Red meat may rule, but it does share space with omnivorous alternatives.

Sugo

Italian

5 Petaluma Blvd. S. (at B St.), Petaluma

Phone: 707-782-9298
Web: www.sugopetaluma.com
Prices: $$

Lunch & dinner daily

Housed behind a well-worn brick façade in Petaluma's Theater District, Sugo Trattoria offers a comely take on dinner and a movie, where classic films silently unfold on a white wall above the open kitchen. If this bit of art house entertainment isn't enough to take your mind off Sugo's strip mall locale, perhaps ambient music and candlelight are enough to transport you at last.

As the name suggests, Sugo's tiered dining room waves its flag for Italy with a hefty selection of bruschetta, including one topped with prosciutto, fig, and Brie; a daily ravioli; and *secondi* starring Californian produce—think pistachio-crusted salmon or artichoke chicken *picatta*. A panzanella salad makes a nice light lunch when paired with five-dollar wines by the glass.

Syrah

Californian ✗✗

B2

205 5th St. (at Davis St.), Santa Rosa

Phone: 707-568-4002
Web: www.syrahbistro.com
Prices: $$$

Lunch Tue – Sat
Dinner nightly

At Syrah, Chef/owner Josh Silver tips his beret to the Rhône with nearly 50 syrah and shiraz labels on the well-edited wine list. Curious oenophiles might enjoy a flight, while those preferring a take-home treat head to Silver's wine shop, Petite Syrah, next door.

It all sounds very French but, in truth, Syrah remains firmly rooted in Sonoma. Housed in Santa Rosa's ivy-clad City 205 building, this warm bistro serves locally sourced fare in an enclosed courtyard shared with a petite salon and a bud-sized florist. The chef, who also owns neighboring Jackson's, is a follower of the Slow Food Movement, so look for dressed up comfort in dishes such as crab cakes with fingerling potato salad and tender chicken potpie with a flaky pastry crust.

Thai Orchid

Thai ✗

D2

1005 Vine St. (at Mill St.), Healdsburg

Phone: 707-433-0515
Web: N/A
Prices: ⊜⊜

Lunch Tue – Sat
Dinner nightly

When savvy foodies need respite from foie gras and duck confit, they head to the local strip mall for authentic, affordable Asian eats. Thai Orchid, at Healdsburg's Vineyard Plaza, is one such retreat, with a modest dining room outfitted with only a few wood tables and simple wall carvings.

Despite an unassuming interior, the cuisine explodes with layers of flavor and heat that may sting a sensitive western palate. Heed the knowing stare of the house matriarch whose warning eyes say, "order mild." The broad menu traverses Thailand from familiar to exotic fare. Kick off the expedition with flavorful coconut soup; travel on to *nua nam tok*, or beef salad with red onions, basil, and mint; or rekindle your love of the land with a perfect pad Thai.

the girl & the fig

D3

110 W. Spain St. (at 1st St.), Sonoma

Phone: 707-938-3634   Lunch & dinner daily
Web: www.thegirlandthefig.com
Prices: $$

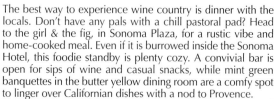

The best way to experience wine country is dinner with the locals. Don't have any pals with a chill pastoral pad? Head to the girl & the fig, in Sonoma Plaza, for a rustic vibe and home-cooked meal. Even if it is burrowed inside the Sonoma Hotel, this foodie standby is plenty cozy. A convivial bar is open for sips of wine and casual snacks, while mint green banquettes in the butter yellow dining room are a comfy spot to linger over Californian dishes with a nod to Provence.

The intricate antique wood bar serves French aperitifs and thoughtful half-glasses to the tasting crowd—paired with a plate of local artisan cheeses. Heartier appetites may indulge in chicken two ways, a crisp-skinned breast and herby leg roulade with roasted root vegetables.

Underwood

A2

9113 Graton Rd. (at Edison St.), Graton

Phone: 707-823-7023   Lunch Tue – Sat
Web: www.underwoodgraton.com   Dinner Tue – Sun
Prices: $$

The tiny town of Graton is the geographical center of Sonoma's West County, and at its center sits Underwood, a hip little hub known to attract the best local winemakers for a sip and a nosh. Its old-school saloon vibe—red vinyl banquettes, zinc- and copper-topped tables, a nickel-topped bar slinging classic cocktails—make Underwood an ideal spot to pop in any time of day or night.

Befitting this Lilliputian town set smack in the middle of sophisticated foodie heaven, Underwood's menu ranges from American classics, including a darn good ham-and-Gruyère sandwich with crispy hot fries, to such global small plates as Vietnamese lettuce cups, white anchovy crostini, or Thai chili clams. On warmer days, locals slurp oysters on the picturesque mini patio.

Willi's Seafood & Raw Bar

Seafood ✗✗

D1

403 Healdsburg Ave. (at North St.), Healdsburg

Phone:	707-433-9191
Web:	www.starkrestaurants.com
Prices:	**$$**

Lunch & dinner daily

A walk beneath the wrought iron archway leads diners through a quaint hedge-lined heated patio straight to Willi's entrance. This upscale tavern, a popular and family-friendly gathering spot just north of Healdsburg's town square, promotes sharing with its small plates served family style. Bright and fresh flavors are featured in the likes of hamachi ceviche with rocoto chili, lime, and *pepitas*; fried oyster Po'boys with celery root rémoulade; and uni and bay scallop "macaroni."

At the long bar, raw oysters, clams, and other chilled seafood make a natural complement for a creative cocktail or good selection of wine by the glass.

Proprietors Mark and Terri Stark also own multiple sibling restaurants in Santa Rosa, including Willi's Wine Bar.

Willi's Wine Bar 😳

International ✗✗

B2

4404 Old Redwood Hwy. (at Ursuline Rd.), Santa Rosa

Phone:	707-526-3096
Web:	www.starkrestaurants.com
Prices:	**$$**

Lunch Tue – Sat
Dinner nightly

Slow down along the Old Redwood Highway where, shrouded by a thick wall of trees, you will turn into a jammed parking lot to find Willi's Wine Bar. One of four eateries from restaurateurs Mark and Terri Stark, this obscure roadhouse is named for the first pioneering spot in Paris to serve American wines to the French. Willi's is popular among local vintners and boasts more than 40 wines by-the-glass (and half-glass). Still, international tapas mingling Asian, French, Mediterranean, and Californian flavors are the real draw, and perfect for groups looking to suit a variety of eclectic tastes. Dishes may include the likes of the Stark's very own "mu-shu bacon"; rabbit rillette with spiced grape chutney; or crispy brandade springrolls with Romesco.

Willow Wood Market Cafe

 Californian

9020 Graton Rd. (at Edison St.), Graton

Phone: 707-823-0233
Web: www.willowwoodgraton.com
Prices: **$$**

Lunch daily
Dinner Mon – Sat

Lulu is your hostess at this darling roadside eatery; its genuine country vibe and hospitality marry well with Californian comfort food. While the budget-friendly café remains a rather tinsel market with quirky knick knacks, fans of Americana will be tickled by the Necco wafers and old-time sundries to go.

Enter this "home" and take a seat. Salads and hot sandwiches are at the ready, but the menu revolves around bowls of "piping hot polenta." The creamy goodness has many guises like garlicky rock shrimp with roasted tomatoes and peppers, but favorites like the black bean soup with a swirl of sour cream or the cheesy skirt steak sandwich will turn back the clock. Nourishing this sense of nostalgia, most items are escorted by crunchy garlic toast.

zazu

Californian XX

3535 Guerneville Rd. (at Willowside Rd.), Santa Rosa

Phone: 707-523-4814
Web: www.zazurestaurant.com
Prices: **$$**

Dinner Wed – Sun

A little red roadhouse in the middle of nowhere—if you can call Sonoma's sprawl of artisan farms and vineyards "nowhere"—pastoral zazu makes the utmost of its environment, serving pick-it-yourself salads from its onsite garden. Knock the dirt off your shoes and duck inside the narrow dining room where boat lights cast a soft glow and husband-wife chefs, John Stewart and Duskie Edwards, provide the extra spark.

The chefs are hog wild for house-made *salumi*, sausage, and bacon and their rustic interior is suited to Californian cuisine with an Italian accent. Start with rich tomato soup and Carmody grilled cheese, and save room for hand-cut pasta with tender braised boar. For dessert, rose-geranium ice cream is a cool accomplice to strawberry-rhubarb crisp.

Zin

 D1

344 Center St. (at North St.), Healdsburg

Phone: 707-473-0946
Web: www.zinrestaurant.com
Prices: $$

Lunch Mon – Fri
Dinner nightly

Wine Country ▶ Sonoma County

 Parked off Healdsburg square, droves of diners unite at diverse Zin for seasonal cuisine. With polished concrete floors, wood beams, high ceilings, and bucolic paintings, this culinary hot spot is *très* cool and casual. Adjacent to the open kitchen at back, zinfandel zealots settle at the bar to ogle a wine list centered on local examples of the zinfandel variety.

The affable staff lays upon your table—set with a wooden ladder-back chair—American classics laced with an eclectic spin. Co-owners Jeff Mall and Scott Silva are sons of the soil whose pastoral psyche shines in fried green beans clothed in a mango salsa; succulent shrimp and Andouille sausage atop a crispy grit cake; and a perfectly sweetened café latte crème brûlée crowned with oatmeal cookies.

Bib Gourmand 😊
indicates our inspectors'
favorites for good value.

Where to**Stay**

Stanyan Park

A1

750 Stanyan St. (at Waller St.)

Phone: 415-751-1000
Web: www.stanyanpark.com
Prices: $$

30 Rooms
6 Suites

Stanyan Park

Victorian-style, reasonable rates, and a view of Golden Gate Park set this small hotel apart. Built in 1905 as one of a dozen lodgings serving visitors to San Francisco's grand park, the Stanyan alone survives in its original function today. Its handsome three-story Queen Anne-style turret marks the corner of Stanyan and Waller streets.

Exploring the 1,017-acre park from here is a breeze, whether you're walking, biking, or driving. This property is also convenient to the UCSF Medical Center.

While Golden Gate Park may be known for the throngs of tie-dyed-T-shirt-clad hippies who staged throbbing rock concerts in the Speedway Meadows during the 1967 "Summer of Love," the hotel across the street has no claims to hipness. The 36 non-smoking rooms set a tasteful, romantic mood with their floral Victorian wallpaper, quiet colors, and classic furnishings. Reserve one of the larger suites (which range up to 900 square feet) if you need more space; you'll have a comfortable living room, a full kitchen, a separate dining room, and two separate bedrooms at your disposal. Continental breakfast and afternoon tea service are on the house.

Inn at the Opera

 C1

333 Fulton St. (at Franklin St.)

Phone: 415-863-8400 or 800-325-2708
Web: www.shellhospitality.com
Prices: $$

30 Rooms

18 Suites

Inn at the Opera

Playing on its proximity to the 1932 Memorial Opera House—home to the San Francisco Opera and the San Francisco Ballet—and the Louise M. Davies Symphony Hall, this 48-room inn is in perfect pitch as a convenient place to stay for performers and theatergoers.

At 215 square feet, there may not be space for a *pas de deux* in the Ballet studio, but this unit does offer a kitchenette with a microwave oven, coffeemaker, and small refrigerator. The Concerto junior suite adds separate sleeping and living areas; bigger still, the Symphony suite sleeps four. Divas can book the Opera suite, the largest accommodation. It can hold a small entourage, with two bathrooms and two separate sitting rooms in addition to the bedroom. Comfy bathrobes, turn-down service, a morning newspaper, and a complimentary continental breakfast are included with any room.

The newly renovated lobby makes a chic place to meet friends; and fine French fare stars nightly at the hotel's on-site restaurant, Ovation at the Opera. Nearby shopping includes the funky shops of Hayes Street, the Westfield San Francisco Centre mall a short distance down Market Street, and the designer boutiques of Union Square, a mere mile away.

San Francisco ▶ Civic Center

Phoenix

601 Eddy St. (at Larkin St.)

Phone: 415-776-1380 or 800-248-9466
Web: www.thephoenixhotel.com
Prices: $$

41
Rooms

3
Suites

Joie de Vivre Hospitality

Bohemian and hip, the Phoenix, admittedly, is not for everyone. It is located at the edge of the Tenderloin neighborhood, an area long known for its mean streets. Today, this diverse district is in transition, and it lures the young and adventurous to its ethnic eateries and nightclubs.

Catering to the rock 'n' roll set, the Phoenix brings in talent that's far from local (think Pearl Jam, the Red Hot Chili Peppers, and The Shins). The hotel is not a quiet place for your grandparents—perhaps not your parents either—since it can get pretty boisterous at times. But for those who want to rub elbows with rock stars by the outdoor heated pool, it's a cool place to hang.

The building retains its 1956 motel configuration, with rooms facing a landscaped central courtyard. Among the courtyard's glorious features, come here to find the amazing pool that incessantly buzzes with even more amazing people. Of the hotel's 44 tropical-toned rooms, the three Deluxe King rooms and the three suites have refrigerators, microwaves and coffeemakers. After enjoying a complimentary continental breakfast by the pool, feel free to quiz the staff on their favorite city sights.

Adagio

A2

550 Geary St. (bet. Jones & Taylor Sts.)

Phone: 415-775-5000 or 800-228-8830
Web: www.thehoteladagio.com
Prices: $$$

169
Rooms

2
Suites

Scott Brooks

A member of the Joie de Vivre Hospitality Group (whose properties include the Carlton, Hotel Kabuki, and the Hotel Vitale among others), the Adagio evokes the quiet grace that its name suggests. This landmark Spanish Colonial Revival structure was built in 1929 as the El Cortez, and knew several different names and owners before it was reopened in 2003.

Clean lines and contemporary furnishings sound a modern note in rooms dressed in tones of walnut brown and terracotta. Almost half of the rooms have dramatic views of the San Francisco cityscape. Foremost among these are the two penthouse suites, located on the 16th floor. The larger of the two, the Bolero Suite, adjoins an outdoor terrace. It offers space galore with a king-size bedroom, a separate living room with fireplace, and a dining table for eight.

Come here often? Take advantage of the Adagio's executive luggage storage program. If you're new to the city, sign up for a complimentary tour—your choice of neighborhoods—with a Golden Gate Greeter. Guests also enjoy free town car service within a two-mile radius of the hotel.

San Francisco ▶ Financial District

Bijou

111 Mason St. (at Eddy St.)

Phone: 415-771-1200 or 800-771-1022
Web: www.hotelbijou.com
Prices: $

65
Rooms

&

Quaint and low-key in the European tradition, the Bijou lies between Union Square and the Tenderloin, and offers good value for its convenient location. In this 1911 hotel, a theater theme and art deco-inspired décor recall the golden years of the silver screen. To illustrate this, each of the 65 rooms is named for a film that was shot in San Francisco.

Rich tones of burgundy, green, and sunny yellow color the well-maintained rooms, which are decorated with still photographs depicting their individual movie motif. Windows are not soundproofed, so if it's absolute quiet you're after, you'll have to sacrifice a street view in a front room for accommodations on the back side of the five-story building (earplugs are provided in all rooms). For security, front doors are locked at 8:00 P.M. each night; guests must show their hotel key card to get in after that time.

Amenities include complimentary wireless Internet access throughout the property, and breakfast pastries, coffee, and tea. Perhaps the best amenity of all here is the nightly double feature. These movies are screened off the lobby in a small theater decked out with vintage, folding velvet-covered seats.

Clift

495 Geary St. (at Taylor St.)

Phone: 415-775-4700 or 800-697-1791
Web: www.clifthotel.com
Prices: $$$

338 Rooms

25 Suites

Clift Hotel

Renowned as "Wonderland for the jet set," the Clift turns the conventional luxury hotel experience upside down. The 1913 Italian Renaissance-style building was reconceived for the 21st century by designer Philippe Starck. True to his style, Starck surprises at every turn in the soaring lobby with a juxtaposition of antique and modern pieces: an Eames chair here; a Salvador Dalí-inspired coffee table there; a 35-foot-high fireplace as a focal point. This play on scale does indeed tend to make guests feel like they've walked into Wonderland.

Things become less surreal in the guestrooms, designed for tranquility in quiet tones of foggy gray, beige, and lavender. English sycamore sleigh beds on a base of polished chrome add whimsy to the sophistication displayed in gauzy silk curtains and Italian percale linens.

Whether you're in town on pleasure or business, the Clift can oblige. The legendary art deco Redwood Room lounge is a hipster haunt swathed in redwood; while the adjacent Velvet Room is open for business in an equally glamorous setting. Doing business is a breeze with the help of a full-service business center, and rooms to support all facets of video production.

San Francisco ▶ Financial District

369

Diva

A2

440 Geary St. (bet. Mason & Taylor Sts.)

Phone: 415-885-0200 or 800-553-1900
Web: www.hoteldiva.com
Prices: $$

116
Rooms

2
Suites

Rien van Rijthoven

Steps from Union Square and across from the Curran and the American Conservatory theaters, Diva preserves its edgy Euro-tech vibe. Charcoal gray, taupe and black lend a hip vibe to the guest rooms, which have been recently enhanced with new bedding and lighting. The ultra-contemporary look uses cobalt blue carpets, streamlined furnishings, contemporary art, and stainless steel accents to make its point. Upgrade your reservation to the Salon floor, and you'll enjoy amenities such as an in-room refrigerator and a complimentary continental breakfast. The Diva has no restaurant, but get your java fix next door at Starbucks.

Kids will go for the Little Diva suites, tailored to the young traveler with pop-art colors, bunk beds, kid-friendly movies, and a karaoke machine for budding American Idols. Parents get the connecting room, so they have their own space, but can easily keep track of the younger members of the family.

Even the meeting room and the Internet lounges are custom designed. The former features a golden onxy and steel underlit buffet, while the lounges credit the likes of skateboarder Pete Colpitts among their designers.

Galleria Park

B3

191 Sutter St. (at Kearny St.)

Phone: 415-781-3060 or 800-792-9639
Web: www.jdvhotels.com
Prices: $$

169
Rooms
8
Suites

Cesar Rubio

Both business and leisure travelers will find a quiet refuge at this 177-room property, which premiered in 1911 as the Sutter Hotel. Taken over by the Joie de Vivre group in 2005, the Galleria Park sits in the heart of the FiDi, a short walk from Union Square and all its fabulous shops.

The lobby is outfitted in a glamorous art deco style, complete with an eclectic collection of furniture and artwork from San Francisco's Lost Art Salon. Likewise, guestrooms have been upgraded with comfy pillowtop mattresses, flat screen TVs, and Frette linens. Shades of chartreuse and plum make a stylish color combination, especially when balanced by clean white trim.

A unique feature, an outdoor jogging track is located on the third floor. Here, you'll also find a landscaped terrace, with benches for relaxing. If jogging's not your thing, you can work out in the little fitness room. The hotel's GPS (Galleria Park Suggests) program offers set packages that provide exclusive access and behind-the-scenes scoops to sights around the city. A free 2-hour guided walking tour of the Financial District is available free of charge to all guests.

San Francisco ▶ Financial District

The Inn at Union Square

440 Post St. (bet. Mason & Powell Sts.)

Phone: 415-397-3510 or 800-288-4346
Web: www.unionsquare.com
Prices: $$

24
Rooms
6
Suites

San Francisco's mecca for shoppers, Union Square is the first place many visitors head for when they arrive in the city. From Saks Fifth Avenue and Neiman Marcus to designer boutiques such as Gucci, Cartier, and Hermès, ways to exercise those credit cards abound around the plaza that was dedicated as a stage for supporters of the Union Army during the Civil War. And it all lies at the doorstep of The Inn at Union Square.

With upscale shopping at your heels, you would expect a hotel with this address to be equally expensive. In this regard, the Inn at Union Square—a certified California Green Lodging—surprises with its affordable rates, especially given the personalized service that the staff provides. The hotel is small, but the 30 rooms and one suite—recently redecorated in tones of cream, sage, and gold—provide all the comforts of home. Goose down pillows and pillow-top mattresses are nice extras for the price.

Intimate sitting areas on each floor boast wood-burning fireplaces lit with crackling fires in the evening, when wine and hors d'oeuvres are offered free of charge. This is also where guests can mingle over the complimentary continental breakfast set out each morning.

San Francisco ▶ Financial District

King George

 A2

334 Mason St. (bet. Geary & O'Farrell Sts.)

Phone: 415-781-5050 or 800-288-6005
Web: www.kinggeorge.com
Prices: $

151
Rooms

2
Suites

King George Hotel

Potted topiary trees and a prominent awning announce the entrance to this Anglophile's hideaway. Opened in 1914, the King George welcomes guests with European flair, beginning with the lobby, where warm tones of yellow, beige, and gold set off a full-size portrait of the hotel's namesake.

English hunting country may come to mind when you check into one of the 153 rooms, colored in a palette of green, gold and burgundy. All accommodations include fun and thoughtful touches like jars of candy. If the sweets aren't sustenance enough, the King George also offers 24-hour room service, catered by an off-site restaurant. Given these comforts, and the hotel's location—a block west of Union Square and convenient to the Moscone Center—rates here are a real deal.

The hotel no longer serves breakfast, but they do set out coffee and tea in the lobby each morning. A proper English tea is available on weekends in the Windsor Tea Room for parties of ten or more; reservations are required. For meals, there are many restaurant options nearby; but for drinks and appetizers, you need not venture farther than Winston's Bar and Lounge. Daily happy hour here features discounted beer and wine.

San Francisco ▶ Financial District

Mandarin Oriental

222 Sansome St. (bet. California & Pine Sts.)

Phone: 415-276-9888 or 800-622-0404
Web: www.mandarinoriental.com
Prices: $$$$

151
Rooms

7
Suites

Mandarin Oriental Hotel Group

The view's the thing at this sumptuous property, which occupies two towers in one of San Francisco's taller buildings, between the 38th and 48th stories. Glass-enclosed sky bridges connect the two towers on each floor, offering spectacular views of the city and beyond.

Exotic touches of the Orient delight at every turn. The lobby's marble floor, for starters, illustrates a stylized Chinese pattern that symbolizes good fortune. On the second floor, Silks restaurant follows suit with Pacific Rim cuisine and silk brocade tablecloths that borrow their design from the robes of the Imperial Chinese Court.

A cinnamon red palette inspires the room décor, enhanced by mahogany furnishings and gold-leaf accents. Every sky-high room claims terrific views from its picture windows. For even better vistas, ask for an Executive Corner room, in which the writing desk cozies up against the window offering a 180-degree cityscape. Or book the Lotus Suite, where you can gaze out the bathroom window at the Golden Gate Bridge while you soak in the tub.

From the hotel, it's a short walk to Embarcadero Center shopping; all the attractions of Fisherman's Wharf are just a quick cable car ride away.

Monaco

A2

501 Geary St. (at Taylor St.)

Phone: 415-292-0100 or 866-622-5284
Web: www.monaco-sf.com
Prices: $$$

169
Rooms

32
Suites

Fred Lichr/Kimpton Hotels

Like every picture, every Kimpton hotel tells a story; the one behind the Monaco is sophisticated world travel. The gold-toned lobby sets the nostalgic tone for 1920s travel with a check-in desk styled like a steamer trunk, and hand-painted ceiling frescoes depicting whimsical skyscapes of hot air balloons and planes. On the landing of the grand staircase, a painting entitled Celestial Lady clearly illustrates that the sky is the limit.

Vibrant fabrics drape over canopy beds in the guestrooms, and cheery striped paper covers the walls. In-room spa services and a yoga channel add cultured touches to please any jet setter. Rock 'n' roll fans can rent the Grace Slick Suite, a shrine to the singer's days with the group Jefferson Airplane and later the Jefferson Starship. If hungry, Grand Café provides a great selection of eats and treats that is sure to please and appease.

For tiny tots, the Kimpton Kids program provides complimentary cribs. Older travelers-in-training receive a welcome gift and a pint-size animal print robe to wear in their room; parents get a list of kid-friendly activities in the city. Even four-legged travelers are welcome here, at no additional cost.

San Francisco ▶ Financial District

Nikko

222 Mason St. (bet. Ellis & O'Farrell Sts.)

Phone: 415-394-1111 or 800-248-3308
Web: www.hotelnikkosf.com
Prices: $$

510
Rooms

22
Suites

Hotel Nikko San Francisco

San Francisco ▶ Financial District

Though large, the Nikko offers a comfortable and convenient stay, with a choice of 12 different types of rooms and suites. At 280 square feet, the Petite queens are best for single occupancy, but may also suit two people in search of a good deal. Deluxe rooms, both king and double/doubles, occupy floors 6 through 21. The Imperial Floors (22, 23, and 24) offer added services and amenities, including restricted access and breakfast served in a private lounge. At the top end, the two bedroom, two bath Imperial Suite measures in at 2,635 square feet. City views are divine, especially from the higher floors. The private, aurally perfect, and sophisticated Rrazz Room theater continues to host myriad world-class entertainers such as Ashford & Simpson, Keely Smith, and the American Idols.

A lovely swimming pool, together with a fitness room and sauna, occupy the very large and bright fifth floor atrium. For your business needs, the well-equipped business center can arrange printing, binding, faxing, translation, and secretarial services. Stop by Nikko's fine dining restaurant, Anzu, for sushi, prime cuts of beef, and a sake martini.

Omni

500 California St. (at Montgomery St.)

Phone: 415-677-9494
Web: www.omnisanfrancisco.com
Prices: $$$$

347
Rooms
15
Suites

Omni Hotels

Located in the heart of the Financial District with a cable car stop right outside, this Omni opened in 2002 in an elegantly renovated 1926 bank building. Though only the original stone and brick façade has been preserved, the spacious wood-paneled lobby, floored in rosy marble, takes its cue and its stylishness from a bygone era.

Spread over 17 stories, the 347 rooms and 15 suites follow suit. They are large and classic in style, with details to match, including Egyptian cotton sheets and well-equipped bathrooms decorated in marble and granite. Most guestrooms feature comfortable furnishings and a well-organized space. For upgraded amenities, reserve on the 16th "signature" floor, where rooms come with a Bose Wave radio and CD player, DVD player, wireless Internet, and a color copier/printer. Specialty accommodations such as Get Fit rooms (furnished with a treadmill and healthy snacks) and a Kids Fantasy Suite, where bunk beds and kids rule in the second bedroom, are also available. Bob's Steak and Chop House will draw the meat-loving guests.

Every Saturday at 10:00 A.M., a guided walking tour departs from the hotel for an overview of the city's history.

San Francisco ▶ Financial District

Rex

A2

562 Sutter St. (bet. Mason & Powell Sts.)

Phone: 415-433-4434 or 800-433-4434
Web: www.thehotelrex.com
Prices: $$

94 Rooms

Joie de Vivre Hospitality

Worldly and sophisticated, the Rex styles itself after the art and literary salons rife in San Francisco in the 1920s and 30s. Don't be surprised to see an author signing books in the dark paneled lobby, or folks gathering here for a poetry reading. This is all part of the hotel's literary mystique. Quotes from various regional authors adorn the walls of the different floors as well as the hotel's cozy bistro, Café Andrée, where breakfast is served to guests each morning.

The artistic theme carries over to the rooms in the custom wall coverings, hand-painted lampshades and contemporary artwork. Pillow-top mattresses, a mini-refrigerator, and a plasma screen TV provide many of the comforts of home.

One of the Joie de Vivre group's pet-friendly properties, the Rex recently dropped its pet weight restrictions and additional fees for four-legged guests. Fido or Fifi will be pampered here with their own food bowls, beds, and yummy treats.

Located one block off Union Square, the Rex is convenient to both upscale shopping and the city's Theater District, which further enhances its artsy appeal. Very affordable rates make the Rex a great choice in this otherwise pricey area of town.

Serrano

405 Taylor St. (at O'Farrell St.)

Phone: 415-885-2500 or 866-289-6561
Web: www.serranohotel.com
Prices: $$

217
Rooms
19
Suites

David Phelps/Kimpton Hotels

It's all fun and games at the Serrano, and the games begin with the Check-In Challenge. If you can beat "the house" in a quick game of 21, you could win a free room upgrade or other prizes; if you lose, your voluntary contribution benefits the local SPCA. The fun continues once you settle in; you can call to order a board game from the hotel's library to be delivered to your room.

The centerpiece of this 1924 Spanish Revival building is its dramatic two-story lobby, where the majestic fireplace, beamed ceilings, wood-paneled columns, Moroccan lanterns, and leafy potted plants stitch together an exotic atmosphere.

Bold Mediterranean colors and large windows combine in the rooms in a play of light and warmth, while Spanish and Moroccan accents echo the whimsical feel of the lobby. In a true flight of fancy, the hotel's Wicked Suite transports guests to the Land of Oz with a purple and green color scheme, and a larger-than-life portrait of the Wicked Witch of the West hanging over the bed.

All the great Kimpton amenities apply, including a nightly wine reception, and coffee and tea service in the lobby each morning. Fusion fare is the order of the day in Ponzu restaurant and lounge.

San Francisco ▶ Financial District

Sir Francis Drake

450 Powell St. (at Sutter St.)

Phone: 415-392-7755 or 800-795-7129
Web: www.sirfrancisdrake.com
Prices: $$$

410
Rooms

6
Suites

Kimpton Hotels & Restaurants

The legend lives on at the Sir Francis Drake, launched in 1928 with its own special brand of luxury. High-tech wonders of that period—such as ice water on tap, an indoor golf course, and a radio in every room—have been supplanted by WiFi, fax services, and a yoga channel on the in-room flat screen TV. Though "The Drake" is now a Kimpton property, the lobby keeps its former grandeur in the marble cladding and vaulted gold-leaf ceilings. Original murals depict the adventures of English explorer Sir Francis Drake, for whom the hotel is named.

Outside, the doormen retain their Beefeater uniforms, a beloved trademark of the hotel since its early days. Inside, rooms have been updated with the Kimpton dash of contemporary style—think striped sage and cream wallpaper and tufted fabric headboards.

Dancing the night away at Harry Denton's Starlight Room may sound like a blast from the past, but it still ranks as a quintessential San Francisco experience. Whether or not you hanker for things historical, the 360-degree view—and classic cocktails—at this 21st floor lounge makes it worth a visit. When you get a yen for pizza, pasta, and panini, drop by Scala's Bistro, adjacent to the hotel.

San Francisco ▶ Financial District

Triton

342 Grant Ave. (at Bush St.)

Phone: 415-394-0500 or 800-800-1299
Web: www.hoteltriton.com
Prices: $$

140
Rooms

Markham Johnson/Kimpton Hotels

If you like hip and eco-friendly, head for this member of the Kimpton group. The Triton's theme—Pop Culture—jumps out at you the moment you step inside the lobby, in the form of fanciful furnishings and whimsical murals in a riot of colors. A rotating selection of work by local artists is on display in the gallery on the mezzanine.

There are no cookie cutter-style rooms here. They come in all sizes, shapes, colors, and comfort levels, so ask for details before you book. Perhaps a standard room meets your needs; the complimentary *New York Times* will update you on world affairs as you sip your morning drink. Other features include iHome docking stations and eco-friendly bath amenities. Or maybe you prefer the panache of a Celebrity Suite, designed by the likes of comedienne Kathy Griffin or rocker Jerry Garcia. Conservation is the name of the game here, where everything is easy on the environment.

Located outside the Chinatown gate—convenient to the Financial District and Union Square—the hotel does not have its own restaurant, but Café de la Presse next door provides room service from its widely appealing French-American bistro menu.

San Francisco ▶ Financial District

Westin St. Francis

335 Powell St. (at Union Square)

Phone: 415-397-7000 or 866-500-0338
Web: www.westinstfrancis.com
Prices: $$$$

1195
Rooms

59
Suites

Westin St. Francis

Doyenne of downtown, the regal St. Francis presides over Union Square as befits a landmark that has graced the square since 1904. In its early days, the hotel was the hub of San Francisco's social scene. "Meet me at the St. Francis" was an oft-heard request, and many a prominent visitor, from presidents to poets, has congregated in the grand 6,000-square foot lobby over the years.

After barely surviving the earthquake and fire in 1906, the hotel built two more wings, and in 1972 a 32-story tower was added behind the main structure. In 2009, all the guest rooms, and the public spaces in the main building were refreshed to the tune of $40 million. The marble-columned lobby now wears modern shades of cream and chocolate brown, while reproductions of the original beaded globe chandeliers glimmer overhead. Even more noteworthy, the 1907 Great Magneta Clock has been returned to its rightful place in the lobby. Pop into the adjacent and aptly named Clock Bar for a snack and a cocktail.

In the rooms, ecru, bronze, and brown tones set off the ornate woodwork, high ceilings, and crystal chandeliers. Westin's signature Heavenly Bed and ergonomic desk chairs hail the modern day.

Drisco

B3

2901 Pacific Ave. (at Broderick St.)

Phone: 415-346-2880 or 800-634-7277
Web: www.hoteldrisco.com
Prices: $$

29
Rooms

19
Suites

Cesar Rubio

With its sunny setting perched high on the north side of California Street, affluent Pacific Heights contains some of the highest priced real estate in the city. It is here that the Hotel Drisco nestles comfortably amid multimillion-dollar mansions and green parks. In the distance, views of the San Francisco skyline stretch out for all to see.

Built in 1903, this member of the Joie de Vivre group makes a quiet haven removed from the bustle of downtown. Recently redecorated guestrooms have a residential ambience with their custom-made furnishings, cast-iron heaters, and white clapboard wainscoting. The daily breakfast buffet (included in the room rates) makes the place feel even more like a B&B. Accommodations vary in size but are consistently graceful in style, and well-appointed with special attention to guests' every comfort. Some rooms offer pleasing city views; others overlook the building's tiny courtyard. A cozy robe and slippers are on hand when you're ready to call it a day.

As for amenities, an on-site workout room and free access to the nearby Presidio YMCA accommodates fitness fiends, while the small business center provides basic services for business travelers.

San Francisco ▶ Marina

Kabuki

1625 Post St. (at Laguna St.)

Phone: 415-922-3200 or 800-533-4567
Web: www.hotelkabuki.com
Prices: $$

218
Rooms

♿

Matthew Millman

An Asian spirit imbues this hotel with Zen-like tranquility, from the sleek lobby to the Japanese garden and koi pond just adjacent.

A renovation in 2007, the year the Joie de Vivre group purchased the hotel, revealed spacious rooms attractively appointed with modern furniture, including working desks and new Serta mattresses. East and West dovetail in lodgings where Japanese artwork and Asian tea kettles mix with flat screen televisions, iPod docking stations/radios, and free high-speed wired and wireless Internet access.

For added luxury, reserve a deluxe corner king room, equipped with extras such as a chaise lounge, a dining table, and a traditional Japanese soaking tub. Also in these rooms, sliding glass doors lead to a wraparound balcony. A stay on the club level will grant you a complimentary continental breakfast.

Located in the heart of Japantown, the reasonably priced Kabuki is also close to Western Addition jazz clubs and Fillmore Street restaurants and boutiques. More traditional experiences await in sake and small plates at on-site O Izakaya Lounge, and in the communal baths at nearby Kabuki Springs and Spa, to which hotel guests have complimentary access.

Laurel Inn

444 Presidio Ave. (at California St.)

Phone: 415-567-8467 or 800-552-8735
Web: www.thelaurelinn.com
Prices: $$

49
Rooms

Joie de Vivre Hospitality

Steps away from Presidio National Park and Sacramento Street shopping, the Laurel Inn borders the quiet residential neighborhood of Laurel Heights. Ignore the bland exterior; inside, the inn tastefully plays on its 1963 pedigree courtesy of its current owners, the Joie de Vivre group.

Designed like urban studio apartments, the 49 sleekly furnished guestrooms include 18 larger units with kitchenettes. The latter are perfect extended stays, for which the hotel offers discounted rates. Be sure to bring the whole family; pets are welcome here, and special treats are provided for them.

Even at the regular rate, this place is a great value. Bold strokes of color enliven the rooms, where large windows open to let in fresh air (the hotel is not air-conditioned). Rooms on the back side of the hotel feature pleasant city panoramas and are quieter than those facing the street, though all are efficiently soundproofed. Amenities—a complimentary continental breakfast and wine hour, concierge services, and access to the fitness center across the street among them—measure up to much pricier hotels.

Next door, Swank Cocktail Club lives up to its name with a cool style and killer drink menu.

San Francisco ▶ Marina

Majestic

1500 Sutter St. (at Gough St.)

Phone: 415-441-1100
Web: www.thehotelmajestic.com
Prices: $

49
Rooms
9
Suites

MICHELIN

Isolated from the downtown bustle, the Majestic embraces its early 20th century heritage with grace and style. Built in 1902 as a private residence, this structure survived the 1906 earthquake to become San Francisco's oldest continuously operated hotel. (The fires that resulted from the quake were stopped a mere two blocks away.)

English and French antiques fill the rooms, while elements such as claw-foot tubs and sumptuously swagged four-poster beds bespeak the charm of the Victorian era. Standard rooms are on the small side, so reserve a junior or a one bedroom suite if you need more space.

When it's time to turn in, don the monogrammed robe provided and nestle in amid the feather pillows. Cookies placed on your bed at turndown assure sweet dreams…just keep an ear out for the mischievous resident ghost, who is said to roam the fourth floor.

Edwardian elegance decks out the lobby with antiques, marble columns, comfy sofas, and etched glass. If you're here on business, make sure you take advantage of the hotel's complimentary sedan service to either the Financial District or Union Square on weekday mornings.

Carlton

A3

1075 Sutter St. (bet. Hyde & Larkin Sts.)

Phone: 415-673-0242 or 800-922-7586
Web: www.hotelcarltonsf.com
Prices: $

161 Rooms

Carlton Hotel

A certified Green Business, the Carlton proudly claims to be the first hotel in San Francisco to be solar powered. In conjunction with the property's other energy-saving measures, 105 solar panels were installed on the hotel's roof in early 2008.

This forward-thinking attitude continues in the ample amenities, which make this place a great value for the price. Afternoon beverages and an evening wine reception are offered gratis, as are shuttle services to and from the San Francisco International airport. Guests also have free wireless Internet access in all the rooms.

The latter are understated and tasteful, their soft colors splashed with accents of persimmon and saffron. Like the hotel's public spaces, they are decorated with photographs of exotic destinations. The higher of the building's seven stories afford unobstructed city views.

Though accommodations are not air-conditioned, rooms keep their cool with ceiling fans on those rare hot days."Peace through travel" is the philosophy espoused by the Carlton's staff, an international team that speaks more than a dozen languages. Another exotic touch, Saha restaurant serves contemporary Middle Eastern cuisine at breakfast and dinner.

San Francisco ▶ Nob Hill

The Ritz-Carlton, San Francisco

600 Stockton St. (bet. California & Pine Sts.)

Phone: 415-296-7465 or 800-241-3333
Web: www.ritzcarlton.com
Prices: $$$$

276 Rooms

60 Suites

The Ritz-Carlton, San Francisco

When it opened in 1909 as the western headquarters of the Metropolitan Life Insurance Company, this neoclassical landmark flanked by a row of stately Ionic columns was lauded as a "Temple of Commerce." A century later, as The Ritz-Carlton, the edifice crowning the eastern slope of Nob Hill can justly be called a temple of luxury.

A museum-quality collection of 18th and 19th century antiques and artwork adorns the public areas. Treasures such as Waterford crystal candelabras, 18th century portraits, and Regency silver abound throughout the hotel.

Restored with European charm, your home-away-from-home here comes with a featherbed and down comforter, a cozy robe and slippers, and a marble bath with a rain showerhead. On the Club Level, a dedicated concierge, five food and beverage presentations, and a private business lounge provide unparalleled pampering.

All the expected amenities apply. Work out in the fitness facility, then relax those tired muscles in the steam room before your massage. Later in the day, the lobby lounge makes a gracious venue in which to linger over afternoon tea or a cocktail before retiring to the splendid Dining Room for fine French cuisine.

The Fairmont

950 Mason St. (at California St.)

Phone: 415-772-5000 or 866-540-4491
Web: www.fairmont.com
Prices: $$$

528
Rooms
63
Suites

The Fairmont San Francisco

This Gilded Age palace atop Nob Hill survives as a monument to James "Bonanza Jim" Fair, who profited mightily off Nevada's Comstock silver Lode, and on whose land the hotel's foundations were laid in 1902. Ironically, The Fairmont was scheduled to open on April 18, 1906, the day the devastating earthquake rocked the city. The structure survived, but the ornate interior was ravaged by fire.

Today, the hotel's public spaces sparkle again with turn-of-the-20th century splendor. The lobby shows off the restoration of architect Julia Morgan's original Corinthian columns, alabaster walls, marble floors, and vaulted gold-trimmed ceilings. Soak up the atmosphere over a meal in the domed Laurel Court. Or, for a different kind of nostalgia, drop by the newly restored Tonga Room, a tiki hideaway, complete with staged rainstorms and live music.

Renovated rooms—divided between the original building and a 23-story tower added in 1961—shine with refined fabrics. Eco-minded folks can choose the Lexus Hybrid Living Suite. In this tower suite, guests enjoy views from wraparound windows, amid furnishings made from organic and recycled materials. Complimentary use of a Lexus hybrid is an added perk.

San Francisco ▶ Nob Hill

Nob Hill

B3

835 Hyde St. (bet. Sutter & Bush Sts.)

Phone: 415-885-2987 or 877-662-4455
Web: www.nobhillhotel.com
Prices: $$

52
Rooms

&

Nob Hill Hotel

Unlike many of its ritzier neighbors, this 1906 hotel named for its lofty location offers prices that are better paired with consumers' current financial belt-tightening. It may not have all the upscale amenities of its brethren, but the Nob Hill Hotel hands out plenty of value for the price.

Rates include an evening wine tasting, access to a 24-hour fitness center, and a continental breakfast. In-room spa services are available, and the hospitable staff can accommodate speakers of Spanish, French, Italian, Greek, and Chinese.

Though small, rooms are clean and individually decorated in a plush crush of romantic Victoriana and period antiques. Some rooms, including two penthouse suites, have private terraces; several suites feature whirlpool tubs. Mini refrigerators and microwaves are provided, along with CD players, hairdryers, and coffeemakers. The atmosphere is hushed and the rooms are quiet, whether they face the courtyard or the street. Smokers beware: a hefty cleaning fee applies if you're caught lighting up in this smoke-free haven.

As an incentive to eat in, guests who choose to dine on Italian food at the on-site Columbini Bistro will receive a complimentary glass of wine.

Orchard Garden

466 Bush St. (at Grant Ave.)

Phone: 415-399-9807 or 888-717-2881
Web: www.theorchardgardenhotel.com
Prices: $$$

86
Rooms

Orchard Garden

Green is more than just a color used in decorating this Nob Hill hotel; it's a way of life. California's first hotel built to U.S. Green Building Council standards, the Orchard Garden prides itself on its commitment to Mother Earth—and its LEED certification.

Opened in 2006 at the top of steep Powell Street, the hotel is constructed of eco-friendly materials including concrete made using the ash that results from recycling coal. Sustainably-grown maple provides the wood for the custom-crafted furniture in the guestrooms, and fabrics all contain recycled content. You won't sacrifice any comfort, though. Stylish rooms are luxuriously outfitted with soft sheets of washable Egyptian cotton, down pillows, plush cotton robes, and Aveda bath products, while a spacious desk leaves lots of room for getting down to business. Your key card also activates the lights and temperature control, adjusting both automatically to save energy when you leave your room.

Downstairs, Roots restaurant makes it easy to be green by choosing local produce, naturally raised meats, and sustainable seafood to craft its American fare. So no matter how you look at it, you can feel good about staying here.

San Francisco ▶ Nob Hill

Argonaut

A1

495 Jefferson St. (at Hyde St.)

Phone: 415-563-0800 or 866-415-0704
Web: www.argonauthotel.com
Prices: $$

239
Rooms

13
Suites

David Phelps/Kimpton Hotels

Over the decades, the area known as Fisherman's Wharf has slowly morphed from a rough-and-tumble port into San Francisco's most visited tourist attraction. The Argonaut Hotel, lodged in a 1907 waterfront warehouse at The Cannery, recalls the neighborhood's hardworking heritage in its original brick walls and massive wood beams.

Likewise, the interior design takes its cue from the area's rich nautical history. Bold stripes and stars in bright marine blue and yellow spiff up the room décor, and all the modern amenities apply. Many rooms look out over the bay and the historic ships of the San Francisco Maritime National Historical Park, whose visitor center shares space with the hotel.

Kids will love the hotel's proximity to the ships berthed at Hyde Street Pier, the rides at the wildly popular Pier 39, and the tasty chocolate treats at Ghirardelli Square. Exhausted adults will no doubt appreciate the hotel's complimentary wine hour at the end of each day.

Named for Jason's mythical ship, the Argonaut is all about adventure. After you've explored all there is to see at Fisherman's Wharf, the Powell-Hyde cable car line (just steps from the hotel's door) will take you on new adventures.

Bohème

444 Columbus Ave. (bet. Green & Vallejo Sts.)

Phone: 415-433-9111
Web: www.hotelboheme.com
Prices: $$

15
Rooms

Hotel Bohème

This quaint boutique hotel at the foot of Telegraph Hill in the heart of North Beach takes its inspiration from the bohemian Beat Generation of the 1950s. And well it might, as poet Allen Ginsberg once slept here. Next door you'll find Vesuvio Café and City Lights Bookstore (founded by poet Lawrence Ferlinghetti), two hangouts still haunted by Beat spirits.

Built in the 1880s and rebuilt after the earthquake, the Victorian structure has been nicely adapted to its current role. Its 15 rooms reflect a certain 1950s countercultural style in their bright colors and eclectic furniture; they are small, romantic, and meticulously clean. Each has a private bath, and all the rooms offer wireless Internet access. About half face Columbus Avenue, which makes for good people-watching, but not much peace and quiet. The surrounding neighborhood is great for strolling and sipping coffee; from here you can walk up Telegraph Hill to Coit Tower and explore up and down the Filbert Steps.

The courteous staff at the Hotel Bohème is glad to help make reservations for restaurants, theater performances, and tours.

San Francisco ▶ North Beach

Four Seasons

757 Market St. (bet. Third & Fourth Sts.)

Phone: 415-633-3000 or 800-819-5053
Web: www.fourseasons.com
Prices: $$$$

231 Rooms

46 Suites

Mary Nichols/Four Seasons San Francisco

Sightseeing may be the only reason to leave the Four Seasons San Francisco, which occupies the first 12 stories of a residential high-rise in the Yerba Buena Arts District. Almost everything else you could wish for lies within the hotel's walls.

Start with the Sports Club/L.A., accessible from the fourth floor. Open to hotel guests, this huge facility has it all: a state of the art gym, exercise studios, a full basketball court, and a junior Olympic-size pool. This is also where you'll find the cocoon-like spa, where signature treatments promise to detoxify and de-stress.

On the fifth floor lobby, Seasons restaurant serves Californian-inspired cuisine for breakfast, lunch, and dinner; while the clubby bar and lounge specializes in small plates and cocktails.

Art is everywhere, as the hotel showcases throughout its public spaces a considerable collection of paintings, sculpture, and ceramics by Bay Area artists. Rooms, as they ascend from the 6th to the 17th floor, offer more and more stunning views of the city. Generously sized, accommodations are done in restful tones with floor-to-ceiling windows. Young guests are welcomed with milk and cookies and child-size bathrobes.

InterContinental

888 Howard St. (at 5th St.)

Phone: 415-616-6500 or 888-811-4273
Web: www.intercontinentalsanfrancisco.com
Prices: $$$

536
Rooms
14
Suites

Rien van Rijthoven/InterContinental Hotels

Contemporary in style and voluminous in size, the InterContinental ranks as one of the city's most sumptuous hotels. The eye-catching landmark pierces the SoMa skyline with its 32-story blue glass tower, and is equally sought out by those traveling on business and pleasure.

The former make good use of the two formal ballrooms and 21 meeting rooms, for a total of 43,000 square feet of flexible meeting space. They also appreciate the hotel's 24-hour business services and close proximity to the Moscone Convention Center.

Leisure travelers get fired up about glorious rooms appointed in rich wood and marble. Large picture windows frame the San Francisco skyline in all its glory. And who wouldn't like the full-service I-Spa and indoor lap pool on the sixth floor?

Down on the lobby level, grappa is the signature cocktail at Bar 888, while local products star in the contemporary American cuisine served at the stellar restaurant Luce (pronounced LOO-chay; Italian for "light").

In these days when recorded phone messages are the norm, the InterContinental offers guests the luxury of pushing a button on their room phone and connecting directly to a customer service manager.

San Francisco ▲ SoMa

The Mosser

54 4th St. (bet. Market & Mission Sts.)

Phone: 415-986-4400 or 800-227-3804
Web: www.themosser.com
Prices: $

166
Rooms

The Mosser

In the hip SoMa district, this family-owned boutique hotel hits a high note with its own recording studio. The only hotel in San Francisco to offer this amenity, The Mosser caters to musicians and media pros with first-rate digital and analog technology in the Studio Paradiso.

There's plenty here to lure non-musicians as well. Within a two-block radius, you can walk to Yerba Buena Gardens and the SF Museum of Modern Art, the Moscone Convention Center, Westfield Centre mall, and the cable car line to Fisherman's Wharf.

With all that action nearby, you might fear that rooms here would be noisy. Happily, this charming 1913 Victorian structure has been retrofitted with double-pane windows to screen out the din. To ensure complete peace, reserve a less expensive room facing the courtyard. The clean, crisp décor includes platform beds, white washed walls, and geometrically-patterned carpet for a comfortable Danish-modern effect. Some rooms feature lovely bay windows with window seats that overlook the street; all are equipped with ceiling fans.

Though all guests at The Mosser enjoy very affordable rates, if you're on a strict budget book one of the 54 economical rooms that share a bath.

San Francisco ▶ SoMa

Palace

2 New Montgomery St. (at Market St.)

Phone: 415-512-1111 or 888-625-5144
Web: www.sfpalace.com
Prices: $$$$

519
Rooms

34
Suites

Palace Hotel

Having celebrated its 100th anniversary in 2009, The Palace reigns as the grand dame of downtown hotels. During its long history, the hotel has entertained such notables as Queen Victoria, Italian inventor Guglielmo Marconi, and President Woodrow Wilson (who gave his League of Nations speech in the Garden Court). Originally built in 1875, the property was destroyed in the 1906 earthquake. The year 1909 marked the unveiling of the new Palace; its centerpiece was the Garden Court, crowned by a stunning leaded-glass dome and flanked by a double row of Italian marble columns. Today you can take breakfast, lunch, brunch, or afternoon tea in this resplendent space, which drips with Austrian crystal chandeliers.

For its anniversary, the hotel upgraded its 553 guestrooms with 37-inch LCD flat screen TVs. Mahogany furniture—including a large work desk—and creamy tones with federal blue accents set a traditional scene in rooms that all boast 14-foot-high ceilings and windows that open.

Classic cocktails are in good company downstairs in Maxfield's Pied Piper Bar, which showcases a mural of the Pied Piper of Hamelin painted for the 1909 reopening by American illustrator Maxfield Parrish.

San Francisco ▶ SoMa

Palomar

12 4th St. (at Market St.)

Phone: 415-348-1111 or 866-373-4941
Web: www.hotelpalomar-sf.com
Prices: $$$

179
Rooms
16
Suites

David Phelps/Kimpton Hotels

Touting a theme of "art in motion," the Palomar flashes its bohemian spirit on the 5th through the 8th floors of a landmark 1908 building. Art is everywhere you look here, on the wall, in niches and nooks, even on the lobby floor—where the parquet displays a trompe l'oeil pattern suggesting the work of M.C. Escher.

In the rooms, taupe alligator-print carpeting lies underfoot, and unexpected bursts of color enliven the contemporary ambience. Every detail in the Magritte Suite—from the blue sky mural on the ceiling to the bowl of green apples set on a table—pays tribute to surrealist painter René Magritte. Downstairs, a recent update has rendered the famed Fifth Floor restaurant a stylish spot to dine on contemporary cuisine.

Located where 4th Street meets Market, the hotel couldn't be better situated. Art museums, shopping, and the Moscone Convention Center are all an easy stroll away. The concierge can direct you to be best of the nearby arts, while the new "What's in Store?" program highlights promotions from stores such as Bloomingdale's, Nordstrom, and Adidas. Packets filled with special savings coupons are available in all the guestrooms to carry with you while you shop.

San Francisco ▶ SoMa

St. Regis

125 3rd St. (at Mission St.)

Phone: 415-284-4000 or 877-787-3447
Web: www.stregis.com
Prices: $$$$

214
Rooms
46
Suites

Joe Fletcher

The fact that the lobby of the St. Regis was conceived by acclaimed Toronto interior designer Yabu Pushelberg, should clue you in to the level of luxury you'll experience here. A neutral palette of beige and gray forms the backdrop for the striated Zebrano wood and Italian travertine marble of the lobby. As you enter the soaring lobby, a striking 16-foot open fireplace catches your eye. From there it's all sleek lines and contemporary art installations.

A landmark 40-story high rise designed by Skidmore, Owings, and Merrill, this building houses the hotel on its first 20 floors, and condominiums above. Next door is the San Francisco Museum of Modern Art; across the street sit all the attractions of Yerba Buena Gardens.

Spacious rooms and suites overlook Yerba Buena Park, or have expansive city views. Exquisite finishes and unique design features pair with Pratesi linens and a touchscreen on the nightstand that controls the room's temperature, curtains, and lighting.

Remède Spa recently introduced customized treatments—does the Stillness Ritual or a Four Hand Massage sound tempting? For dining, Chef Hiro Sone's modern fusion cuisine delights palates downstairs at the scrumptious Ame.

San Francisco ▶ SoMa

Vitale

8 Mission St. (bet. Steuart St. & The Embarcadero)

Phone: 415-278-3700 or 888-890-8688
Web: www.hotelvitale.com
Prices: $$$

180
Rooms

20
Suites

Cesar Rubio

Flagship of the Joie de Vivre group, the Vitale occupies a prime piece of real estate across the street from the Ferry Building—its marketplace teeming with gourmet delights—and the elegant Embarcadero promenade. All the attractions and eateries of Market Street, Rincon Hill, and the Financial District are easily accessible from the hotel.

An understated luxury permeates the public spaces. Rich wood paneling, rough-hewn stone columns, large softly curtained windows, and sleek furnishings create a Scandinavian modern aspect in the lobby. Luminous and well-soundproofed rooms wear soothing tones that play off the natural light that streams in from large windows. Ask for a water view room, and you'll look out on San Francisco Bay by day, and an awesome silhouette of the Bay Bridge all lit up by night.

Since the hotel's name translates to "vitality" in Italian, you'll want to save time for a trip to the YMCA next door (guests get free passes), then to the penthouse spa to unwind. Your pets will be equally pampered here with special toys and treats. When it's time to eat, you need go no farther than the hotel lobby for stylish Italian fare at Americano restaurant.

San Francisco ▶ SoMa

W - San Francisco

C2

181 3rd St. (at Howard St.)

Phone: 415-777-5300
Web: www.whotels.com
Prices: $$$

404
Rooms

W San Francisco

San Francisco ▶ SoMa

Part of a hotel chain that has become known for its innovative and eclectic contemporary ambience, the W San Francisco finds a fitting and well-situated home in the hip and artsy enclave that is the city's SoMa district.

Each of the recently redesigned rooms boasts a panorama of the city, along with such Asian-inspired details as platform beds, Chinese checkers, and origami butterflies. Signature pillow-top mattresses and a Sweet Dreams pillow menu assure comfort when you turn in for the night, and window nooks make great places to take in the cityscape or curl up with a good book. Lemon and sage bath amenities come courtesy of the hotel's 5,000-square foot Bliss Spa.

The octagonal, three-story Living Room, as W calls their lobby, has been refreshed with eye-catching artwork and textured walls. Comfy seating around a redesigned modern fireplace offers a hip spot to meet and greet, while live DJ music entertains from Wednesday through Saturday evenings. Lighting colors change throughout the evening, adding another dimension to this airy public space.

Continuing the alphabetic W theme, XYZ restaurant and lounge indulges diners with organic cocktails and modern Californian cuisine.

Claremont Resort & Spa

41 Tunnel Rd., Berkeley

Phone: 510-843-3000 or 800-551-7266
Web: www.claremontresort.com
Prices: $$$

263
Rooms
16
Suites

Bob Bryant Photography

Surrounded by 22 lovely landscaped acres in the hills overlooking San Francisco Bay, this gleaming, white, castle-like edifice has been pampering guests since 1915. The grand tradition of 19th century resort spas continues here today, as The Claremont fulfills its promise to wrap guests in elegance.

If you like lodgings with plenty of activity, the Claremont is for you. Start with the fitness facility, where weight equipment, aerobics classes, and personal training are available. Then there are the ten tennis courts (six of which are lit for evening play), and two heated pools—one dedicated to lap swimming, the other to recreation. For families, the hotel features a Kids Club, with babysitting services, games, movie nights, and other activities tailored to the young set.

Dining options include the Paragon Bar and Café, where live jazz entertains guests Thursday through Saturday nights. For a more refined experience, Meritage overlooks much of the Easy Bay. Chef Josh Thompsen's seasonal Californian cuisine keeps up with the posh surroundings.

Accommodations offer three degrees of comfort, all luxurious. One caveat: Request a quiet room since some of them face a loud, refuse area.

Lafayette Park

3287 Mt. Diablo Blvd. (bet. Carol Ln. & Pleasant Hill Rd.), Lafayette

Phone: 925-283-3700 or 877-283-8787
Web: www.lafayetteparkhotel.com
Prices: $$

138
Rooms

Lafayette Park

Sister property to the Stanford Park hotel, the Lafayette Park displays all the splendor of a French château, just off the I-24 freeway. Indeed, that's what this stately structure, with its mansard roofs and turrets, brings to mind.

Beginning with the three-story domed lobby, common areas exude elegance. Wings of the hotel surround a lovely central courtyard, ideal for relaxing to the sound of a trickling fountain. Stucco walls frame the tranquil outdoor heated pool, which is flanked on one end by a small full-service spa, and on the other by a well-equipped fitness room.

Traditional American style defines the oversized guestrooms, decked out with cherrywood furnishings, granite vanity countertops, and ample work desks; many rooms have fireplaces and vaulted ceilings. Beware bargain room rates; you get what you pay for here (for a few more dollars a night you can ensure that you overlook the courtyard). Friendly service takes on a laid-back California attitude, and occasionally misses the mark, but for high style and comfort, the Lafayette Park stands out as a welcome upscale alternative to the corporate chain hotels that predominate in this area.

East Bay

Casa Madrona

801 Bridgeway, Sausalito

Phone: 415-332-0502 or 800-288-0502
Web: www.casamadrona.com
Prices: $$$

63
Rooms

Casa Madrona Hotel & Spa

Climbing up Sausalito's hillside from the waterfront, Casa Madrona envelops the best of old and new within a charming complex well-situated for exploring both San Francisco and the northern wine country. Of course, Sausalito affords ample opportunities of its own for waterfront dining and shopping in chic boutiques.

Accommodations, from historic suites to contemporary rooms, satisfy a range of tastes. Highest in terms of vantage point, the 1885 Casa Madrona mansion crowns the complex, offering bewitching bay views. Victorian style pervades the rooms; most romantic are the bay view chambers furnished with wood-burning stoves and private, flower-bedecked balconies.

A covey of quaint cottages have been built into the hillside since 1976. Connected by brick pathways lined with flowers and waterfalls, these rooms may be either contemporary or historic in décor. Last but not least, ultramodern rooms populate the newest wing of the hotel. Four-poster king-sized beds and large, luxurious bathrooms with oversized soaking tubs fill these rooms.

When you're not in your room, you can treat yourself to a rejuvenating session at the hotel's spa, and fine Northern Italian dishes at Poggio.

Marin

Cavallo Point

601 Murray Circle (at Fort Baker), Sausalito

Phone: 415-339-4700 or 888-651-2003
Web: www.cavallopoint.com
Prices: $$$$

142
Rooms

Kodiak Greenwood

Some hotels pin their appeal on history, others on their setting, while some tout their eco-friendly efforts. Cavallo Point boasts all of these enticements and more. On the grounds of Fort Baker, this lodge-like property offers incredible views of the Golden Gate Bridge, the bay, and the city skyline.

Rooms seesaw between classic and contemporary. The former are housed in the original fort buildings, while the latter occupy new structures. None of the facilities are air-conditioned, but who needs it when constant bay breezes cool the site? Meals at Murray Circle restaurant feature outstanding Californian cuisine from talented chef, Joseph Humphrey. Aside from eating, guests can visit the healing arts center and spa or enroll in the on-site cooking school. There's a complimentary shuttle to the center of Sausalito, but for those craving more exercise, the surrounding Marin Headlands contain a web of hiking trails.

In addition to the normal hotel taxes, Cavallo Point levies an extra fee on its guests. This money goes toward the operation of Golden Gate National Recreation Area, in which the property is located. To save a few bucks, insist on self versus valet parking.

Marin

The Inn Above Tide

30 El Portal (at Bridgeway), Sausalito

Phone: 415-332-9535 or 800-893-8433
Web: www.innabovetide.com
Prices: $$$

29
Rooms

The Inn Above Tide

Every room in this bayfront beauty boasts spectacular water views that extend across to San Francisco, Alcatraz, and Angel Island. As you go up the price scale, king rooms add gas fireplaces, while accommodations in the deluxe category feature private decks that extend out over the bay and provide comfy teak chairs for waterside reflection.

Standard amenities encompass plush robes and slippers, Bvlgari toiletries, and DVD players with access to the hotel's film library. Another thoughtful touch, each sandy-toned room comes with a pair of binoculars for honing in on the scenery. And if that's not enough, a complimentary continental breakfast is served in the guest lounge adjacent to the small lobby—or the staff will deliver it to your room, if you prefer.

At happy hour, wine and cheese are on tap, gratis of course! A short menu of in-room spa services can be arranged for a fee.

The city is just a short ferry ride away, but there's plenty to keep you occupied in Sausalito. Stroll the waterfront and check out the shops, then have a leisurely lunch in one of the bayside restaurants. The inn's concierge can arrange a host of other activities, including biking, boating, and wine tours.

Marin

The Ritz-Carlton, Half Moon Bay

1 Miramontes Point Rd. (at Hwy. 1), Half Moon Bay

Phone: 650-712-7000 or 800-241-3333
Web: www.ritzcarlton.com/hmb
Prices: $$$$

239
Rooms
22
Suites

The Ritz-Carlton, Half Moon Bay

Overlooking miles of rugged Pacific coastline from its bluff-top perch 30 miles south of San Francisco, the Ritz-Carlton Half Moon Bay presents a convincing argument for leaving the city.

Start with the public spaces, where plush furnishings, large stone fireplaces, and a collection of fine art recall the grand seaside lodges of the 19th century. All of this, however, pales before the magnificent ocean views, seen through floor-to-ceiling windows.

Then there are the accommodations, done in subdued tones so as not to distract from the scenery. Of the total number, two-thirds of the rooms have coastal views, and from every one you can see the green fairways of the hotel's golf links. Marble bathrooms and feather beds with down duvets are standard amenities.

Follow the path to the secluded beach, where relaxing is de rigueur. Beyond the beach, six lighted tennis courts, jogging trails, a basketball half court, and two oceanside golf courses insure you'll never be bored. That's not to mention the fitness facility and the lavish spa.

With all this activity, you're bound to work up an appetite. Take care of that with tasty Californian cuisine at Navio—along with an ocean view, naturally.

Peninsula

Rosewood Sand Hill

2825 Sand Hill Rd. (at I-280), Menlo Park

Phone: 650-561-1500 or 888-767-3966
Web: www.rosewoodsandhill.com
Prices: $$$$

91 Rooms

32 Suites

Rosewood Hotels & Resorts

It might be possible to have the best of both worlds after all, or at least while staying at Rosewood Sand Hill. This new luxury resort is just minutes off I-280 in Silicon Valley, but its serene setting on 16 sprawling acres with views of the nearby Santa Cruz Mountains feels a million miles away from it all.

The resort blends a laid-back Californian ranch style with a contemporary elegance. The accommodations are decorated with soothing earth tones, and amenities (king beds, spacious desks, walk-in closets) are especially thoughtful. Bigger is always better when it comes to bathrooms, and these modern chrome-fitted spaces with large marble tubs and oversized showers don't disappoint.

The grounds are immaculate, and courtyard gardens and landscaped patios are a pleasant buffer between resort buildings. Downtime is cherished, especially at the state of the art Sense Spa and beautiful outdoor heated pool. The garden view fitness center is especially well appointed, and after those feel-good endorphins kick in, treat yourself to a trinket at high-end Stephen Silver jewelry.

Madera is quickly becoming a destination unto itself for its local wood-fired cuisine.

Peninsula

Stanford Park

C4

100 El Camino Real (at Sand Hill Rd.), Menlo Park

Phone: 650-322-1234 or 866-241-2431
Web: www.stanfordparkhotel.com
Prices: $$$

134
Rooms
29
Suites

Stanford Park Hotel

In contrast to the Spanish-inspired archways and red tile roofs of Stanford University, the Stanford Park hotel, located just adjacent, stands out with its dark cedar shingles and crisp white trim. English Colonial is the style displayed by this four-story lodging, which makes a convenient retreat for university visitors.

Spacious and residential in feel, sparkling clean guest rooms flaunt a traditional ambience—cultivated by vaulted ceilings, granite fireplaces, and canopied beds in many of them. Courtyard rooms have vaulted ceilings and views of the manicured gardens or the heated lap pool. Spa robes, CD players, and coffeemakers number among the many room amenities, and the on-site gym sees to your fitness needs.

When happy hour rolls around, drop by the Lounge at the Park for a classic cocktail or a glass of wine—from California, of course. A menu of small plates will tide you over until dinner. Then it's off to the hotel's Duck Club Restaurant for delightful Californian cuisine served in a cozy contemporary setting.

Antiques and museum-quality objets d'art grace the lobby, which contains a library of literary masterpieces for guests' use—a nod to the hotel's erudite neighbor.

Peninsula

Cypress

10050 S. De Anza Blvd. (at Stevens Creek Blvd), Cupertino

Phone: 408-253-8900 or 800-499-1408
Web: www.thecypresshotel.com
Prices: $$

224 Rooms

David Phelps/Kimpton Hotels

You can count on the Kimpton group to deliver luxury, and the Cypress is no exception. You get the idea when you stroll through the entrance colonnade, where urns hold sculpted topiaries, and clusters of comfortable seating invite you to relax.

In the rooms, bold contemporary style echoes the creative spirit of Silicon Valley in polka dot wallpaper, striped drapery fabric, and bright sculptural headboards. Yet warm colors soothe the psyche, and new beds fitted with Frette linens cushion the body. A morning newspaper and WiFi Internet access all come with the hotel's compliments—as does a nightly wine reception and a 24-hour fitness facility.

Being in the heart of Silicon Valley, the Cypress provides ample space for meetings—5,000 square feet to be exact. The Parkview Ballroom boasts an adjoining patio perfect for cocktail receptions. When it's time to get down to business, the Boardroom accommodates 25 for private meetings, and a second ballroom can be subdivided to provide more space. Catering and room service are provided by the adjacent Park Place restaurant, whose recently renovated dining room is a stylish oasis of neutral tones and for fresh American cuisine.

De Anza

233 W. Santa Clara St. (bet. Almaden Blvd. & Notre Dame Ave.), San Jose

Phone: 408-286-1000 or 800-843-3700
Web: www.hoteldeanza.com
Prices: $$

80
Rooms

20
Suites

Anthony Abuzeide

Recognizable by its pink façade, the Hotel De Anza provides pleasant downtown San Jose digs for both business and leisure travelers. A neutral palette and blonde wood furniture warm the bedrooms without overdoing it. Two TVs, three phones, and a DVD/VCR (videos are complimentary) furnish each room. On the lower level, the business center offers a range of services, and the hotel can accommodate meetings of up to 70 people. In the rooms, a large glass-topped desk ensures adequate work space; wireless Internet access is available for an extra fee.

La Pastaia restaurant, off the lobby, serves Italian cuisine in a colorful taverna setting. Even more attractive is the Hedley Club Lounge with its sophisticated art deco design—an ideal spot for a cocktail. And lest you go hungry, cookies and fresh fruit are available throughout the day in the comfortable pastel-hued lobby; purified ice and water are on tap on each floor above. In fact, the De Anza even features a "Raid Our Pantry" service offering sandwiches and snacks to satisfy those late-night munchies.

Last but not least, your petite pet—15 pounds or less—can accompany you here.

South Bay

Valencia

355 Santana Row (bet. Olin Ave. & Tatum Ln.), San Jose

Phone: 408-551-0010 or 866-842-0100
Web: www.hotelvalencia-santanarow.com
Prices: $$$

196
Rooms

16
Suites

Hotel Valencia

A plethora of shopping, dining, and entertainment options lie just outside your door when you check into this gracious hacienda, set smack in the middle of Santana Row. Shopping is the draw for many of the guests here, but young Silicon Valley business types also find the Valencia a fitting and well-located haven.

Contemporary Cal-Med describes the hotel's shiny style, including the spacious third floor lobby, which feels like a lounge with its low lighting, comfy couches, and hidden nooks. Service is friendly and informal, in keeping with a young Californian sensibility.

Whether your stay is for business or pleasure, you'll find ample room in the well-kept accommodations that sport plenty of counter space for the paper chase, as well as a leather club chair and ottoman for chilling out. Soundproofing is a minus; light sleepers may be bothered by hallway noise or clamor from the street outside.

Best perks? The complimentary breakfast served at the glorious open air restaurant, and the sunny rooftop pool. On the seventh floor, Cielo lounge serves up impressive Silicon Valley views with its cocktails, a buzzing happy hour spot in warm weather.

South Bay

412

Auberge du Soleil

180 Rutherford Hill Rd. (off the Silverado Trail), Rutherford

Phone: 707-963-1211 or 800-348-5406
Web: www.aubergedusoleil.com
Prices: $$$$

31
Rooms

21
Suites

Erhardt Pfeffer

Olives aren't the only things that thrive on the sunlit slopes of Rutherford Hill. Tucked in among the silvery trees are the cottages of the "Inn of the Sun," a favorite Napa Valley hideaway that has been flourishing for 25 years.

Over the years, the property has catered increasingly to well-to-do sybaritic visitors. Auberge du Soleil opened with its much-acclaimed restaurant in 1981; the hotel was added a few years later. Then came the spa in 2000. Here, the valley's signature product is pressed into service for signature treatments such as a grape seed crush body exfoliation. Unlike many hotel spas, this one is open exclusively to resort guests.

Scrambling down the hillsides, sophisticated rooms and suites all occupy cottages with private terraces and surroundings that could just as well be Mediterranean. King, or Maison, rooms measure 520 square feet and feature fireplaces and large bathrooms with luxurious soaking tubs. Suites at least double that space, adding a separate living room, a dining table, butler's pantry, and full-size refrigerator.

Toasting the setting sun with a glass of Napa Valley wine on the restaurant's breezy terrace is a wine country must before you leave.

Wine Country ▶ Napa Valley

AVIA Napa

1450 1st St. (at School St.), Napa

Phone: 707-224-3900
Web: www.aviahotels.com/hotels/napa
Prices: **$$**

83
Rooms

58
Suites

Glen Coburn, Glen Coburn Photography

If you're craving a taste of the wine country but not feeling the farmhouse vibe, AVIA Napa is the hotel for you. This urbane hideaway is perfect for city slickers who wish to enjoy the wine, food, and vistas of Napa without leaving their chic city lifestyles behind. Set in downtown Napa, Avia offers a different slant on the wine country lifestyle. You won't look out over vineyards, but you can hit up the famous Oxbow Public Market for tasty provisions or take a short stroll to visit the shops, galleries, and award-winning restaurants of this culinary capital.

There's no need to go far for good food though, since AVIA's Kitchen and Wine Bar serves a yummy breakfast buffet and offers sophisticated, locally sourced cuisine at dinner. The Terrace, outfitted with porch swings and a fire pit, is plain heavenly for sipping a glass of wine.

Avia is distinctly Californian, offering a countrified chic design in its public spaces. Where else would you find a farmhouse-type table reception area juxtaposed with bordello-style antique mirrors and red velvet seating? The rooms and suites flaunt a more modern approach and are accented with soothing earth tones and sleek, contemporary styling.

Bardessono

C2

6526 Young St. (at Finnell Rd.), Yountville

Phone: 707-204-6000 or 877-932-5333
Web: www.bardessono.com
Prices: $$$$

62
Suites

Sammy Todd Dyess

What's greener than grape vines in Napa? Bardessono, a 62-room hotel that stands out as a feat of eco-engineering. Constructed with 100,000 square feet of salvaged wood, the hotel uses photovoltaic solar collectors to create electricity, and geothermal wells to heat the rooms and water. Motion sensors turn off lights when guests are not in residence; settings are automatically restored when they return. Stone paths lined with flowering plants meander between the low-rise buildings that compose the complex.

Guest suites are tranquil sanctuaries, well-appointed with organic cotton bed linens, deep soaking tubs, and private patios or balconies. The carefully thought-out design places a comfy sitting area in front of the gas fireplace and the flat screen TV. Bathrooms conceal a massage table for in-room spa treatments, but there's also a full-service spa for those who desire a more in-depth experience.

For exercise, you can swim in the rooftop pool, or use one of the complimentary bicycles to explore the valley. And while the hotel lies within an easy walk of some stellar restaurants, you won't go wrong if you stay on-site to dine on contemporary Cali fare in the main restaurant.

Wine Country ▶ Napa Valley

415

The Carneros Inn

4048 Sonoma Hwy., Napa

Phone:	707-299-4900 or 888-400-9000
Web:	www.thecarnerosinn.com
Prices:	$$$$

76
Rooms

10
Suites

Mark Hundley

Located at the southern gateway to the Napa Valley, the Carneros wine region wins raves for sparking wine, chardonnay, and pinot noir. The appellation takes its moniker from the Spanish word for "sheep," animals that once grazed on the hillsides where straight rows of grapevines now grow. The inn named for this region fits well into this pastoral setting, its 86 cottages punctuating 27 acres of vineyards. Use of water recycling and geothermal heating and cooling systems for all of the guest accommodations respect the local environment.

The property is set up like a small village, with many gardens and paths crisscrossing the site. Walking is the preferred manner of transportation to get to the spa, the meeting halls, or any of the three restaurants. The latter include the Hilltop dining room, the casual Boon Fly Café, and Farm, which gathers its ingredients from the surrounding farms and ranches.

Natural light bathes tastefully decorated cottages, where Italian bedding and wood-burning fireplaces set the scene for a tranquil stay. In the bathrooms you'll find heated slate floors and deep soaking tubs. Two infinity pools and two hot tubs provide additional places to relax.

Lavender

2020 Webber St. (bet. Yount & Jefferson Sts.), Yountville

Phone: 707-944-1388 or 800-522-4140
Web: www.lavendernapa.com
Prices: $$

8
Rooms

Lavender

Napa Valley finds the south of France at this enticing gray clapboard house, trimmed in bright blue and nested amid a profusion of lavender and roses. Inside, Provençal prints and vibrant colors create a sunny palette worthy of Avignon.

You'll find joie de vivre in each of the inn's eight spacious guestrooms, all cheerfully decorated with country charm à la française. Two rooms are located in the main house. The remaining six cottage rooms surround the house and garden; each has its own private entrance and patio. After a day of wine tasting or biking around the valley, slip on the comfy robe provided and kick up your feet in front of the gas fireplace in your room. For a true romantic getaway, ask for room No.7; its private patio comes with an outdoor jetted spa tub.

The little things that can add up elsewhere are included here: a buffet breakfast; afternoon wine, tea, and hors d'oeuvres; freshly baked cookies; and chocolates with turndown service. The wraparound porch and the fragrant terrace garden make perfect spots to enjoy your morning coffee or an afternoon glass of wine.

Guests have pool privileges at neighboring Maison Fleurie, also a member of the Four Sisters Inns group.

Wine Country ▶ Napa Valley

Maison Fleurie

6529 Yount St. (at Washington St.), Yountville

Phone: 707-944-2056 or 800-788-0369
Web: www.maisonfleurienapa.com
Prices: $$$

13
Rooms

Maison Fleurie

Oozing French country charm inside and out, the "Flowering House" makes the perfect romantic wine country getaway. This member of the Four Sisters Inns welcomes guests amid Provençal-inspired fabrics and furnishings, and a huge stone fireplace in the lobby. Constructed in 1849, back when the valley was known for growing walnuts and olives, the rustic main house contains 7 of the property's 13 rooms. Elsewhere on the grounds, two Carriage House rooms have private entrances, while those in the Bakery Building boast fireplaces and whirlpool tubs.

Before setting out to explore the valley, whether by car or complimentary mountain bike, you'll need a hearty breakfast. The inn complies with a spread of hot and cold dishes—perhaps a quiche, a potato casserole and soft-boiled eggs, along with fresh fruit, cakes, toast, and English muffins. Drop by the lobby lounge for wine and hors d'oeuvres each evening. A small refrigerator in the common area offers complimentary soft drinks all day.

True to its name, Maison Fleurie abounds in lovely landscaped flora, from the roses that surround the hot tub area, to the grape vines that climb the walls and trellises scattered around the pastoral grounds.

Wine Country ▶ Napa Valley

Meadowood

900 Meadowood Ln. (off the Silverado Trail), St. Helena

Phone: 707-963-3646 or 800-458-8080
Web: www.meadowood.com
Prices: $$$$

41
Rooms
44
Suites

Meadowood Napa Valley

Serenity prevails in the 85 cottages and lodges nestled on 250 acres of wooded hills off the Silverado Trail. What is now a world-class resort began in the 1960s as a small club for local winemakers. It still doubles as a chic country club for Napa notables, and its décor and ambience say as much.

When there's a chill in the air, guests bunk in secluded cottages, warmed by wood-burning stone fireplaces. White wainscoting and exposed beams lend a bucolic feel, while glorious French doors lead to private decks perfect for soaking in nature's bounty.

The valley's most famed product is celebrated in Meadowood's wine-education program. Lessons begin at the afternoon wine reception, where all guests are invited to a complimentary tasting of two local wines. More in-depth tastings, conducted by the resort's master sommelier, are offered for a fee. But, don't miss an evening at The Restaurant at Meadowood, where the superb cuisine pays homage to the area's farm-to-table tradition.

If you find yourself with time to spare, the grounds also encompass a nine-hole golf course, seven tennis courts, two croquet lawns, two lap pools, and a fitness center and relaxing spa...with its own spa menu!

Wine Country ▶ Napa Valley

Napa River Inn

500 Main St. (at 5th St.), Napa

Phone: 877-251-8500
Web: www.napariverinn.com
Prices: $$$

68
Rooms

Napa River Inn

Surrender your car keys at check in at the Napa River Inn, since you won't need to drive anywhere once you're ensconced within this historic property. All of Napa's charms—art galleries, top-notch restaurants, Summer Chef's Markets, and area wineries—are within reasonable distance from this hotel located on the River Walk. The charming Napa Valley Wine Train, which skirts through the countryside vineyards, is also just steps away.

The Napa River Inn is an exquisite, independently owned hotel hidden inside the Napa Mill, a National Registered Landmark built in 1884. This former warehouse shares its special history but it's far from stuck in the past. Guests are treated to luxurious accommodations featuring the finest in everything from high quality linens to the latest technology.

This intimate property impresses with its bountiful amenities, including four restaurants. Sweetie Pies provides fresh baked goods for complimentary breakfast, Angèle and Napa General Store have the country-chic style down pat, and Celadon shares a worldly cuisine. Feelin' groovy? Silo's Jazz Club is a cool cat's heaven. Imbibed too much Chardonnay? Opt for one of 25 treatments at the refreshing spa.

Rancho Caymus Inn

1140 Rutherford Rd. (off Hwy. 29), Rutherford

Phone: 707-963-1777 or 800-845-1777
Web: www.ranchocaymus.com
Prices: $$

25
Rooms
1
Suite

Rancho Caymus Inn

Wine Country ▶ Napa Valley

Owned for some 20 years by the Komes family, who runs Flora Springs winery, Rancho Caymus captures the spirit of the early days of Alta California in both its name and its hacienda-style buildings. The name comes from a sprawling *rancho* built on this site in the 1830s, after Spanish general Mariano Vallejo awarded this land to pioneer George Yount (for whom the town of Yountville is christened).

The inn's buildings, each of which bears the name of a historic Napa Valley personality from Robert Louis Stevenson to Black Bart, house one- and two-bedroom suites. Hand-carved black walnut headboards, 100-year-old reclaimed oak ceiling beams, and white stucco walls imbue the accommodations with a sound sense of the past. Standard amenities, such as televisions, air conditioning, a wet bar, and a refrigerator, cater to modern comfort. Many of the rooms have beehive fireplaces, and private outdoor balconies or sitting areas. Designed as "split levels," the sleeping areas are set up a step in each room.

Complimentary continental breakfast is served each morning in the main dining room. Like The Rutherford Grill, there are several great restaurants in the immediate area.

Solage

A1

755 Silverado Trail (at Rosedale Rd.), Calistoga

Phone: 707-226-0800 or 866-942-7442
Web: www.solagecalistoga.com
Prices: $$$$

83
Rooms
6
Suites

Solage Calistoga

There's no place like wine country to indulge in the good life, and Solage capitalizes on what is best about this area. The first property from Auberge Resorts' new Solage Hotels & Resorts brand, this eco-friendly cottage-style resort and spa spreads out over 20 acres off the Silverado Trail.

The resort's 89 rooms are tucked inside bungalows that fashion urban lofts in a pastoral environment. Modern amenities (WiFi, flat screen TV, iPod docking station, mini refrigerator) mix with vaulted ceilings, contemporary furniture, polished concrete floors, and semi-private patios. Colors run to leafy greens, and sizes range from one bedroom studios to spacious suites. Each cottage is equipped with a pair of bikes for exploring.

Guests want for little here. There's a large outdoor heated pool flanked by cabanas, and a state of the art fitness center where classes are complimentary. Solbar restaurant serves up healthy Californian cuisine for breakfast, lunch, and dinner. But the pièce de résistance is the resort's 20,000-square foot spa. And this being Calistoga—a small town with a big reputation for its mineral-rich mud—a visit to the spa's signature Mud Bar is an absolute must.

Villagio Inn & Spa

6481 Washington St., Yountville

Phone: 707-944-8877 or 800-351-1133
Web: www.villagio.com
Prices: $$$

86
Rooms

26
Suites

Villagio Inn & Spa

Tuscan style defines the two-story buildings and the grounds of elegant Villagio, where sybarites want for little. Fluffy duvets, fine linens, and cozy robes make for cushy quarters, swathed in Tuscan gold tones and warmed by fireplaces when it's cold outside. Room rates include a champagne breakfast, afternoon tea, and Friday evening wine tastings.

Some of the valley's best restaurants are literally steps from the complex, but if intent on an evening indoors, room service can oblige with a Tuscan Carpet Picnic for two. This in-room treat fosters romance with wine country cuisine, candlelight, Italian music, and throw pillows to sit on.

If work is the reason you're here, Villagio accommodates business functions with 26,000 square feet of meeting space—but it's not unusual for break out meetings to take place in the adjacent vineyard.

Treat yourself to an evening of relaxation at Spa Villagio. This luxurious 3,000-square foot plush retreat has separate wings for men and women, and offers Swiss showers, steam and dry saunas, and outdoor thermal soaking tubs. Treatments pamper with everything from a hot stone massage to the signature facial that features a mask of crushed pearls.

Wine Country ▶ Napa Valley

Vintage Inn

C2

6541 Washington St., Yountville

Phone: 707-944-1112 or 800-351-1133
Web: www.vintageinn.com
Prices: $$$

72
Rooms

8
Suites

Vintage Inn

Wine Country ▶ Napa Valley

Sharing a 23-acre estate with Villagio, the Vintage Inn is the older of the two, but is no less charming in its Gallic demeanor. A Provençal feel pervades the grounds, abloom in season with lavender and roses. Paths and footbridges connect the two-story French country-style buildings within this intimate complex.

A complimentary bottle of wine welcomes guests to airy rooms with vaulted ceilings, where French antiques, toile de Jouy fabrics, plush robes, and down duvets set the tone for luxurious comfort. Every room boasts a wood-burning fireplace and a bathroom equipped with an oversized whirlpool tub.

A signature of both properties, a lavish champagne breakfast comes compliments of the house. You won't need lunch after tackling a buffet laden with egg dishes, quiche, salmon mousse, fresh fruit, homemade breads, and pastries. At dinnertime you need only meander Washington Street to sample Yountville's justly famous restaurant lineup, which encompasses Bouchon, The French Laundry, Redd, and Ad Hoc. Michael Chiarello's regional Italian restaurant, Bottega, is right next door at V Marketplace.

For those "aah" moments, guests at Vintage Inn have access to Villagio's spa.

Duchamp

421 Foss St. (at North St.), Healdsburg

Phone: 707-431-1300 or 800-431-9341
Web: www.duchamphotel.com
Prices: $$$

6
Rooms

David Duncan Douglas

Wine Country ▶ **Sonoma County**

French Dada artist Marcel Duchamp was known for his unconventionality, and so this small hotel echoes the artist's spirit by its departure from conventional wine country accommodations. A not-so-well-kept secret within minutes of Healdsburg's downtown plaza, the Duchamp displays a sleek, modern aspect that trumps country charm.

Owner Pat Lenz—an artist herself—and her husband, Peter, named the hotel's six freestanding bungalows after modern artists (the seventh bungalow serves as a reception area). The design of each reflects the style of namesakes such as Picasso and Warhol. The grouping surrounds a heated swimming pool with a sundeck and Jacuzzi.

Each room is large and minimalist in style, with whitewashed walls and decorative murals to add a spark of color. French doors let in natural light, and lead out to a private patio. King beds and down comforters promise a good night's rest; white tiles dress the large bathrooms, which highlight two washbasins and a spacious shower.

Convenient to the wineries of the Russian River, Dry Creek, and Alexander valleys, the hotel offers a unique amenity: the innkeepers will arrange private tastings at nearby Duchamp Winery, which they also own.

El Dorado

405 1st St. W. (at W. Spain St.), Sonoma

Phone: 707-996-3220 or 800-289-3031
Web: www.eldoradosonoma.com
Prices: $$

27
Rooms

Erin Kunkel

Laid out by Mariano Vallejo in 1835, Sonoma Plaza holds a lot of history in its eight acres. Among the historic structures that flank this square, the El Dorado hotel nods to the area's past while furnishing guests with a reasonably priced place to stay in the wine country.

Light and color set the hotel's 27 rooms aglow; the 23 accommodations in the main building, and the four independent bungalows were recently refurbished in a clean simple style. French doors open onto private balconies or terraces and admit a wash of sunlight into the rooms. Some look over the historic plaza; others face the restaurant terrace, which is shaded by a fig tree. Every Friday evening, the hotel holds a complimentary wine tasting in the lobby, spotlighting wineries from El Dorado Kitchen's extensive wine list.

The property recently applied a range of green initiatives, from using non-toxic cleaning products and environmentally-friendly bath amenities to employing solar panels to collect heat for the small pool. Following suit, the hotel's popular restaurant—El Dorado Kitchen—has formed a partnership with local Benziger Winery Biodynamic Farms to grow organic produce for the seasonal menu.

The Fairmont
Sonoma Mission Inn & Spa

C3

100 Boyes Blvd. (bet. Arnold Dr. & Hwy. 12), Sonoma

Phone: 707-938-9000 or 800-441-1414
Web: www.fairmont.com
Prices: $$$

166
Rooms

60
Suites

Fairmont Sonoma Mission Inn

With a tradition built around a hot mineral spring discovered by Native Americans eons ago, the Fairmont Sonoma Mission Inn flaunts its tie to these healing 135-degree waters, which flow from 1,100 feet directly beneath the Inn.

No place on-site is this more evident than at the 40,000-square foot spa, where mineral baths are integral to the rejuvenating treatments. The Bathing Ritual begins with an exfoliating shower and includes soaks in two mineral pools.

The sprawling resort models itself after the San Francisco Solano Mission, erected in the Sonoma Valley in 1824. Located in the main building, Heritage Rooms are done up in French country décor. Wine country rooms, spread throughout the complex, display a graceful contemporary style. Mission Suites set the mood with two-person Jacuzzi tubs, wood-burning fireplaces, and a complimentary bottle of wine.

A careful steward of the land, the hotel strictly limits its use of pesticides and herbicides. Rooms have been retrofitted with energy-efficient light bulbs, and low-flow shower heads. Even the restaurants, the casual Big 3 and reputed Santé for fine dining, use organic and sustainable products from local purveyors whenever possible.

Wine Country ▶ **Sonoma County**

427

Farmhouse Inn

7871 River Rd. (at Wohler Rd.), Forestville

Phone: 707-887-3300 or 800-464-6642
Web: www.farmhouseinn.com
Prices: $$$$

6
Rooms

12
Suites

Tai Power Seeff

Make "country" the operative word when visiting the wine country and head for the charming Farmhouse Inn. This gracious getaway has definitely cornered the market on peace and quiet.

Set in an idyllic area of Forestville in the Russian River Valley, the Farmhouse Inn is surrounded by groves of trees and miles of vineyards. Away from it all and offering just 8 cottages, 2 guestrooms in the main house, and 8 rooms in the barn, this hideaway is the ultimate retreat. The cottages, with pale yellow and white trim, and impeccable flower beds, exude an Anne of Green Gables charm, while inside they are graciously appointed with a mod rustic style. This isn't your grandfather's farmhouse, so you won't be forsaking any of your city slicker comforts.

The Farmhouse Inn blends down home appeal with sophisticated touches. Farm-fresh breakfasts, locally made and organic bath and beauty products, and cookies and milk delivered to guests each afternoon are among the country charms, while the full-service spa and wine tasting classes with Sonoma's only Master Sommelier are seriously.

Gaige House Inn

C3

13540 Arnold Dr. (at Railroad St.), Glen Ellen

Phone: 707-935-0237 or 800-935-0237
Web: www.gaige.com
Prices: $$$

12
Rooms
11
Suites

Paul Dyer

Built in the 1890s by Glen Ellen's butcher at the time—a man with the surname of Gaige—this Sonoma County landmark now cossets visitors to the area in luxurious accommodations designed with an Asian flair.

With a full menu of spa services, an expanded continental breakfast (included in the rates), and a lovely heated swimming pool, this new member of the Joie de Vivre group merits a detour off the beaten track. It is located just north of Sonoma, couched amid three acres of lush gardens along Calabazas Creek. The cottage suite that overlooks this creek through its floor-to-ceiling windows features a private deck for reveling in the natural setting. Offering true tranquility, stand-alone Zen suites are the inn's largest, showing off Japanese-inspired elements such as an interior atrium garden and a large granite soaking tub. Standard rooms, all 10 of which are located in the main house, bespeak a luxury all their own. In some, tatami mats cover hardwood floors, and rice paper screens decorate the walls; others feature fireplaces.

Unwind and treat yourself to indulgent body treatments such as the Thai herbal poultice massage, enjoyed in your room, or in the Spa Loft.

Wine Country ▶ Sonoma County

429

Healdsburg

D1

25 Matheson St. (at Healdsburg Ave.), Healdsburg

Phone: 707-431-2800 or 800-889-7188
Web: www.hotelhealdsburg.com
Prices: $$$$

51
Rooms

4
Suites

Hotel Healdsburg

Natural elements of wine country combine in this three-story garden hotel to create a serene retreat on Healdsburg's town square. Spacious rooms are decorated with soothing wine country tones, Tibetan wool carpets, and pecan wood floors; most have French doors leading to private balconies. Teak platform beds dress in down duvets and Frette linens. In the oversize bathrooms, you'll find Italian glass tile, walk-in showers, separate soaking tubs, and organic bath amenities courtesy of the hotel's full-service spa.

A hearty breakfast comes with your stay. Whether you plan on wine tasting, getting acquainted with the shops and wine bars around the square, or working out in the hotel's fitness room and relaxing by the olive- and cypress tree-shrouded pool afterwards, the selection of baked goods, smoked salmon, eggs, cereals, and fruit will fortify you for the day's activities.

Dining options are plenty in downtown Healdsburg, but you can eat just as well on-site. Check out the grappa bar in the lobby before retiring to the Dry Creek Kitchen for seasonal Californian fare; or walk down the street to their new sibling and sustainable inn, h2hotel, and grab a bite at Spoonbar.

Honor Mansion

14891 Grove St. (bet. Dry Creek Rd. & Grant St.),

Phone: 707-433-4277 or 800-554-4667
Web: www.honormansion.com
Prices: $$$

13
Rooms

The Honor Mansion

Romance waits behind the façade of this restored 1883 house, located less than a mile away from the tony boutiques, tasting rooms, and fine restaurants lining Healdsburg's downtown plaza. Owners Cathi and Steve Fowler have anticipated guests' every need in the 13 individually decorated rooms and suites. Rooms in the main house vary in size and style, while four separate Vineyard Suites (the priciest accommodations) foster *amore* with king-size beds, gas fireplaces, and private patios complete with your own whirlpool (robes and rubber ducky included). On the four-acre grounds, landscaped with rose gardens and zinfandel vines, you'll find a lap pool, a PGA putting green, bocce and tennis courts, a croquet lawn, and a half basketball court.

Following the Fowlers' hospitable lead, the staff will provide you with a picnic basket and a list of places to pick up picnic fare. They'll also make arrangements for everything from private winery visits to poolside massages. A hearty multicourse breakfast, and an afternoon wine and hors d'ouevres reception are included in the room rate.

On weekends, count on a minimum stay of two nights in low season, and four nights in high season.

Les Mars

27 North St. (bet. Foss St. & Healdsburg Ave.), Healdsburg

Phone: 707-433-4211 or 877-431-1700
Web: www.lesmarshotel.com
Prices: $$$$

16
Rooms

Les Mars

Good things come in small packages, as Les Mars—just off Healdsburg's central square—proves beyond the shadow of a doubt. The hotel only has 16 rooms, but each is a study in old-world elegance. Perhaps your room will wear a classic Parisian décor, draped in warm earth tones and a four-poster canopy bed. Or maybe you prefer a regal red and burgundy palette, with a jetted hydrotherapy soaking tub. There are also chambers in the grand chateau style, impeccably dressed in French toile underneath 20-foot-tall beamed ceilings. Whatever your preference, in all the rooms you'll revel in period antiques, a gas fireplace, marble bath, and sumptuous Italian linens.

Attention to detail reveals itself in vases of fresh flowers on each floor, Bulgari bath amenities, and locally produced artisan cheeses offered at the nightly wine reception. Owned by the Mars family, the place oozes luxury, from the 17th century Flemish tapestry that hangs in the lobby to the hand-carved walnut panels and leather-bound books that line the library.

You owe it to yourself to book a meal at neighboring Cyrus, which makes an equally posh setting in which to linger over Chef Douglas Keane's delicious preparations.

Madrona Manor

1001 Westside Rd. (at West Dry Creek Rd.), Healdsburg

Phone: 707-433-4231 or 800-258-4003
Web: www.madronamanor.com
Prices: $$$

17
Rooms
5
Suites

Madrona Manor

Built for San Francisco businessman John Paxton, the stately, three-story Victorian mansion has graced this wooded knoll above the vineyards of the Dry Creek Valley since 1881. Whether your pleasure is simply strolling along sun-dappled paths lined with flowers, having an elegant dining experience, or visiting some of California's finest wineries, you will be well-situated to do all of those things here.

Of the 22 handsome rooms on-site, 9 are located in the historic landmark mansion itself; all of these have king-size beds and fireplaces. Four large rooms on the second floor boast original antique furniture; two of them have balconies. The remainder of the rooms and suites are scattered around the eight-acre wooded grounds in buildings such as the original carriage house and school house. All accommodations are individually decorated with an eye to Victorian style, and are fitted with pillow-top mattresses and terrycloth robes. To foster tranquility, there are no TVs in any of the rooms.

Guests need not leave the property to find creative contemporary cuisine. Nightly menus are based on market-fresh ingredients, including vegetables, herbs, and fruit from the on-site gardens.

Wine Country ▶ Sonoma County

Vintners Inn

 4350 Barnes Rd. (at River Rd.), Santa Rosa

Phone: 707-575-7350 or 800-421-2584
Web: www.vintnersinn.com
Prices: $$$

44 Rooms

Vintners Inn

An idyllic wine country retreat just north of Santa Rosa, this small lodging focuses on romance—with weddings frequently held here. There are many charming settings a couple can choose from to tie the knot, given that the four picturesque Tuscan-style structures that compose the Vintners Inn cuddle in the midst of a 90-acre vineyard. And with catering by the acclaimed John Ash & Co. restaurant on-site, it's a sure bet that the food and wine will include some of the best products of the Sonoma Valley.

Cozy nests feathered with down bedding, bathrobes, and a complimentary bottle of wine roost on the two floors of the tile-roofed buildings. All have either private patios or balconies, and second-floor chambers boast vaulted ceilings and exposed wood beams. Windows look out on either the surrounding vineyards or the brick-paved courtyard and central fountain around which the structures are arranged. Rates include a buffet breakfast.

In 2009, Vintner's Inn was awarded the highest honor in the State of California's Green Lodging Program, thanks to the efforts of owners Don and Rhonda Carano (of Ferrari-Carano Winery) in minimizing waste, recycling, and conserving energy.

You know
the MICHELIN guide

...DO YOU REALLY
KNOW **MICHELIN?**

● Data 31/12/2009

MICHELIN
A better way forward

The world No.1 in tires with 16.3% of the market

A business presence in over **170 countries**

A manufacturing footprint
at the heart of markets

In 2009 **72** industrial sites in **19** countries produced:

- **150** million tires
- **10** million maps and guides

Highly international teams

Over **109 200** employees* from all cultures on all continents

including **6 000** people employed in R&D centers in Europe, the US and Asia.

*102,692 full-time equivalent staff

The Michelin Group at a glance

Michelin competes

At the end of 2009

Le Mans 24-hour race
12 consecutive years of victories

Endurance 2008
- 6 victories on 6 stages in Le Mans Series
- 12 victories on 12 stages in American Le Mans Series

Paris-Dakar
Since the beginning of the event, the Michelin group has won in all categories

Moto Endurance
2009 World Champion

Trial
Every World Champion title since 1981 (except 1992)

Michelin, established close to its customers

○ **68 plants in 19 countries**

- Algeria
- Brazil
- Canada
- China
- Colombia
- France
- Germany
- Hungary
- Italy
- Japan
- Mexico
- Poland
- Romania
- Russia
- Serbia
- Spain
- Thailand
- UK
- USA

● **A Technology Center spread over 3 continents**

- Asia
- Europe
- North America

◐ **2 Natural rubber plantations**

- Brazil

Our mission

To make a sustainable contribution to progress in the mobility of goods and people by enhancing freedom of movement, safety, efficiency and pleasure when on the move.

Michelin committed to environmental-friendliness

Michelin, world leader in low rolling resistance tires, actively reduces fuel consumption and vehicle gas emission.

For its products, Michelin develops state-of-the-art technologies in order to:
- Reduce fuel consumption, while improving overall tire performance.
- Increase life cycle to reduce the number of tires to be processed at the end of their useful lives;
- Use raw materials which have a low impact on the environment.

Furthermore, at the end of 2008, 99.5% of tire production in volume was carried out in ISO 14001* certified plants.

Michelin is committed to implementing recycling channels for end-of-life tires.

*environmental certification

**Passenger Car
Light Truck**

Truck

Michelin
a key mobility enabler

Earthmover

Aircraft

Agricultural

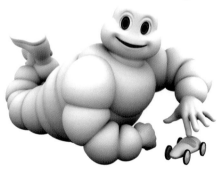

Two-wheel   **Distribution**

Partnered with vehicle manufacturers, in tune with users, active in competition and in all the distribution channels, Michelinis continually innovating to promote mobility today and to invent that of tomorrow.

Maps and Guides   **ViaMichelin, travel assistance services**   **Michelin Lifestyle, for your travel accessories**

MICHELIN
plays on balanced performance

- **Long tire life**
- **Fuel savings**
- **Safety on the road**

... MICHELIN tires provide you with the best performance, without making a single sacrifice.

The MICHELIN tire pure technology

1 Tread
A thick layer of rubber provides contact with the ground. It has to channel water away and last as long as possible.

2 Crown plies
This double or triple reinforced belt has both vertical flexibility and high lateral rigidity. It provides the steering capacity.

3 Sidewalls
These cover and protect the textile casing whose role is to attach the tire tread to the wheel rim.

4 Bead area for attachment to the rim
Its internal bead wire clamps the tire firmly against the wheel rim.

5 Inner liner
This makes the tire almost totally impermeable and maintains the correct inflation pressure.

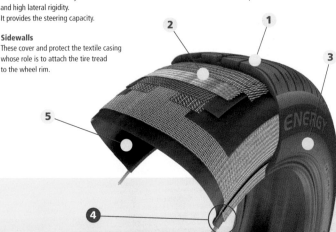

Heed
the MICHELIN Man's advice

To improve safety:

- I drive with the correct tire pressure
- I check the tire pressure every month
- I have my car regularly serviced
- I regularly check the appearance of my tires (wear, deformation)
- I am responsive behind the wheel
- change my tires according to the season

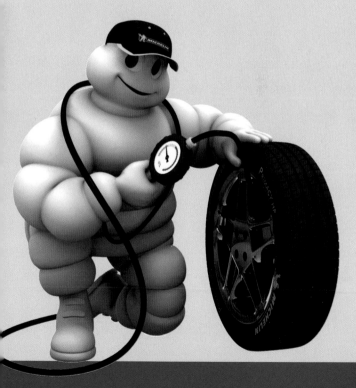

www.michelin.com
www.michelin.(your country extension – e.g. .fr for France)

● Where to **Eat**

 Where to **Stay**

Alphabetical List of Restaurants

Restaurants by Cuisine

Afghan

Kabul	✗✗	238

American

Ad Hoc	✗✗	295
AKA	✗✗	295
Bix	✗✗	117
Blue Plate	✗✗	84
Bounty Hunter	✗	303
Brannan's Grill	✗✗	303
Brick & Bottle	✗✗	214
Brown Sugar Kitchen	😊 ✗	175
Buckeye Roadhouse	✗✗	215
Bungalow 44	✗✗	215
BurgerMeister	✗	17
Cuvée	✗✗	307
Digs Bistro	✗✗	181
Fish & Farm	✗✗	51
FIVE	😊 ✗✗	185
Flora	✗✗	185
Gott's Roadside	✗	312
Home	✗	22
Market	😊 ✗✗	313
Maverick	✗	89
Mission Beach Café	✗✗	90
Monti's Rotisserie	😊 ✗✗	349
Mustards Grill	✗✗	316
Nick's on Main	✗✗	275
900 Grayson	✗	194
Park Chow	✗✗	136
Prospect	✗✗✗	158
Rutherford Grill	✗✗	319
Salt House	✗✗	160
Sauce	😊 ✗✗	38
SR24	✗✗	201
Tavern at Lark Creek	😊 ✗✗	225

1300 on Fillmore	✗✗✗	39
Town Hall	✗✗	161
Wexler's	✗	60
Woodward's Garden	✗	98
Zin	✗	361

Asian

Betelnut	😊 ✗	65
Champa Garden	✗	177
Chinois	✗✗	336
Crustacean	✗✗✗	105
EOS	✗✗	19
E&O Trading Compagny	✗✗	50
house (the)	✗	120
Mingalaba	✗	243
Namu	✗	135
O Chamé	✗	195
Red Lantern	✗	246

Barbecue

BarBersQ	😊 ✗✗	298

Basque

Iluna Basque	🍲	120
Piperade	✗✗	122

Brazilian

Espetus Churrascaria	✗	32
Pampas	✗✗	275

Burmese

Burma Superstar	😊 ✗	129
Mandalay	✗	133

Californian

Adagia	✗✗	168
Applewood	❄ ✗✗	331

Cambodian

Caribbean

Chinese

Indexes ▶ Restaurants by Cuisine

Cuisines by Neighborhood

SAN FRANCISCO

Castro

American
BurgerMeister	🍴	17
Home	🍴	22

Asian
EOS	🍴🍴	19

Californian
Frances	❀ 🍴🍴	20
Starbelly	☺ 🍴🍴	26

Chinese
Eric's	🍴	19
Henry's Hunan	☺ 🍴	22

French
L'Ardoise	🍴	25

Gastropub
Alembic (The)	🍶	16
Magnolia Pub	🍴	25

Indian
Kasa	🍴	24

Italian
Incanto	☺ 🍴🍴	23

Japanese
Eiji	🍴	18
Hama Ko	🍴	21
Kamekyo	🍴	23

Mexican
Chilango	🍴	17
La Corneta	🍴	24

Peruvian
Fresca	🍴🍴	21

Seafood
Anchor Oyster Bar	🍴	16

Spanish
Contigo	🍶	18

Civic Center

American
Sauce	☺ 🍴🍴	38
1300 on Fillmore	🍴🍴🍴	39

Brazilian
Espetus Churrascaria	🍴	32

Californian
CAV	🍴🍴	31
Jardinière	🍴🍴🍴	33
Nopa	☺ 🍴🍴	35

Indian
Indian Oven	🍴	32

Japanese
Domo	☺ 🍴	31
Otoro	🍴	36
Sebo	🍴	38
Yoshi's	🍴🍴	40

Mediterranean
Absinthe	🍴🍴	30
paul k	🍴🍴	37
Zuni Café	🍴🍴	40

Mexican
Nopalito	🍴	35

Middle Eastern
Jannah	🍴🍴	33

Pizza
Little Star Pizza	🍴	34
Patxi's	🍴	37

Seafood
Bar Crudo	🍶	30

Thai
Lers Ros	🍴	34
Thep Phanom	🍴	39

Vietnamese
Pagolac	🍴	36

Indexes ▶ Cuisines by Neighborhood

MARIN

Sonoma County

Indexes ▶ Cuisines by Neighborhood

Starred Restaurants

Within the selection we offer you, some restaurants deserve to be highlighted for their particularly good cuisine. When giving one, two, or three Michelin stars, there are a number of elements that we consider including the quality of the ingredients, the technical skill and flair that goes into their preparation, the blend and clarity of flavours, and the balance of the menu. Just as important is the ability to produce excellent cooking time and again. We make as many visits as we need, so that our readers may be assured of quality and consistency.

A two or three-star restaurant has to offer something very special in its cuisine; a real element of creativity, originality, or "personality" that sets it apart from the rest. Three stars – our highest award – are given to the choicest restaurants, where the whole dining experience is superb.

Cuisine in any style, modern or traditional, may be eligible for a star. Due to the fact we apply the same independent standards everywhere, the awards have become benchmarks of reliability and excellence in over 20 countries in Europe and Asia, particularly in France, where we have awarded stars for 100 years, and where the phrase "Now that's real three-star quality!" has entered into the language.

The awarding of a star is based solely on the quality of the cuisine.

✿ ✿ ✿

Exceptional cuisine, worth a special journey.

One always eats here extremely well, sometimes superbly. Distinctive dishes are precisely executed, using superlative ingredients.

✿ ✿

Excellent cuisine, worth a detour.

Skillfully and carefully crafted dishes of outsanding quality.

✿

A very good restaurant in its category.

A place offering cuisine prepared to a consistently high standard.

Bib Gourmand

Indexes ▶ Bib Gourmand

⬭ ⬭ Under $25

Brunch

Late Dining

Alphabetical List of Hotels

Notes

Notes

Notes

Notes

Notes

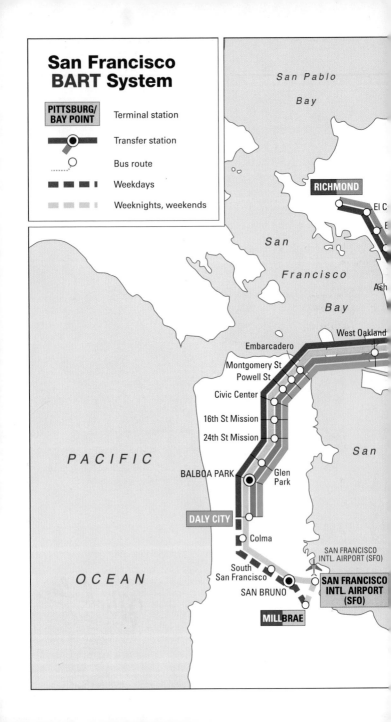

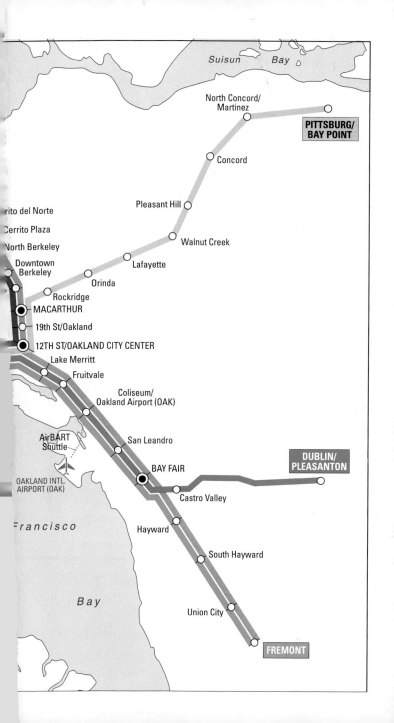

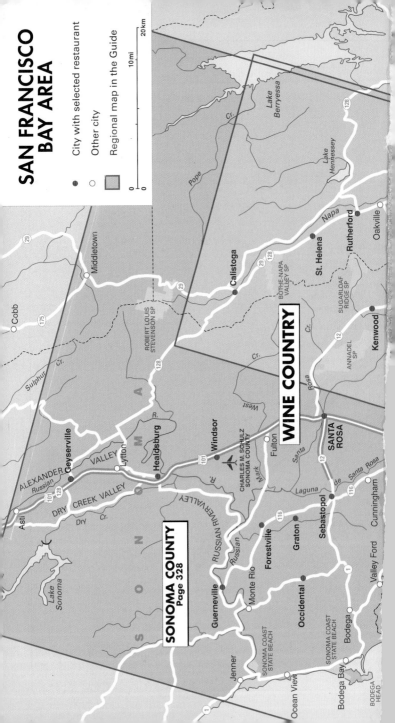